ELIMINATING THE PROPERTY TAX IN TEXAS:
A DETAILED FISCAL ANALYSIS

by

Richard D. Cunningham

TEXAS CENTER FOR ECONOMICS, LAW & POLICY

SEPTEMBER 2010

TEXAS CENTER FOR ECONOMICS, LAW & POLICY

The Texas Center for Economics, Law & Policy conducts analysis of and advocacy for public policies promoting liberty, constitutional government, and fiscal and monetary responsibility. Areas of current study include state and local tax reform, monetary systems and policy, and key issues in federal/state relations.

Inquiries may be directed to:

> Texas Center for Economics, Law & Policy
> Houston, Texas
> contact@tcelp.org

The views and opinions expressed in this report reflect those of the author and do not represent, and should not be construed in any way to represent, the views and opinions of any other person, group or entity, whether or not named herein.

ISBN 978-1-931276-26-9

LSI PUBLISHING, LLC,
Houston, Texas, USA.

Printed in the United States of America

TABLE OF CONTENTS

APPENDIX A

Table A1

Table A2

Table A3

Table A4

Table A5

Table A6

Table A7

ELIMINATING THE PROPERTY TAX IN TEXAS:
A DETAILED FISCAL ANALYSIS

by Richard D. Cunningham

INTRODUCTION

The subject of property tax reform continues to command both interest and controversy in Texas political debate. The 2010 Texas Republican gubernatorial primary brought heightened visibility to this issue both within and outside of the state for one candidate's platform position to eliminate the Texas local *ad valorem* property tax and to expand state and local sales and use taxes in its place. This particular suggestion stemmed philosophically from concern for the preservation of liberty and protection of private property rights, including the right of property owners to be free from confiscatory and arbitrary taxation.[1] But it likewise embraced the fiscal and economic benefits seen as likely to result.[2]

The proposal continued a long tradition of efforts along similar lines. On a more limited basis, a proposal called "Proposition Zero" in the mid-1980's would have raised the sales-tax rate by 1 cent and exempted the first $100,000 of residential property valuation for purposes of school property taxes.[3] In 2003, the Texas Senate passed an initiative to finance a near-elimination of local school property taxes by expanding the range of transactions subject to the general sales tax, and introducing a new state-level property tax at levels much lower than prevailing local rates.[4] The proposal did not become law, although key elements were incorporated by the legislature into its 2006 expansion of Texas' Foundation School Program,[5] through which a reformulation of the Texas business franchise tax and changes to the cigarette tax would finance a limited $7 billion shift of the burden of funding local school districts from local property tax revenues to state tax revenues, with a corresponding reduction in local school district M&O

---

[1] D. Medina, *Protecting Texas Property*, Sept. 24, 2009; http://www.medinafortexas.com/propertyTax.php (accessed June 24, 2010).

[2] *Frequently Asked Questions on Debra Medina's Proposed Texas Tax Policy Reforms*, http://www.medinafortexas.com/propertyTax.php (accessed June 24, 2010).

[3] Patrick K. Graves, *Revamping State Taxes: Options and Implications*, p.3, Texas House of Representatives, House Research Organization Focus Report (February 26, 2003).

[4] *See* S.B. No. 2, 78 R.S. (2003); Sen. Comm. Rep. *Bill Analysis* (March 2, 2003), http://www.capitol.state.tx.us/BillLookup/Text.aspx?LegSess=78R&Bill=SB2 (accessed June 24, 2010).

[5] Tex. Educ. Code sec. 42.001 *et seq.*

(maintenance and operations) property taxes.[6] The Texas Conservative Coalition (TCC), a leading conservative caucus in the Texas legislature, has worked for years to achieve property tax relief through appraisal and/or revenue caps, enhanced protections for property owners' rights, and dedication of other tax revenues (such as the franchise tax, the motor vehicle sales and use tax, and tax on cigarettes and other tobacco products) to reduction of local school districts' M&O property tax rates. In 2007, the TCC's Research Institute advocated complete elimination of the M&O property tax, with an expanded sales tax as a "particularly" interesting candidate for producing substitute revenues,[7] and followed in 2009 with a Task Force Report affirming the sales tax as its preferred alternative and exploring the long term fiscal, legislative and constitutional considerations involved.[8] On the other hand, the Austin-based Center for Public Policy Priorities (CPPP), which has long favored a personal income tax in Texas,[9] has staunchly opposed replacing the property tax with the sales tax, arguing that Texas businesses would be rendered less competitive, the burden on middle-class families would be increased, and public education would be harmed by the instability of the sales tax's revenue stream and the loss of local control over funding and decision-making.[10]

Talmadge Heflin, Director of the Center for Fiscal Policy at the Texas Public Policy Foundation (TPPF) and former Chairman of the Texas House Appropriations Committee, took the property tax reform discussion even further by advocating the complete elimination of all *ad valorem*

---

[6] *See* Texas Taxpayers and Research Association (TTARA) Research Foundation, *Property Tax Relief. The $7 Billion Reality*, (August 2008), http://www.ttara.org/docs/Property_TaxReliefReport_08_08.pdf (accessed June 24, 2010); Texas Legislative Budget Board, *Foundation School Program Fiscal and Policy Studies*, p.1 (March 2009), http://www.lbb.state.tx.us/Public_Education/FoundationSchool_FiscalPolicy_0309.pdf (accessed June 24, 2010.

[7] *See TCCRI Statement on the M&O Property Tax*, (December 7, 2007), http://www.txccri.org/publications/MO_Statement_2-7-07.pdf (accessed June 24, 2010).

[8] *Final Report of the TCCRI Property Tax Task Force*, pp.18-26 (February 2009), http://www.txccri.org/publications/TCCRI_Property_Tax_Task_Force_Report.pdf (accessed June 24, 2010.

[9] Dick Lavine, *The Best Choice for a Prosperous Texas: A Texas-Style Personal Income Tax*, Center for Public Policy (October 2006), http://www.cppp.org/files/7/Texas_Trilogy_update.pdf (accesed June 24, 2010).

[10] Dick Lavine, *Replacing Property Taxes With Sales Taxes Would Be Bad For Texas Businesses, Families, And Public Education*, Center for Public Policy Priorities Policy Page No. 07-307 (December 12. 2007), http://www.cppp.org/files/7/Sales_TaxPolicy_Page307.pdf (accessed June 24, 2010). *See also* George R. Zodrow, *An Economic Evaluation of Alternative Sources of Tax Revenue for the State of Texas*, n.68, Report Prepared for the Texas Joint Select Committee on Public School Finance pp. 45-47 (March 12, 2004), http://bush.tamu.edu/research/faculty/TXSchoolFinance/papers/GRZ_TX_Rev_Options_03-12-04.pdf (accessed June 24, 2010) (addressing the merits of actually expanding the property tax to include non-residential property); *cf.* George R. Zodrow, *Texas Tax Options (January 2006)* (reviewing and updating conclusions in his earlier report), http://www.bakerinstitute.org/publications/wp_2006002.pdf (accessed June 24, 2010).

property taxes,[11] an idea more fully considered in the April 2009 study commissioned by the TPPF and prepared by Arduin, Laffer & Moore Econometrics (the "Arduin-Laffer study").[12] The TPPF's advocacy on this topic focused in particular on the economic benefits to be derived from such reform, while simultaneously emphasizing the fundamental liberty interests at stake.[13] In this spirit, the Arduin-Laffer study provided valuable insight into the pro-growth benefits to be gained by converting Texas' public finances from the inefficient, inconsistent, and bureaucracy-laden collection of taxes based on individual assessments of property value to the one-time assessment of taxes imposed relative to market price at the point of sale. Simply by implementing a revenue-neutral expansion of the existing state and local sales and use tax system in substitution for the existing local property tax system, the study showed that increased macroeconomic efficiencies could yield an increase of aggregate personal income in Texas by as much as $52 billion over five years, including the possibility of a net gain of between 127,700 and 312,700 new jobs over that same period.[14]

Relying as it did on aggregate, statewide proxies for its overall revenue and tax rate calculations, however, the Arduin-Laffer study could not undertake to examine the comparative effects of such a proposal on individual taxing jurisdictions at the county and local levels. Nor could it offer recommendations on how the proposed increase in sales tax collections -- and hence the political power over their expenditure -- would be allocated among the state and the thousands of counties, cities, school districts, special purpose districts and metropolitan transit authorities that currently levy property and sales taxes in Texas. Since in reality these considerations would dictate the prospects for and course of such reform, a careful examination of actual revenue streams, tax bases and local economic conditions in these various jurisdictions might prove beneficial to the debate. The present report undertakes to accomplish this to a certain degree, and in the process concludes not only that this reform should be both fiscally and politically feasible, but also that it could put to rest funding and constitutional problems that have long plagued the Texas public school finance system.

---

[11] T. Heflin, *The Case for Converting from Property Taxes to Sales Taxes*, (March 2008); http://www.texaspolicy.com/pdf/2008-03-PB04-propertytaxes-th.pdf (accessed May, 2010).

[12] Arduin, Laffer & Moore Econometrics, Enhancing Texas' Economic Growth Through Tax Reform – Repealing Property Taxes and Replacing The Revenues with a Revised Sales Tax, (April 2009); http://www.texaspolicy.com/pdf/2009-04-taxswap-laffer-posting.pdf (accessed May, 2010).

[13] T. Heflin, *Texas Can Put a Halt to Onerous Property Tax*, Houston Chronicle, Feb. 5, 2010; http://www.chron.com/disp/story.mpl/editorial/outlook/6853878.html (accessed May, 2010).

[14] Arduin-Laffer Study pp. 3, 16.

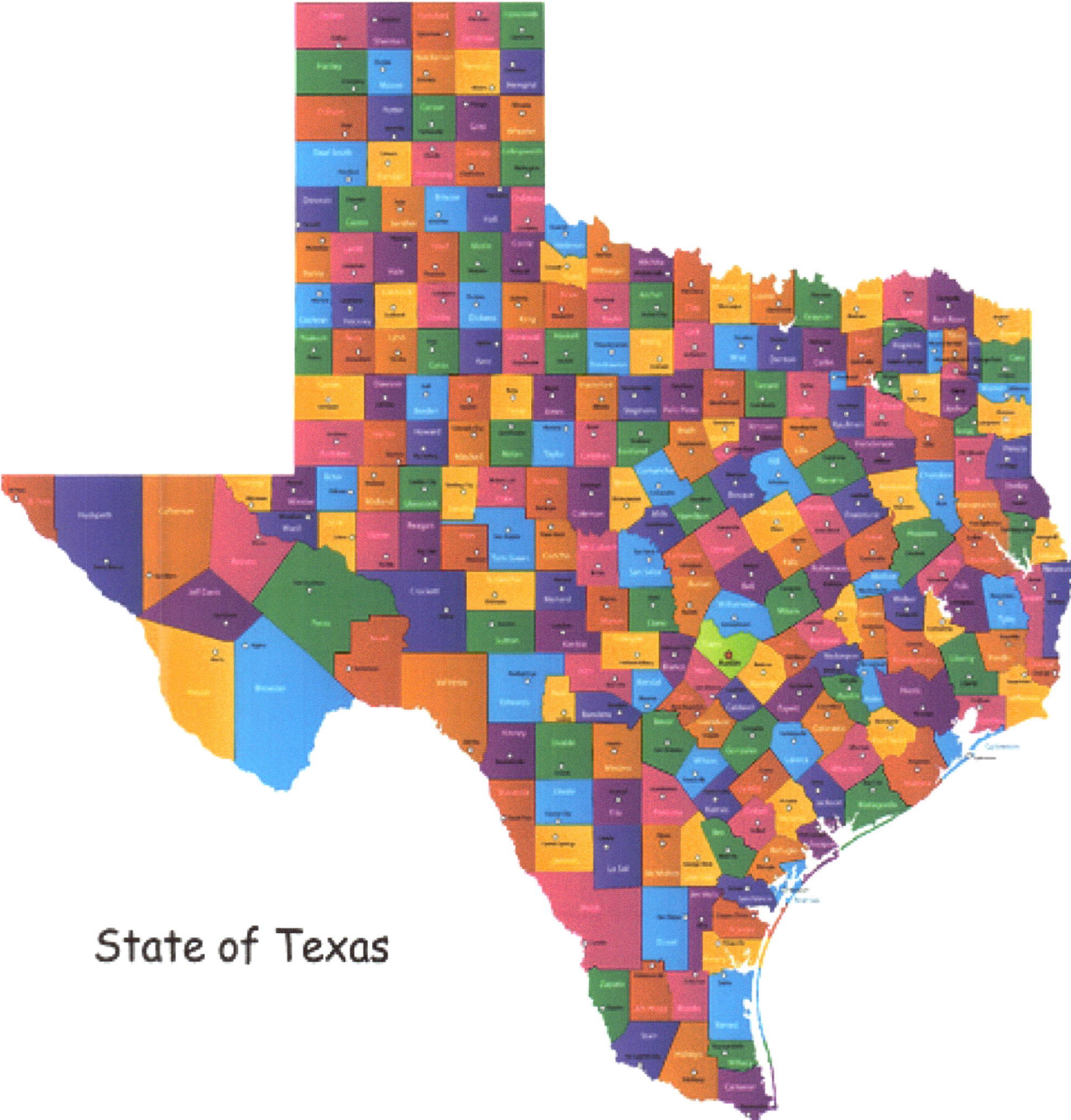

State of Texas

EXECUTIVE SUMMARY

This report recommends a substantial reform and rationalization of Texas' current property, business franchise and sales tax system. In short, we propose the complete elimination of the local *ad valorem* property tax in those jurisdictions where it is feasible to do so, full elimination of the business franchise or "margins" tax, and elimination of the portions of the current state sales tax that in fact currently fall on Texas business and industry. In their place, we propose the adoption of a two-tier system consisting of the "**Consumption Sales Tax**" and the "**Business Sales Tax**".

Proposed New Sales Taxes
(pro forma 2008)

Tax	Rate
Consumption Sales Tax	7.5%
Business Sales Tax	2.525%

The Consumption Sales Tax would represent a slight variation of the state and local sales and use tax currently in place, modified in the scenario presented here to increase its rate from 6.25% to 7.5% and to exempt from its coverage purchases by persons and entities for the purpose of use in a trade or business, but otherwise retaining the primary exclusions, exemptions and administrative processes that reflect current sales tax policy and practice. The exemption would be available to those purchasers who present a satisfactory "Business Use Exemption Certificate", subject to audit and enforcement similarly to current exemption certificates such as those utilized by government agencies, non-profit organizations and entities purchasing goods for resale.

The Business Sales Tax would consist, in the scenario presented here, of a 2.525% across-the-board tax on all sales by businesses taking place in or apportioned to Texas, the payment of which would be the responsibility of the selling business, based on quarterly reports and remittances, and subject to an annual *de minimus* threshold. Except for gross insurance premiums, which are already subject to a gross receipts tax, no other major exclusions, exemptions or limitations would apply, save for discounts or other customary incentives deemed appropriate and authorized by law to facilitate collections and administration.

This report does not undertake to analyze the feasibility of replacing also the current taxes on sales of specific products such as motor vehicles, natural gas, and gasoline, which are for analytical purposes assumed to be covered by the proposed Business Sales Tax. It should be noted that these three sources in particular represent around $2.5 billion, $1.8 billion and $2.3 billion, respectively, of projected tax revenues under the current sales tax for fiscal 2011, of which the cumulative incidence on businesses is estimated at $3,116,000,000.[15] If the current tax on these items were to be eliminated rather than an exemption created for them under the Business Sales Tax,[16] our estimated taxable sales base for the proposed Business Sales Tax suggests that the foregone revenues of $3.116 billion could have been replaced by an incremental increase of 0.158 percentage points in the proposed Business Sales Tax rate, for a total 2.683% tax on business sales. Such sales would by definition already be exempted from the Consumption Sales Tax as part of the current sales tax systems' effort to prevent double taxation, though this need not necessarily remain so. In other words, the current taxes on these items could be phased out altogether, to be replaced by the proposed Business Sales Tax and Consumption Sales Tax. In most cases, sales to businesses of such currently taxed items would enjoy a tax rate reduction at either the proposed 2.525% or the hypothetical 2.6783% rates (although, as a flat, $0.20 per gallon excise tax, the gasoline tax's percentage burden varies with the products' price per gallon). Since our proposed 7.5% Consumption Sales Tax rate is higher than what would likely be the current blended rate of all such taxes combined, our proposed Consumption Sales Tax rate might be able to be lowered when applied to the increased taxable sales base, assuming that we seek to replace tax revenues from consumer sales with the new consumption tax on a dollar for dollar basis.

To the extent deemed necessary or appropriate to achieve desired revenue targets, this report also poses for consideration the adoption of a 5% tax on the purchase of residential property located within the State of Texas by any person or entity intending to occupy or lease the property for residential purposes, and on the sale to such persons or entities of labor, services, goods and materials to construct or improve any such residential property. We estimate that such a tax would in 2008 have yielded just over $3.46 billion in general revenues. As a consumption-oriented tax imposed near the end, rather than the beginning, of the chain of commerce and distribution, such a tax would represent an economically principled improvement over taxes on sales of natural gas, gasoline and motor vehicles to businesses, for example. The residential property tax might for this reason be seen as the means by which current taxes on

---

[15] See Texas Comptroller of Public Accounts, *Tax Exemptions & Tax Incidence 2009*, pp. 60-64 (February 2009) (*"Tax Exemptions & Tax Incidence 2009"*).

[16] $2,023,225,790,000 during fiscal year 2008.

the sales of such items are eliminated, so as to be able to keep Business Sales Tax and Consumption Sales Tax rates at more or less the levels proposed here. This idea is presented only for consideration, however. Analysis shows that our policy aims can be achieved within the parameters proposed without resorting to imposition of a new residential property sales tax.

Revenues from these new taxes would have to be allocated in ways both new and familiar to Texas legislators and policymakers. In the case of counties, analysis shows that county-level property taxes could be phased out entirely by permitting county governments to receive local allocations averaging around one-half percent of the taxable Business Sales sourced in their jurisdictions. In the case of municipalities, just over half of the cities and towns studied would be unable successfully to replace municipal property tax revenues in their entirety by reliance exclusively on locally-generated Business Sales tax revenues. For these jurisdictions, which we estimate to represent only about $1.7 billion, or 4.41%, of the total property taxes levied statewide, we recommend retention of their existing property tax systems, subject to enhanced legislative and constitutional protections for affected taxpayers. The property tax would be abolished in the remaining municipalities, however.

This report advocates critical review and rationalization of the more than 1600 special purpose districts that litter the Texas landscape, particularly by focusing on the extent to which their financing needs might be more effectively supplied through county-level tax revenues. All but two of the top 39 counties by population could replace the entire 2008 special purpose district property tax levies from within their boundaries by assessing an incremental tax on local Business Sales of less than one-half percent, and the highest of these rates – in Fort Bend County – is only 1.12%. In fact all but 13 could accomplish this transition with a tax of less than one-quarter percent. Even where issues of responsiveness or accountability dictate that current special purpose districts retain their geographic configurations and administrative autonomy, their financing might still be amenable to inclusion in a county-managed system of revenue generation and formula-based allocation. Such a system might be patterned to varying degrees after the system by which state revenues are allocated by formula for use by local school districts, while still retaining local political control and accountability -- at least at the level of county government. If implemented throughout the state, this reform would effectively abolish property taxes in all Texas special purpose districts, relieving property owners of an aggregate $4,952,734,969 in property taxes, or 12.7% of 2008 property taxes levied statewide.

Texas' school district property taxes represent $21,233,517,226, or 54.47%, of the entire 2008 property tax levies statewide and, subject to limited local optionality, this report proposes to abolish all of them. The present, highly developed Foundation School Program, through which state general revenues are allocated to school districts in accordance with strict formulas tied to enrollment, demographics and other relevant factors, in principle serves as a means of permitting some degree of local property tax relief. As such, the program provides a robust "foundation," if you will, for scaling the program to support the full cost of a "basic" education, subject only to the availability of state general revenues to fund it. The two-tier sales tax system described in this report has been designed so as to generate revenues sufficient in the aggregate to fully replace the local *ad valorem* property tax on a pro-forma, statewide basis during fiscal 2008. These revenues would be available and sufficient for full property tax relief in school districts, even after allowing for local tax allocations to replace other property taxes in other local jurisdictions. In the final analysis, the state has a constitutional mandate to "make suitable provision for" free public education to Texas children; this report proposes the means by which to do so.

Even so, allocation formulas would require careful maintenance and review to prevent the state's "basic" education funding from being used for or diverted to local "enrichment" facilities, programs and activities, whether directly or indirectly. For this reason the enabling legislation might identify current or potential interest and sinking (I&S) obligations or projections, either by category or by jurisdiction, that would be ineligible for substitution with state funding. In turn, local districts might retain a minimal right to burden themselves with property taxes in order to fund such programs, but subject to strict limitations both on amounts and voter referendum requirements.

At the same time, we recommend revisiting the current structure of Texas school districts which in many cases are conceived, expanded and gerrymandered – often across city or even county lines – for reasons that have far more to do with the ongoing quest to command a sufficient taxable property base than with effective teaching, responsive relationships with the local community, or personal accountability for teachers and faculty. How much more responsive to the needs of students and parents might school districts be if, rather than being organized into bureaucracy-laden leviathans encompassing populations in the millions, they were instead organized at the truly local, community level, with direct political accountability to the voters being served, and freed from the feudal imperative of having to capture their own sources of financing? The harm in persisting to try to finance public schools through the local property tax extends beyond the evils inherent in the tax itself, and beyond the system's constitutional infirmities. Texans are ready for a fresh start in their relationships with state and local government. Perhaps our public school districts offer a fruitful place to begin.

We have crafted these proposals based on 2008 data (the most recent year for which complete data is available) in such a way as to achieve revenue neutrality in the study year.[17] Subsequent changes in Texas' economic performance, collected tax revenues and spending requirements may require modification of proposed rates in order to maintain revenue neutrality for any subsequent target year. In particular, no effort is made by this report to project the adjustments

Summary of Property Taxes Abolished
(pro forma 2008)

Tax Jurisdictions	Property Taxes Abolished	%	Property Taxes Retained	%	Total	% of Aggregate
Top 39 Counties	$4,784,390,135.00	100%	$0.00	0%	$4,784,390,135.00	12.27%
Remaining Counties	$1,558,314,768.00	100%	$0.00	0%	$1,558,314,768.00	4%
Municipalities in Top 39 Counties	$4,378,086,064.89	73.32%	$1,592,877,943.11	26.68%	$5,970,964,008.00	15.32%
Remaining Municipalities	$351,985,605.41	73.32%	$128,062,833.59	26.68%	$480,048,439.00	1.23%
SPD's in Top 39 Counties	$4,569,780,623.00	100%	$0.00	0%	$4,569,780,623.00	11.72%
Remaining SPD's	$382,954,346.00	100%	$0.00	0%	$382,954,346.00	0.98%
Subtotal:	$16,025,511,542.30	90.30%	$1,720,940,776.70	9.70%	$17,746,452,319.00	45.53%
School Districts	$21,233,517,226.00	100%	$0.00	0%	$21,233,517,226.00	54.47%
Aggregate Property Taxes Statewide	$37,259,028,768.30	95.59%	$1,720,940,776.70	4.41%	$38,979,969,545.00	100%

in proposed rates that might be required to address anticipated operating deficits in the 2010-2011 period or beyond. It is worth pointing out, however, that growth projections for the Texas economy in general may lend themselves to more precise estimation when viewed as statewide aggregates for business sales in general, as compared to being viewed with respect to each local jurisdiction and on an industry-by-industry, or product-by-product, basis. If so, this would enhance the accuracy of revenue projections under the proposed Business Sales tax, at least,

---

[17] We have left intact the recommended rate of 2.525% for the Business Sales Tax in order to maintain consistency throughout the presentation, but leaving in place $1.7 billion of property taxes actually permits a rate reduction toward 2.44% while maintaining revenue neutrality statewide. Doing so, however, would in turn increase the number of municipalities that would have to retain their property tax, unless we attenuate the actual permitted rate reduction. At 2.525%, the additional $1.7 billion in revenues would be available to apply to reduction or elimination of other business taxes not examined here.

thereby equipping policymakers with a more effective fiscal planning tool. Subject to these considerations, the underlying structure of these proposals should be valid and workable for 2011 and beyond.

This report is intended to facilitate serious dialogue on elimination of the property tax in Texas by providing some insight into the detailed fiscal circumstances that prevail in the individual local jurisdictions involved. In that spirit, our specific proposals represent one possible scenario, subject to fine-tuning, certainly, and possibly to substantial revision, as legislative deliberation and policy analysis progress. We know that, as long as any portion of the property tax system remains in place, its attendant ills will likewise remain, as will the potential for its creeping resurrection. At the same time, we accept that local conditions and practical considerations in many municipalities, in particular, do not permit the complete abolition of the system as their primary source of revenues. Even so, the proposals set forth in this report would have completely abolished property taxes for all but 237 of the 3942 counties, municipalities, special purpose districts and school districts in the State of Texas, representing more than 95% of the entire 2008 property taxes levied statewide. If even part of such reforms might realistically be put into practice, then they are worth serious consideration. This effort and this debate require that we try to reconcile important but competing public values, not the least of which include individual liberty and the protection of private property.

DISCUSSION AND ANALYSIS

I.   INTRODUCTION

A.   Overview of Texas State and Local Tax System

Texas' state and local tax system presently consists of a hodgepodge of different assessments, fees and schemes operating at various levels of government. Having evolved more out of immediate need and/or political expedience than a coherent governing philosophy, these systems create a variety of inefficiencies, inequities, economic distortions, and opportunities for abuse and bureaucratic oppression. On occasion these effects may neutralize one another; more often they tend to exacerbate one another.

The *ad valorem* property tax system, in effect at the county and local levels essentially in its current form for many decades, imposes an annual assessment on owners of real and tangible property within each taxing district's boundaries, based on the corresponding appraisal district's annual determination of that property's value. Property taxes provide in most cases the primary means of financing school district facilities and operations, city and county governments, and nearly two thousand so-called "special purpose districts", organized to provide services such as hospital and emergency response, crime control, residential utility and infrastructure development, water control and management, and others. Laws and regulations governing the property tax have acquired over time numerous limitations, exemptions, and exceptions to shift its incidence away from certain favored groups, and judicial intervention and public pressure have endeavored to roll back its burden in certain jurisdictions. The Texas property tax provides the single largest source of tax revenue to government in the state of Texas, and represents one of the most economically burdensome systems of its kind in any U.S. state.

The sales and use tax system, assessed at both the state and participating local levels, imposes a one-time tax on the sale to or use by Texas residents and businesses of certain items of tangible personal property and, to a lesser extent, certain enumerated types of services. Developed throughout the United States as a replacement or supplement for diminished property tax revenues in the wake of the Great Depression,[18] state retail sales and use taxes are designed to function principally as a tax on consumption.[19] Texas' laws and regulations contain numerous exemptions, exclusions and interpretations designed to steer the tax away from business inputs, while at the same time serving various other social and economic policy aims. Sales and use taxes, or simply "sales taxes" as referred to in this report, produce the second largest source of tax revenue to Texas' state and local governments combined, and represent the single largest source of tax revenue for Texas' state government.

The so-called "Franchise" or "margins" tax, adopted in its current form effective for periods beginning 2008, constitutes in effect a blended "gross receipts" and "income" tax, in which businesses must annually remit a percentage of their entire gross revenues, determined in most cases net of either the business's cost of goods sold, total employee compensation, or a flat 30% of total revenue. Subject to numerous exemptions for certain federal, non-profit or other favored classes of businesses or organizations, as well as a variety of deductions, exclusions, credits, refunds and accounting procedures designed to moderate its impact on small businesses or otherwise promote specific state policies, the franchise tax applies at every level of business activity throughout the chain of state commerce, and to most forms of businesses not otherwise specifically exempted.

In addition to these tax systems, the Texas Comptroller's office administers almost sixty other sales and excise taxes, fees and assessments, including taxes on the sale of boats, batteries, manufactured housing and motor vehicles, taxes on the production or distribution of cement, sulphur, crude oil and natural gas, gasoline and diesel fuel, tobacco products, oysters and even

---

[18] *See* John L. Mikesell, *The Future of American Sales and Use Taxation*, THE FUTURE OF STATE TAXATION, 15 (David Brunori, ed. 1998).

[19] John F. Due summarized the essential philosophy of a consumption tax as follows:

> "If a sales tax is to be a truly general consumption tax, it should apply to all expenditures for personal consumption purposes but not to any transactions involving use in business activity. Exclusion of any personal consumption purchases favors those persons with disproportionate expenditures on these goods, leads to economic distortions by shifting purchases and production from taxed to untaxed goods, reduces revenue at given rates, and, as is well known, complicates compliance and administration. Inclusion of purchases for production purposes is contrary to the philosophy of the tax, results in haphazard and uncertain distribution of the tax burden, affects choice of production processes, and, from a state's standpoint, may adversely affect economic development"

John F. Due, *Sales Tax Exemptions – the Erosion of the Tax Base*, REVENUE ADMINISTRATION, 1982, PROCEEDINGS OF THE FIFTIETH ANNUAL MEETING OF THE NATIONAL ASSOCIATION OF TAX ADMINISTRATORS, 50, 200 (1982). *See also* JEROME R. HELLERSTEIN & WALTER HELLERSTEIN, STATE TAXATION (3d ed. 2002); Wayne G. Eggert, *Globalization of the Marketplace: Sales and Use Tax Implications,* SALES TAXATION: CRITICAL ISSUES IN POLICY AND ADMINISTRATION, 143, 150 (William F. Fox, ed., National Tax Association – Tax Institute of America, 1992).

controlled substances (e.g., marijuana), and taxes on inheritances, insurance policies, hotel occupancy, pari-mutuel betting and sexually oriented businesses, to name a few. Revenues from some of these taxes are dedicated by law to particular uses; others are received into the general fund and available for general government purposes. Since many of them either constitute or function as sales and use taxes in their own right, certain exemptions under the general sales tax laws often prevent them from being taxed under both systems.[20] But their rates and applicability do not necessarily coincide with those of the general sales tax, and in some cases there is otherwise little evident correlation or coordination between the policies they reflect and the policies and incentives embodied in the tax systems described above.

B.   Scope of Report; Methodology

This report undertakes to evaluate the fiscal ramifications associated with proposals to eliminate the Texas property tax system in favor of a broadened, simplified sales and use tax system. Particular attention will be devoted to the consequences of any such reform to the individual county and local governments and other taxing jurisdictions that currently rely on the property tax, and, where necessary, specific revenue alternatives will be considered or recommended as a means of addressing individual jurisdictions the composition of whose local economies do not render them amenable to such reform. No effort will be made to recommend modifications to the several dozen miscellaneous excise and other taxes described above. A truly comprehensive reform would undertake to expand, remove or harmonize these taxes with a broadened general sales tax system, but this is presently beyond the scope of this report. At an appropriate point in the analysis, consideration will also be given to the nature and disadvantages of the state franchise tax, including the possibility of its elimination along with the state and local property tax. The role of state government in school finance and administration will be examined as a necessary component of a comprehensive revenue solution. But this report's primary focus is and will remain the property and sales tax systems, and its conclusion will highlight specific considerations dictated by local conditions in the various local tax jurisdictions.

---

[20] *See* Texas Tax Code, Section 151.308, "Items Taxed by Other Law". This is not always the case; fireworks are subject to both the sales tax and a special fireworks surtax, for example. *See* Texas Tax Code, Section 161.001 *et seq.*

The analysis will examine in detail all Texas counties estimated to have a population in excess of 100,000 in 2008 (a total of 39 counties), based on the population estimates provided by the Texas Association of Counties – County Information Project. (See **Table 1**.) According to our analysis of data retrieved from the Texas Comptroller's online database, the 2008 property taxes collected in these 39 counties represent more than 84% of the $38.98 billion in property taxes collected statewide that year, and the taxable 2008 sales in all industries made in these same counties represent more than 88.6% of the $1.464 billion of aggregate taxable sales in all industries statewide. The remaining 205 counties and their respective fiscal situations are addressed in this report on an aggregate basis for purposes of simplification; as a group, these rural counties appear to have more in common fiscally with one another than with the more populous counties.

The methods used to draw inferences from the available data rely to a large extent on a static, rather than dynamic, view of local fiscal and economic conditions. We did employ the 2008 IMPLAN® input-output model for Texas[21] to assess certain key issues. In an economy as large as that of the State of Texas, such analysis provides useful insight into overall relationships and interdependencies. But, owing to the nature of the data utilized, the methods of its collection, and the limitations of the input-output model itself, these models'

Table 1 – Top 39 Counties by Population

County	Population
Harris	3,980,602
Dallas	2,411,921
Tarrant	1,749,974
Bexar	1,621,304
Travis	998,561
Collin	763,438
El Paso	738,416
Hidalgo	721,275
Denton	637,516
Fort Bend	532,609
Montgomery	431,238
Williamson	395,146
Cameron	389,164
Nueces	320,319
Brazoria	301,228
Galveston	288,489
Bell	285,598
Lubbock	265,372
Jefferson	242,201
Webb	235,937
McLennan	230,849
Smith	201,160
Brazos	174,864
Johnson	153,889
Hays	149,424
Ellis	147,909
Ector	131,180
Midland	129,159
Wichita	127,701
Taylor	126,651
Potter	121,143
Grayson	118,786
Gregg	117,665
Guadalupe	117,341
Randall	114,291
Parker	112,054
Comal	110,119
Tom Green	107,445
Kaufman	100,399

[21] See text and notes, *infra*, at nn. 135 -142.

predictive qualities diminish when applied to small, local sub-economies, particularly those characterized by proportionately high levels of cross-border flows in goods, services, capital and labor, and in any case they tend to be of limited value when comparing the income effects of alternate tax schemes considered on the basis of revenue neutrality. Similarly, we do not undertake to project our findings for 2008 into future tax periods. To the extent that economic contraction or other factors have affected fiscal balances at the state or lower level, these effects would have to be taken into account in translating this report's recommendations into detailed policy going forward. Nevertheless, we are satisfied that this static approach provides useful insight into the factors that will determine the success or failure of any particular reform at the local level, and clear direction as to both the challenges of local property tax reform and the potential solutions.

C.   Guiding Philosophy

Finally the guiding philosophy underlying this report embodies the recognition that (1) taxes at levels sufficient to meet public need represent a necessary but not sufficient condition to good government, (2) the system through which government extracts revenue from its host economy should be selected for its efficiency of administration, simplicity (i.e., low cost) of compliance, breadth of coverage, and neutrality of effect on economic decision-making and allocation of resources,[22] and (3) all other things being equal, a system that creates a more favorable climate for private sector job creation and growth, that renders government more transparent and more accountable to its citizens, and that preserves or promotes fundamental liberty interests, should be preferred over any other.

We start from the premise that the tax on real and tangible property represents one of the most inefficient, anti-growth, anti-liberty forms of taxation available to government. It punishes businesses, industry and individuals alike with taxes that stay more or less the same regardless

---

[22] Professor John Mikesell of Indiana University's School of Public and Environmental Affairs has condensed what he describes as the "broad expectations of revenue policy" into "yield, equity, economic efficiency, collectability, and transparency." *See* John L. Mikesell, *The Prospects for General Sales Taxation in American State and Local Government Finance: Challenges for a Fiscal Workhorse Unready for the New Millenium*, 16 J. PUB. BUDGETING, ACCOUNTING & FINANCIAL MANAGEMENT 6 (Spring 2004). A 1997 Texas House of Representatives report on the Texas tax system summarized the "standards for evaluating any system of taxation" as including, in part: "equitable distribution of the tax burden, economically efficient taxes that promote growth, ease of administration, and accountability." Patricia Tierney Alofsin & John J. Goodson, *The Tax System and Public School Financing in Texas*, p.9, TEXAS HOUSE OF REPRESENTATIVES, HOUSE RESEARCH ORGANIZATION SPECIAL FOCUS (March 24, 1997). These standards and expectations form the basis of our analysis as well.

of whether or to what extent the taxpayer actually generates revenues or income with which to pay them. It suffers gross inconsistency in its application from taxpayer to taxpayer, and requires the creation, staffing and funding of bureaucratic fiefdoms throughout the state in which tax assessors enjoy the power to exercise undue discretion over who does and does not receive favorable treatment and, more insidiously, the taxable value of property to be taxed. It in effect turns homeowners into squatters in their own homes, requiring over the course of their lifetimes that they pay most or all the value of their property to the government for the privilege of living there. It drives the elderly out of homes for which they have cared and saved their entire lives. It depresses the value of property and imposes a disproportionate burden on capital-intensive industries, thereby retarding growth in the very industries that are best able to generate Texas jobs. It hurts our economy, it hurts families, it breeds disrespect for state government, and it disenfranchises Texas citizens who lack the connections or the resources to challenge the appraisers' findings or mount a judicial challenge to their relentless grab for more revenues.

Some may argue that the property tax is really just a tax on the consumption of the benefits afforded by real property ownership, and at just over 2% of value per annum, for example, is three times less burdensome than the corresponding 6.25% sales tax on consumption of personal goods and services. To make this an honest comparison, however, we must place the two on "apples to apples" footing, which requires that we measure the annual property tax against the value of real estate "consumption" that occurs during a single year with respect to the property being taxed. Viewed in this way, the amount consumed may be seen as the economic equivalent of the property's annual depreciation or, more generously, its equivalent rental value. Assuming a price-to-net rental ratio of 8 (meaning that a landlord could purchase the property expecting to recover his full investment within eight years of ownership), the economic value to the owner of occupying and using the property could be said to equal 12.5% of its initial market value each year. A two percent annual tax on the *initial* value of the property would represent 2/12.5, or 16% of the real estate value "consumed" in that year. Obviously, a 16% tax on consumption represents more than twice the economic burden as a 6.25% tax on consumption. Running this same estimate instead against annual depreciation, which under ordinary accounting principles would usually be 3.33% per year (a 30 year depreciable life) for real property, we find that the two percent annual tax represents 2/3.33, or 60% of the real estate value "consumed" in that year -- nearly ten times the economic burden as a 6.25% tax on consumption. Even if we assume that the true value of the "consumption" increases above straight-line depreciation due to inflation or local economic growth, it is unlikely that such factors will escape the appraiser's keen attention with each succeeding revaluation, which may be expected to rise in response. This comparison places in stark relief the true nature of the property tax as a punitive measure against an institution thought to represent the "American dream" and a foundation for individual liberty.

Contrast this system with the retail sales tax system, with which it currently stands side by side in Texas. For its transparency, its ease of administration, its neutrality of effect on business decision-making, and its care for individual liberty, the retail sales tax in theory knows no equal. Uniquely American in its provenance, the modern retail sales tax is fundamentally different in character from most other forms of taxation. As stated by Professor Mikesell:

> The essential logic of the American sales tax is that of a tax on consumption expenditure. It is not a good proxy for other taxes. It is not an income tax; such taxes assign burdens among taxpayers according to net income, generally defined "as equal consumption during a given period, plus increases in net worth." It is not a selective excise; these taxes, like those on alcoholic beverages or tobacco products, apply to transactions that, for reasons of equity or social impact, merit extraordinary or putative tax burden. It is not a general gross receipts, transactions, or turnover tax; such taxes, although precursors of the American sales tax, strike each exchange in the production/distribution chain virtually without exception for type or use of purchase, not even excluding purchases for resale or of ingredients to become physical parts of an item to be sold. The American sales tax represents a method of taxing according to consumption expenditure. If some other distribution of the cost of government is desired, some handle other than the retail sales tax should be applied.[23]

Recent economic trends have caused observers to question the continued viability of the retail sales tax in its present form, however. The rise of ecommerce, in which consumers make growing percentages of their purchases from vendors located outside of their home states,[24] combined with the failure of the tax (either by design or in practice) effectively to reach many if not most consumer services, has eroded the retail sales tax's base on a relative basis and

---

[23] See John L. Mikesell, *The Sales and Use Taxation of Services in Public Finance Theory*, attached as Appendix A to Report of Price Waterhouse, *Analysis of Selected Tax Policy Alternatives Using the Florida Multitax Simulation Models*, submitted to the Florida Taxation and Budget Reform Commission, Oct 8, 1991 (footnotes omitted), accessible at http://legacy.library.ucsf.edu/tid/ggr12f00.

[24] Comment, *Internet Taxation Without Physical Representation?: States Seek Solution To Stop e-Commerce Sales Tax Shortfall*, 50 ST. LOUIS L.J. 893 (Spring, 2006); Comment, *Surfing Around The Sales Tax Byte: The Internet Tax Freedom Act, Sales Tax Jurisdiction And The Role Of Congress*, 12 ALB. L.J. SCI. & TECH. 619 (2002)

produced substantial inefficiencies and inequities in its application.[25] Related to this is the extent to which products that formerly were delivered in tangible, and therefore taxable form, are now delivered electronically, such as music, software, videos and other media and information. The exemptions created to spare lower income citizens the brunt of its burden (groceries, health care, education, etc.) have been demonstrated to benefit middle and higher income citizens at least as much if not more, to the point of materially diminishing the breadth of the tax base and renewing calls instead for a program of means-tested rebates or credits, or even a household consumption tax measured and reported by households as a function of net, post-savings income.[26] The tendency of lawmakers to expand its base to tax business inputs as well as individual consumption likewise undermines its claim to embody the qualities associated in theory with a pure consumption tax.[27]

But state and local government must be financed somehow. In choosing how to do so, the question to be asked is whether our choice advances our fundamental political values and policy goals better than any other or, if not, whether it lends itself to being improved upon to serve those values and goals more effectively. It has been argued that sound public finance requires diversified sources of tax revenues, such as a mixture of property, income and sales taxes, on the theory that a more stabilized revenue stream will result, and that the "defects of each tax tend to 'average out' and reduce taxpayer dissatisfaction."[28] Our view is that an imperfect tax is not made more perfect by afflicting taxpayers with an even worse one, and that cyclical variability in revenues from a less diverse tax system may be addressed through flexibility in rates and a willingness on the part of government to constrain spending during tough economic times, just as its constituents must do. By these standards, the Texas sales and use tax, for which we already have a well-functioning administrative infrastructure in place, seems to offer the best starting point.

---

[25] See generally Kirk J. Stark, *Florida Services Tax: The Uneasy Case For Extending The Sales Tax To Services*, 30 FLA. ST. U.L. REV. 435 (Spring 2003); Rich McKeown, *Questioning the Viability of the Sales Tax: Can It Be Simplified to Create a Level Playing Field?* 2000 B.Y.U.L. Rev. 165 (2000); Hal R. Varian, *Taxation of Electronic Commerce*, 13 HARV. J. LAW & TECH. 639 (2000). Stark highlights this point in the context of products such as music and video that are being sold increasingly in intangible, downloadable format. *See* Stark at 446.

[26] *See* Stark, *supra* n. 25, at 460-62; GEORGE R. ZODROW, STATE SALES AND INCOME TAXES: AN ECONOMIC ANALYSIS 80-98 (1999)

[27] *See* Stark, *supra* n. 25, at 456-57.

[28] *See, e.g.*, Alofsin and Goodson, *supra*, n.22.

II.   TEXAS PROPERTY AND SALES TAX REVENUES

A.   Composition of Texas Economic and Taxable Sales Activity

Strictly speaking, the Texas sales and use tax operates as a tax either upon the *sale in Texas* of a covered product,[29] in which case the in-state vendor is expected to collect and remit the tax for the benefit of the state, or upon the *use in Texas* of a covered product purchased from a retailer,[30] in which case either the consumer is expected to voluntarily report and remit the tax due, or the retailer – if it does business in Texas – is expected to collect and remit the tax on behalf of the consumer. States are barred by constitutional principles from taxing businesses lacking a physical presence in the state,[31] so collection of the use tax directly from in-state consumers is seen as the means by which a fair distribution, or "distributional equity," is achieved between Texans' purchases from in-state and out-of-state businesses. In reality, use taxes in general are widely ignored or even unknown to many, and experts and tax authorities have had little expectation of being able to change this without personally oppressive enforcement means against which voters would likely rebel.[32] As a result, outside of sales by established out-of-state vendors with sufficient presence in Texas to be required to collect the tax from consumers, the use tax is better thought of as a tax on purchases that are otherwise reportable by consumers under other regulatory regimes (such as vehicle purchases). For the fourth quarter of 2009, the Texas Comptroller reports that use tax purchases from both in-state and out-of-state vendors amounted to only eight percent of the aggregate purchases by Texans to which the sales and use tax is applicable. The theoretically collectible figure probably is much higher.

Over the past decade, however, an organized, cooperative effort among over forty participating U.S. states has been underway to at least partially address this issue. In fall 1999, the National Governor's Association (NGA) and the National Conference of State Legislatures (NCSL)

---

[29] Texas Tax Code Section 151.052.

[30] Texas Tax Code Sections 151.101 through 107.

[31] *See* Quill Corp. v. N. Dakota, 504 U.S. 298; 112 S. Ct. 1904; 119 L. Ed. 2d 91 (1992).

[32] *See* Michael Mazerov, *A Five-Year Extension of the Internet Tax Moratorium Would Further Erode the Tax Base of State and Localities*, 21 ST. TAX NOTES 957, 957 n.1 (2001); Stark, supra n. 25, at n. 49 ("Noncompliance with use tax obligations is nearly universal--in fact, most consumers are not even aware of the requirement to pay state use taxes for items purchased tax-free from out-of-state vendors. Use taxes collected from consumers tend only to be effective where there is some sort of information-reporting obligation associated with the out-of-state purchase, as in the case of automobiles purchased out-of-state for use in the taxing state.").

organized the "Streamlined Sales Tax Project" (or "SST"), pursuant to which participating states would conform their tax legislation to certain key uniform standards, and large, multistate online or mail-order vendors would voluntarily participate in a unified tax collection and distribution arrangement with participating states.[33] Once the system has proven itself fair and effective, the project's organizers hoped that Congress would enact legislation authorizing states to tax vendors on the basis of the principles and procedures it establishes. A 2004 study by The Progress and Freedom Foundation, however, found that the maximum increase in total sales tax collections nationwide would reach only $4.8 billion, and in the process participating states would lose to non-participating states around $29 billion of the $123 billion in potentially affected sales, costing jobs, personal income, and resulting losses in other state tax revenues.[34] Even so, the study estimated that, after taking all of these effects into account, Texas stood to gain approximately $415 million in net additional sales tax revenues from participating. The Texas Comptroller has recently estimated that sales tax revenues lost to online sales stands at around $600 million,[35] which at a 6.25% sales tax rate represents a lost taxable sales base of $9.6 billion. So far, twenty three of the 44 participating states have enacted legislation conforming their taxes to the SST system; and compromise by the SSTP on local origin sourcing rules may have paved the way for Texas to do so as well.[36] This figure will be revisited at an appropriate point in this report; otherwise, this report will focus primarily on the "sales tax" component of the sales and use tax based on reported aggregate and local taxable sales.

The Texas sales tax currently applies with varying exceptions to over twenty different industry classifications, ranging from the "Retail Trade" and "Accommodations and Food Service" to "Mining", "Manufacturing", "Insurance" and other diverse industries.[37] **Table 2** sets forth a full

[33] See "Streamlined Sales Tax -- Frequently Asked Questions", http://www.streamlinedsalestax.org/index.php?page=faqs (accessed 6/20/10).

[34] See THOMAS M. LENARD AND STEPHEN MCGONEGAL, TAXATION OF ONLINE SALES: COMPETING WITH THE STREAMLINED SALES TAX PROJECT, PROGRESS ON POINT PERIODIC COMMENTARIES ON THE POLICY DEBATE (Release 11.16 September 2004)

[35] Maria Halkias, States consider taxing Internet sales to help boost revenues, Dallas Morning News, Wednesday, April 14, 2010.

[36] The SSTP amended its rules in 2007 to permit local jurisdictions to tax sales transactions on the basis of the "origin" of the sale, rather than its "destination", and Texas recently amended its statute to conform. See "An Act Relating to the Sales and Use Tax", Tex. H.B. No. 3319 (80R), signed into law 6/15/2007.

[37] These classifications are based directly on the statistical classifications used in the North American Industry Classfication System (NAICS). See http://www.window.state.tx.us/taxinfo/sales/naics_coding.htm and http://www.census.gov/eos/www/naics/index.html.

listing of these classifications and the aggregate statewide sales of potentially taxable goods and services reported for each in 2008, including the component of such sales that was subject to the Texas state sales and use tax under then-applicable law.[38] The $1.4 trillion aggregate

Table 2

Texas Sales and Use Tax Base by Industry Classification (2008)

NAICS Industry Classification	Gross Sales ($US)	Percentage of Aggregate	Amount Subject to State Sales Tax ($US)	Percentage of Aggregate
Accommodation and Food Services	38,878,826,745.00	2.67%	33,628,041,444.00	11.27%
Administrative and Support and Waste Management and Remediation Services	25,513,349,163.00	1.75%	9,003,223,094.00	3.02%
Agriculture, Forestry, Fishing and Hunting	1,626,342,251.00	0.11%	137,798,442.00	0.05%
Arts, Entertainment, and Recreation	4,686,780,758.00	0.32%	3,520,605,955.00	1.18%
Construction	89,625,721,676.00	6.16%	12,979,673,981.00	4.35%
Educational Services	1,072,145,977.00	0.07%	290,961,342.00	0.10%
Finance and Insurance	8,740,308,660.00	0.60%	1,380,634,504.00	0.46%
Health Care and Social Assistance	13,851,472,468.00	0.95%	658,470,525.00	0.22%
Information	23,723,862,353.00	1.63%	13,634,133,647.00	4.57%
Management of Companies and Enterprises	2,894,078,079.00	0.20%	821,034,687.00	0.28%
Manufacturing	329,668,249,016.00	22.67%	21,423,023,305.00	7.18%
Mining	28,746,438,242.00	1.98%	12,276,653,428.00	4.11%
Professional, Scientific, and Technical Services	49,840,697,869.00	3.43%	6,288,390,853.00	2.11%
Public Administration	3,496,241,699.00	0.24%	1,479,530,213.00	0.50%
Real Estate and Rental and Leasing	18,591,364,150.00	1.28%	7,254,603,231.00	2.43%
Retail Trade	341,151,078,619.00	23.46%	132,246,835,419.00	44.32%
Transportation and Warehousing	23,288,438,431.00	1.60%	2,464,929,188.00	0.83%
Unclassified Establishments	30,574,617.00	0.00%	1,253,040.00	0.00%
Utilities	78,652,849,846.00	5.41%	8,422,863,919.00	2.82%
Wholesale Trade	346,247,060,625.00	23.81%	22,735,434,438.00	7.62%
Other Services (except Public Administration)	23,822,610,327.00	1.64%	7,753,546,872.00	2.60%
Aggregates	**1,454,148,491,571.00**	**100.00%**	**298,401,641,527.00**	**100.00%**

"Gross Sales" figure for all of these industry classifications combined approximates the total reported sales of all Texas business outlets required to file a sales tax return in 2008, [39] and the

---

[38] Source: Texas Edge Data Center: Taxable Sales Report 2008 (run for all industry classifications in all Texas counties, http://www.texasahead.org/texasedge/run_report.html (accessed July 15, 2010).

[39] This "gross reported sales" figure does not serve as an effective measure of the size of the state's economy; it excludes large amounts of sales by firms having no obligation to file a sales tax return, and, not being offset by the value of imports and transfer payments, it overstates the state's true economic output as captured by the customarily

corresponding percentage column represents the percentage of this aggregate represented by that particular industry. Note that the two industries responsible for the majority (55.59%) of 2008 taxable sales in Texas – "Retail Trade" and "Accommodations and Food Services" -- represented only 23.46% and 2.67%, respectively, of the state's aggregate reported gross sales. "Accommodations and Food Services," together with "Arts, Entertainment and Recreation" and "Information," represent the only classifications for which the majority by value of sales transactions are currently taxable; Retail Trade transactions come in a close fourth at 38.7% taxable. All seventeen other classifications are overwhelmingly not subject to sales tax under current law. This of course is a function of how current laws, exemptions and exclusions were crafted; by design they are intended to function primarily as a tax on "consumption", and therefore to cause the burden to fall disproportionately on purchasers from those four industries. This effect can be seen in reverse in the "Wholesale Trade" and "Manufacturing" industries, the gross sales percentages of which (23.81% and 22.67%, respectively) dwarf their corresponding taxable sales percentages (7.62% and 7.18%). Taken together, though, Retail Trade, Accommodations and Food Services, Wholesale Trade and Manufacturing alone accounted in 2008 for 72.61% of the state's reported gross sales, and 70.39% of its currently taxable sales.[40] All seventeen other industry classifications combined represent less than 30% of the aggregate in both categories. Determining the extent to which the state's economy might support a substantial increase in the sales tax burden, therefore, whether through an increase in sales rates, or an expansion of the taxable sales base, or both, will lead us to examine closely most if not all of these four largest industry classifications, if for no other reason than the fact that – as Willie Sutton famously observed – "that's where the money is." But first we should understand exactly the extent to which the current taxable sales base will – or will not -- support the effort.

---

used (and more meaningful) "gross domestic product" figure, reported as $1,226,493,000,000 in the Texas Comptroller's 2009 annual financial report (Texas Comptroller of Public Accounts, *Comprehensive Annual Financial Report for the State of Texas for the Fiscal Year Ending August 31, 2009*, p.246 (February 2010) ("CAFR 2009")), or as $1,223,511,000,000 by the U.S. Bureau of Economic Analysis (http://www.bea.gov/regional/gsp, accessed 9/4/10).

[40] As stated in NAICS Clarification Memorandum No. 1, NAICS Sector 42 - Wholesale Trade, Scope and Implementation Guidelines for U.S. Statistical Agencies, quoting the US NAICS Manual, 1997, p. 375, "The wholesaling process is an intermediate step in the distribution of merchandise. Wholesalers are organized to sell or arrange the purchase of (a) goods for resale (i.e., goods sold to other wholesalers or retailers), (b) capital or durable nonconsumer goods, and (c) raw and intermediate materials and supplies used in production. Wholesalers sell merchandise to other businesses and normally operate from a warehouse or office."

B.   The Magnitude of the Challenge – Limiting New Sales Taxes to the "Retail Trade" Alone

Rather than starting by looking at the state's entire economic base all at once, it is instructive to look first at the principal component of the sales tax base -- the "Retail Trade" component. **Table 3** illustrates, for the 39 most populous counties, the average ratio of property taxes levied in 2008 to the retail sales taxes that, based upon reported economic activity in currently taxable retail sales, would be nominally collectible from taxable sales activity in those counties at the standard state sales tax rate of 6.25%. This ratio represents a measure of the "tax effort" that would be required to replace locally-sourced property tax revenues with locally-sourced sales tax revenues, stated as a function of the current state sales tax rate. As **Table 3** shows, 2008 property tax collections in these 39 counties averaged 4.126[41] times the retail sales taxes nominally collectible in these counties at the current state sales tax rate of 6.25%.[42] The deviation from this average among the counties studied ranges from a negative 3.157 to a positive 3.327 percentage points, reflecting the fact that some counties in 2008 enjoyed a disproportionately higher taxable sales base (such as Randall County, with a Nominal Property-to-Sales Tax Ratio of 0.97), while others have a disproportionately lower sales tax base (such as Ellis County, with a Nominal Property-to-Sales Tax Ratio of 7.454). If local property tax levies within those counties were to be entirely replaced by an increase in sales tax rates on currently taxable retail sales in those counties, an incremental, new set of county, municipal, school district. and/or other special purpose district sales taxes on retail sales would have to be imposed in each such county that would aggregate to a weighted average of 4.126 times the

---

[41] This ratio is close to, but somewhat lower than, the 4.716 ratio for aggregate collections and sales in all counties statewide.

[42] The figures are given as "nominally collectible" because various exemptions, exclusions, discounts and enforceability issues would operate to reduce actual collections below the theoretical figure produced simply by multiplying the tax rate by most general measures of aggregate economic activity. However, as a check on the overall reliability of our approach to this data, we may compare the aggregate statewide "nominally collectible" sales tax of $18,650 102,595.44 (.0625 times $298,401,641,527) for calendar year 2008 with the somewhat higher actual Texas state sales tax collections reported for fiscal year 2008 of $21,640,855,000. *See* Texas Comptroller of Public Accounts, *Comprehensive Annual Financial Report for the State of Texas for the Fiscal Year Ending August 31, 2008,* p.240 (February 2009) ("*CAFR 2008*"). This comparison gives us confidence that our methodology does not reflect a bias to *overstate* aggregate potential revenues,at least, so the difference will be disregarded for present purposes.

Table 3

Comparison of Texas Property Taxes and Retail Sales Tax Potential

Top 39 Counties by Population	Property Taxes ($US)	Retail Sales ($US)			Nominal Property-to-Sales Tax Ratios and Deviations	
County	Actual Property Taxes Levied in all in-county Taxing Jurisdictions	Gross Retail Sales	Amount Retail Sales Subject to State Sales Tax	Nominal State Retail Sales Taxes Collectible @ 6.25%**	Nominal Property to Sales Tax Ratios	Deviation from Average
Harris	7,424,792,202.00	58,095,979,469.00	24,086,870,092.00	1,505,429,380.75	4.932	0.806
Dallas	4,397,201,734.00	39,190,875,873.00	13,835,748,562.00	864,734,285.13	5.085	0.959
Tarrant	3,229,775,699.00	25,031,557,837.00	10,640,745,969.00	665,046,623.06	4.856	0.730
Bexar	2,424,607,729.00	22,065,065,918.00	9,197,025,274.00	574,814,079.63	4.218	0.092
Travis	2,212,177,208.00	14,590,240,588.00	6,739,295,625.00	421,205,976.56	5.252	1.126
Collin	1,625,200,541.00	11,620,605,700.00	5,221,775,770.00	326,360,985.63	4.980	0.853
El Paso	776,219,957.00	8,373,575,223.00	3,554,677,134.00	222,167,320.88	3.494	(0.633)
Hidalgo	630,820,030.00	8,046,333,037.00	3,651,101,584.00	228,193,849.00	2.764	(1.362)
Denton	1,112,293,529.00	10,265,553,636.00	2,693,778,364.00	168,361,147.75	6.607	2.480
Fort Bend	1,033,756,774.00	6,411,390,246.00	2,320,069,038.00	145,004,314.88	7.129	3.003
Montgomery	694,388,205.00	7,506,383,112.00	2,727,350,004.00	170,459,375.25	4.074	(0.053)
Williamson	720,717,112.00	5,731,336,574.00	2,316,779,278.00	144,798,704.88	4.977	0.851
Cameron	310,598,230.00	3,549,291,431.00	1,735,667,921.00	108,479,245.06	2.863	(1.263)
Nueces	460,611,557.00	3,967,294,163.00	1,958,269,720.00	122,391,857.50	3.763	(0.363)
Brazoria	531,231,383.00	3,140,693,964.00	1,483,367,678.00	92,710,479.88	5.730	1.604
Galveston	562,250,562.00	2,973,274,750.00	1,478,170,036.00	92,385,627.25	6.086	1.960
Bell	284,099,889.00	5,060,283,207.00	1,491,643,051.00	93,227,690.69	3.047	(1.079)
Lubbock	286,035,178.00	4,314,265,772.00	1,770,421,544.00	110,651,346.50	2.585	(1.541)
Jefferson	453,082,674.00	3,636,487,404.00	1,702,920,167.00	106,432,510.44	4.257	0.131
Webb	297,282,029.00	3,263,269,534.00	1,347,939,036.00	84,246,189.75	3.529	(0.598)
McLennan	261,135,700.00	3,132,710,749.00	1,182,424,458.00	73,901,528.63	3.534	(0.593)
Smith	232,386,408.00	3,213,139,338.00	1,394,484,546.00	87,155,284.13	2.666	(1.460)
Brazos	217,901,059.00	2,357,523,728.00	1,116,396,372.00	69,774,773.25	3.123	(1.003)
Johnson	222,901,862.00	3,003,042,260.00	574,717,346.00	35,919,834.13	6.206	2.079
Hays	220,149,276.00	1,980,867,657.00	1,087,616,288.00	67,976,018.00	3.239	(0.888)
Ellis	222,448,255.00	1,291,922,225.00	477,501,022.00	29,843,813.88	7.454	3.327
Ector	179,242,089.00	2,565,276,845.00	1,028,973,292.00	64,310,830.75	2.787	(1.339)
Midland	201,922,071.00	2,354,901,780.00	1,166,322,742.00	72,895,171.38	2.770	(1.356)
Wichita	126,291,681.00	1,685,873,259.00	760,604,112.00	47,537,757.00	2.657	(1.470)
Taylor	131,517,411.00	2,052,776,914.00	907,461,366.00	56,716,335.38	2.319	(1.808)
Potter	230,253,556.00	2,568,936,172.00	1,123,916,375.00	70,244,773.44	3.278	(0.849)
Grayson	139,841,988.00	1,429,175,967.00	628,500,481.00	39,281,280.06	3.560	(0.566)
Gregg	154,726,834.00	2,653,449,171.00	1,154,678,393.00	72,167,399.56	2.144	(1.982)
Guadalupe	144,974,346.00	998,216,882.00	430,308,923.00	26,894,307.69	5.391	1.264
Randall	25,265,410.00	1,300,609,261.00	416,844,543.00	26,052,783.94	0.970	(3.157)
Parker	177,529,185.00	1,671,509,400.00	530,180,376.00	33,136,273.50	5.358	1.231
Comal	184,196,942.00	1,401,927,830.00	598,782,869.00	37,423,929.31	4.922	0.796
Tom Green	87,322,380.00	1,504,327,379.00	671,547,643.00	41,971,727.69	2.081	(2.046)
Kaufman	137,719,555.00	1,584,881,554.00	352,840,703.00	22,052,543.94	6.245	2.119
				Average ratio:	4.126	
Subtotals:						
39 Largest	32,764,868,230.00	285,584,825,809.00	115,557,717,697.00	7,222,357,356.06	4.537	
All other counties:	6,215,101,315.00	55,566,252,810.00	16,689,117,722.00	1,043,069,857.63	5.958	
Statewide Total:	38,979,969,545.00	341,151,078,619.00	132,246,835,419.00	8,265,427,213.69	4.716	

current state sales rate of 6.25%, or 25.79%. This excludes any sales taxes being currently assessed by these local jurisdictions under current Texas law (up to 2% altogether).[43] Using the broader figures for effecting this conversion in all counties statewide, the incremental, new local taxes would have to amount to a figure aggregating to a weighted average of 4.716 times the current state sales rate of 6.25%, or 29.47%. In the alternative, for illustration purposes, we could also assume that local rates remain unchanged, and that instead the entire increase occurs in the state sales tax rate, the incremental revenues from which would be allocated to local property tax relief in proportion to need. In that case, the new state sales tax rate would equal 29.47 percentage points plus the current 6.25, for a new state sales tax rate of 35.72%. In either case, once state and local rates are cumulated in individual jurisdictions, the resulting figure of 35% or higher would almost certainly encounter fatal popular opposition, and deservedly so. This is too high for a state-wide transition from property to sales taxes to be shouldered by currently taxable retail sales alone.

Pausing to consider this idea's other implications, though, we can see that the more populous counties (those with populations in excess of 100,000) have a stronger relative retail sales base as a group than do the less populous counties. As illustrated in **Table 4**, the theoretical imposition in all counties of our hypothetical, incremental, new tax of 29.47% on in-county taxable retail sales would generate a surplus of roughly $1.3 billion over their aggregate levies under the current property tax regime, while the least populous counties would in the aggregate face a corresponding shortfall of roughly $1.3 billion. This shortfall represents a full 20% of the property taxes currently levied by the various taxing jurisdictions within these less-populated counties. Closing this gap through those counties' resources alone would require the imposition of punitively higher sales taxes as compared to the larger counties, and in some counties would perhaps even be mathematically impossible. Such contrasts will resurface when looking at the broader "all-industry" sales figures (see below).

C.   Increasing the Sales Tax Rate on All Currently Taxable Sales

If currently taxable Retail Trade sales are simply insufficient to sustain a sales tax-based replacement of local property taxes, what happens if instead the incremental, new sales taxes are spread across currently taxable sales in all industry classifications? **Table 5** shows that, in

---

[43] See text and note at n.45, *infra.*

Table 4
County-by-County Comparison of Hypothetical
New Sales Taxes (Retail Trade only)

County	Actual Property Taxes Collected (all in-county Jurisdictions)($US)	Hypothetical New Local Sales Taxes Collectible @ 29.47% ($US)	Resulting Local Surplus (Deficit) by County
Harris	7,424,792,202.00	7,098,400,616.11	(326,391,585.89)
Dallas	4,397,201,734.00	4,077,395,101.22	(319,806,632.78)
Tarrant	3,229,775,699.00	3,135,827,837.06	(93,947,861.94)
Bexar	2,424,607,729.00	2,710,363,348.25	285,755,619.25
Travis	2,212,177,208.00	1,986,070,420.69	(226,106,787.31)
Collin	1,625,200,541.00	1,538,857,319.42	(86,343,221.58)
El Paso	776,219,957.00	1,047,563,351.39	271,343,394.39
Hidalgo	630,820,030.00	1,075,979,636.80	445,159,606.80
Denton	1,112,293,529.00	793,856,483.87	(318,437,045.13)
Fort Bend	1,033,756,774.00	683,724,345.50	(350,032,428.50)
Montgomery	694,388,205.00	803,750,046.18	109,361,841.18
Williamson	720,717,112.00	682,754,853.23	(37,962,258.77)
Cameron	310,598,230.00	511,501,336.32	200,903,106.32
Nueces	460,611,557.00	577,102,086.48	116,490,529.48
Brazoria	531,231,383.00	437,148,454.71	(94,082,928.29)
Galveston	562,250,562.00	435,616,709.61	(126,633,852.39)
Bell	284,099,889.00	439,587,207.13	155,487,318.13
Lubbock	286,035,178.00	521,743,229.02	235,708,051.02
Jefferson	453,082,674.00	501,850,573.21	48,767,899.21
Webb	297,282,029.00	397,237,633.91	99,955,604.91
McLennan	261,135,700.00	348,460,487.77	87,324,787.77
Smith	232,386,408.00	410,954,595.71	178,568,187.71
Brazos	217,901,059.00	329,002,010.83	111,100,951.83
Johnson	222,901,862.00	169,369,201.87	(53,532,660.13)
Hays	220,149,276.00	320,520,520.07	100,371,244.07
Ellis	222,448,255.00	140,719,551.18	(81,728,703.82)
Ector	179,242,089.00	303,238,429.15	123,996,340.15
Midland	201,922,071.00	343,715,312.07	141,793,241.07
Wichita	126,291,681.00	224,150,031.81	97,858,350.81
Taylor	131,517,411.00	267,428,864.56	135,911,453.56
Potter	230,253,556.00	331,218,155.71	100,964,599.71
Grayson	139,841,988.00	185,219,091.75	45,377,103.75
Gregg	154,726,834.00	340,283,722.42	185,556,888.42
Guadalupe	144,974,346.00	126,812,039.61	(18,162,306.39)
Randall	25,265,410.00	122,844,086.82	97,578,676.82
Parker	177,529,185.00	156,244,156.81	(21,285,028.19)
Comal	184,196,942.00	176,461,311.49	(7,735,630.51)
Tom Green	87,322,380.00	197,905,090.39	110,582,710.39
Kaufman	137,719,555.00	103,982,155.17	(33,737,399.83)
Top 39	32,764,868,230.00	34,054,859,405.31	1,289,991,175.31
All other counties:	6,215,101,315.00	4,918,282,992.67	(1,296,818,322.33)
Statewide Total:	**38,979,969,545.00**	**38,973,142,397.98**	**(6,827,147.02)**

the 39 most populous counties, the average Nominal Property-to-Sales Tax Ratio for currently taxable sales activity in all industry classifications equals 2.116; in other words, 2008 property tax levies in these counties averaged just over twice the sales taxes nominally collectible in these counties on all industry classifications at the current state sales tax rate of 6.25%. The deviation from this average among the counties studied ranges from a negative 1.567 to a positive 1.590 percentage points, reflecting the fact that some counties in 2008 enjoyed a disproportionately higher taxable sales base (such as Randall County, with a Nominal Property-to-Sales Tax Ratio for all industry classifications of 0.549), and some enjoyed disproportionately higher property tax levies (such as Ellis County, with a Nominal Property-to-Sales Tax Ratio for all industry classifications of 3.706). If local property tax levies within those counties were to be entirely replaced

Table 5

Comparison of Texas Property Taxes and All-Industry Sales Tax Potential

Top 39 Counties by Population	Property Taxes ($US)	All Industry Sales ($US)			Nominal Property-to-Sales Tax Ratios and Deviations	
County	Actual Property Taxes Levied in all in-county Taxing Jurisdictions	Gross Sales All Industries	Amount Sales All Industries Subject to State Sales Tax	Nominal State Sales Tax Collectible (@ 6.25%)	Nominal Property-to-Sales Tax Ratios	Deviation from Average
Harris	7,424,792,202.00	390,075,906,868.00	66,228,067,406.00	4,139,254,212.88	1.794	(0.323)
Dallas	4,397,201,734.00	230,484,532,972.00	45,103,918,133.00	2,818,994,883.31	1.560	(0.557)
Tarrant	3,229,775,699.00	80,940,529,982.00	22,536,184,922.00	1,408,511,557.63	2.293	0.177
Bexar	2,424,607,729.00	116,798,126,142.00	20,538,534,214.00	1,283,658,388.38	1.889	(0.228)
Travis	2,212,177,208.00	51,319,217,510.00	14,915,399,213.00	932,212,450.81	2.373	0.257
Collin	1,625,200,541.00	30,345,719,038.00	9,520,283,283.00	595,017,705.19	2.731	0.615
El Paso	776,219,957.00	23,436,234,374.00	5,969,496,449.00	373,093,528.06	2.080	(0.036)
Hidalgo	630,820,030.00	15,225,146,912.00	5,424,962,356.00	339,060,147.25	1.860	(0.256)
Denton	1,112,293,529.00	26,250,222,840.00	5,126,246,372.00	320,390,398.25	3.472	1.355
Fort Bend	1,033,756,774.00	17,393,091,224.00	4,738,274,659.00	296,142,166.19	3.491	1.374
Montgomery	694,388,205.00	23,972,394,489.00	5,126,934,883.00	320,433,430.19	2.167	0.051
Williamson	720,717,112.00	14,724,542,672.00	5,117,262,615.00	319,828,913.44	2.253	0.137
Cameron	310,598,230.00	6,721,478,397.00	2,732,037,466.00	170,752,341.63	1.819	(0.297)
Nueces	460,611,557.00	31,689,740,650.00	4,175,178,215.00	260,948,638.44	1.765	(0.351)
Brazoria	531,231,383.00	8,873,017,577.00	2,504,725,703.00	156,545,356.44	3.393	1.277
Galveston	562,250,562.00	41,392,961,872.00	2,552,249,304.00	159,515,581.50	3.525	1.408
Bell	284,099,889.00	11,843,553,185.00	2,394,567,804.00	149,660,487.75	1.898	(0.218)
Lubbock	286,035,178.00	11,263,238,320.00	3,154,837,009.00	197,177,313.06	1.451	(0.666)
Jefferson	453,082,674.00	40,593,669,773.00	3,527,801,025.00	220,487,564.06	2.055	(0.061)
Webb	297,282,029.00	6,318,802,191.00	2,030,770,177.00	126,923,136.06	2.342	0.226
McLennan	261,135,700.00	9,703,729,985.00	2,148,097,043.00	134,256,065.19	1.945	(0.171)
Smith	232,386,408.00	7,252,217,677.00	2,598,837,709.00	162,427,356.81	1.431	(0.686)
Brazos	217,901,059.00	5,230,842,968.00	2,041,566,611.00	127,597,913.19	1.708	(0.409)
Johnson	222,901,862.00	7,077,604,681.00	1,296,433,117.00	81,027,069.81	2.751	0.635
Hays	220,149,276.00	4,573,892,433.00	1,792,286,763.00	112,017,922.69	1.965	(0.151)
Ellis	222,448,255.00	4,970,216,055.00	960,290,640.00	60,018,165.00	3.706	1.590
Ector	179,242,089.00	8,422,916,311.00	2,720,472,922.00	170,029,557.63	1.054	(1.062)
Midland	201,922,071.00	9,034,486,892.00	3,579,085,031.00	223,692,814.44	0.903	(1.214)
Wichita	126,291,681.00	3,974,253,947.00	1,304,289,601.00	81,518,100.06	1.549	(0.567)
Taylor	131,517,411.00	4,982,780,396.00	1,566,678,078.00	97,917,379.88	1.343	(0.773)
Potter	230,253,556.00	7,916,537,939.00	2,125,627,774.00	132,851,735.88	1.733	(0.383)
Grayson	139,841,988.00	3,031,271,428.00	1,058,152,090.00	66,134,505.63	2.115	(0.002)
Gregg	154,726,834.00	12,127,588,240.00	2,576,383,005.00	161,023,937.81	0.961	(1.155)
Guadalupe	144,974,346.00	3,434,024,657.00	760,572,882.00	47,535,805.13	3.050	0.933
Randall	25,265,410.00	2,757,471,509.00	736,323,139.00	46,020,196.19	0.549	(1.567)
Parker	177,529,185.00	4,566,245,357.00	1,032,214,308.00	64,513,394.25	2.752	0.635
Comal	184,196,942.00	6,435,815,713.00	1,358,147,681.00	84,884,230.06	2.170	0.054
Tom Green	87,322,380.00	4,001,161,170.00	1,175,603,562.00	73,475,222.63	1.188	(0.928)
Kaufman	137,719,555.00	3,232,193,261.00	638,097,923.00	39,881,120.19	3.453	1.337
				Average ratio:	2.116	
Subtotals:						
39 Largest counties:	32,764,868,230.00	1,289,155,184,346.00	264,248,793,164.00	16,515,549,572.75	1.979	
All other counties:	6,215,101,315.00	161,761,113,964.00	33,514,750,440.00	2,094,671,902.50	2.967	
Statewide Total:	38,979,969,545.00	1,454,148,491,571.00	298,401,641,527.00	18,650,102,595.44	2.090	

TEXAS CENTER FOR ECONOMICS, LAW & POLICY

by an increase in sales tax rates on currently taxable sales in all industry classifications in those counties, an incremental, new set of county, municipal, school district, and/or other special purpose district sales taxes on sales in all industry classifications would have to be imposed in each such county aggregating to an average of 2.116 times the current state sales rate of 6.25%, or 13.23%. Using the broader figures for effecting this conversion in all counties statewide, the incremental, new local taxes would have to amount to a figure aggregating 2.09[44] times the current state sales rate of 6.25%, or 13.0625%. As before, we could in the alternative assume that local rates remain unchanged, and that instead the entire increase occurs in the state sales tax rate, the incremental revenues from which would be allocated to local property tax relief in proportion to need. In that case, the new state sales tax rate would equal 13.0625 percentage points plus the current 6.25, for a new state sales tax rate of 19.3125%. Either scenario would represent a substantial lessening of the incremental

Table 6
County-by-County Comparison of Hypothetical New Sales Taxes ($US - All Industry Classifications)

County	Actual Property Taxes Collected (all in-county Jurisdictions)($US)	Hypothetical New Local Sales Taxes Collectible @ 13.0625%	Resulting Local Surplus (Deficit) by County
Harris	7,424,792,202.00	8,651,041,304.91	1,226,249,102.91
Dallas	4,397,201,734.00	5,891,699,306.12	1,494,497,572.12
Tarrant	3,229,775,699.00	2,943,789,155.44	(285,986,543.56)
Bexar	2,424,607,729.00	2,682,846,031.70	258,238,302.70
Travis	2,212,177,208.00	1,948,324,022.20	(263,853,185.80)
Collin	1,625,200,541.00	1,243,587,003.84	(381,613,537.16)
El Paso	776,219,957.00	779,765,473.65	3,545,516.65
Hidalgo	630,820,030.00	708,635,707.75	77,815,677.75
Denton	1,112,293,529.00	669,615,932.34	(442,677,596.66)
Fort Bend	1,033,756,774.00	618,937,127.33	(414,819,646.67)
Montgomery	694,388,205.00	669,705,869.09	(24,682,335.91)
Williamson	720,717,112.00	668,442,429.08	(52,274,682.92)
Cameron	310,598,230.00	356,872,394.00	46,274,164.00
Nueces	460,611,557.00	545,382,654.33	84,771,097.33
Brazoria	531,231,383.00	327,179,794.95	(204,051,588.05)
Galveston	562,250,562.00	333,387,565.34	(228,862,996.67)
Bell	284,099,889.00	312,790,419.40	28,690,530.40
Lubbock	286,035,178.00	412,100,584.30	126,065,406.30
Jefferson	453,082,674.00	460,819,008.89	7,736,334.89
Webb	297,282,029.00	265,269,354.37	(32,012,674.63)
McLennan	261,135,700.00	280,595,176.24	19,459,476.24
Smith	232,386,408.00	339,473,175.74	107,086,767.74
Brazos	217,901,059.00	266,679,638.56	48,778,579.56
Johnson	222,901,862.00	169,346,575.91	(53,555,286.09)
Hays	220,149,276.00	234,117,458.42	13,968,182.42
Ellis	222,448,255.00	125,437,964.85	(97,010,290.15)
Ector	179,242,089.00	355,361,775.44	176,119,686.44
Midland	201,922,071.00	467,517,982.17	265,595,911.17
Wichita	126,291,681.00	170,372,829.13	44,081,148.13
Taylor	131,517,411.00	204,647,323.94	73,129,912.94
Potter	230,253,556.00	277,660,127.98	47,406,571.98
Grayson	139,841,988.00	138,221,116.76	(1,620,871.24)
Gregg	154,726,834.00	336,540,030.03	181,813,196.03
Guadalupe	144,974,346.00	99,349,832.71	(45,624,513.29)
Randall	25,265,410.00	96,182,210.03	70,916,800.03
Parker	177,529,185.00	134,832,993.98	(42,696,191.02)
Comal	184,196,942.00	177,408,040.83	(6,788,901.17)
Tom Green	87,322,380.00	153,563,215.29	66,240,835.29
Kaufman	137,719,555.00	83,351,541.19	(54,368,013.81)
Top 39 counties:	32,764,868,230.00	34,600,850,148.24	835,981,918.24
All other counties:	6,215,101,315.00	4,377,864,276.23	(1,337,237,038.78)
Statewide Total:	38,979,969,545.00	38,978,714,424.46	(1,255,120.54)

[44] The actual calculated ratio is 2.090067298. For convenience, all textual and chart references, and most chart calculations, will be limited to the second decimal point; this will result in rounding error in certain summation cases, which will be noted below.

percentage burden from a retail trade-only tax, but either still would yield cumulative state and local tax rates in individual locales in excess of 19%, in addition to any sales taxes being currently assessed by local jurisdictions under current law.

Does expanding the incremental, new sales taxes in this way to all industries do anything to narrow the gap between the 39 most populous counties and the rest of the state? No. In fact **Table 6** shows that the least populous counties would have faced budget deficits aggregating almost $1.84 billion in 2008 had they suddenly converted from a property-based revenue system to a sales tax-based system as described in the paragraph immediately above. This shortfall represents 28% -- more than a quarter – of the property taxes that were actually collected in those counties in 2008. Once again, the relatively smaller base of taxable retail and other industry sales in the less populous counties would, upon conversion to the new sales tax system, force them to impose even higher sales tax rates than their more populous counterparts or else face severe revenue shortfalls. We will return to this point once more in articulating specific statewide proposals, but first let us examine the local impact of our assumptions in more detail.

III.   ANALYSIS OF INDIVIDUAL LOCAL TAX JURISDICTIONS USING THE CURRENTLY TAXABLE SALES BASE

A.   "Dual-Tax" Jurisdictions

Under current law, counties, cities and special purpose districts in many cases, together with certain transit authorities, have been granted and have exercised authority to impose local sales and use taxes within their jurisdictions, as long as the aggregate state and local sales tax rate does not exceed 8.25% in any one location.[45] Of the 2099 separate, individual local tax jurisdictions in the 39 Texas counties studied that in 2008 collected or at least levied an *ad valorem* property tax, 464 assessed both a property tax and a sales and use tax, while the remainder assessed the property tax only. Of these 464 "dual-tax" jurisdictions, data is available and meaningful for 461 of them, consisting of 427 cities, towns or villages, 16 counties, and 18

---

[45] Cities are permitted ¼ to 2%, Counties ½ to 1.5%, Transit Authorities ¼ to 1%, and Special Purpose Districts 1/8 to 2% (*see* Texas Comptroller of Public Accounts, http://www.window.state.tx.us/taxinfo/local/index.html (accessed Sept. 10 2010).

special purpose districts (or "SPDs"),[46] which together account for $6,832,566,185 of 2008's property tax levies, or 20.85% of the aggregate property taxes levied in all 39 counties combined, and 17.5% of the aggregate 2008 local property tax levies statewide. The other 79.15% of property taxes levied in these 39 counties were levied by municipalities, school districts, municipal utility districts, public utility districts, water control districts, emergency services districts, and other special-purpose districts that do not also currently assess sales and use taxes. For this reason, we do not have direct information regarding the taxable sales activity for most such "property-tax-only" districts.[47] The Comptroller's office also does not publish taxable sales data for special purpose districts directly, but we do have direct sales activity data for all cities and counties, so we would by definition have such data for any SPDs having boundaries co-extensive with either. As it happens, only one of the 18 dual-tax SPDs noted -- Ector County Hospital District – falls into this category (its boundaries are co-extensive with Ector County).[48] The boundaries of the 17 others are not co-extensive with any city or county, but for these the Comptroller's office provides the 2008 sales tax allocations and their applicable sales tax rates, enabling us to derive an overall taxable sales activity estimate from those figures for each such SPD.[49] We can, therefore, compare the property tax revenues with actual or potential sales tax revenues for all 461 dual-tax jurisdictions with available data in the top 39 counties by population, all as set out in **Table A1** (in **Appendix A**)[50]

---

[46] Source data obtained from Texas Comptroller of Public Accounts, *Texas Edge Data Center,* http://www.texasahead.org/texasedge (custom reports accessed frequently during 2010), Texas Comptroller of Public Accounts, *Texas Sales and Use Tax Rates* (January 2008), and Texas Comptroller of Public Accounts, *Window on State Government,* http://www.window.state.tx.us/taxes (accessed frequently during 2009-2010). To place this in perspective, there were 126 special purpose districts throughout the State that assessed a sales tax as of January 1, 2008 (Source: Texas Comptroller of Public Accounts, *Texas Sales and Use Tax Rates* (January 2008)). Today the number of SPD's assessing a sales tax has risen to 174 (Source: Texas Comptroller of Public Accounts, *Local Sales and Use Tax,* http://www.window.state.tx.us/taxinfo/local/spd.html, accessed June 5, 2010).

[47] One possible way to compile such data might be to use the sales data that the Comptroller's office makes available by zip codes. But zip codes often do not coincide with the boundaries of particular districts, and in fact frequently overlap or are overlapped by multiple districts, so it would represent an approximation at best.

[48] Of the 126 SPDs in these top 39 counties that as of January 1, 2008 did impose sales taxes, 48 had boundaries that were co-extensive with a city, and 19 had boundaries co-extensive with a county. As noted above, however, only 18 are dual-tax jurisdictions.

[49] The annual sales tax allocation figures for 2008 tend to be higher than would be predicted by reliance on full-year taxable sales activity and January 1, 2008 sales tax rates alone. In many cases this is attributable to increases in the rates or imposition of new taxes that took place during the course of the year (which are not incorporated into our data); in others it may be attributable to timing differences, overlap in datasets, etc. We ran this same calculation as an accuracy check in the case of SPD's for which we know both the allocations and the taxable sales base, and found the extrapolation bias to run approximately 25% over actual taxable sales. The SPD extrapolations included in the analysis presented have been corrected for this bias.

[50] For cities whose territories overlap the boundaries of two or more counties, the property tax collections and sales tax allocations for such cities have been aggregated in Table A3 for clarity.

As a general proposition, the available sales tax allocations in these jurisdictions correlate very well with the absolute amount of property taxes currently being levied. This makes sense upon first impression, since we might expect that jurisdictions with higher levels of taxable property will tend to have higher levels of economic activity. In fact this correlation in 2008 equaled 0.954035, indicating an almost direct one-to-one relationship, as illustrated in **Figure 1** below, albeit a widely scattered one. In the dual-tax jurisdictions, assuming that any requisite rate increases occur at the local and not the state level, the local components of sales taxes generated within their boundaries would have to increase in order to replace property tax collections. Since current sales tax collections are presumably already spoken for in current budgets, these increases would take the form of incremental, new sales taxes (or at least sales tax rate increases) in addition to any current sales taxes, ignoring for present purposes any revenues that might also be generated through changes in the law governing other local taxes, fees and charges, or indirect effects that might reduce revenues under the existing laws governing such taxes, fees and charges. Assuming that the rate increases adopted were to apply uniformly to all currently taxable sales in all industry classifications, such increases could

Figure 1
Correlation between 2008 Local Property Tax Levies and Sales Tax Allocations

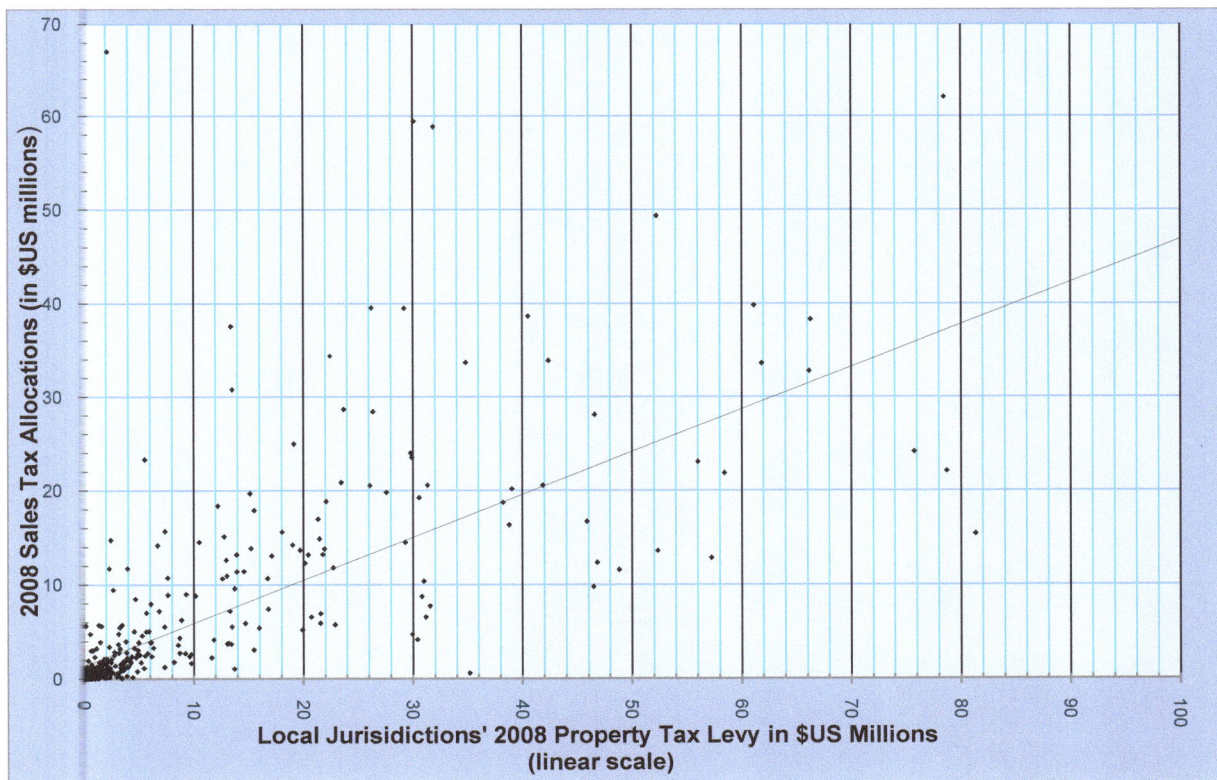

be measured as a simple multiple of the local sales taxes currently being collected in such jurisdictions. This multiple is designated in this report as the "Replacement Factor" or "RF", since it is a measure of the tax effort that would be required to replace locally-sourced property tax revenues in a given taxing jurisdiction (such as a county, municipality, or special purpose district) with locally-sourced sales tax revenues, stated as a function of the local sales taxes currently imposed by that jurisdiction. As seen in **Table A1**, set forth in **Appendix A** to this report, the affected jurisdictions' RFs range from fractions as low as 0.005 (for the City of Lytle in Bexar County), to multiples as high as 59.9865 (City of Fairview), 134.6035 (City of Ransom Canyon), and even 1361.8869 (City of Lakeside), illustrating the extreme disparity among jurisdictions in this regard. **Figure 2** gives a graphical illustration of the distribution of these RFs among the jurisdictions (up to a maximum RF of 35), showing that the highest concentration of RFs lies in the range of 0 to 5, but that a large number of outliers appear at higher levels.

Figure 2
Distribution of Replacement Factors Among Local Tax Jurisdictions

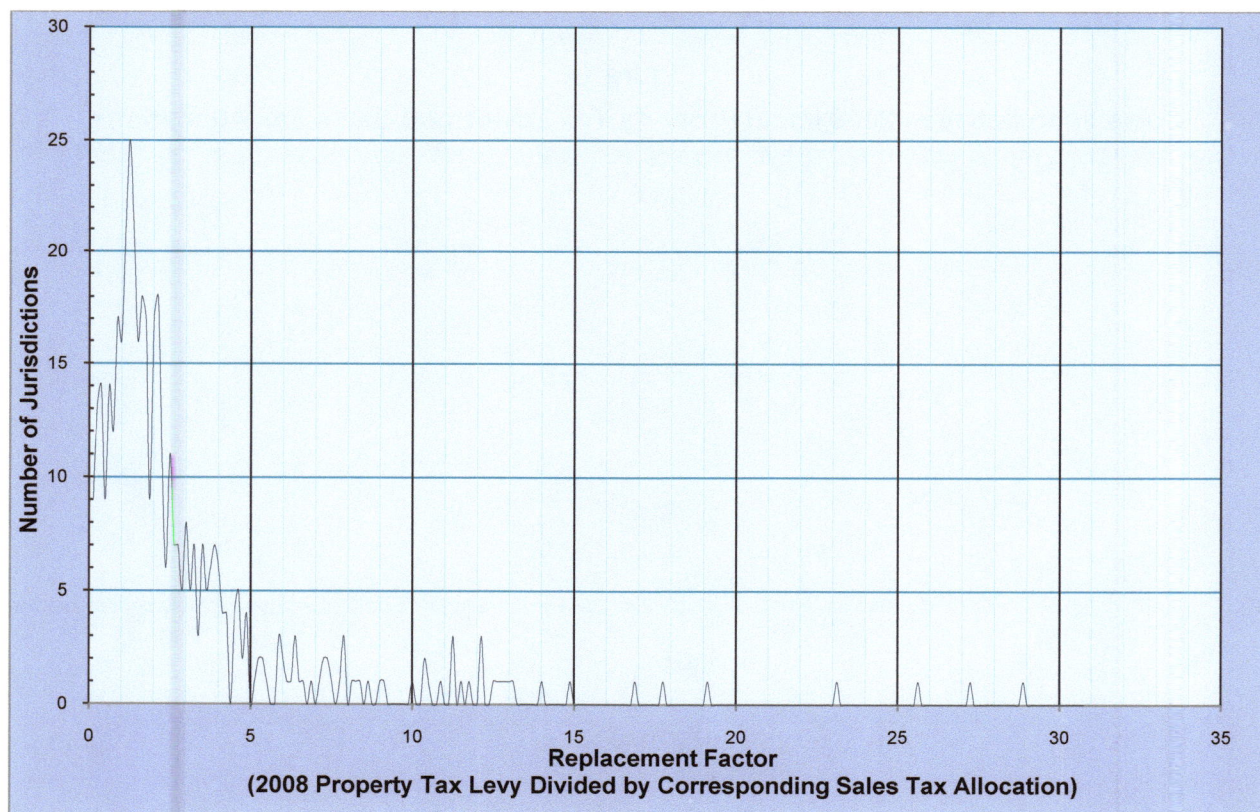

Replacement Factor
(2008 Property Tax Levy Divided by Corresponding Sales Tax Allocation)

Unlike the relationship between property tax levies and sales tax allocations, however, there is virtually no correlation between local property tax levies and the corresponding RFs; in fact our calculated correlation of 0.066685 was very close to zero, or purely random (see **Figure 3** below). We therefore cannot draw any meaningful rules of thumb about the proportional increases in local sales tax effort required to replace local property taxes based solely on the amount of property taxes to be replaced. The variability of this requisite incremental tax effort need not necessarily be interpreted to reflect the jurisdictions' relative wealth, or their capacities to generate tax revenues; it may in certain cases reflect merely the policy choice that was made

Figure 3

Correlation between 2008 Local Property Tax Levies and Corresponding RFs

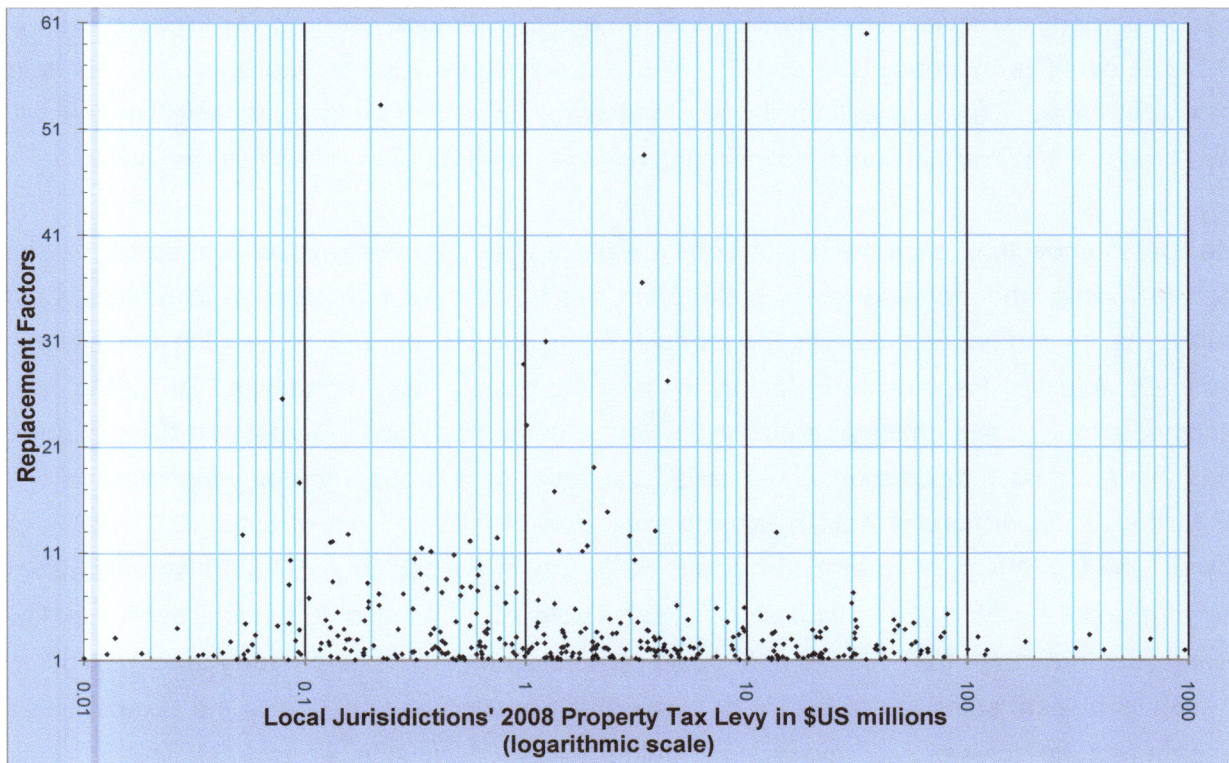

within the constraints of existing law to rely more on one form of tax than another. For example, the sales tax rate imposed by the dual-tax special purpose districts ranges from a low of 0.125% to a high of 2%. Some of the variability in RFs for these jurisdictions is a direct result of these different local tax policy choices.

Such differences may be smoothed out for purposes of analysis by comparing the known or imputed overall taxable sales base within these jurisdictions with the applicable sales tax rates as reported by the Texas Comptroller's office.[51] By then adjusting the sales tax allocations to those that would have been realized had the sales tax rates been uniform throughout all of these jurisdictions, we can obtain a more straightforward comparison of their relative *potential* for generating sales tax revenue from transactions taxable under current law. Although we cannot literally compare "replacement factors" in jurisdictions with no current sales tax, this same technique also enables us to consider on a *pro-forma* basis more than two dozen additional jurisdictions from within the top 39 counties that do not currently assess a sales tax and therefore would otherwise have been excluded from the analysis. **Table A2** (in **Appendix A**) reflects these calculations, using a normalized sales tax rate of one percent per jurisdiction. Altogether, the 488 jurisdictions analyzed to produce **Table A2** account for $10,886,912,294.00 of 2008 property tax levies, which is 33.2% of the entire 2008 local property tax levies in the top 39 Texas counties by population, and 27.9% of the aggregate 2008 local property tax levies in the entire State of Texas. If we can develop a workable transition for these jurisdictions, we will have presented a practical plan for eliminating nearly one-third of Texas' *ad valorem* taxes.

The figures show that, once the jurisdictions are placed on a nominally equal one percent sales tax rate footing, the increase in sales tax effort required for each jurisdiction to replace local property taxes can be measured as the product of that one percent rate times such jurisdiction's nominally adjusted Replacement Factor. In other words, our new, normalized RF rating now becomes simply a straightforward statement of the percentage point increase in the sales tax rates that each such jurisdiction would have to impose. As a group, the non-weighted average RF for these jurisdictions is 4.32[52], ranging from lows of 0.007 (Town of Lytle), 0.014 (City of Luling), and 0.019 (City of Heath), to highs of 53.3 (City of Pelican Bay), 67.3 (Town of Ransom Canyon) and 82.3 (Village of Tiki Island).[53] (See **Table A2.**) Of these 488 jurisdictions, the 414 having RFs that range from .005 to 6.25 could completely replace their property tax by imposing an additional local sales tax of 6.25% or less without making any change to the taxable sales base. In fact the non-weighted average RF of these 414 jurisdictions is only 2.50. This includes all the counties examined, nearly all the SPD's, and most towns and cities. Even at this

---

[51] The Comptroller does not collect or report taxable sales data collected in connection with the Texas sales tax with respect to school districts, or with respect to special purpose districts that do not currently assess a sales tax. However, available data does include gross and taxable sales in each county and municipality. Such data may be used to estimate potential sales taxes collectible in jurisdictions not currently assessing a sales tax, provided their boundaries are coincident with the jurisdictions for which we do have reported data.

[52] Excluding the two outlying data points of 120 and 1362 for the City of Fairview and the Town of Lakeside, respectively.

[53] Again excluding Fairview and Lakeside.

seemingly reasonable level, though, the possibility exists of introducing exaggerated differences in the sales tax rate structures of immediately neighboring jurisdictions, which in turn carries the potential to introduce undesirable, or at least unintended, distortions in local economics and demographics. There also would be instances where some of the higher-rate jurisdictions would actually be co-located, and their rates therefore compounded. Examples include several towns and cities in Ellis, Fort Bend and Galveston Counties, where combined county and city rates could reach as high as 10% or more in many cases, not including any SPD or transit rates, and also not including the 6.25% statewide sales tax. This problem alone is significant enough to warrant closer attention.

The remaining 74 jurisdictions, however, pose a much more serious issue. Having as they do a disproportionately low base of taxable sales activity relative to taxable property valuations, their transition away from property taxes could be traumatic. A cursory glance at the list of cities in **Table A2** reveals this particularly striking fact: many small, well-known suburban or "bedroom" communities (such as the cities of Piney Point Village, Hilshire Village, and Fairview, for example) start from the disadvantage of having deliberately minimized commercial and industrial development within their boundaries; indeed, this is part of their appeal to residential property owners. In order to maintain their police, fire, and emergency protection, public facilities, public administration and other community services, such jurisdictions theoretically would be forced to impose sales tax rates upwards of 30%, 40%, 50% or more, rates which would inevitably drive those few local commercial establishments that do exist into neighboring jurisdictions or out of business altogether, or at a minimum expose the local governments to catastrophic fiscal consequences in the event of a major local business failure. In reality such rates would never be approved by either voters or elected public officials. Referring again to **Table A1 (**which indicates current actual sales tax rates), we can see that these estimates are more or less representative of the amounts by which these jurisdictions would have to increase their actual current sales tax collections, depending on how far above or below 1% their current tax rate lies. Even if these particular municipalities were to double their taxable base and quintuple their rates with no dynamic effect on their taxable sales base, the resulting 10-fold increase in sales tax allocations would still be woefully inadequate.

Similarly, although most SPD's examined would not need new sales tax rates exceeding 2% or so, the Travis County Emergency Services District #8 would require a sales tax rate increase of 12.6 percentage points beyond its current 1% sales tax rate, and the Cibolo Canyon Special Improvement District in Bexar County would have to adjust its sales tax rate to 44.69% in order to replace its property tax revenues and still fund those current and projected expenditures supported by its 2008 1.5% sales tax. If we assume that these findings are representative of the SPDs that do not currently impose a sales tax, we can estimate that approximately two-eighteenths, or 254, of the 2291 Texas SPDs reported in the U.S. Census Bureau's 2007 Governments Integrated Directory[54] would require prohibitively high sales tax rates in order to replace property taxes through local taxable sales alone. However, it is likely that the number is much higher, given that the SPD's that do not currently impose a sales tax have evolved to their current situation precisely as a function of the availability within their designated boundaries of an adequate taxable property base, and without regard to the available taxable sales base.

B.   Summary

We may draw encouragement from our finding that every county, most cities, and many special purpose districts in the 39 counties studied could transition away from reliance on property taxes by imposing a relatively modest tax on those locally-generated sales that are taxable under current law. However, assuming for discussion purposes that 6.25% represents the maximum incremental local sales tax rate (i.e., incremental to any existing local sales tax rates) determined to be "acceptable" by policymakers and voters, 74 or more of the 488 jurisdictions specifically examined would simply be unable to make this transition by reliance on locally-generated sales tax revenues alone. And even this limited progress toward a solution fails to ascertain the detailed effects in each of the 1457 remaining single-tax jurisdictions n the counties studied, including school districts, all of which together account for a full two-thirds of the property taxes currently levied in those 39 counties. Overall, the attempt to expand revenues by the additional aggregate two-fold increase needed,[55] as demonstrated earlier, would push the average cumulative state and local sales tax burden in various locales to 19% or more. Assuming that these figures would be politically unacceptable, something more is required.

IV.   BROADENING THE TAXABLE SALES BASE

As the Arduin-Laffer study demonstrated, and as further illustrated above, the problem of the unacceptably high sales tax rate required in some jurisdictions to replace the property tax persists as long as nothing is done to broaden the sales tax base. Arduin-Laffer posed several

---

[54] *See* http://harvester.census.gov/gid/gid_07/options.html, (accessed 6/10/10).

[55] 2.090067298.

possible scenarios, particularly in reference to the Federation of Tax Administrators' 2007 survey of state sales tax incidences, exemptions and exclusions. Hypothesizing that Texas might expand the sales tax to cover all items of goods or services shown by the survey to be subject to such a tax in at least one other state, Arduin-Laffer concluded that Texas could have increased its aggregate sales tax collections in 2006 by roughly $32.5 billion dollars with a relatively less objectionable average statewide state and local tax rate of approximately 8.8%. [56]

Arduin-Laffer's analysis, however, focused on aggregate state-wide results of aggregate, state-wide reforms. It did not undertake to consider the differential impact of any such reforms on the different local taxing jurisdictions within the state, or the political ramifications that would inevitably result. This does not represent a shortcoming in the study's methodology; it simply was beyond its scope. But such an analysis is critical to an understanding of how such reforms could be implemented in practice, if at all. This section will address this element to an additional degree.

A.   The Magnitude of Base Expansion Needed

Working our way backward from the known quantity of property tax collections that must be replaced, the figures in **Tables 5 and 6** may be read to imply that, by expanding the percentage of all-industry sales subject to new local sales taxes by a factor of 2.09 (the statewide ratio of property taxes levied to state sales taxes nominally collectible at 6.25%), the aggregate 2008 property tax levies of $38.98 billion could have been replaced entirely with new local sales taxes at a weighted average rate equal to the state's current 6.25% tax rate. This would mean expanding the taxable sales base for such local taxes across all industry classifications from 20.52% to 42.89% of the state's entire aggregate reported gross 2008 sales. Whether such a contemplated expansion is realistic or not remains to be seen. Assuming its feasibility, however, the presumed base expansion would also apply to current local sales tax rates in the 39 counties studied (which rates currently range from 0.5% to 2.0%); their enhanced contribution to the effort would enable us to accomplish the desired increase in revenues with either a lower expansion factor, or a lower incremental rate, or some combination of both.

First let us solve for the reduced expansion factor required after taking into account both the new revenues attributable to the new, incremental local rate (weighted average 6.25%) and the

---

[56] Arduin-Laffer Study, pp. 19-20.

enhanced revenues attributable to the current local rates.[57] Assuming that, by legislative or constitutional mandate, the incrementally enhanced, or "windfall," sales tax revenues realized by local jurisdictions under current tax rates as a direct result of this base expansion, less the amounts required to phase out their own property taxes, are dedicated to the statewide property tax relief pool, and further assuming that this expansion were to take place proportionately to existing taxable sales in each individual jurisdiction,[58] our calculations show this revised expansion factor to be 1.81.[59] Under this scenario, the enhanced revenues under existing local sales taxes and the new revenues under the incremental new local sales taxes in the dual-tax jurisdictions examined under Section III would have the effect of increasing from 414 to 450 the number of jurisdictions for which the requisite property tax replacement rate would fall below the 6.25% target. The non-weighted average of these 450 jurisdictions' incremental new rates would be only 1.27%, and 169 of these jurisdictions would require no new sales taxes at all. In the alternative we may also calculate the reduced incremental new rates required given the previously assumed 2.09 expansion factor.[60] Making the same assumptions as above, the revised incremental local rate would come to an aggregate cumulative statewide weighted

---

[57] $B_e = T/(T_1 + T_2)$

where

   B_e = Taxable sales base expansion factor required to achieve targeted increase in total taxes collected

   T = Total targeted sales taxes to be collected

   T_1 = Taxes nominally collectible at the presumed incremental sales tax rate (in this case 6.25%) on the pre-expansion taxable sales base

   T_2 = Taxes actually collected through current local sales taxes at the effective weighted average local sales tax rate on the pre-expansion taxable sales base

[58] This is an unrealistic assumption, as will be further discussed in Section V.A. below.

[59] 1.813787976. Since we have not taken into account enhanced revenues from existing sales taxes in any counties outside of the most populous 39, this figure would actually be lower on a statewide basis, but we will use 1.81 for discussion purposes.

[60] $R' = (R/T_1) \times (T/B_e - T_2)$

where

   R' = The revised incremental sales tax rate required to achieve the revised targeted total taxes collected given a presumed base expansion factor and presumed intial incremental sales tax rate

   R = The presumed initial incremental sales tax rate on the pre-expansion taxable sales base

   T = The total targeted sales taxes to be collected

   T_1 = Taxes nominally collectible by local jurisdictions at the initial presumed rate "R" on the pre-expansion taxable sales base

   T_2 = Taxes actually collected through current local sales taxes on the pre-expansion taxable sales base

   B_e = The presumed base expansion factor

average of 4.128%[61] (rather than 6.25%), in addition to the existing local sales tax rates of 0.5% to 2.0%.[62] Under this scenario, 465 of the 488 local jurisdictions examined would require new, incremental sales tax rates of below 6.25%, with such rates having a non-weighted average of only 1.177%, and with 193 of these 465 jurisdictions requiring no incremental new sales taxes at all.

Once again, however, the foregoing calculations assume no expansion of the taxable state sales tax base and no new allocations of state tax revenues to local property tax relief. If the overall sales tax base were to be expanded as described above for *both* state and local sales tax collections, the state's incremental sales tax revenues under its existing rate could theoretically be made available to offset the otherwise requisite local rate increases. Applying our presumed factor of 2.09[63] to state sales taxes nominally collectible at 6.25%, for example, state sales tax collections at the currently applicable rate would increase by that same factor, to an amount equal to $38,979,969,545. The incremental revenues available from the state for local property tax relief would therefore equal $20,329,866,949.56, which would in turn permit a reduction in incremental, new local rates to an aggregate weighted average of only 1.88%.[64] How that burden would affect individual local jurisdictions would depend entirely on how local property tax relief is allocated from state coffers. If we were to assume that none of the state funds would be allocated to the 488 jurisdictions examined, the impact to them would be the same as given in the example above (using the 2.09 base expansion factor).

As summarized in **Table 7** below, these calculations furnish to us the lower and upper boundaries of the taxable sales base and overall weighted average rates theoretically required to replace the local *ad valorem* property tax with the Texas state and local sales tax under four key scenarios. The first and fourth scenarios presented, in which either the state sales tax rate is increased (Scenario 1), or the taxable sales base is expanded for both the state and local sales taxes (Scenario 4), squarely present the question of how power over access to and use of the state's increased revenues would be distributed between state government, on the one hand, and county and local authorities, on the other. This issue will be addressed in the context of special purpose districts and school districts in Section VI below, but first we need to

---

[61] 4.128⁻38%.

[62] Again, this estimate ignores the fact that other counties' sales tax revenues would likewise be enhanced and thereby reduce the required rate further still.

[63] Using the more precise 9 decimal figure.

[64] 1.8836846%.

understand the differential local effects of different base expansion scenarios.

Table 7

Theoretical Boundaries of Rates and Taxable Sales Base for Modified Texas Sales Tax

Scenario	Expansion Factor	Boundary Condition		State Sales Tax Rate	Local Sales Tax Rates	
					Statewide Weighted Average	Individual Jurisdictions[3]
1. No change in taxable sales base	N/A	State:	Max	19.3125%	Current local sales taxes[1]	Current local sales taxes[1]
		Local:	Min			
		State:	Min	6.25%	13.0625%[2] plus current local sales taxes	See Table A2 plus current local sales taxes[1]
		Local:	Max			
2. Expanded taxable sales base (local changes only)	1.81	N/A		6.25%	6.25%[2] plus current local sales taxes[1]	See Table A2 plus current local sales taxes[1]
3. Expanded taxable sales base (local changes only)	2.09	N/A		6.25%	4.128%[2] plus current local sales taxes[1]	See Table A2 plus current local sales taxes[1]
4. Expanded taxable sales base (changes in both state and local base and rates)	2.09	State:	Max	9.24%	Current local sales taxes[1]	Current local sales taxes[1]
		Local:	Min			
		State:	Min	6.25%	1.88%[2] plus current local sales taxes[1]	See Table A2 plus current local sales taxes[1]
		Local:	Max			

1 If any.

2 On an aggregate, statewide weighted average basis.

3 Individually for the 488 local jurisdictions studied

4 Increased by the indicated expansion factor, either for the local taxable sales base only or for the entire statewide base, as applicable

B.   Classifications Eligible for Inclusion

As will be seen, the precise local effects will depend on precisely how the legislature chooses to achieve the desired base expansion. Referring again to **Table 1**, we can see that, of the $341.15 billion in gross sales classified in the "Retail Trade" reported in the State of Texas in 2008, only $132.25 billion -- or roughly 38.8% -- were subject to the sales tax. As suggested from our analysis of retail sales described above, however, expanding taxable sales even to 100% of the "Retail Trade" would be insufficient to produce a tolerable overall sales tax rate in most locales, even though 100% coverage would mean complete elimination of the exclusions or exemptions currently designed to minimize the tax's impact on lower-income taxpayers, avoid double taxation, remain within the constitutional limits of state taxation, and facilitate collections and enforcement. The remaining three predominantly taxed classifications (Accommodation and Food Services (gross 2008 sales $38.88 billion), Arts, Entertainment and Recreation (gross 2008 sales $4.69 billion), and Information (gross 2008 sales $23.72 billion)), represent too small a cross-section of the state's economy to provide a significant boost to the tax base. Altogether, the untaxed components of these three industry classifications amount to only $16.5 billion, which at a 6.25% rate represents only $1.03 billion of potential added tax revenue.

For a more detailed view of potential sources of expanded revenues, we may turn to the Texas Comptroller's "Tax Exemptions & Tax Incidence" report.[65] In this report, the Comptroller estimates the "value" of the various exemptions, exclusions and discounts available under Texas' sales tax regime (as well as under various other state and local tax regimes). "Value" in this context is understood to mean the theoretical tax revenues foregone by virtue of such exemptions and other accommodations.[66] According to the 2009 report, the value of all such sales tax-related items was projected to aggregate $30,009,800,000 for fiscal year 2009 (September 1, 2008 through August 31, 2009), falling into the three categories set forth in **Table 8** below.[67]

"Exclusions" represent those categories of transactions that under current law would by definition not be subject to the sales tax; typical exclusions would consist of sales of intangibles, sales or rentals of property, and sales of most types of services. Most proposals to expand the

Table 8

Value of Sales Tax Exemptions, Exclusions, and Discounts (Fiscal 2009)

Item	Value
Exemptions	$24,454,000,000
Exclusions	$5,366,000,000
Discounts	$189,500,000
Total:	$30,009,800,000

taxable sales base focus on adding one or more of these transaction categories to the list of taxable transactions. Based on the Comptroller's estimate, however, expanding the base to cover even all such exclusions would yield only $5.3 billion of additional revenue. "Discounts"

---

[65] The Texas Comptroller is required by law to prepare and present this report regularly. *See* Tex. Govt. Code, sec. 403.014.

[66] *Tax Exemptions & Tax Incidence 2009*, p.3.

[67] Id.

represent the very modest incentives offered by the Comptroller to encourage timely payment or prepayment of sales tax remittances by businesses. They serve a valuable role in the overall context of administration and collectability, and in any case do not represent enough value to be meaningful for our purpose. The largest of these categories, "Exemptions," represents transactions that would be taxable under applicable law but for the existence of particular exceptions created by law or regulation for various policy reasons. Well-known examples of such exemptions include subsistence-related items as such as groceries, residential gas and electric utilities, and prescription and over-the-counter drugs, but they also include sales to non-profit and governmental organizations, as well as exemptions crafted to prevent taxing the same item more than once as it passes through commerce or under multiple Texas tax regimes, or otherwise to retain the tax's character as a tax primarily upon consumption. In fact, of the entire $24.4 billion worth of "exemption" categories, four of these meeting the characteristics just described account for a full $21.2 billion of the total (see **Table 9** below). Since these represent fundamental state policies incorporated into the current system, we should not expect to realize significant additional tax revenues from modifications to the "exemptions" category unless we are prepared to alter fundamentally the character of the tax and the economic and social policies embodied by it.

Table 9

Value of Major Sales Tax Exemptions (Fiscal 2009)

Item	Value
Items Taxed by Other Laws	$8,102,900,000
Property Used in Manufacturing	$11,000,800,000
Food for Home Consumption	$1,378,200,000
Residential Gas & Electricity:	$791,600,000
Total:	$21,273,500,000

Amplifying on the analysis of the "Exclusions" category, the Center on Budget Policies and Priorities in July, 2009, published a study by Michael Mazerov entitled "Expanding Sales Taxation of Services: Options and Issues," (the "Mazerov Study")[68] in which the author explored the types and amounts of sales transactions classified as "services" that currently remain untaxed in various states, but that might reasonably be subjected to the sales tax. The study

---

[68] Michael Mazerov, "Expanding Sales Taxation of Services: Options and Issues," http://www.cbpp.org/files/8-10-09sfp.pdf (accessed 6-14-10). The Mazerov study made broadly generic assumptions about Texas' contribution to the national GDP in various service categories, then used those assumptions to estimate the amount of specific categories of services transactions not currently subject to tax in Texas, but that might "feasibly" be subjected to the sales tax after taking into account "distributional, practical and/or political" considerations. See Mazerov Study at p. 4. The use of this estimate should be regarded as indicative only.

observed that, in expanding the sales tax to cover services, policymakers have tended to try to optimize competing economic, political and fiscal needs by avoiding taxation of services that are purchased "almost exclusively by businesses (like advertising and accounting)", and focusing the sales tax instead on "household services (like haircuts) or mixed household/business services (like landscaping)."[69] Reasoning that the preferred expansion of taxable services would include "all services consumed by households except: housing, health care, education, transit, legal, funeral, and certain banking and insurance services,"[70] the Mazerov Study concluded that the aggregate sales of such "feasibly taxable" services in Texas probably amount to approximately $123,239,000,000. Applying the state sales tax rate of 6.25% to this figure, Mazerov's analysis implies that eliminating all feasibly taxable services from the "exclusions" category would yield roughly $7.7 billion of additional state sales tax revenues. This figure compares somewhat generously with the Comptroller's $5.3 billion estimate, which was reached even while including some of the categories excluded by Mazerov's assumptions.[71] Given the discrepancy, this report will use the Comptroller's estimates as its primary basis, and will regard the Mazerov figure as a suggested upper limit.

Looking at the "Tax Incidence" section of the Comptroller's report, we find the Comptroller's itemization of the proportions in which consumers, as opposed to business and industry, directly experience the tax relief associated with some, but not all, of these exclusions.[72] Viewed in reverse, this itemization enables us to estimate the amounts of net tax revenues that might have been realized by taxing each category after exempting sales of services to businesses that in one way or another go into products or services that themselves will be sold further into the chain of commerce. Using the principles for inclusion or exclusion articulated by the Mazerov Study as our guide, and applying them to the figures presented by the Comptroller, we find that the Comptroller offers this incidence analysis for only four categories of potential interest to us; these are summarized in **Table 10**. The remaining exclusion categories listed in the Comptroller's report that should be considered (as per the Mazerov Study's principles), but that are *not* addressed by the Comptroller's incidence analysis, consist of those set forth in **Table 11**.

---

[69] Id. at vii.

[70] *See* Mazerov Study, p. 5, footnote to Table 1

[71] *See Tax Exemptions & Tax Incidence 2009*, pp. 12-14. The Comptroller's estimate included professional services such as health care services, legal services, accounting and audit services, and architectural and engineering services Those five categories alone accounted for $2.6 billion of the Comptroller's $5.3 billion estimate.

[72] *See* the "Incidence Analysis" Tables 1 through 17 on pages 47-55 of *Tax Exemptions & Tax Incidence 2009*, itemizing these proportions by both dollar value and percentage for each major category.

Table 10

Tax Incidence of Certain Excluded Service Categories

Currently Excluded Category	Comptroller's Estimated Tax Value of Incidence on Consumers in Fiscal 2011[73]	Adjusted Tax Value of Incidence on Consumers in Fiscal 2008[74]	Estimated Annual Sales Volume for Calendar 2008[75] (inferred at 6.25% sales tax rate)
Residential Construction Labor	$446,800,000	$428,013,918	$6,848,222,686
Real Estate Brokerage and Agency Services	$82,100,000	$78,648,036	$1,258,368,582
Freight Hauling	$64,900,000	$62,171,225	$994,739,598
Automotive Maintenance and Repair	$246,400,000	$236,039,905	$3,776,638,473
Totals:	$840,200,000	$804,873,084	$12,877,969,339

Assuming that the tax incidence of the categories in **Table 11** falls entirely on consumers these figures suggest that an expansion of the Texas taxable sales base to include "feasibly taxable" services, if imposed in such way as to ensure that they are taxed only once at the point of consumption, would have resulted in an incremental increase in 2008 of $24,308,307.52 in taxable sales activity, or $1,519,269,220 of incremental state sales tax revenues at 6.25% (**Tables 10 & 11** combined). This hardly seems worth the effort, considering that we are striving for incremental revenues an order of magnitude larger than this figure, and it may not even be entirely feasible. In fact, considering the relatively low levels of incremental revenues to be expected from some of these newly taxed services, their relatively high enforcement and compliance burdens may suggest that they should not be taxed at all. Professor Randall Holcombe addressed this issue in the context of the Florida services tax, for example, arguing that a tax on services supplied in particular by individuals with low levels of tax, accounting or bookkeeping sophistication or resources, "such as teenagers who cut lawns for their neighbors for a fee" and "[b]abysitters," would either drive them out of business or turn them into tax

---

[73] Source: *Tax Exemptions & Tax Incidence 2009*, Tables 1 through 17, pp. 47-45.

[74] In the absence of directly reported 2008 data, this estimate was obtained by adjusting the Comptroller's projected 2011 incidence estimates down in proportion to the fraction of the Comptroller's projected 2011 aggregate sales tax revenues ($22,590,700,000.00) (*see Tax Exemptions & Tax Incidence 2009*, Incidence Analysis Table 1, p.47) represented by the known aggregate sales tax revenues for fiscal 2008 ($21,640,855,000) (*see* CAFR 2008, p. 240), or 0.958.

[75] This estimate, necessary to conform to the calendar year basis of our other data, ignores any discrepancy that may exist between fiscal year and calendar year figures.

evaders.[76] Such considerations suggest that the cost-benefit analysis would favor exemption of sales by sole proprietors at least, or service firms with annual revenues below a certain *de minimus* threshold, in a manner similar to the approach taken by Texas to its latest version of the business franchise tax.

Table 11
Aggregate Tax Value of Remaining Excluded Service Categories

Currently Excluded Category	Comptroller's Estimated Tax Value of Service Exclusions in Fiscal 2009[77]	Adjusted Estimated Tax Value of Service Exclusions in Fiscal 2008[78]	Estimated Annual Sales Volume for Calendar 2008[79] (inferred at 6.25% sales tax rate)
Barber and Beauty Services	$82,700,000	$85,118,226	$1,361,891,612
Funeral Services	$57,200,000	$58,872,582	$941,961,308
Child Day Care Services	$206,700,000	$212,744,102	$3,403,905,637
Miscellaneous Personal Services	$14,800,000	$15,232,766	$243,724,255
Financial Services Brokerage	$143,800,000	$148,004,847	$2,368,077,555
Other Financial Services	$61,100,000	$62,886,621	$1,006,185,943
Other Transportation (except scheduled passenger)	$24,700,000	$25,422,251	$406,756,020
Veterinary Service	$47,600,000	$48,991,869	$783,869,900
Car Washes	$32,900,000	$33,862,027	$541,792,431
Travel Arrangements	$13,800,000	$14,203,525	$227,256,400
Interior Design	$8,800,000	$9,057,320	$144,917,124
Totals:	$694,100,000	$714,396,136	$11,430,338,184

Let us therefore also consider another suggestion that has been made to expand the sales base – the proposal to impose a one-time tax on the *purchase* of residential or commercial property, imposed at the time of sale, rather than the annual tax currently imposed on the continuing ownership of such property. According to the Texas A&M University Real Estate Center (the "Real Estate Center"), 2008 sales of existing residential housing (single family, townhouses and condominiums) aggregated $44,524,894,984 in dollar volume in the 47 Texas major

---

[76] Randall G. Holcombe, "Forum: Florida Services Tax: Taxing Services," 30 Fla. St. U.L.Rev 467, 473-474 (Spring 2003)

[77] Source: *Tax Exemptions & Tax Incidence 2009*, Table 3, p.13.

[78] In the absence of directly reported 2008 data, this estimate was obtained by adjusting the Comptroller's projected 2009 figures (*see Tax Exemptions & Tax Incidence 2009,* Table 3, p.13) higher in proportion to the multiple of the Comptroller's reported aggregate sales & use tax revenues for fiscal 2009 ($21,026,034,000.00) represented by the corresponding aggregate 2008 figure ($21,640,855,000.00), or 1.029 (*see* CAFR 2009, p.240).

[79] *See* n 75, *supra.*

metropolitan areas for which the Real Estate Center maintains data, for an average sale price of $191,597, as illustrated in **Table 12**.[80] Adding as a proxy for new home sales the figures for

Table 12

Total 2008 Sales of Residential Housing in Texas

Category	Number of Units Sold/Permits Granted	Average Price/Value Per Unit	Total Dollar Volume	Potential Sales Tax Revenues (@ 6.25%)
Existing Residential Housing Sold	232,388	$191,597	$44,524,894,984	$2,782,805,936.50
New single family permits	81,107	$174,100	$14,120,728,700	$882,545,543.75
New 2-4 Family Permits	2,979	$75,500	$224,914,500	$14,057,156.25
New 5+ Family Permits	46,918	$74,600	$3,500,082,800	$218,755,175.00
Totals:	**363,392**	**$171,635**	**$62,370,620,984**	**$3,898,163,811.50**

building permits granted in 2008,[81] we find that the total dollar volume of residential housing sold in Texas in 2008 may be estimated at approximately $62.4 billion. To illustrate the potential contribution to revenues of a 6.25% one-time tax on all such sales,[82] which is no more than around three years' worth of annual *ad valorem* taxes paid by many Texas homeowners in these jurisdictions, note that an additional $3.9 billion in tax revenue would have been generated in the 47 metropolitan areas reported by the Real Estate Center. Assuming otherwise that the all-industry taxable sales base is increased by a factor of 1.81 as described in Scenario 2 above, revenues from this residential property sales tax would, for example, have permitted a reduction in the incremental new weighted average local sales tax rate on all other sales from 6.25% to 5.25%, or in the alternative permit still further reductions in the expansion factor for other categories of taxable sales or services.[83] As suggested by our previous analysis, a reduction of this size would at the margin have a substantial impact on the number of local jurisdictions able to sustain this transition.

---

[80] Texas A&M University Real Estate Center, "Texas MLS Residential Housing Activity," http://recenter.tamu.edu/Data/hs/hs800a.htm, accessed May 13, 2010.

[81] Texas A&M University Real Estate Center, "Building Permit Activity," http://recenter.tamu.edu/data/databp.html, accessed July 11, 2010.

[82] This assumes that all such sales consisted of sales to persons who intended to reside in or rent out the properties (as opposed to developers, builders and investors not intending to rent).

[83] Assuming for the present discussion that it would be applied proportionately to property tax relief in all taxing jurisdictions.

Imposing a tax on the sale to consumers or landlords of residential property would suggest also imposing the same tax on new residential construction labor and residential repair and remodeling labor rendered to such persons so as not to introduce direct tax distortions into the homeowner's decision to buy or build. The Comptroller's 2009 Tax Exemptions report projects that including these categories in the state sales tax would add $492.6 million to projected state tax revenues in fiscal 2011,[84] which, after adjusting for the difference between actual 2008 and projected 2011 sales tax revenues,[85] suggests an estimated incremental taxable sales base increase in 2008 of approximately $7.55 billion between them. However, in order to avoid double or multiple taxation of residential construction labor on homes intended for resale, it would be necessary to maintain as an exemption the current exclusion for residential construction services rendered to builders or developers. The Comptroller's report provides insight into the potential size of such an exemption from its indication that $45.8 million of the projected 2011 initial incidence of the exclusion for residential construction labor falls on the finance and real estate industry, with the remainder falling directly on consumers.[86] Adjusting for the translation to 2008 figures, extrapolating this figure's corresponding taxable sales base, and correcting for the "resale" exemption just described, therefore, we may assume that the

Table 13

Results of Including Sales of Residential Properties and Construction, Repair & Remodeling Services

Currently Excluded Category	Comptroller's Estimated Tax Value in Fiscal 2011	Adjusted Tax Value in Fiscal 2008[87]	Estimated Annual Sales Volume for Calendar 2008 (reported or inferred)
Sales of Residential Housing	N/A	$3,898,163,811.50	$62,370,620,984.00
New residential construction	$362,000,000[88]	$346,779,405.24	$5,548,470,483.87
Residential repair and remodeling	$130,600,000[89]	$125,108,813.05	$2,001,741,008.82
Initial Incidence of Residential Construction Exclusion on Real Estate Industry	($45,800,000)[90]	($43,874,300.44)	($701,988,807.08)
Totals:	N/A	$4,326,177,729.35	$69,218,843,669.61

---

[84] *Tax Exemptions & Tax Incidence 2009*, Table 3, p.13.

[85] *See* n.78, *supra.*

[86] *Tax Exemptions & Tax Incidence 2009*, Table 11, p.52.

[87] *See* n.74, *supra.*

[88] Comptroller's projection for Fiscal 2011. *See* n.84, *supra.*

[89] *See* n.88, *supra.*

[90] Comptroller's projection for Fiscal 2011. *See* n.86, *supra.*

incremental taxable sales base obtained by introducing a tax on residential property sales, construction, repair and remodeling to consumers and landlords would increase the statewide taxable sales base by $69.2 billion, as illustrated in **Table 13**. After netting out from the figures in **Table 10** the amounts for residential construction that are also represented in **Table 13**, we conclude that the net increase in the taxable sales base achieved by expanding the range of potentially taxable services to consumers as set forth in **Tables 10 & 11,** and by including transactions relating to the construction, repair and sale of residential housing as set forth in **Table 13**, would in 2008 have amounted to $86.7 billion of newly taxable sales activity, or $5.4 billion of potential additional sales tax revenues at 6.25%, as set out in **Table 14**.

Table 14

Combined Incremental Revenues and Taxable Sales Base from Expanded Coverage of Selected Services and Sales of Residential Properties

Newly Taxable Transactions	Incremental Tax Revenues in 2008	Incremental Taxable Sales Base in 2008
Initial Excluded Service Categories (Table 10)	$804,873,084.00	$12,877,969,339.00
Remaining Excluded Service Categories (Table 11)	$714,396,136.00	$11,430,338,184.00
Residential housing transactions (Table 13)	$4,326,177,729.35	$69,218,843,669.61
Eliminate double-counting of residential construction labor	($428,013,918.00)	($6,848,222,686.00)
Totals:	$5,417,433,031.35	$86,678,928,506.61

The Arduin-Laffer Study also contemplated taxing sales of commercial and industrial property in the same way as residential property.[91] This might in theory produce still further revenue gains, but in practice it may be expected that the imposition of a new tax on the sale of commercial or industrial properties would induce widespread adoption of special-purpose corporate or other entity-based ownership structures by their owners, effectively negating (or at least complicating enforcement of) any revenue gains on future dispositions of the ownership through such entities. Once the property-tax based incentives for individuals to hold record title to their homesteads are abolished along with the property tax, in fact, even some homeowners might consider adopting such techniques. However, the cost and relative complexity of such methods would limit their practical usefulness to homeowners in general, for reasons similar to those that in practice have discouraged adoption of such techniques by consumers for their automobile purchases, and it would be easier to administer a "look-through" rule that disregards such

---

[91] Arduin-Laffer Study, p.19, estimating approximately $23 billion in annual commercial property sales in Texas based on national commercial property sales in the U.S. and Texas' share of the national economy, as compared to the $66 billion in residential property sales estimated by Arduin-Laffer based on National Association of Realtors and U.S. Census Bureau data.

techniques for residential owners than for commercial or industrial owners. But even accepting the Arduin-Laffer estimates for adding both residential and commercial property sales to the tax base, a tax on property sales in 2008 would not, under our assumptions so far, enable politically meaningful reductions in the local sales tax rates required to replace the property tax, at least not without making still broader changes to the system.

Interim Summary.   Of the $1.454 trillion in reported gross sales of all industries in the State of Texas, only $298.4 billion, or 20.5%, were subject to the sales tax in 2008. We have shown that it is not possible to achieve a doubling of the base for local sales taxes by expanding coverage of sales in industry classifications already predominantly subject to tax. Eliminating selected services-related exclusions for sales to consumers and imposing a new state tax on transactions relating to the sale, construction, repair or improvement of residential real property would yield an estimated maximum taxable sales base increase of about $86.7 billion (or the equivalent of around $5.4 billion in additional sales tax revenues at an average local incremental rate increase of 6.25%), all while remaining faithful to the core policies embodied in current sales tax exclusions and exemptions. But this would still leave state and local governments collectively short of the requisite tax revenues by around $28.4 billion, and the expansion to currently excluded consumer services could be expected to increase compliance burdens and administrative costs by amounts disproportionately high in relation to the potential revenues to be realized. Viewed another way, this change would yield a base expansion factor of only 1.29,[92] far short of even our more modest goal of 1.81 described in **Table 7**. As suggested in the initial section of this report, therefore, meaningful expansion of the base may require considering the inclusion of sales by large industry classifications not predominantly subject to the sales tax under current law, such as Manufacturing (gross 2008 sales $329.67 billion), or the Wholesale Trade (gross 2008 sales $346.25 billion), either through the reduction or elimination of exemptions and exclusions currently designed to minimize the initial incidence of the Texas sales tax on sales to business and industry, or by adoption of a new category of business sales taxes altogether.

C.   Limiting or Removing Current Exemptions and Exclusions for Sales to Business & Industry

Referring again to the Comptroller's tax incidence analysis, we may identify several potentially

---

[92] 1.290477385.

taxable categories of goods or services sold to businesses by their projected 2011 incidence on industry, as shown in **Table 15**. Other categories of service taxes excluded from the

Table 15

Tax Incidence of Certain Additional Sales Exemptions & Exclusions ($US millions)[93]

NAICS Industry Classification Affected	Gas & Electricity	Property Used in Manufacturing	New Non-Residential Construction Labor	Legal Services	Architectural & Engineering Services	Real Estate Brokerage and Agency Services	Freight Hauling	Automotive Maintenance & Repair
Mining	76.0	0.0	15.7	10.8	12.6	0.8	2.6	0.2
Utilities & Transportation	63.6	303.7	23.1	33.1	26.7	7.7	43.8	11.8
Construction	24.3	0.0	5.3	8.1	164.9	2.0	15.6	4.2
Manufacturing	672.3	11,108.6	32.9	29.1	54.5	3.8	100.9	19.8
Trade (Wholesale and Retail)	0.0	0.0	58.7	17.4	5.3	25.1	6.3	4.2
Information	0.0	0.0	10.6	7.5	39.2	2.7	2.3	0.9
Finance, Insurance & Real Estate	0.0	0.0	7.8	48.1	30.5	31.2	5.0	1.1
Other Services	0.0	268.7	57.5	121.5	54.9	78.7	14.3	15.0
Projected 2011 Totals:	**836.2**	**11,681.0**	**211.6**	**275.6**	**388.6**	**152.0**	**190.8**	**57.2**
Adjusted 2008 Totals:	801.0	11,189.9	202.7	264.0	372.3	145.6	182.8	54.8
Estimated 2008 Sales Volume (@ 6.25%)	12,816.7	179,037.8	3,243.2	4,224.2	5,956.2	2,329.7	2,924.4	876.7

Comptroller's incidence analysis, but the initial incidence of which would likely be borne predominantly by business and industry, include those described in **Table 16**. Finally, we may also consider those additional exemptions specified in the Texas Tax Code for the sales of goods to business or industry that are *not* (i) directly tied to the production, manufacture and distribution of food for home consumption, water, health care, education, or governmental

---

[93] Source: *Tax Exemptions & Tax Incidence 2009*, pp. 47-55, Tables 2 through 17. Since it is our intention to maintain the exemption for food and activities directly related to food production and distribution, we have excluded from this summary the tax incidence on the agriculture industry of the exemption or exclusion categories listed.

Table 16

Tax Value of Certain Additional Service Exclusions ($US millions)[94]

Category	Comptroller's Estimated Tax Value in Fiscal 2011	Adjusted Tax Value in Fiscal 2008[95]	Estimated Annual Sales Volume for Calendar 2008[96] (inferred at 6.25% sales tax rate)
Accounting and audit services	226.60	217.07	3,473.16
Management consulting and public relations	200.70	192.26	3,076.18
Contract computer programming	143.50	137.47	2,199.46
Research and development laboratory services	142.10	136.13	2,178.00
Economic and sociological research	23.00	22.03	352.53
Testing labs	55.20	52.88	846.07
Billboard advertising	28.50	27.30	436.83
Employment agency services	36.20	34.68	554.85
Temporary labor supply	54.40	52.11	833.80
Totals:	910.20	871.93	13,950.88

Table 17

Tax Value of Certain Additional Exemptions ($US millions)

Category	Comptroller's Estimated Tax Value in Fiscal 2009	Adjusted Tax Value in Fiscal 2008	Estimated Annual Sales Volume for Calendar 2008 (inferred at 6.25% sales tax rate)
Timber operations (equipment)	20.20	20.79	332.65
Information and data processing services	37.40	38.49	615.90
Enterprise projects (refunds)	17.70	18.22	291.48
Sales tax refund for economic development	8.70	8.95	143.27
Totals:	84.00	86.46	1,383.30

---

[94] Source: *Tax Exemptions & Tax Incidence 2009*, p 13., Table 3.

[95] See n 33, *supra*.

[96] See n 34, *supra*.

Table 18

Estimated 2008 Potentially Taxable Sales to Business and Industry in Selected Categories of Exemptions & Exclusions ($US millions)

Category		Adjusted Tax Value in Fiscal 2008		Estimated Annual Sales Volume for Calendar 2008 (@ 6.25%)
Accounting and audit services		217.1		3,473.2
Architectural & Engineering Services		372.3		5,956.2
Automotive Maintenance & Repair		54.8		876.7
Billboard advertising		27.3		436.8
Contract computer programming		137.5		2,199.5
Economic and sociological research		22.0		352.5
Employment agency services		34.7		554.9
Enterprise projects (refunds)		18.2		291.5
Freight Hauling		182.8		2,924.4
Gas & Electricity		801.0		12,815.7
Information and data processing services		38.5		615.9
Legal Services		264.0		4,224.2
Management consulting and public relations		192.3		3,076.2
New Non-Residential Construction Labor		202.7		3,243.2
Property Used in Manufacturing				
Materials used in manufacturing	10,266.7		164,266.9	
Manufacturing machinery & equipment	606.4		9,702.2	
Packaging and wrapping supplies	316.8		5,068.7	
Property Used in Manufacturing Subtotals:		11,189.9		179,037.8
Real Estate Brokerage and Agency Services		145.6		2,329.7
Research and development laboratory services		136.1		2,178.0
Sales tax refund for economic development		9.0		143.3
Temporary labor supply		52.1		833.8
Testing labs		52.9		846.1
Timber operations (equipment)		20.8		332.7
Totals:		14,171.4		226,743.2

operations (ii) beyond the reach of Texas taxing authority for, or exempted by policy in support of, interstate or foreign commerce, jurisdictional or similar considerations, (iii) intended for resale in substantially recognizable form, (iv) excluded for reasons of enforcement practicality (such as occasional sales), (v) estimated by the Comptroller in her Tax Exemptions report, or (vi) otherwise subject to tax. We also may eliminate sales tax refunds for "corporate welfare" and property tax-related economic development incentives. All of these remaining items are set forth in **Table 17.** Combining the information set forth in **Tables 15, 16 and 17** gives us the summary set forth in **Table 18** of the estimated aggregate 2008 sales to business and industry that we might consider subjecting to the current Texas sales tax. Whether and to what extent the categories set forth in **Table 18** should in fact be subjected to tax depends upon numerous considerations. First, as noted in Section IV.B. above, care should be given to the relationship between the marginal increase in compliance burden imposed on the state's new taxpayers and the marginal increase in revenues to be anticipated as a result. In comparison with the expansion of the sales tax to currently untaxed consumer services, it is reasonable to expect that the providers of currently untaxed business services will as a group be more sophisticated and better positioned to efficiently establish new compliance and collection procedures than would many independent or small providers of consumer services. Nevertheless this factor merits attention on a service-by-service basis even in the case of business services.

Another consideration is the extent to which such taxes are likely to be imposed multiple times on the same identifiable commodity or service, or its embedded cost, as it passes through the chain of commerce. In an effort to minimize this possibility, the Tax Code provides an exemption to the sales tax for purchases of goods being purchased for "resale". [97] The Comptroller is unable to provide an estimate as to how much tax value may be attributed to this particular exemption,[98] but for this reason no value is attributed to it in **Table 18**, which therefore represents the result of retaining this exemption as a matter of policy. To the extent that they are not rendered to one another, services in the classifications derived from **Table 16** would in principle be subject to the sales tax only once. Like "freight hauling" in the example given above, subsequent renditions of any particular type of service would themselves be subject to tax, but any one incidence of such service could be received only once, and therefore taxed only once, although their accounting cost would be amortized over the value of the purchasing enterprise's resulting productive outputs. The same may be said of most of the categories derived from **Table 15**, with the exception of "Property Used in Manufacturing", which could theoretically be resold in successive forms through multiple iterations.

In order to extract taxable value from sales to manufacturers without completely abandoning the principle of avoiding multiple instances of the same tax on the same commodity or its

---

[97] Texas Tax Code Section 151.302.

[98] *See* Texas Comptroller of Public Accounts, *Tax Exemptions & Tax Incidence 2007*, p.4, Table 2 (February 2007) ("*Tax Exemptions & Tax Incidence 2007*").

derivatives, it might make sense to assess the tax only once upon an input's first entry into the manufacturing sector. Such a system could be administered by reference to the vendor's and purchaser's NAICS Sector Codes, and it could, for example, exclude products bought and then modified or resold, while at the same time capturing the initial stage of transforming initial inputs. Section 151.318 of the Texas Tax Code, which contains the "property used" exemption for manufacturing, provides a lengthy list of numerous items of materials, equipment and supplies to which the exemption applies. Only one of these items specifically targets property that will become an ingredient or component of the resulting product, however;[99] the remainder covers a wide range of materials and items that by their nature would tend to be consumed in the manufacturing process, or that would be purchased once and used by the manufacturer over the course of producing multiple outputs.[100] While the Comptroller's estimates include a breakdown of "property used in manufacturing" to "materials used", "machinery and equipment", and "packaging supplies,"[101] they do not provide more detailed estimates that would enable us to distinguish among the elements of the $10.267 billion "materials used" sub-category.

In order to compensate for our inability to discriminate meaningfully among the components of Manufacturing's "materials" estimates, we may turn to data provided by the U.S. Department of Commerce's Bureau of Economic Analysis, which maintains a database of annual industry economic accounts and input-output relationships at the U.S. national level, and on May 25, 2010 released a revision of these statistics for the periods 2001 through 2008.[102] Based on its report entitled "The Use of Commodities by Industries after Redefinitions (1987, 1992, 1997 to 2008)"[103], we may estimate the proportions in which, nationally at least, various classifications of commodities made up the manufacturing industry's "materials" inputs. Unfortunately, the data does not in all ways indicate the uses to which those materials were put (i.e., whether transformed or consumed, for example, or recognizably incorporated into a resulting product). The BEA's database also includes a detailed listing of the intermediate inputs acquired by each industry classification during the reporting year, divided generally into "durable" and "non-

---

[99] *See* Texas Tax Code Section 151.318(a)(1) ("tangible personal property that will become an ingredient or component part of tangible personal property manufactured, processed, or fabricated for ultimate sale").

[100] *See* Texas Tax Code Section 151.318(a)(2)-(11), (b), (n) and (t).

[101] *See Tax Exemptions & Tax Incidence 2009*, p. 5, Table 2.

[102] *See* http://www.bea.gov/industry/iotables. *See also* Matthew M. Donahoe, Edward T. Morgan, Kevin J. Muck, and Ricky L. Stewart "Annual Industry Accounts: Advance Statistics on GDP by Industry for 2009 Revised Statistics for 1998–2008, Comprehensive Revision," Survey of Current Business Vol. 90, No. 6 (Bureau of Economic Analysis, June 2010).

[103] *See* http://www.bea.gov/industry/iotables (accessed June 15, 2010).

durable" goods, but even this data does not adequately convey the intended or resulting uses of those inputs. Similarly, the U.S. Census Bureau publishes its "Annual Survey of Manufactures"[104], which provides a measure of the major categories of expenditures[105] (machinery and equipment, packaging, goods bought and resold, fuel and electricity, etc.) of the "Manufacturing" NAICS industry classification during each year surveyed, both at the state and national levels. While the 2008 survey, released March 30, 2010,[106] does provide this data for the Texas manufacturing industry, it likewise does not set forth the detailed makeup of those portions of the "materials" acquired, such as raw materials, semi-finished inputs and expendable other supplies, that might or might not have become an "ingredient or component" of resulting products.

However, the BEA data does enable us to determine that, of the entire 2008 acquisitions of intermediate inputs by the U.S. Manufacturing industry, 49.08% consisted of re-acquisitions from the Manufacturing industry itself to support or supply further manufacturing activity, while others came from Agriculture (6.37%), Mining (15.56%), Wholesale Trade (6.99%), the Retail Trade (0.33%), and Scrap and Used Goods (0.12%).[107] Further analysis, illustrated in **Table 19** below, shows that 97.8% by value of all goods and materials inputs into the Wholesale Trade not obtained from the Wholesale Trade itself came from the Manufacturing industry, and 1.44% came from the Retail Trade.[108] Similarly, 98.36% of goods and materials inputs into the Retail Trade not obtained from the Retail Trade itself came from the Manufacturing and Wholesale Trade industries. This suggests that nearly all manufacturing inputs sourced from the Retail and Wholesale Trade industries consisted of goods and materials previously manufactured and then resold in either recognizable or derivative form. And although roughly four-fifths of all external inputs by value in the Agriculture and Mining industries came from the Manufacturing industry, it

---

[104] *See* U.S. Census Bureau, "Sector 31: Annual Survey of Manufactures: Geographic Area Statistics: Statistics for the United States and States: 2008 and 2007," http://www.census.gov/manufacturing/asm/index.html (accessed June 15, 2010).

[105] The survey details the manufacturing industry's aggregate expenditures on "materials" and "purchased fuels", as well as on capital expenditures for such items as "autos, trucks etc. for highway use," "computer and data processing equipment", and other "machinery and equipment.

[106] *See* U.S. Census Bureau, "Sector 31: Annual Survey of Manufactures: Geographic Area Statistics: Supplemental Statistics for the United States and States: 2008 and 2007," http://www.census.gov/manufacturing/asm/index.html (accessed June 15, 2010).

[107] Source: U.S. Dept. of Commerce, Bureau of Economic Analysis, The Use of Commodities by Industries after Redefinitions for 2008, at n.103, *supra* (accessed June 15, 2010). The remaining inputs came from services such as (i) Professional and Business Services, (ii) Transportation and Warehousing, (iii) Financial, Insurance Real Estate, Rental & Leasing, etc.

[108] Source: BEA, The Use of Commodities by Industries after Redefinitions for 2008, *supra* n.107.

is reasonable to suppose that such previously manufactured items were predominantly not re-sold in recognizable form as part of those industries' outputs. For simplicity, therefore, we will treat all manufacturing inputs from the Wholesale and Retail Trades as industry-internal inputs, and all manufacturing inputs from the Agriculture and Mining industries as industry-external inputs.

Table 19

2008 U.S. Industry Goods and Materials External Input Percentages by Industry and Commodity Source (excludes inputs from within same industry)

Commodity Source	Agriculture, Forestry, Fishing & Hunting	Mining	Manufacturing	Wholesale Trade	Retail Trade
Agriculture, forestry, fishing, and hunting	0.00%	0.00%	21.68%	0.03%	1.04%
Mining	1.38%	0.00%	52.97%	0.72%	0.59%
Manufacturing	80.35%	86.00%	0.00%	97.82%	71.28%
Wholesale trade	17.35%	12.50%	23.81%	0.00%	27.08%
Retail trade	0.96%	1.35%	1.12%	1.44%	0.00%
Scrap, used and secondhand goods	-0.04%	0.14%	0.41%	0.00%	0.00%
Totals:*	100.00%	100.00%	100.00%	100.00%	100.00%

* Percentages may not add due to rounding

In addition, the BEA data also enables us to determine that, of the total 2008 commodity output of the U.S. manufacturing industry, 33.81% was re-acquired by that industry as intermediate inputs for further manufacturing activity.[109] Likewise, intermediate manufacturing inputs obtained from the Wholesale and Resale Trades amounted to 19.96% and 1.01% of their respective total commodity outputs. Assuming that all of the foregoing percentage relationships held true for the Texas economy in 2008, and referring back to the aggregate gross sales figures in **Table 2**, we might therefore infer that $184,017,374,187.11 worth of previously manufactured items were consumed as inputs by the Texas Manufacturing industry.

Turning, then, to the Census Bureau's 2008 Annual Survey of Manufactures, (see n. 104 above), we find that total "cost of materials" for the Texas manufacturing industry (NAICS Sector

---

[109] Source: BEA The Use of Commodities by Industries after Redefinitions for 2008, *supra* n.107. Other portions of manufacturing output were consumed by the Wholesale Trade (1.7%), the Retail Trade (1.04%), Construction (10.33%), Mining (2.23%) and Agriculture, Forestry, Fishing & Hunting (2.39%)

code 31) equaled $450,004,458,000.[110] This figure includes all parts, components, containers, raw materials, semi-finished goods, scrap and supplies, products bought and sold in the same condition, fuels consumed for heat and power, purchased electricity, and contract work, but as a measure of operating costs it excludes capital expenditures for machinery and equipment. Adding the $15,512,184,000 of costs for such machinery and equipment (excluding buildings and other structures) brings the total to $465,516,642,000.00.To arrive at a figure that excludes categories of expenditures otherwise covered in **Table 17**, we must then deduct from this the amount known to apply to gas and electricity ($18,037,571,000), and to limit the figure to purchases of actual goods and materials we must also deduct contract work ($6,676,441,000). This yields a net total cost of goods and materials inputs of $440,802,630,000.[111] Subtracting from this our estimated $184 billion of previously manufactured items, we estimate that $256,735,255,812.89 -- 58.25% -- of the Texas manufacturing industry's goods and materials inputs (excluding gas, electricity, buildings & structures) were obtained from outside the manufacturing industry. Applying this percentage to the Comptroller's reported figure for the tax value of the exemption for "property used in manufacturing" described in **Table 19**, this calculation suggests that $6,518,116,750 of tax value, or $104,289,868,000 of potentially taxable activity, consists of the initial acquisition of goods and materials by the Manufacturing industry, enabling us to revise **Table 19** to appear as **Table 20** below.

Based on the estimates derived above, this principled modification of the "property used" exemption would theoretically contribute more than $6.5 billion of additional sales tax revenues, for a total increase in Texas state sales tax collections from sales to business and industry of approximately $9.5 billion at the 6.25% rate.

D.   "Consumption" Sales Taxes versus "Business" Sales Taxes

This is the point at which theory confronts reality. The most compelling arguments in favor of the retail sales tax draw on its character as a tax on consumption. Unlike taxes on income or property accumulation, the incentives created by such a tax actually favor those behaviors – thrift, savings, investment -- that have been demonstrated to produce economic growth, jobs

---

[110] *See* U.S. Census Bureau, "Sector 31: Annual Survey of Manufactures: Geographic Area Statistics: Statistics for the United States and States: 2008 and 2007," http://www.census.gov/manufacturing/asm/index.html (accessed June 15, 2010).

[111] *See* n.110, *supra*.

and generally higher levels of prosperity across all socio-economic classes.[112] This premise underlay the Arduin-Laffer study's projections of income and jobs creation associated with its proposal. Consumption taxes tend to be more transparent, as well, necessarily rendering elected officials and their appointees more responsive, or at least more accountable, to the concerns and needs of taxpaying citizens. And consumption taxes are generally less costly,

Table 20

Revised Estimated 2008 Potentially Taxable Sales to Business and Industry in Selected Categories of Exemptions & Exclusions ($US millions)

Category	Adjusted Tax Value in Fiscal 2008	Estimated Annual Sales Volume for Calendar 2008 (@ 6.25%)
Accounting and audit services	217.1	3,473.2
Architectural & Engineering Services	372.3	5,956.2
Automotive Maintenance & Repair	54.8	876.7
Billboard advertising	27.3	436.8
Contract computer programming	137.5	2,199.5
Economic and sociological research	22.0	352.5
Employment agency services	34.7	554.9
Enterprise projects (refunds)	18.2	291.5
Freight Hauling	182.8	2,924.4
Gas & Electricity	801.0	12,816.7
Information and data processing services	38.5	615.9
Legal Services	264.0	4,224.2
Management consulting and public relations	192.3	3,076.2
New Non-Residential Construction Labor	202.7	3,243.2
Property First Used in Manufacturing	6,518.1	104,289.9
Real Estate Brokerage and Agency Services	145.6	2,329.7
Research and development laboratory services	136.1	2,178.0
Sales tax refund for economic development	9.0	143.3
Temporary labor supply	52.1	833.8
Testing labs	52.9	846.1
Timber operations (equipment)	20.8	332.7
Totals:	$9,499.8	$151,995.40

---

[112] These arguments are stressed, of course, by proponents of a national consumption-based tax. *See, e.g.,* David Altig et al., *Stimulating Fundamental Tax Reform in the United States*, 91 AM ECON. REV. 574, 593 (2001); *see also* Dale W. Jorgenson & Peter J. Wilcoxen, *The Economic Impact of Fundamental Tax Reform,* UNITED STATES TAX REFORM IN THE 21ST CENTURY, at 55, 87-88 (George R. Zodrow & Peter Mieszkowski eds. 2002).

inefficient and intrusive to collect.[113] Eliminating both income and property tax systems in favor of a consumption-based tax system can liberate individual taxpayers from the complexities, inequities, and oppressive bureaucracies associated with such other systems, while at the same time freeing businesses and business owners from a major source of operating complexity and inefficiency.

1.   The Disadvantages of Taxing Business Inputs

Taxing goods or services sold as inputs to other businesses, on the other hand, gives rise to a host of principled objections, as has been well documented in the literature on this subject.[114] A sales tax on inputs would accumulate through subsequent stages as each successive manufacturer or distributor pays through the price of its inputs the taxes borne by its predecessors. This process is referred to as tax "pyramiding" or "cascading," and it entails the conceptually distinct but related consequence that subsequent impositions of the tax apply as well to the value of taxes previously paid, i.e., a tax-on-tax.[115] Expanding the Texas sales tax to all purchases of business inputs would amount to repeal of the exemption for products purchased "for resale"[116] or for use in manufacturing.[117] Even items that can be purchased and used by a business only once, such as gas and electricity, freight hauling (a particular shipment can be shipped only once), or a particular rendition of accounting or legal services, would be subject to pyramiding to the extent that the purchaser of those inputs resells its own output to other Texas businesses subject to similar taxes. The accounting cost of the items carries forward through successive links in the chain of commerce, because all businesses operating at break-even or better will be charging a price sufficient to cover the cost of their inputs in order to remain in business.[118] In all cases, therefore, the pyramiding taxes become a part of each succeeding vendor's cost structure, until they are finally embedded in the price of the product as

---

[113] Provided that authorities do not undertake significant efforts to enforce the "use" tax directly against consumers – *see* text and notes at n. 32, *supra*.

[114] *See generally,* Andrew Chamberlain & Patrick Fleenor, *Tax Pyramiding: The Economic Consequences of Gross Receipts Taxes* (Tax Foundation, Inc. Spec. Rpt. No. 147, Dec. 2006)

[115] While the literature is not completely consistent in this respect, this report will use the "pyramiding" term exclusively to refer to both elements of the phenomenon described.

[116] *See* Texas Tax Code Sec. 151.302.

[117] *See* Texas Tax Code Sec. 151.318.

[118] While it is true that in a dynamic, economic sense the burden of the newly imposed tax may fall to varying degrees on other inputs (such as labor in the form of reduced wages) or to the enterprise's owners (in the form of reduced profit), thereby moderating the net impact to consumers, we are focused for illustration purposes on the burden in its static, accounting sense once equilibrium has been achieved.

sold to in-state consumers or out-of-state purchasers.

At higher levels, pyramiding of business input taxes produces serious harm to the state's economy. The pyramided taxes place exporters at a competitive disadvantage to their untaxed foreign competitors,[119] and those sectors most susceptible to pyramiding[120] could see a punitively higher escalation of input costs before the product finally exits Texas commerce. The pyramiding effect creates artificial advantages for enterprises that integrate vertically, or that produce goods and services requiring fewer manufacturing stages than their competing substitutes, or that simply choose to import more of their inputs than their competitors. This incentivizes businesses to organize themselves and their processes in ways that otherwise would be economically inefficient, thereby reducing consumer welfare through relatively higher prices, reduced output, and misallocation of capital and labor resources. Since the pyramided taxes are embedded without fanfare in the product's ultimate retail price, the system lacks the transparency needed for consumers to appreciate the hidden extent to which their elected leaders have burdened them with the cost of state and local government through their retail purchases.[121] And, to add insult to injury, the consumer presumably would be paying the standard retail sales tax on top of those embedded input taxes, as well. Of course, introducing a sales tax to businesses or entire industries that to date have been exempt from its application produces substantial compliance and enforcement complications as well. Proposals to tax business services, in particular, tend to produce well-organized protests from influential business groups, usually tied to the objecting groups' self interest, of course, but at the same time grounded in genuine economic concerns associated with the particular pyramiding and administrative problems associated with the tax in question.[122]

---

[119] In reality, nearly all businesses are subject to taxation of some kind in the jurisdictions in which they operate. The question of tax competitiveness is necessarily a relative one.

[120] See discussion in Section IV.E. below.

[121] As stated by Professor Mikesell, for example,

> The fundamental logic of retail sales taxation is challenged by the inclusion of business purchases in the base. Including these purchases distorts business choices and can harm economic development efforts. . . . The tax paid by businesses is hidden from the view of the business customers who ultimately pay it, being certainly less transparent than the tax added to consumer prices at the cash register . . . .

Mikesell, THE FUTURE OF STATE TAXATION at 24.

[122] See generally JOHN F. DUE & JOHN L. MIKESELL, SALES TAXATION: STATE AND LOCAL STRUCTURE AND ADMINISTRATION (Urban Inst. Press 2d ed. 1994) (1983); Walter Hellerstein, Florida's Sales Tax on Services, 41 NAT'L TAX J. 1 (1988) William F. Fox & Matthew Murray, Economic Aspects of Taxing Services, 41 NAT'L TAX J. 19, 19 (1988); Michele E. Hendrix & George R. Zodrow, Forum: Florida Services Tax: Sales Taxation of Services: An Economic Perspective 30 FLA. ST. U.L. REV. 411 (Spring 2003) **

Complex accounting, reporting and refunding practices could be adopted in the manner of the European-style value-added tax (or "VAT") to ensure that each incremental assessment down to the retail level was credited with the previous assessments and disclosed to subsequent purchasers, thereby avoiding pyramiding, assuring equitable treatment of participants throughout the chain of distribution, and providing transparency to consumers who ultimately must bear the economic burden. The administrative burden of a VAT system represents a step in the opposite direction from simplification, however, and as a political matter the VAT may be an idea whose time has not yet come in Texas. Besides, it may fairly be questioned whether either solution – i.e., a VAT or a business inputs sales tax without value-added elements -- adopted in the quest to keep the nominal retail tax rate below some arbitrarily selected target, would be any better than charging a proportionately higher rate only once at the point of consumption. All other things being equal, the disadvantages of the business inputs sales tax would seem to be sufficient to disqualify it from consideration.

2.   The Trade-off between Business Input Taxes and Retail Consumption Taxes

But all other things are never equal. We have shown that aggregate weighted average sales tax rates would have to exceed 19% in order to replace the property tax while preserving all existing major sales tax exemptions and exclusions. We recognize intuitively that consumers would likely chafe at nominal sales tax rates approaching even 15%, and economic principles reinforce this perception, since the incentive for any economic actor – including a consumer – to adjust its behavior increases in proportion to the marginal tax imposed on such behavior. A cumulative state and local sales tax of 19% would provide potent psychological and financial incentives for the consumer to make alternate purchasing decisions (to drive across jurisdictional boundaries to shop, for example), or even engage in evasion (such as by ordering from out-of-state vendors and failing to remit the applicable use tax). The very misallocation of resources we have sought to avoid within the business-to-business sector would be induced many times over within the retail sector. And without expanding coverage of sales by the Manufacturing and Wholesale Trade classifications, in particular, the entire economic base of sales remaining for consideration in all of the fifteen remaining classifications (excluding the four already addressed above) would only amount to $298,579,066,136.00. This still would fall approximately $27 billion short of the base required for a 2.09 expansion factor, even allowing for no exclusions, exemptions or discounts in the coverage for those classifications.

Furthermore, the decision to exempt or exclude from the sales tax certain sales to Texas businesses occupying an initial or intermediate position in the chain of distribution places beyond reach substantial value in goods and services ultimately destined for export to other states and countries, since no in-state sale to consumers will occur to which the sales tax could be applied. While constitutional considerations in effect bar the state from taxing export transactions in a way that discriminates against them relative to non-export transactions, this bar would not prevent the state from taxing a Texas manufacturer or wholesaler on its own purchase of goods and services, or imposing the burden of a business sales tax on the exporter itself rather than on the out-of-state purchaser, just as it does not prevent the state from imposing a business franchise tax or, through its county and local taxing authorities, an *ad valorem* property tax on such exporters. According to the U.S. Census Bureau Foreign Trade Division's December 2008 report on U.S. international Trade in Goods and Services,[123] Texas exported a total of $192,143,600,000 worth of goods and services to non-U.S. jurisdictions in 2008, of which $156,552,500,000 consisted of manufactured commodities, $12,369,500,000 consisted of non-manufactured commodities (such as agricultural, forestry, fishery products, mineral commodities, scrap, waste and used or second-hand merchandise), and $23,221,700,000 consisted of re-exports. Just to put matters in perspective, 6.25% of these sales would have amounted to $12,008,975,000.00. This represents the tax value theoretically foregone by being unable to apply a Texas sales tax at these exports' point of final distribution. Reducing this figure by the value added in the final stage of pre-export production and/or distribution, it also represents the tax value theoretically lost by the policy choice not to tax inputs to that final stage.

Let us also not lose sight of the reality currently faced by Texas businesses and industry. If necessary state and local government revenues cannot be generated by the retail sales tax alone, they will inevitably be generated by other taxes. At the present time, Texas' state and local governments already tax resident businesses with a modified gross receipts tax (the business franchise tax), an annual *ad valorem* property tax, as well as numerous other excise taxes, severance taxes, other forms of gross receipts taxes, licensing fees and other charges and assessments, which in many cases themselves induce the very pyramiding and distortions described above. Even the sales tax itself falls to a very substantial degree directly on business and industry, as discussed in more detail below.

---

[123] FT900 Supplemental Exhibit 2, "Origin of Movement of U.S. Exports of Goods by State by NAICS-Based Product Code Groupings," (issue date February 11, 2009)

3.   The Burden on Business Inputs from the Current *Ad Valorem* Property Tax

Leaving aside particular development incentives and abatement programs, every business that owns property in Texas, whether real or tangible, must pay an annual *ad valorem* tax with respect to that property, at effective rates that change frequently, on a taxable base valued in the first instance by government fiat, under a system in which the taxpayer bears the practical (even f not the legal) burden of disproving the government's dictate and challenging it in court on a recurring, annual basis if necessary. According to the Comptroller's 2007 Tax Exemptions & Incidence Report, for example, just under one half of the projected 2009 local school property tax's initial burden would fall on Texas consumers ($9,748,400,000.00), but the majority of this burden would fall on Texas businesses ($10,227,900,000.00) before making its way to households, as set forth in **Table 21**.[124]

Table 21

Initial Incidence of Current Texas School Property Tax by Industry ($US millions)

NAICS Industry Classification	Comptroller's Estimated Initial Tax Incidence in Tax Year 2009	Percent of Total	Adjusted Tax Incidence for Tax Year 2008	Estimated 2008 Incidence of Non-School Property Taxes
Agriculture	243.2	1.2	258.51	212.96
Mining	1,079.9	5.4	1,147.86	958.31
Utilities & Transportation	1,538.2	7.7	1,635.01	1,366.48
Construction	99.9	0.5	106.19	88.73
Manufacturing	1,578.1	7.9	1,677.42	1,401.97
Trade (Wholesale and Retail)	898.9	4.5	955.47	798.59
Information	699.2	3.5	743.20	621.13
Finance, Insurance and Real Estate	3,136.3	15.7	3,333.68	2,786.19
Other Services	958.9	4.8	1,019.25	851.83
Government	0.0	0.0	0.00	0.00
Subtotal	10,227.9	51.2	10,871.60	9,086.18
Individual Consumers	9,748.4	48.8	10,361.92	8,660.27
Total:	$19,976.3	100.0%	$21,233.52	$17,746.45

If we adjust these figures upward in proportion to the actually higher 2008 school property tax

---

[124] Adapted from "Incidence Analysis Table 36", in *Tax Exemptions & Tax Incidence 2007*, p. 68. Totals do not add, reportedly due to rounding.

levies,[125] and if we assume that these same proportions prevailed for the remaining $17,746,452,319.00 of Texas 2008 local property tax levies, this means that Texas businesses already bore an annual initial tax burden on capital goods inputs of $19,957,780,000 through 2008 local property taxes alone. Nothing about these taxes are designed to, or should be expected to, minimize their impact on those industries most susceptible to pyramiding of input taxes. And since the tax is applied every year to the same property regardless of whether it was purchased in that year, the same capital inputs are being taxed, not just twice, but many, many times over the useful life of the assets, dramatically penalizing capital intensive industries relative to a tax imposed only once at the time of purchase. The property tax even pyramids through the application of subsequent assessments against real and tangible property inputs held by businesses whose input prices bear the embedded costs of their suppliers' previous property tax assessments. As noted in the introductory pages of this report, if measured in relation to the useful value "consumed" by the owning business during each taxable year, rather than the asset's initial purchase price, the effective rate of the property tax exceeds its nominal rate by as much as an order of magnitude or more. This system is costly, arbitrary, bureaucratic and especially burdensome to capital-intensive businesses that must compete with other businesses located in more favorable tax jurisdictions – i.e., the very same high technology and job-creating industries that Texas policymakers profess to want to attract. It also drives the costs of finished products higher, which increased costs are then borne by the consumer without transparency. Replacement of this system with a broadly diversified, simplified sales tax on business inputs would in principle represent a substantial improvement.

4.   The Burden on Business Inputs from the Current Business Franchise Tax

Since 2008, Texas businesses have been subject to the Texas business "franchise" or "margins" tax, which the Comptroller reports to have generated $4,712,183,000 in 2008 tax collections.[126] Of course, all of this tax's initial incidence fell by definition on business and industry, but for our own estimate of its incidence by industry classification, we have noted that the Comptroller's 2009 tax incidence analysis projects business franchise tax collections of

---

[125] The Comptroller's 2007 forecast for school property tax collections in Tax Year 2009 of $19,976,300,000 closely approximates the reported actual school property tax levies during Fiscal Year 2008 of $21,233,517,226. (*See* Texas Comptroller of Public Accounts, *Annual Property Tax Report, Tax Year 2008, Revised Edition*, p.3, Exhibit 4 (Feb 2010).

[126] CAFR 2009, p. 240. Again, this assumes no difference between the Comptroller's 2007 forecast for fiscal 2009 and the actual levies for 2008.

$4,495,200,000 for Tax Year 2011,[127] whereas the 2007 forecast for Tax Year 2009 projected only $2,819,900,00.[128] For this reason it would likely be more meaningful to use the industry sector incidence forecast from the Comptroller's 2009 report as the basis for our tax incidence estimates for Fiscal Year 2008, as set forth in **Table 22.**[129]

Although imposed as a function of a business's gross receipts, the Texas franchise tax purports to function more as a net receipts, or "margins" tax, by permitting businesses to make one of three standardized deduction calculations before applying the tax to the result; in this sense it functions more as a "blended" gross receipts and net income tax. But if these deductions were intended to moderate the impact of the tax in relation to businesses' actual profitability, they are very blunt instruments indeed. The cost of goods sold, or employee wages and salaries, or a flat 30% deduction must necessarily yield widely varying net incidence ratios on businesses affected, whether measured in relation either to their gross receipts or their net income, and they cannot be said in any true sense to represent a fair estimation of actual profit margins for all taxpayers. By attempting to hybridize a gross receipts calculation with a net income calculation, the Texas franchise tax offers a poor representation of either. In terms of its distributional equity, it must make perfect sense to those few businesses whose net incomes happen to equal exactly the remainder after deducting one of the three available deductions

Table 22

Initial Incidence of Current Texas Business Franchise Tax by Industry ($US millions)

NAICS Industry Classification	Comptroller's Estimated Initial Tax Incidence in Fiscal 2011	Percent of Total	Adjusted Tax Incidence for Tax Year 2008
Agriculture	18.0	0.40	18.87
Mining	440.5	9.8	461.76
Utilities & Transportation	310.2	6.9	325.17
Construction	233.8	5.2	245.09
Manufacturing	849.6	18.9	890.61
Trade (Wholesale and Retail)	777.7	17.3	815.24
Information	215.8	4.8	226.22
Finance, Insurance and Real Estate	570.9	12.7	598.46
Other Services	1,078.60	24.1	1,130.66
Government	0	0	0
Subtotal	4,495.10		4,712.08
Individual Consumers	0	0	0
Total:	**$4,495.20**	**100.00%**	**$4,712.18**

---

[127] See *Tax Exemptions & Tax Incidence 2009*, p.56, Table 18.

[128] See *Tax Exemptions & Tax Incidence 2007*, p.56, Table 18.

[129] Adapted from "Incidence Analysis Table 18", in *Tax Exemptions & Tax Incidence 2009*, p. 56. Totals do not add, reportedly due to rounding.

from their gross receipts, but for everyone else its real impact is chaotic and fundamentally inequitable. A business compelled by its own cost structures to select the 30% deduction, if its actual profitability equals only 10% of its gross receipts, pays as a percentage of net income twice the tax as a similar business making a 20% profit; a business making no profit pays infinitely more. Similar inequities prevail between the three different categories of business taxpayers if the incidence is measured as a function of gross receipts instead. The tax is applied to each successive taxpayer in the chain of distribution, with the corresponding pyramiding effects being affected inconsistently by the three standardized deductions, since of course they do not actually quantify franchise taxes previously paid in the chain of distribution. The tax's only saving grace lies in the absolutely low percentage rates (0.5% for wholesalers and retailers, 1.0% for all others) at which it is applied. These low nominal rates minimize the absolute size of the negative distributional effects, and perhaps may be credited with the attenuated opposition met by this tax from the Texas business community. Measured in relation to net income, of course, a pure "gross sales" or "gross receipts" tax likewise yields widely differing incidence ratios, but at least it is predictable, simple to administer, and -- as a function of gross receipts -- the same for every taxpayer. In fact, depending on the levels of revenues generated by the sales tax reforms contemplated by this report, repeal of the margins tax along with the property tax would represent a particularly attractive *quid pro quo*, behind which many Texas businesses might very well rally.

5.   The Burden on Business Inputs from the Current State and Local Sales Tax

The Texas sales tax system as currently configured, moreover, already directs nearly half of the aggregate state sales tax burden to intermediate business inputs. The Comptroller's 2007 tax incidence analysis shows that $9,468,600,000 of the $21,117,700,000 in state sales taxes projected under then-current law for Tax Year 2009 would initially fall upon industry, rather than consumers, as illustrated in **Table 23** below.[130] If we adjust these figures upward in proportion to the actually higher 2008 state sales tax collections,[131] this means that Texas businesses in 2008 already bore an annual initial tax burden on business inputs of $9,703,170,000 through 2008 state sales taxes alone. Whatever other arguments may be mustered for maintenance of the

---

[130] Adapted from "Incidence Analysis Table 1", in *Tax Exemptions & Tax Incidence 2007*, p. 47. Totals do not add, reportedly due to rounding.

[131] The Comptroller's 2007 forecast for state sales tax collections in Tax Year 2009 of $21,117,700,000 closely approximates the reported actual state sales tax collections during Fiscal Year 2008 of $21,640,855,000 (see CAFR 2009, p.240.

curren: sales tax system, shielding sales of business inputs from its reach cannot be among them.

Table 23
Initial Incidence of Current Texas Sales Tax by Industry
($US millions)

NAICS Industry Classification	Comptroller's Estimated Initial Tax Incidence in Fiscal 2009	Percent of Total	Adjusted Tax Incidence for Tax Year 2008
Agriculture	56.3	0.3	57.69
Mining	647.6	3.1	663.64
Utilities & Transportation	1,402.0	6.6	1,436.73
Construction	131.0	0.6	134.25
Manufacturing	905.0	4.3	927.42
Trade (Wholesale and Retail)	1,053.9	5.0	1,080.01
Information	982.6	4.7	1,006.94
Finance, Insurance and Real Estate	841.0	4.0	861.83
Other Services	3,449.2	16.3	3,534.65
Government	0.0	0.0	0.00
Subtotal	$9,468.6	44.8	9,703.17
Individual Consumers	11,649.0	55.2	11,937.58
Total:	$21,117.7	100.0%	$21,640.86

6.   The Combined Burden of All Current Major Taxes on Business and Industry

Putting all of this together, we can readily see that Texas businesses in 2008 paid more than $34.3 billion dollars in pyramiding, incentive-distorting, export industry-burdening taxes that opponents of business input sales taxes would prefer to avoid, as summarized in **Table 24** below,[132] and this does not include the effect of any of the local sales taxes, excise taxes, minerals severance or production taxes, or other business taxes currently in effect. All of these taxes necessarily would ultimately come to rest on households, either within or outside the state, as reflected in the Comptroller's analysis, but not before they have first been borne by Texas businesses, both large and small. Part of the property tax paid by an office equipment manufacturer, for example, would be embedded in the cost of that equipment to an accounting services firm, which would pay additional property tax on the value of that equipment during each year of its useful life, even as both the factory and the services firm must pay business franchise taxes on the portion of their net revenues represented by that embedded property tax.

---

[132] Aga n, this assumes no difference between the Comptroller's 2007 forecast for fiscal 2009 and the actual levies for 2008.

And, somewhere in the chain of distribution, nearly one-half of Texas' total state sales taxes are being assessed, at least in part, on sales of goods or services the taxable values of which

Table 24

Taxes Initially Incident to Texas Businesses in 2008 ($US)[133]

NAICS Industry Classification	Local School Property Taxes	Local Non-School Property Taxes	Current Texas State Sales Taxes	Texas Business Franchise Taxes	Total
Agriculture	258.51	212.96	57.69	18.87	548.03
Mining	1,147.86	958.31	663.64	461.76	3,231.57
Utilities & Transportation	1,635.01	1,366.48	1,436.73	325.17	4,763.39
Construction	106.19	88.73	134.25	245.09	574.26
Manufacturing	1,677.42	1,401.97	927.42	890.61	4,897.42
Trade (Wholesale and Retail)	955.47	798.59	1,080.01	815.24	3,649.31
Information	743.2	621.13	1,006.94	226.22	2,597.49
Finance, Insurance and Real Estate	3,333.68	2,786.19	861.83	598.46	7,580.16
Other Services	1,019.25	851.83	3,534.65	1,130.66	6,536.39
Government	0	0	0	0	0
Subtotal	10,876.59	9,086.19	9,703.16	4,712.08	34,378.02
Individual Consumers	10,361.92	8,660.27	11,937.58	0	30,959.77
Total:	$21,238.51	$17,746.46	$21,640.74	$4,712.08	$65,337.79

include these embedded property taxes and business franchise taxes. And make no mistake – the very citizens we seek to protect from the Texas retail sales tax by exempting sales of groceries, medicine and utilities are fully participating through their retail purchases in the property taxes, sales taxes and franchise taxes currently being paid by grocery, pharmaceutical and power distribution companies. While any proposed reform should stay as true as possible to key economic ideals, including the minimization of double taxation, economic distortion, and tax "pyramiding" and "cascading," the system Texas already has is certainly no blank slate; in fact, it seems overdue for substantial rationalization. The critical question is how to quantify the relative impact of a sales tax on business inputs.

E.   "Pyramiding" Factors and Texas Input-Output Analysis

Not every taxed input leads to the same degree of pyramiding as every other. Capital equipment used in manufacturing, for example, which would be sold only once and then consumed over

---

[133] Totals do not add, reportedly due to rounding.

time by the manufacturer who purchased it, would be amortized over its entire productive capacity and over its entire useful life. If a one million dollar piece of equipment, taxed upon acquisition at the state sales tax rate of 6.25%, produced one million units of retail output over time, each unit of output might theoretically reflect in its sales price only 6.25 cents of the initial $62,500 sales tax paid by the manufacturer. If the finished product's price were $10.00 per unit, this would represent an incremental, amortized burden of only six tenths of a percent per unit. If the price were $2.00 per unit, the embedded, amortized tax burden would be just over three percent per unit. Subsequent acquisitions by other companies of these outputs for use as machinery or equipment in manufacturing operations, if taxable, would add to the cumulative embedded tax burden in amounts that depend on the output's cost, productivity, useful life, and the degree to which its derivative outputs themselves contribute to or become part of subsequent business operations and outputs. The same could be said of any material consumed in the course of manufacturing operations, depending upon the consumption rate per unit of output and the subsequent course of those outputs through commerce. But in either case the dilutive effect of the machinery's productivity, or the finite amount of material consumption required for a single output stage, would establish an upper limit on the extent of pyramiding involved.

On the other hand, inputs physically incorporated or transformed into productive output and resold on a value added basis (such as petrochemical feedstocks or early-stage automotive engine components) would be characterized by higher pyramiding factors if they passed through subsequently taxable stages of manufacture or distribution. The only limit on such pyramiding would in fact be the number of subsequent taxable stages through which such outputs must pass before coming to rest at the consumer or export level. Even so, the finished product or service would almost never derive entirely from inputs on which a sales tax had been incurred; services of in-house employees (in other words, payroll costs) are not subject to sales tax, for example.[134] The fractional contribution of taxable inputs to the finished product or service would usually be diluted, sometimes substantially, by the contribution of such non-taxable inputs. For all of these reasons, actual pyramiding effects would have to be predicted empirically, and would exhibit high degrees of variability among industry sub-classifications and among products and services.

---

[134] Of course payroll costs are subject to numerous other federal and state taxes, which themselves must be passed through the finished product.

The Washington state legislature in 2002 commissioned a study of the state's "Business and Occupations" tax, which included an analysis of the tax's pyramiding effects. The Washington tax is classified by the U.S. Census Bureau as a sales tax because, although -- like the Texas franchise tax -- it is imposed with respect to gross business receipts, it allows no deduction for payroll costs, costs of goods sold, or other operating expenses.[135] In this sense it is more like the Texas retail sales tax, except of course that it applies to all sales by businesses and not just retail sales. Using IMPLAN®[136] input-output data and known figures for B&O tax revenues, the Washington study found that the theoretical measure of "tax pyramiding" associated with the Washington B&O tax varied along a continuum from 1.4 to 6.7, with most falling well below 4.[137] Interestingly for Texans, the Committee found that "tax pyramiding is more prevalent in petroleum refining than in any other industry in the state."[138] The breadth of the tax enables its rates to be exceptionally low, however; the tax applies at a rate of 1.5% for certain services, and below 0.5% for other activities (0.484% for manufacturing and wholesaling, for example)[139] For this reason, even in manufacturing businesses found to be subject to the highest degree of pyramiding, this tax would yield an effective overall tax rate (or, viewed another way, the amount of tax actually embedded in the final product's price) of no more than 3.25%; in most cases it would be substantially lower.[140] These absolutely low actual rates minimize the potential for distortion in the economic incentives affecting businesses, because in the short run relatively few alterations to otherwise sensible business practices could be justified by a marginal tax

---

[135] *See* I Tax Alternatives for Washington State: A Report to the Legislature, Ch. 3, p.13, Washington State Tax Structure Study Committee, William H. Gates Sr., Chair (November 2002), http://dor.wa.gov/content/aboutus/statisticsandreports/wataxstudy/Volume_1.pdf (last accessed 6/20/2010).

[136] Minnesota IMPLAN Group Inc. economic modeling software and data, derived primarily from data reported or developed by the U.S. Department of Commerce's Bureau of Economic Analysis ("BEA") and Census Bureau, and the U.S. Department of Labor's Bureau of Labor Statistics.

[137] II Tax Alternatives for Washington State: A Report to the Legislature, p. 41 Appendix C-12, Table 1, Washington State Tax Structure Study Committee, William H. Gates Sr., Chair (November 2002), http://dor.wa.gov/content/aboutus/statisticsandreports/wataxstudy/Volume_2.pdf (last accessed 6/20/2010). The study estimated the average pyramid factor to be 2.5 across all industries. I Tax Alternatives, *supra* n.135, Ch.9, pp.110-11. *See also* A. Chamberlain & P. Fleenor, *Tax Pyramiding: The Economic Consequences of Gross Receipts Taxes,* at pp. 4-5 (Tax Foundation, Inc., Dec. 2006), describing results of the Washington study.

[138] Washington Research Council Special Report, *B&O Tax Pyramiding in Petroleum Distribution,* (January 13, 2010), http://www.researchcouncil.org/docs/PDF/WRCTaxes/BOTaxPyramidingInPetroDist.pdf (last accessed June 20, 2010).

[139] I Tax Alternatives, *supra* n.135, Ch.3, p.13.

[140] The Washington Tax Structure Committee ultimately recommended the value added tax as the most suitable replacement for the B&O tax, if such a replacement were desired by the legislature. I Tax Alternatives, *supra*, n.135, Introduction & Summary, p. 5. The primary reason identified was the desire to remove the element of pyramiding from the system. *See id.*

savings of only 0.484% (as compared to 6.25%, for example), and the relatively low resulting effective rates minimize the marginal impact on consumers at the retail level.[141]

Simplifying the methodology employed in the Washington study to derive a roughly estimated pyramiding factor for Texas' industries in 2008,[142] and utilizing the recently released 2008 data available from IMPLAN® and Version 3.0 of the IMPLAN® software, we have estimated that the average 2008 pyramiding ratios in various industry classifications for a pure gross receipts tax on Texas businesses would have been as set forth in **Table 25.** Listed as they are by overall NAICS classification, these averages conceal the roughly two dozen underlying sub-classifications with estimated pyramiding factors in the range of 4 to 10, such as petroleum refineries (5.98), wet corn milling (7.65), and chocolate manufacturing (9.64), but the large majority of these sub-classifications fall within in the range of 1 to 4, as can be seen in **Table A3** in **Appendix A**.[143]

---

[141] This does not mean that that even such low marginal rates have no distorting effect on the economy. In the context of long-term decisions to invest or restructure, based on small variations in projected profit margins, even rates of 1% or below can be influential. *See* Tax Pyramiding, *supra* n. 137, at p.7. But it is far from clear that these distorting effects would be any greater than those caused by the Texas local property tax, state business franchise tax, or the host of other business and excise taxes currently imposed in this state, and in any case they would certainly be less than those caused at rates of 6.25% or more.

[142] The Washington study utilized known tax collections under the existing B&O tax and an input-output matrix calculation to determine the effective tax rate on the value of total output in each industrial sector, and then to determine the effective tax rate on value added. The ratio of the two effective rate solutions was taken to represent the factor by which the B&O tax experienced pyramiding on business-to-business sales in each sector of Washington's economy. In our case, having no existing nominal sales tax on all business inputs to examine (the Texas franchise tax's varying deductibles render it unsuitable as a standardized measure), we hypothesized the imposition of a gross sales or "gross receipts" tax on all sales by Texas businesses at a given nominal rate, and then calculated the effective tax rate of resulting nominal tax proceeds in relation to (1) that industry's value added component of total output and (2) that industry's total output excluding imports (because the tax would not be collected on sales by non-Texas businesses to Texas importers). We included final demand by households on the assumption that the tax would apply at that level also. Dividing the first result by the second yields a ratio that should roughly approximate the estimated pyramiding factor that would be associated with an across-the-board, uniform gross sales (or gross receipts) tax imposed on sales by every industry in Texas in 2008. Mathematically, the tax variable factors out of this simplified equation, allowing the pyramiding ratio to be determined simply as the ratio of the industry's total output (less imports) to its value added. Substantial disparities exist between the Comptroller's reported 2008 gross sales figure ($1,454,148,491,571) and the IMPLAN® model's industry output figures, due in part to the fact that NAICS classifications of sales activity are based on the "primary business activity" of the vendor), whereas Texas sales tax inclusions, exclusions and exemptions may be based variously on this or other factors such as nature or characteristics of the product or service being sold, the identity of the purchaser thereof, or the purposes for which the purchase is being made. *See* Texas Tax Code Title 2, Subtitle E, Chapter 151. Also, sales figures reported for sales tax purposes necessarily exclude substantial portions of in-state sales activity that simply are not subject to sales tax. However, the "gross receipts in Texas" reported for franchise tax purposes ($2,430,050,718,294) bear much closer resemblance to the IMPLAN®/BEA total output figure for Texas ($2,595,578,438,656), confirming the IMPLAN® model data's value as a proxy for the known, potentially taxable sales base as measured by the Comptroller's reporting methods and practices.

[143] It should be noted also that our study took a static view of the situation in 2008, focusing only on the direct effects of a proposed sales or gross receipts tax imposed on all sales of products by Texas businesses in the 19 non-governmental NAICS industry classifications, and we ignored the potential for indirect or induced effects, including

These calculations now permit an assessment of the potential for pyramiding associated with a proposed expansion of Texas' 6.25% sales tax to include sales of business inputs. Removal of the current exemption for sales of property to be used in manufacturing, for example, which as we saw in **Table 9** is estimated by the Comptroller to represent $11 billion in foregone 2008 sales tax revenues, would produce an average effective tax rate on such property of 19.06%.[144] In petroleum refining the effective rate could in some cases exceed 37%. And if the nominal

Table 25

Estimated Pyramiding Ratios for Sales Tax on Business Inputs to Texas Business & Industry in 2008

NAICS Industry Classification	Pyramiding Ratio
11 Ag, Forestry, Fish & Hunting	1.93
21 Mining	1.44
22 Utilities	1.32
23 Construction	1.81
31-33 Manufacturing	3.05
42 Wholesale Trade	1.38
44-45 Retail trade	1.36
48-49 Transportation & Warehousing	1.52
51 Information	2.06
52 Finance & insurance	1.72
53 Real estate & rental	1.33
54 Professional- scientific & tech svcs	1.49
55 Management of companies	1.53
56 Administrative & waste services	1.37
61 Educational svcs	1.61
62 Health & social services	1.38
71 Arts- entertainment & recreation	1.89
72 Accommodation & food services	1.60
81 Other services	1.57

the possibility of any changes in collections of other taxes that currently burden those industries. We likewise ignored other changes in investment, consumption or asset deployment patterns that might result over the long term. We assumed that intermediate commodity demand was sufficiently inelastic at the volumes and price ranges examined as to exhibit no substitution effects or output reduction from the initial imposition of the business input tax; in other words, the tax could be passed in full to subsequent stages of manufacture or distribution without affecting underlying outputs and intermediate purchases, and that incremental retail margins remain unchanged regardless of pricing formulas defined as a percentage function of cost. Finally, we assumed that final household demand for all goods and services in question remains completely inelastic over the range of prices in question, meaning that the volume of Texas-produced goods and services purchased remains constant while the incremental embedded taxes are paid for by households either out of savings or by reducing purchases of their directly imported goods and services.

[144] The 3.05 pyramiding factor multiplied by the 6.25% state sales tax rate.

sales tax rate were to be increased as contemplated by this report, the impact on manufacturing would be multiplied proportionately. Such punitively high effective tax rates would force manufacturing operations to integrate vertically or to import larger percentages of their inputs from outside of Texas, or drive many of them out of business altogether. This result cannot be justified economically or rendered acceptable politically, particularly as a means of achieving less than sufficient levels of additional sales tax revenue. The only complete way to avoid this consequence in the context of a tax on sales of business inputs is to convert to a European-style value-added tax system, with its attendant accounting, reporting and other administrative complexities. But as we observed in the case of the Washington gross receipts tax, the absolute levels of tax pyramiding diminish in proportion to the applicable pyramiding factor as nominal rates are lowered. So, assuming that Texans would opt decisively against a value-added tax solution, a willingness to consider differential retail and business sales tax rates may yet permit a solution that incorporates business-to-business sales in a broadened, simplified Texas sales tax, and eliminates both the local property tax and the state business franchise tax. The business sales tax rates in such a two-tier solution ought to be maintained at substantially lower nominal levels than the consumption tax rates, so as to minimize the effects of pyramiding, while the tax's breadth of application should be sufficient to generate the levels of revenue required.

F.   Proposed Comprehensive Reform – The Two-Tier Texas Business and Consumption Sales Tax

1.   The "Business Sales" Tax

The current Texas business franchise tax system requires reporting entities to disclose considerable information about their business receipts and taxable sales base that otherwise is not reflected in the sales tax-related "Gross Sales" figures tabulated in **Table 2.**[145] The data collected includes and identifies separately those items that would be reported by a corporation on lines 1(c) and 4 through 10 of the U.S. Internal Revenue Service Form 1120, such as, for example, revenues from dividends, interest, rents, royalties, and gains and losses on sales of investment or capital assets, as well as all gross sales or "receipts" from the entity's trade or

---

[145] Texas Tax Code Sec. 171, Subchapter C, "Determination of Taxable Margin; Allocation And Apportionment."

business[146] without regard to their coverage under state sales tax rules and regulations. It also includes income from partnerships and similar entities in which the reporting entity owns an interest, and certain federal income tax credit, recapture or accounting items.[147] After excluding from the total revenues reported federal or non-U.S. sourced dividends and interest, items already being reported for franchise tax purposes by other reporting entities, Medicare and Medicaid reimbursements, and certain other U.S. or Texas-sanctioned deductions,[148] the taxpayer reports a "Total Revenues" figure that, after being reduced by one of three available deduction formulas, then is treated as the entity's taxable "margin".[149] United States constitutional law requires, however, that state taxation of businesses engaged in interstate commerce be fairly apportioned to business activity within the taxing state,[150] so the Texas franchise tax rules and regulations also provide for the taxpayer to report a separately calculated figure for "gross receipts" from "business done in this state"[151] which figure is then divided by still another reported figure for "gross receipts" from "its entire business" everywhere.[152] The resulting ratio is then used as the factor by which to apportion the entities' calculated "margin" to Texas for purposes of applying the relevant tax rate and determining the tax liability.

Ordinarily the "Total Revenues" reported will be identical or nearly identical to the "Gross Receipts Everywhere" figure,[153] unless the entity is one of a few special cases for which certain additional adjustments are made that inflate the "receipts" figure beyond what it would have been if calculating taxable "revenue" only.[154] In the case of lending institutions and security broker dealers, this difference can be enormous, because for them "Gross Receipts" includes the underlying value of debt instruments or securities sold by the entity in the course of its

---

[146] *See* Texas Tax Code Sec. 171.105; Texas Administrative Code Title 34, Part I, Rule 3.587 ("Margin: Total Revenue")

[147] *See* U.S. Internal Revenue Service, Instructions for Form 1120, p.8, http://www.irs.gov/pub/irs-pdf/i1120.pdf, (accessed 9/8/10).

[148] *See* Texas Tax Code Sec. 171.1011; Texas Administrative Code Title 34, Part I, Rule 3.587(e).

[149] *See* Texas Tax Code Sec. 171.101(a).

[150] Complete Auto Transit, Inc. v. Brady, 430 U.S. 274 (1977).

[151] *See* Texas Tax Code Sec. 171.103 (referred to in Comptroller's office parlance as "Gross Receipts in Texas" or "Texas Receipts").

[152] *See* Texas Tax Code Sec. 171.105 (referred to as "Gross Receipts Everywhere").

[153] *See* Texas Tax Code Sec. 171.1055.

[154] *See* Texas Tax Code Sec. 171.106.

business,[155] while "Total Revenues" captures the proceeds of such sales only to the extent of the gain, commission, fee or other net income realized by the entity from the transaction.[156] And although the "Receipts in Texas" determination applies well-established regulatory standards for determining which transactions should and should not be deemed to take place "in" Texas,[157] the taxpayers do not report separately the components of "Receipts in Texas" that we intend to exclude for present purposes. For these reasons, the "Total Revenue" figure will serve our needs better in deriving a proxy for potentially taxable business sales in Texas than would the "Receipts in Texas" figure. Since the sales tax by its nature would not and should not extend to such items as dividends, interest, capital gains and loss, royalties or partnership income, we first determine the extent to which pre-apportionment "Total Revenues" would be reduced by their exclusion,[158] followed by our apportionment to Texas of the adjusted Total Revenues figure, using the imputed apportionment factor for each industry classification from known aggregates. Utilizing data for 2008 recently obtained from the Comptroller's office,[159] this methodology yields a net base of transactions potentially amenable to a business sales tax of $2,062,379,049,042, including proceeds from all rental activity to the extent currently included within the business franchise tax liability calculations.

Based on Texas' experience with the business franchise tax, moreover, it is clear that certain other exemptions or discounts that make sense in the context of the franchise tax would continue to make sense in the context of a simplified, broad-based "business sales" tax. The small business exception[160] and the small business deduction,[161] for example, exist both to ease

---

[155] See Texas Tax Code Sec. 171.106(f) & (f-1).

[156] "Total Revenue" for the "finance" industry in 2008 was reported to the Comptroller for franchise tax purposes at $1.4 trillion, whereas "Gross Receipts Everywhere" for that industry were reported at $122.8 trillion. Source: Texas Comptroller of Public Accounts, Revenue Estimating Division, "Margin Data for 2008 Reports" (internal spreadsheet run June 22, 2010).

[157] See Texas Tax Code Secs. 171.103, 171.1055, 171.106; Texas Administrative Code Title 34, Part I, Rule 3.591("Margin: Apportionment").

[158] This effort is complicated by the fact that the statutory deductions from Total Revenue reportable by taxpayers include revenues in the categories to be excluded (e.g., certain dividends, interest, and income from partnerships and similar entities), but without the taxpayer specifying any such distinctions. This creates the potential for deducting the same item more than once as we attempt to adjust the data. Since most of the authorized deductions appear to fall under the categories we intend to exclude from taxable revenues, we address this problem by applying the reported deductions to reduce the revenues to be excluded first, and then applying any remainder to revenues to be included. This is only a marginally satisfactory solution to the lack of data, however.

[159] Source: Texas Comptroller of Public Accounts, Revenue Estimating Division, "Margin Data for 2008 Reports" (internal spreadsheet run June 22, 2010).

[160] Texas Tax Code Sec. 171.002(d):

the disproportionately higher burden of compliance on firms with low annual sales, and to promote the growth of small business as a matter of economic policy. While the second of these objectives may be out of place in a system aimed at neutrality in economic policy, the first has intrinsic merit as a matter of tax administration policy; certainly the argument can be made to limit the regulatory compliance burden on most sole proprietorships and very small firms.[162] The small business exception taxability threshold for the franchise tax in 2008 stood at $300,000, was increased to $1,000,000, and is now scheduled to fall back "permanently" to $600,000 in 2012.[163] With the new "business sales" tax's streamlined new structure, and given our proposal to retain the graduated "small business discount" feature of the current franchise tax, $300,000 offers a reasonable compromise between the competing goals of relieving small business from undue tax and regulatory burdens, on the one hand, and maximizing breadth of participation in the "business sales" tax, so we would propose to retain the threshold at that level.[164]

The exemption for insurance companies should be retained because they are already subject to a tax on gross premiums under a separate statutory regime.[165] The exemption for investments in open-end investment firms (i.e., mutual funds)[166] should be retained, as well, because (1) their "sales" by nature do not truly represent productive commercial activity, and (2) to tax them would place Texas-based mutual funds in a uniquely inferior competitive position to those in most other states, while providing discriminatory tax treatment against mutual fund investors

---

"(d)   A taxable entity is not required to pay any tax and is not considered to owe any tax for a period if:
(1)   the amount of tax computed for the taxable entity is less than $1,000; or
(2)   the amount of the taxable entity's total revenue from its entire business is less than or equal to $1 million or the amount determined under Section 171.006 per 12-month period on which margin is based."

The exception described in clause (2) was $300,000 in 2008, and is scheduled to revert to $600,000 in 2012.

[161] Texas Tax Code Sec. 171.0021 ("Discounts from Liability for Small Businesses")(providing graduated discounts of the tax liability as the business's annual revenues falls below certain statutory levels).

[162] Recall Professor Holcombe's "babysitters" and teenage lawnkeepers, *supra*, n.76

[163] See n. 160, *supra*.

[164] The challenge of applying such an exemption during periods in which taxpayers transition through the threshold can be met by allowing the determination to be made retrospectively, either annually or quarterly, or through refunds, as appropriate. Neither solution completely shields from the administrative burden those firms whose sales fluctuate around or near the threshold, but those who are and with good reason expect to remain below will still benefit.

[165] Texas Tax Code Sec. 171.052 (exempting those insurance firms required to pay a gross premium receipts tax under required to pay an annual tax under Chapter 4 or 9 of the Texas Insurance Code.

[166] Texas Tax Code Sec. 171.055

relative to direct investors in corporate securities.[167] And of course the exemption for governmental agencies, non-profit organizations, cooperatives and similar organizations would remain appropriate policy.[168]

Referring once again to the Comptroller's 2009 Tax Exemptions and Incidence Report, and adjusting its figures to reported 2008 franchise tax levels, we estimate that the taxable base under the proposed business sales tax, after taking these limitations and exemptions into account, would approximate $2,023,225,790,000.[169] This would yield on average approximately $20,232,257,900 in tax revenues for every percentage point of the "business sales" tax's nominal rate.[170] **Table 26** sets forth how these taxes and exemptions would be allocated among industry classifications.

Table 26

Estimated Incidence of Proposed New Business Sales Tax and Exemptions in 2008 ($US millions)

NAICS Industry Classification	Apportioned Gross Texas Business Sales	Business Sales Exemptions	Taxable Business Sales
Agriculture	9,037.28	619.62	8,417.66
Mining	297,468.81	465.98	297,002.84
Utilities & Transportation	120,670.69	693.28	119,977.41
Construction	116,997.11	2,302.94	114,694.17
Manufacturing	390,684.48	894.91	389,789.58
Trade (Wholesale and Retail)	590,864.66	15,050.91	575,813.75
Information	43,829.78	286.66	43,543.12
Finance, Insurance and Real Estate	121,518.60	6,080.00	115,438.60
Other Services	371,307.63	12,758.97	358,548.66
Totals:	2,062,379.05	39,153.26	2,023,225.79

---

[167] *See* Letter dated July 15, 2010 from Keith Lawson, Senior Counsel, Investment Company Institute, to Chair & Vice Chair of the Ways and Means Committee, Texas House of Representatives, http://www.ici.org/pdf/24427.pdf, (accessed September 7, 2010).

[168] Texas Tax Code Secs. 171.057 through 171.187.

[169] This assumes only statistically insignificant variations in the average credits and deductions taken by taxpayers under the current business franchise tax, since we are treating the actual tax revenues and the Comptroller's estimate of actual exemption "values" as a proxy for the relative gross sales of businesses falling within and without these various exemptions. It also likely overstates the magnitude of sales attributable to the exemptions because their tax value was determined by reference to a slightly larger tax base than the one we are using in our calculations. Gross sales by exempted open-end investment companies, insurance firms and non-profit enterprises appear to have been excluded from the Comptroller's base revenue estimates for the franchise tax referenced in n. 141, *supra.* For this reason no adjustment was made for these in our own estimates of the post-exemption "business sales" tax base.

[170] Assuming inelasticity of demand and no long term changes in investment or production patterns.

In view of the pyramid factors calculated in the previous section, it may be expected that the effective burden of these taxes would fall disproportionately on products sold by industry classifications such as "Manufacturing", which upon final sale would experience the tax at an average effective rate of 3.05% for every percentage point of nominal tax rate. Certain sub-classifications would feel the effects even more severely (petroleum refining, for example at an effective rate of 5.98%), and in extreme cases the legislature would be justified in allowing such classifications a partial exemption or rate relief. In order to provide a mechanism to monitor and measure these effects on an ongoing basis, we would recommend including in the business sales tax reporting procedures an accounting by the taxpayer both for sales taxes collected on sales as well as sales taxes paid on purchases of inputs. It should be recognized, though, that even in the few cases of high pyramid factors, the effective tax rate at the point of final demand is not substantially different from the rates that were under consideration in Section III above. Nevertheless, if nominal rates are maintained at levels low enough to keep these effects in check, the direct tax relief experienced by these sectors as a result of reform might substantially if not entirely offset any resulting burden. We will explore this question further momentarily.

2.   The "Consumption Sales" Tax

For the retail or "consumption" tier of the proposed consumption and business sales tax, only limited reforms of the current state sales tax would be required. As shown in **Table 23**, $9.7 billion of Texas state sales tax collections fell directly upon business and industry in 2008. In order to complete the transformation of the retail sales tax to a pure consumption tax, a new, blanket exemption could be created for sales to purchasers who intend to use the item in the course of conducting a trade or business. Purchasers could present a "Business Use" exemption certificate modeled after the sales and use tax exemption certificates currently required for purchasers intending to avail themselves of the exemptions for sales "for resale" or to governmental agencies or non-profit organizations. The use of such certificates would be subject to audit and review as is currently provided in the cases just mentioned, and falsification would be subject to criminal and/or civil penalties just as it is today. This blanket exemption would render obsolete some of the current exemptions and exclusions intended to abate the tax's impact on sales of business inputs, but it would do so in a comprehensive and more straightforward manner than is reflected in current Texas statutes and regulations. Given the administrative and enforcement challenges associated with expanding the tax to purchases by consumers of various services that are currently excluded from its application, particularly in view of the relatively small amounts of additional revenues that might result (see discussion in

Section IV.B. above), there would be ample reason to leave such services exempt from the "consumption" tier of the new tax.

3.   The "Residential Property Sales" Tax

Finally, to the extent that these reforms are almost but not quite sufficient to generate the requisite revenues at politically acceptable nominal rates, the proposed tax on sales of residential property and related services discussed in Section IV.B. could be introduced as well. Assuming a fixed nominal rate of 5% on such sales, Texas could expect to have realized incremental tax revenues of $3,460,942,183 on the 2008 taxable sales base of $69,218,843,669.61 calculated in Section IV.B. above. Five percent of the property's initial value represents approximately two to three years' worth of annual property taxes in typical major metropolitan area jurisdictions, and is lower even than the standard six percent commission usually collected by sales agents out of sales proceeds. Given the prospect for complete relief from the annual *ad valorem* property tax, homeowners and rental property owners might view this as a favorable trade-off. However, it must also be recognized that front-loading the tax costs of home ownership in this way could present an undue challenge to home buyers if rates are not kept at a low enough level to approximate the *ad valorem* taxes that otherwise would have been paid within the first couple of years or so. Given the potential for higher sales tax rates on all other consumer transactions, there is likely to be an upper limit to taxpayers' appetites for such trade-offs.

4.   Overall Impact of the Proposed New Tax System

The net impact of these proposed reforms on Texas consumers and businesses may be assessed by referring once more to the "Incidence" data set forth in **Table 24** above. This data enables us to compare for each industry classification the tax relief that would be realized by business and industry directly from abolition of the local property tax, the state sales tax on sales of business inputs, and the Texas business franchise tax altogether. We may then compare that to the initial incidence tax burden that would result for each industry from the imposition of a new, broadly-based tax on gross sales in that industry, using reported gross sales in each industry as the direct proxy for taxable sales. Modifying the current sales tax to make it a pure tax on consumption, making the simplifying assumption that no other changes are made to the state sales tax as currently configured, and – if necessary -- including an estimate for the tax revenues that would result from adoption of the proposed residential property sales and service tax, we are able to generate a comprehensive overview of the tax relief and new tax burdens that would result from these proposed reforms.

Table 27 presents such an overview for one revenue-neutral scenario consisting of a 2.525% "Business Sales" tax and a 7.5% "Consumption Sales" tax. Under this scenario we may comfortably omit the "Residential Property Sales" tax and its attendant administrative and political challenges. The "Total Tax Relief" column reflects the sum of the initial incidence tax burdens reflected in the "Local School Property Taxes" column, the "Local Non-School Property Taxes Column", the "Current Texas Sales Taxes" column, and the "Texas Business Franchise Taxes" column of **Table 24** above. Each of these burdens would be eliminated under our proposed reform, with the exception of the estimated $11.93758 billion of Texas state sales taxes currently borne by individual consumers, which would now be included under the new "Consumption Sales" tax. The "Total Tax Increase" column of **Table 27** illustrates the initial incidence on each group of the new taxes being proposed, while the "Net Change in Tax Burden" column illustrates which groups stand to benefit directly from such reform, which are

Table 27

Overview of Proposed Two-Tier Consumption and Business Sales Tax Solution in 2008 ($US millions)[171]

NAICS Industry Classification	Business Sales Tax (2.525%)	Consumption Sales Tax (7.5%)	Residential Property Sales Tax (0%)	Total Tax Increase	Total Tax Relief	Net Change in Direct Tax Burden
Agriculture	212.55	0.00	0.00	212.55	548.03	(335.48)
Mining	7,499.32	0.00	0.00	7,499.32	3,231.57	4,267.75
Utilities & Transportation	3,029.43	0.00	0.00	3,029.43	4,763.39	(1,733.96)
Construction	2,896.03	0.00	0.00	2,896.03	574.26	2,321.77
Manufacturing	9,842.19	0.00	0.00	9,842.19	4,897.42	4,944.77
Trade (Wholesale and Retail)	14,539.30	0.00	0.00	14,539.30	3,649.31	10,889.99
Information	1,099.46	0.00	0.00	1,099.46	2,597.49	(1,498.03)
Finance, Insurance and Real Estate	2,914.82	0.00	0.00	2,914.82	7,580.16	(4,665.34)
Other Services	9,053.35	0.00	0.00	9,053.35	6,536.39	2,516.96
SubTotals:	51,086.45	0.00	0.00	51,086.45	34,378.02	16,703.43
Individual Consumers	0.00	14,325.10	0.00	14,325.10	30,959.77	(16,634.67)
Total:	51,086.45	14,325.10	0.00	65,411.55	65,337.79	73.76

---

[171] Totals do not add, reportedly due to rounding.

likely to incur a larger initial incidence tax burden, and by how much. Based on our estimates, this combination of rates would have yielded a small surplus of $73.76 million over the amount needed to eliminate property taxes, franchise taxes and the portion of the current state sales tax borne by business and industry in 2008. While some may be concerned that the proposed system in effect shifts a substantial portion of the initial tax burden from consumers to business, it should be noted that the largest component of this shift is being directed toward those sectors with the lowest pyramiding factors – i.e., the wholesale and retail trade sectors. Indeed, the retail sector occupies a place in the chain of distribution closer to the consumer than any other, which serves to minimize pyramiding effects, and the wholesale sector lies not far behind.[172] As long as Texas citizens understand that they will ultimately bear the "business sales" tax from all industries in the price they pay for goods and services, these reforms stand to deliver a substantial improvement in the quality of Texans' relationship with, and their treatment at the hands of, their state and local governments.

G.   Summary

The principal arguments against expanding the sales tax's application to business inputs relate to the problems of double or multiple taxation, tax pyramiding and lack of transparency to consumers, who ultimately bear the cost of such taxes whether they are aware of it or not. Such flaws should, to the maximum extent feasible, be minimized in any proposed reform of the current state tax system. However, against this goal must be balanced (1) the need to remedy the other economic and social harm caused by the taxes we are attempting to replace, and (2) the recognition that the current property tax, the current business franchise tax, and even the current sales tax fall directly on, and therefore burden inputs to, business and industry to a substantial degree. We have minimized the potential consequences of pyramiding by proposing a two-tier rate system with dramatically lower rates for sales to businesses, and we have shown that this proposal achieves revenue neutrality for the study year at nominal rates that seem well within the limits of political feasibility. It may be suggested that the legislature might exercise some discrimination in distinguishing between those inputs for which pyramiding remains a

---

[172] As stated in NAICS Clarification Memorandum No. 1, NAICS Sector 42 - Wholesale Trade, Scope and Implementation Guidelines for U.S. Statistical Agencies, quoting the US NAICS Manual, 1997, p. 375, "The wholesaling process is an intermediate step in the distribution of merchandise. Wholesalers are organized to sell or arrange the purchase of (a) goods for resale (i.e., goods sold to other wholesalers or retailers), (b) capital or durable nonconsumer goods, and (c) raw and intermediate materials and supplies used in production. Wholesalers sell merchandise to other businesses and normally operate from a warehouse or office."

serious economic issue and those for which it does not. In doing so, however, all of the relevant policy considerations should be considered, including the maintenance of an economic environment favorable to investment and job growth, the maximization of simplicity, efficiency, transparency and neutrality in the chosen system of tax reporting and collections, the generation of sufficient tax revenues to support state and local government, and, of course, the protection of property, property owners and the fundamental liberty interests of our citizens. With these goals well in reach, let us examine the effect of the proposed reforms on individual local taxing jurisdictions.

V.   ANALYSIS OF INDIVIDUAL LOCAL JURISDICTIONS UNDER THE PROPOSED TWO-TIER SALES TAX SYSTEM

In Sections III.A. and IV.A., we compared the relative effects of theoretical, uniform increases in sales tax rates or the taxable base under the current Texas state sales tax in those jurisdictions that impose both a property tax and a sales tax, at least in the cases of jurisdictions for which we have data sufficient to establish or approximate the taxable sales base. In order to perform a similar analysis of those jurisdictions under the proposed two-tier sales tax solution, we must generate an estimate for each jurisdiction of the potential taxable sales base of both the proposed Consumption Sales tax and the proposed Business Sales tax. This represents more of a challenge.

A.   Industry Classification Concentration Differentials Among Jurisdictions

Our previous analysis assumed that changes in the nominal sales tax rate or the taxable sales base would take place uniformly from jurisdiction to jurisdiction in proportion to those jurisdictions' current relative taxable sales bases. As illustrated by a quick comparison between **Tables 3** and **5** above, however, the local economies of different counties are comprised of differing concentrations of activity among the various industry classifications. The same is true of the individual local property tax jurisdictions within those counties – municipalities, hospital and emergency districts, municipal utility districts, etc. In converting to a revenue system based solely on sales taxes imposed within their respective boundaries, these jurisdictions would see differential results caused, not only by their differing levels of overall taxable economic activity, but also by their different relative concentrations of industries. **Table 2**, for example, which sets out gross and taxable sales by industry classification, tells only part of the story. Its figures are taken in the aggregate from all counties throughout the state; they do not convey any information about the differences in composition of economic activity among Texas' counties and other local tax jurisdictions. Such differences could produce dramatically different appetites for sales and property tax reform among such jurisdictions, depending on exactly how the industry classifications affected are concentrated therein.

Illustrating this point, **Table A4** (in **Appendix A**), like **Table 2,** sets forth Texas' 2008 "Gross Sales" and "Taxable Sales" by industry classification but, in contrast to **Table 2**, it also breaks these figures down by county. **Table A5** (in **Appendix A**) provides more insight into the "Taxable Sales" component, expressing that information as a percentage of each county's total taxable sales, with an indication of the ratio that each county's percentage bears to the average among all counties for each industry classification. The most striking aspect of this comparison lies in the variability among counties of the relative concentrations of different industries within each county's boundaries. To illustrate the impact of this variability, suppose for the sake of discussion that an increase in sales tax rates were to be limited to sales only in certain targeted industry classifications. In Hidalgo County, for example, where taxable Retail Trade sales comprise more than 67% of that county's taxable sales base, it is apparent that a simple, three percentage point increase in the sales tax rate applicable to currently taxed Retail Trade transactions would produce a two percent increase in total sales tax revenues from Hidalgo County (i.e., 3% of 67%). In Dallas County, on the other hand, where taxable Retail Trade sales comprise only 30.68% of the county's taxable sales base, the same three percentage point rate increase would yield only a 0.92% percent increase in total sales tax revenues – only half the tax collection results obtained for the same tax effort, as measured by tax rate percentage points. Looked at another way, if the Retail Trade were the only classification being modified, Dallas County's various taxing jurisdictions would have to impose an aggregate sales tax increase on Retail Trade sales of 6.51 percentage points in order to increase their aggregate sales tax collections by the same percentage achieved in Hidalgo County by a mere 3 percentage point aggregate rate increase. A quick survey of **Table A5** reveals that this scenario repeats itself to varying degrees in nearly every county and in every industry classification. As welcome as the relief from property taxes might be in all counties, the magnitude of the differentials in corresponding sales tax adjustments required to obtain that relief -- if sourced at the local level – arguably poses a serious practical and political obstacle.

The math dictates that the same results would obtain from any proposed increase or decrease in the taxable sales base, but with an additional twist. As demonstrated above, each county starts with its own unique taxable sales base in each of the various industry classifications.

Whether the legislation provides for this expansion to occur in only one classification, or to occur to varying degrees in multiple classifications, these same percentage differentials will produce similarly different results. Counties relatively rich in the industries targeted for expansion of taxable transaction types will see more generous expansion of their tax revenues, while counties in which those industries are not as highly concentrated will lag behind. They will be forced to impose higher rates, or to seek state legislative authorization to expand the taxable transaction types still further, or to pursue other revenue sources altogether. The twist lies in the the additional likelihood that the specific transaction types chosen for addition to a given industry classification's taxable sales base will themselves be unevenly distributed among the counties. Put another way, it is highly *unlikely* – to the point of practical impossibility -- that the legislature could successfully craft a combination of newly taxable transaction lists that happens to result in identically proportional increases in a given industry classification's tax base across county lines, or for that matter across municipal or special purpose district lines within any given county. For this reason, any attempt to increase the taxable sales base by selective targeting of different industry classifications and sub-classifications can be expected to yield wildly varying and possibly unforeseeable results among the jurisdictions affected.

As expected, the same "lumpiness" observed in the distribution of industry concentrations and taxable sales among counties also prevails among cities as well. As we did with respect to counties in the preparation of **Table A5,** we studied Texas' 2008 reported "Gross Sales" and "Taxable Sales" by industry classification and individual jurisdiction with respect to each city that in 2008 imposed a property tax and was situated within one of the top 39 counties by population. Space limitations prevent inclusion of a table showing here the breakdown in dollars for all such 433 cities and towns, but **Tables A6 and A7** (in **Appendix A**) describe each such jurisdiction's 2008 taxable sales in each industry classification as, first, a percentage of each city's total taxable sales in all classifications (**Table A6**), and, second, the percentage that such taxable sales represent of the gross sales in the same classification (**Table A7**). Once again, the variability of these percentages – in other words, the variability of the relative concentrations of different industries within each city's boundaries -- represents the most striking aspect of this comparison. In Baytown, for example, a well-populated city whose economy depends largely on nearby petrochemical plants and related activity, 68.7% of the city's 2008 taxable sales derived from the "retail trade" classification. Galena Park, on the other hand, situated only a few minutes from Baytown, but home to the Port of Houston and the Houston Ship Channel, derived 74.4% of its 2008 taxable sales from the "wholesale trade". As in the example given for Hidalgo and Dallas Counties above, any attempt to expand or contract the range of taxable sales in either such classification would yield dramatically different percentage changes in tax revenue for these two cities.[173] And though it might be feasible to craft a list of newly taxable sales for each classification specifically designed to increase taxable sales in one classification and city by a similar percentage to that in the other classification and city, there are hundreds of other jurisdictions and nearly two dozen other industry classifications yielding millions of potential points of disparity that simply could not be solved at the same time.

These considerations highlight two fundamental limitations in our ability to forecast distributional effects from the proposed two-tier sales tax solution. First, the proposal to convert the existing sales tax to a pure consumption tax by adopting a blanket "business use" exemption will have different results in different jurisdictions, depending upon whether the previously taxed "business" purchases are more or less highly concentrated in the jurisdictions being considered. The Comptroller's Tax Exemptions & Tax Incidence report for 2007 does describe an allocation among industry classifications of the business-incident portion of the sales tax, which we will use to fine-tune our analysis, but the published data provides only the most general guidance as to the overall distributional effect among industries statewide. It does not permit more detailed allocations among industries within counties, much less among jurisdictions within those counties. For these reasons we will allocate the consumption sales tax's projected reduction in taxable sales base in proportion to the extent to which reported taxable sales are currently concentrated in each such jurisdiction and classification, keeping in mind that this allocation represents only a rough approximation.

Second, the taxable base for the proposed "Business Sales" tax, by virtue of the fact that it has been derived from data obtained through reporting under the current business franchise tax, necessarily differs in its geographic distribution from that of "gross sales" figures reported under the current sales tax regime. While the sales tax is reported by sales outlets on a per-outlet basis, the franchise tax is reported instead on an aggregated basis by individual entities with respect to all of their outlets wherever located,[174] and on a unitary basis by business enterprises with respect to all of the sales effected through all of their affiliated entities,[175] in all cases

---

[173] A 10% increase in coverage by value in Retail Trade would presumably produce a 6.87% increase in Baytown's sales tax revenues with no change in rate (making the unrealistic assumption that the newly taxable transactions are proportionately distributed among remaining non-taxable transactions in Baytown). Galena Park, with only a 6.4% concentration of "retail trade" taxable sales, would of course see only a 0.64% revenue.increase under similar assumptions.

[174] Texas Tax Code Sec. 171.0002, "Definition of Taxable Entity."

[175] Texas Tax Code Sec. 171.1014, "Combined Reporting: Affiliated Group Engaged in Unitary Business."

subject to proper apportionment to Texas. The distribution of reported franchise tax liability among industry classifications in local jurisdictions, or among smaller jurisdictions within individual counties, may have only the most tenuous of relationships with the distribution of the taxable sales base among those jurisdictions under the proposed Business Sales tax.

Our estimates suggest that the proposed "Business Sales" tax would in 2008 have enjoyed a taxable sales base of approximately $2.023 trillion, with the corresponding ability to generate $51.086 billion in new tax revenues at a 2.525% tax rate. In the aggregate, this amount alone would have been more than sufficient to replace the $38 billion of 2008 local property tax levies throughout the State of Texas, plus the estimated $4.7 billion of franchise tax revenues. As noted above, however, due to the way in which current franchise tax data is collected and reported, we do not have meaningful information establishing the geographic distribution of the taxable base for business sales as calculated in Section IV.F. In fact, information obtained from the Comptroller's office suggests that approximately one-half of this sales base is attributable to out-of-state taxpaying entities that report no specific geographical Texas nexus at all. We do have the distribution of "gross sales" figures for data reported under the sales tax procedures, though, and it might be reasonable to suppose that the geographic and industry identifiers associated with gross sales reported for franchise tax and sales tax purposes would show a greater correlation with one another at the county level, at least, than at the levels of smaller political subdivisions, just as we might expect the data distribution to be even more smooth when compared at larger regional or state levels. Absent any more authoritative guidance on this point, we will for simplicity treat the proposed "Business Sales" tax's estimated taxable base as being distributed among Texas' jurisdictions in proportion to the distribution known for 'gross sales" reported in connection with the sales tax. Taking care to calculate such proportions separately for each NAICS industry classification helps to minimize any inherent bias in the distribution attributable to inherent structural differences in the two databases (such as the franchise tax database's much more complete representation of service-related revenues)

B.   The Local Tax Jurisdictions Revisited

Returning to the 488 local tax jurisdictions examined in Section III, we find that 456 of them provide data sufficient to conduct a meaningful comparison of their relative tax revenue potential under the proposed two-tier sales tax solution. Thirty-nine of these consist of the top 39 counties that are the subject of our focus, 416 consist of cities or municipalities in those counties, and one consists of a local hospital district. Based on the assumptions described above, we developed estimates for the taxable sales base in each of these jurisdictions under both the proposed Business Sales tax and the proposed Consumption Sales tax, and from these estimates we derived pro-forma figures for the resulting tax revenues that might have been generated locally in each of these jurisdictions in 2008.

Beginning with the proposed Consumption Tax, we first estimated the revenues that would have resulted at the existing 2008 nominal local sales tax rate in each such jurisdiction, and then compared that to the revenues associated with an increase in that local tax rate by an amount equal to the difference between the current statewide rate of 6.25% and our proposed statewide Consumption Tax rate of 7.5%. In other words, we posited that each local jurisdiction would receive as part of its local tax allocation the full increase in revenues attributable to the 1.25% increase in this statewide rate. Relying on the Consumption Tax alone, all 456 jurisdictions would have faced a deficit in their attempt to replace the property tax with locally generated sales tax revenues at current rates, and only one jurisdiction would have generated a surplus at the increased local Consumption Tax rate (the City of Creedmoor, Travis County, generating a surplus of $136,790 over its 2008 property tax levy of $78,750 and its 2008 sales tax allocation of $111,431). This compares unfavorably with the results reported in Section III, where

Table 28

Estimated 2008 Surplus at Target Business Tax Rate and unchanged Consumption Tax Rate ($US millions)

Tax Jurisdiction	Surplus	Percent of Total
Harris County	$14,283,783,309.29	20.04%
City of Houston	$11,530,744,092.12	16.17%
Dallas County	$6,857,875,297.39	9.62%
City of Dallas	$3,617,735,949.55	5.07%
Bexar County	$2,845,098,378.69	3.99%
City of San Antonio	$2,436,246,616.30	3.42%
Jefferson County	$2,341,419,650.76	3.28%
Tarrant County	$2,196,923,470.75	3.08%
City of Beaumont	$1,468,118,231.22	2.06%
Travis County	$1,182,154,921.07	1.66%
Galveston County	$1,147,323,104.49	1.61%
City of Texas City	$1,029,415,177.32	1.44%
City of Austin	$974,388,058.05	1.37%
Nueces County	$940,823,542.17	1.32%
City of Irving	$831,988,365.91	1.17%
Total:	$53,684,038,165.09	75.30%

we relied on rate adjustments in the current sales tax system, but this is understandable in substantial part because the proposed Consumption Tax exemption for "trade or business use" sales excludes a large proportion of revenues otherwise included in the Section III analysis. In any case, it demonstrates that local revenue neutrality cannot be achieved by reliance on the Consumption Tax rate differential alone.

As expected, however, expanding the revenues under consideration to include those resulting from assessment of the proposed Business Sales tax brings a swell of additional monies available for property tax relief. By dedicating to local use the Business Sales tax revenues generated locally at the target 2.525% rate, and maintaining the current local sales tax rate as the new Consumption Tax rate, 283 of the 456 jurisdictions examined would have realized a net surplus after eliminating their property tax and providing for the sales tax revenues already being generated. Such surpluses ranged from a low of $413.36 (in the City of Happy, Potter County) to highs of $14,283,783,309.29 and $11,530,744,092.12 in Harris County and the City of Houston, respectively. Indeed, the collective surpluses generated in the top 15 jurisdictions showing a surplus aggregated over $53.6 billion, as shown in **Table 28,** or 75.3% of the aggregate surplus of all such jurisdictions. Furthermore, additional calculation shows that increasing the local sales tax allocation to include the 1.25% increase in the Consumption Tax rate over the 2008 sales tax rate only manages to increase from 283 to 294 the number of jurisdictions that could show a surplus at the targeted Business Sales tax rate. Clearly, attempts to tinker with the Consumption Tax rate to this end will be of negligible value to our overall objectives. From this point forward,

Table 29
Revenue-Neutral County Business Sales Tax Rate in Top 39 Counties

Tax Jurisdiction	Revenue-Neutral Business Sales Tax Rate
Jefferson County	0.096%
Dallas County	0.135%
Gregg County	0.148%
Nueces County	0.169%
Harris County	0.180%
Ector County	0.185%
Midland County	0.189%
Galveston County	0.243%
Bexar County	0.255%
Ector County Hospital District	0.294%
Tarrant County	0.329%
Johnson County	0.342%
Tom Green County	0.370%
Taylor County	0.391%
Potter County	0.395%
El Paso County	0.405%
Denton County	0.418%
Parker County	0.442%
Lubbock County	0.453%
Smith County	0.467%
Collin County	0.481%
Bell County	0.493%
McLennan County	0.505%
Montgomery County	0.516%
Comal County	0.542%
Wichita County	0.560%
Travis County	0.632%
Cameron County	0.686%
Ellis County	0.750%
Brazoria County	0.755%
Guadalupe County	0.848%
Brazos County	0.873%
Williamson County	0.899%
Grayson County	0.904%
Webb County	0.905%
Hidalgo County	0.910%
Randall County	0.942%
Fort Bend County	0.956%
Hays County	0.990%
Kaufman County	1.022%

therefore, our analysis assumes that all local Consumption Sales tax rates remain at the 2008 sales tax rate levels, and that any increases in revenues associated with the rise from 6.25% to 7.5% flow into the state's general revenues.

Given their surpluses, there is no actual need to allocate the full benefit of the Business Sales tax to these 283 jurisdictions, so we also calculated for all of them the local portion of the tax for which they would have to receive allocations in order to achieve revenue neutrality. The local rate thus calculated ranges from a low of 0.056% (again, the City of Creedmoor, Travis County) to a high of 2.503% (City of Joshua, Johnson County), with an average among those jurisdictions of only 1.073%, and with the overwhelming majority (214) under 1.5%. The counties themselves are particularly well positioned for this transition. Only one of the 39 counties reviewed would have required a Business Sales tax rate of over 1% (see **Table 29**). In fact the average county-level Business Sales tax rate required to achieve revenue neutrality among the top 39 counties by population would be 0.527%. In other words, every one of the 39 most populous Texas counties, and even one special purpose district, could eliminate their property tax entirely by adoption of our proposed Business Sales tax at a local rate of around one-half percent, on average.

The remaining 243 surplus jurisdictions consist of municipalities, each of which necessarily is co-located, or "stacked," with at least one county, and in some cases they are divided among two or even three counties. So it is useful also to conduct this same measurement on a cumulative basis, taking into account the full tax burden that would be imposed on sales in any given location. As we would expect, we find that fewer jurisdictions can achieve revenue neutrality if the combined or "stacked" local Business Sales tax rate is capped at the targeted 2.525% rate. There are 210 municipalities in this group that are located in a single county, so it is possible to state a single combined rate for those cities. The stacked revenue neutral rates for those 210 jurisdictions would have averaged 1.64% in 2008, but 30 of them would have exceeded the hypothetical 2.525% cap; the average of those 180 falling at or below that cap would have been 1.446%. An additional 33 municipalities that are in surplus when measured individually are actually spread among multiple counties. When measured on a stacked basis in locations within their primary county's jurisdiction, the number in surplus drops to 28; measured in the county with the highest revenue neutral rate, that number drops even further to 26. From these calculations, we may conclude that, of the 243 municipalities in the top 39 counties that could achieve revenue neutrality on an individual basis with local allocations from the Business Sales tax capped at 2.525%, only approximately 206 would remain entirely neutral once their combined city and county rates are considered. Bear in mind, also, that this calculation does not take into account any special purpose districts or metropolitan transit authority districts; their addition could be expected to reduce the number still further. The figure of 206 therefore represents an estimated upper limit on the number of completely revenue-neutral municipalities after taking into account stacked local tax rates; the actual number might be lower than that. To the extent that the aggregate 2.525% Business Sales tax applied to sales in any given jurisdiction exceeds the amounts required for local revenue neutrality, however, that excess could in principle be available to the state as part of its general revenues.

For the 172 individual jurisdictions that would have been in deficit even if they had received allocations of all of their locally generated Business Sales tax revenues, the required rate for revenue neutrality quickly assumes impossible proportions. Starting from a low of 2.56% (the City of Meadows Place, Fort Bend County) the rate rises above 10% after the first 124 jurisdictions, 20% after 18 more, and 100% only 18 more after that. In fact, as anticipated by our analysis in Section III, 12 individual jurisdictions can be identified for which, mathematically speaking, their local Business Sales tax rate would have to equal or exceed by many times the entire taxable sales base in order to replace their local property tax, as illustrated in **Table 30**.

Table 30
Theoretical Revenue-Neutral Business Sales Tax Rate for Deep-Deficit Jurisdictions

County	Tax Jurisdiction	Revenue-Neutral Business Sales Tax Rate
Harris	City of Bunker Hill Village	118.4%
Ellis	City of Oak Leaf	149.7%
Ellis	City of Pecan Hill	207.9%
Fort Bend	City of Beasley	216.8%
Harris	City of Shoreacres	253.6%
Ellis	City of Milford	264.9%
Collin	City of Weston	285.4%
Travis	City of Point Venture	570.8%
Bexar	City of Grey Forest	650.1%
Lubbock	City of Ransom Canyon	765.6%
Tarrant	City of Lakeside	1707.1%
Montgomery	City of Stagecoach	2032.5%

As discussed previously, it is obviously not meaningful to talk of reliance on locally generated sales tax revenues to replace the property tax in jurisdictions such as these because they and, to a lesser extent, many other jurisdictions owe their very existence to the availability of the property tax. Even if it were possible to do so, attempts to alter the economic mix of such jurisdictions in order to enhance the taxable sales base would likely be opposed by residents for whom that mix provides the reason for residing there in the first place. Whether by circumstance or by conscious design, more than 200 of the 456 local tax jurisdictions we have examined would be unable to achieve local revenue neutrality at the statewide revenue-neutral target Business Sales tax rate of 2.525%, once the effects of stacking or co-location of cities and counties are taken into account. As suggested in Section III, this may also prove true in the more than 1600 special purpose districts throughout Texas, most of which were conceived and contoured around the available property tax base without regard to the availability, if any, of a taxable sales base. Indeed, the proliferation of these districts in many cases results directly from competition among existing cities, districts and local groups for access to property tax revenues, or as a defensive response to the encroachments of "outsiders" on the local property tax base. The resulting clusters of districts providing the same or similar services within the same counties offer an example of how the determination to finance public services through highly localized revenue sources may in some cases foster administrative inefficiency and complicate the introduction of principled tax reform based on county-wide or even broader revenue sources. The same might be said of school districts, as well. The promise of the Arduin-Laffer study, taken as a high-altitude photograph of Texas' economic landscape, struggles to contend with the ground-level realities in local jurisdictions.

C.   The Central Policy Dilemma

A second look at **Table 28** offers further insight into this point. More than three-quarters of the net fiscal surpluses we calculated for our proposed two-tier sales tax in all the top 39 counties' local tax jurisdictions originated in only seven Texas cities and eight Texas counties. Since our proposal rests on the premise of achieving overall, statewide revenue neutrality, the cumulative fiscal surpluses among all the affected jurisdictions necessarily will, on a statewide basis, equal the cumulative fiscal deficits among them. That being the case, it is clear that any proposal to finance the complete elimination of property tax through the establishment or expansion of a sales tax must of necessity depend, directly or indirectly, upon revenues generated in a very few jurisdictions to finance deficits in many others.

This represents the central dilemma in crafting public finance policy. Revenues collected from particular citizens and businesses for general government purposes may not – and often do not – find application to expenditures that directly or immediately benefit the particular taxpayers themselves. This fact can be relied upon to generate ongoing contention and controversy in public policymaking, a fresh example of which may be found in recent years' debates over Texas' public school finance system and the so-called "Robin Hood" financing scheme (to which we will return shortly). In all cases, the qualitative question to be addressed is whether and to what extent the larger governmental need is sufficiently compelling, or the benefit to citizens sufficiently generalized or intangible, as to justify the seemingly disproportionate tax burden imposed on the relative few.

This question will occupy a central position in any legislative debate on these or any similar reform proposals, and it will figure prominently in the discussion regarding school finance set forth in Section VI below. At the risk of anticipating some of this debate, it may be suggested that cities such as Houston, Dallas, San Antonio, Beaumont, Texas City, Austin and Irving would justifiably object to the imposition of a tax on their citizens and businesses to finance directly the conduct of city government in large numbers of the other 1145 municipalities in the State of Texas. The same may be said of counties such as Harris, Dallas, Bexar, Jefferson, Tarrant, Travis, Galveston and Nueces with respect to the purely local services and functions of hospital, water, municipal utility and other special purpose districts situated outside their boundaries. But for those purposes that comprise an inherent function or responsibility of state government, a broadly based tax borne in a principled, equitable way by similarly situated citizens and businesses throughout the state may very well be justified, even advisable, even if it means that locally generated revenues from that tax are absorbed predominantly for local purposes in some jurisdictions, while being transferred predominantly to state coffers in others. The Business Sales tax component of the proposed two-tier sales tax might therefore be introduced as a flat, statewide rate, but with highly differentiated local allocation formulas for counties and municipalities, depending on their unique fiscal and economic conditions.

D.   Selective Elimination by Jurisdiction

For those jurisdictions that can be expected to achieve revenue neutrality with combined local allocations of less than the target statewide Business Sales tax rate, the implementing legislation could identify those jurisdictions specifically, setting forth in a table the percentage rates permitted for each such jurisdiction. These rates in turn would have been derived from a detailed calculation of the required revenue-neutral rate in the foreseeable future following introduction, modified as appropriate to allow for projected debt service on existing bonds, scheduled expenditures, and anticipated changes in the taxable sales base. In order to provide some degree of flexibility in future years, the initial target cap might be set somewhere below the statewide level of 2.525%, with provision for increases up to that or a lower level upon approval by local voters at the ballot. No jurisdiction would be permitted to forecast a surplus in the year of introduction, so these rates would likely be unique for almost every such jurisdiction, and any revenues in excess of the permitted local rate up to the mandated statewide rate cap would be retained in the state's general revenues. But, upon introduction, these jurisdictions would have a new source of revenues, tied to underlying economic activity, and the *ad valorem* property tax would by statute and constitutional amendment, if necessary, be abolished within their boundaries. Based on our analysis of the year 2008, and assuming the stacked local Business Sales rate cap is set at the same statewide 2.525% level, we estimate that taking this approach in the local tax jurisdictions examined would abolish the *ad valorem* property tax in its entirety in jurisdictions representing $9,647,332,021, or 24.75% of the entire 2008 property tax levies in the State of Texas, including all 39 counties, almost 216 municipalities, and one special purpose district.[176]

For those jurisdictions that cannot be expected to achieve revenue neutrality within the mandated local Business Sales tax rate caps, there is no reason in principle why local allocations could not be made to these jurisdictions up to the permitted limit, provided that the local property tax in those jurisdictions undergoes a mandated reduction or phase-down. The necessary calculations and table could be prepared as with the other jurisdictions, but in this case the local jurisdictions would be permitted to retain the local property tax to the extent, and only to the extent, required to maintain projected revenue neutrality. Strict statutory and/or constitutional limitations could be placed on their appraisal district practices, local property tax rates, exemptions and other parameters, in order to ensure that the taxpayers' initial gains are not dissipated through creeping post-reform expansion. In the local tax jurisdictions examined, we estimate that this approach would have reduced 2008 property tax levies by approximately $292,316,000, a reduction so small as to cast doubt on the value of the legislative effort required to achieve it. This diminutive sum reflects the equally diminutive $625,188,580 of 2008 property tax levies in the 172 municipalities we identified as "deficit" jurisdictions. It might be preferable at these levels, simply as a matter of practicality, to abolish the property tax in those

---

[176] This estimate does not reflect the effect of stacking special purpose districts and metropolitan transit districts for which jurisdiction-specific taxable sales data is not available. As noted earlier, including those districts would tend to reduce the number of jurisdictions in this category.

jurisdictions where it is feasible to do so, and to leave it in those jurisdictions where it is not. Depending on the boundaries of the municipalities and special purpose districts affected, such a compromise admittedly blunts the effort to dismantle, or at least dramatically scale back, operations of the county appraisal districts encompassing those jurisdictions, despite our having successfully abolished the *ad valorem* tax at the county level.

Further progress might be achieved, however, through critical review and rationalization of the various special purpose districts that litter the Texas landscape, particularly by focusing on the extent to which their financing might be more effectively designed and administered on a county-wide basis, at least. To the extent that even a small percentage of the more than 1600 such districts could be consolidated and funded through the county-wide taxable sales base, even more property taxes and county appraisal offices could be phased out altogether. With this thought in mind, we examined in detail the 2008 property tax levies reported for all special

purpose districts in the top 39 counties by population, and then compared those with the county-wide taxable Business Sales tax base estimates we developed previously for analysis of the local tax jurisdictions. As shown in **Table 31**, the aggregate 2008

Table 31

Aggregate 2008 Property Tax Levies from in-County Special Purpose Districts

Counties	2008 SPD Property Tax Levies
Top 39	$4,564,251,928
Statewide	$4,952,734,969

property tax levies reported for all special purpose districts in the top 39 counties amounted to just over $4.5 billion, or roughly 92.2% of the entire property tax levies reported for special purpose districts throughout the state. By calculating the incremental Business Sales tax percentage that would have to be added to the tax on all taxable sales throughout each of these 39 counties in order to replace the property tax levies from in-county special purpose districts, we can place in some perspective the magnitude of the overall policy challenge posed by these districts.

If we are prepared to consider the matter on a county-wide basis, **Table 32** illustrates that they really pose no challenge at all. All but two of the top 39 counties could replace the entire 2008 special purpose district property tax levies from within their boundaries by assessing an incremental tax on local Business Sales of less than one-half percent, and the highest of these rates – in Fort Bend County – is only 1.12%. In fact all but 13 could accomplish this transition with a tax of less than one-quarter percent. Even where issues of responsiveness or accountability dictate that current special purpose districts retain their geographic configurations

Table 32

Incremental Business Sales Tax Rates Required to Replace County and Special Purchase District 2008 Property Taxes in Top 39 Counties by Population

County	County Replacement Rate	Estimated Taxable Business Sales Base	Cumulative in-County SPD 2008 Property Tax Levies	County-Wide SPD Replacement Rate	Cumulative County/SPD Replacement Rate
Jefferson	0.00096	$96,386,829,106.59	$49,808,176.00	0.0005	0.0015
Dallas	0.00135	$286,966,877,599.54	$661,537,680.00	0.0023	0.0037
Gregg	0.00148	$20,966,513,944.30	$4,321,738.00	0.0002	0.0017
Nueces	0.00169	$39,940,643,293.97	$74,253,949.00	0.0019	0.0036
Harris	0.00180	$609,066,009,318.48	$1,545,306,338.00	0.0025	0.0043
Ector	0.00185	$18,555,028,343.18	$21,179,284.00	0.0011	0.0030
Midland	0.00189	$19,366,646,208.87	$31,108,540.00	0.0016	0.0035
Galveston	0.00243	$50,273,070,791.57	$59,552,452.00	0.0012	0.0036
Bexar	0.00255	$125,325,272,859.12	$429,563,491.00	0.0034	0.0060
Tarrant	0.00294	$100,051,157,455.29	$470,353,272.00	0.0047	0.0080
Johnson	0.00329	$12,386,762,167.70	$4,766,590.00	0.0004	0.0038
Tom Green	0.00342	$6,669,113,467.03	$187,507.00	0.0000	0.0037
Taylor	0.00370	$7,482,765,079.07	$163,646.00	0.0000	0.0039
Potter	0.00391	$9,259,903,143.45	$19,974,690.00	0.0022	0.0061
El Paso	0.00395	$33,008,532,931.59	$110,027,300.00	0.0033	0.0074
Denton	0.00405	$29,650,693,583.67	$33,600,844.00	0.0011	0.0053
Parker	0.00418	$8,059,595,321.85	$21,164,335.00	0.0026	0.0070
Lubbock	0.00442	$12,289,282,869.39	$18,927,736.00	0.0015	0.0061
Smith	0.00453	$10,611,461,706.42	$17,931,299.00	0.0017	0.0064
Collin	0.00467	$36,195,045,722.28	$64,276,137.00	0.0018	0.0066
Bell	0.00481	$12,294,262,326.99	$16,441,979.00	0.0013	0.0063
McLennan	0.00493	$10,801,686,156.16	$16,379,686.00	0.0015	0.0066
Montgomery	0.00505	$28,427,550,884.16	$141,946,007.00	0.0050	0.0102
Comal	0.00516	$6,711,111,155.34	$7,876,439.00	0.0012	0.0066
Wichita	0.00542	$4,793,808,830.37	$492,137.00	0.0001	0.0057
Travis	0.00560	$62,439,578,814.65	$221,306,830.00	0.0035	0.0099
Cameron	0.00632	$7,953,092,342.94	$33,037,225.00	0.0042	0.0110
Ellis	0.00686	$5,392,056,653.81	$1,725,586.00	0.0003	0.0078
Brazoria	0.00750	$12,108,505,830.65	$95,790,502.00	0.0079	0.0155
Guadalupe	0.00755	$3,894,656,995.12	$9,466.00	0.0000	0.0085
Brazos	0.00848	$6,411,141,867.01	$576,476.00	0.0001	0.0088
Williamson	0.00873	$17,420,965,819.87	$52,827,257.00	0.0030	0.0120
Grayson	0.00899	$3,264,901,874.20	$12,109,123.00	0.0037	0.0128
Webb	0.00904	$7,248,772,463.60	$23,504,357.00	0.0032	0.0123
Hidalgo	0.00905	$17,580,859,149.20	$58,454,702.00	0.0033	0.0124
Randall	0.00910	$2,682,096,873.70	$0.00	0.0000	0.0094
Fort Bend	0.00942	$19,959,718,058.38	$223,156,912.00	0.0112	0.0207
Hays	0.00956	$5,281,971,823.09	$12,854,706.00	0.0024	0.0123
Kaufman	0.00990	$3,319,876,233.46	$7,757,534.00	0.0023	0.0126

and administrative autonomy, their financing might still be amenable to inclusion in a county-managed system of revenue generation and formula-based allocation. In a very real sense, this process would look very much like the process by which the State of Texas expanded the business franchise tax in order to provide local property tax relief to taxpayers in Texas school districts. In the case of the special purpose districts, however, this solution offers the more favorable element of retaining local political control and accountability, at least at the level of county government. If adopted, this reform would effectively abolish property taxes in all special purpose districts in the 39 most populous counties, which we estimate to represent an additional $4,569,780,623, or 11.7% of the aggregate 2008 property taxes levied statewide. If this success could be replicated in the remaining counties, abolition of special purpose district property taxes statewide would relieve property owners of an aggregate $4,952,734,969 in property taxes, or 12.7% of the statewide total.[177]

Increasing the base rate for the county-level Business Sales tax, however, would be expected to affect the number of municipalities able to achieve revenue neutrality when rates are measured on a stacked basis. Returning to those calculations, we find in fact that the county-level tax increase required to replace property taxes in the special purpose districts reduces from 180 to 156 the number of municipalities situated within a single county that are able to achieve revenue neutrality within the proposed 2.525% combined rate cap. Likewise, of the additional 33 multi-county municipalities that are in surplus when measured individually, we find that this rate increase reduces from 28 to 25 the number able to achieve tax neutrality within the 2.525% combined cap when measured in locations within their primary county's jurisdiction, and from 26 to 23 the number when measured in the county with the highest revenue neutral rate From these calculations, we may conclude that, of the 243 municipalities in the top 39 counties that could achieve revenue neutrality on an individual basis with local allocations from the Business Sales tax capped at 2.525%, only approximately 179 (as compared to our previous estimate of 206) would remain entirely neutral once the counties increase their base rate to accommodate property tax relief for special purpose districts and all local rates within each jurisdiction are considered together. We calculate the net effect of this change as being to reduce from $9,647,332,021 to $9,162,476,199.89 the 2008 property tax levies represented by the counties and municipalities for which we can achieve combined revenue neutrality, which when added to the $4,569,780,623 figure for special purpose districts comes to $13,732,256,822.89 in county, municipality and special purpose district property taxes abolished by these proposed reforms.

---

[177] Texas Comptroller of Public Accounts, *Annual Property Tax Report Tax Year 2008, Revised Edition*, p.2, Exhibit 2 (February 2010).

This figure represents 41.9% of the 2008 property tax levies in the top 39 counties by population, and 35.2% of the state's entire 2008 local *ad valorem* property taxes.

The 172 municipalities unable to achieve neutrality on an individual basis, combined with the additional 65 unable to do so on a stacked basis, together represent approximately $1,592,877,943.11, or 26.68% of the estimated $5,970,964,008 in 2008 property tax levies of all municipalities in the top 39 counties by population. If this proportion holds for all municipalities in the rest of the state, we estimate that the property tax levies represented by municipalities that would be permitted to retain their existing property tax system would amount to $128,062,833.59 of the $480,048,439 in municipal 2008 property tax levies in the remaining counties, for a total of $1,720,940,776.70 of the $6,451,012,447.00 in municipal 2008 property tax levies statewide, as summarized in **Table 33**.

Table 33
Summary of Property Taxes Abolished (Pro Forma 2008)

Tax Jurisdictions	Property Taxes Abolished	%	Property Taxes Retained	%	Total	% of Aggregate
Top 39 Counties	$4,784,390,135.00	100%	$0.00	0%	$4,784,390,135.00	12.27%
Remaining Counties	$1,558,314,768.00	100%	$0.00	0%	$1,558,314,768.00	4%
Municipalities in Top 39 Counties	$4,378,086,064.89	73.32%	$1,592,877,943.11	26.68%	$5,970,964,008.00	15.32%
Remaining Municipalities	$351,985,605.41	73.32%	$128,062,833.59	26.68%	$480,048,439.00	1.23%
SPD's in Top 39 Counties	$4,569,780,623.00	100%	$0.00	0%	$4,569,780,623.00	11.72%
Remaining SPD's	$382,954,346.00	100%	$0.00	0%	$382,954,346.00	0.98%
Subtotal:	$16,025,511,542.30	90.30%	$1,720,940,776.70	9.70%	$17,746,452,319.00	45.53%
School Districts	?	?	?	?	$21,233,517,226.00	54.47%
Aggregate Property Taxes Statewide	?	?	?	?	$38,979,969,545.00	100%

Although we would not have successfully extinguished the property tax in all municipalities, we would have made respectable progress. But we still would have not addressed the single group of jurisdictions responsible for the majority of Texas' property tax levies. This brings us to the longstanding effort to reform Texas' school financing system on a sustainable, constitutional basis.

VI.   TEXAS SCHOOL FINANCE REFORM

A.   The Current State of Texas School Finance

Perhaps the most controversial aspect of the current local property tax system has been its role in school finance. For several decades, the legislature, the school districts and the courts have struggled to balance the fundamental obligation to minimize disparities among districts in per-pupil spending (or, more to the point, funding) for the basic educational curriculum, on the one hand, with the political imperative to avoid forcing wealthier districts to shoulder most of the burden of statewide education, on the other. The Texas Constitution, in particular, plays a key role in the judicial treatment of this issue, since it effectively prohibits the state from forcing local districts to impose property taxes in amounts mandated to meet state revenue distribution requirements.[178] But the disproportionate destruction of property value associated with punitively higher rates in the wealthier districts also has forced a general recognition that the state's economic resources could be more productively employed in the quest to provide public school education to Texas pupils.[179] The Texas Supreme Court ruled in November 2005 that the state had instituted a system that in effect subordinated to state control the school districts' discretion over their own local property tax rates in violation of article VIII, section 1-e of the Texas Constitution.[180] This led to further controversy and, ultimately, to a series of legislative acts intended to at least partially address the problem.

In 2008, school districts in the top 39 counties levied $17,313,933,664 in property taxes, representing 52.84% and 44.42%, respectively, of the 39-county and statewide property tax levies, with $21,233,517,226 being levied by school districts statewide. The state legislature allocates portions of the motor vehicle sales tax, collection of tobacco products' tax increases and portions of franchise taxes to a so-called "Property Tax Relief Fund," which is used to make transfer payments to local school districts to enable them to reduce property taxes on their residents. In fiscal 2009 (ending August 31, 2009), the Comptroller's unaudited report indicates that $2,536,209,130.94 of such payments were made based on revenues of $2,538,176,123.05, leaving a balance of $3,003,882,629.23 available for property tax relief payments in 2010-2011.

---

[178] *See* Neeley v. W. Orange-Cove Consol. Indep. Sch. Dist., 176 S.W.3d 746 (Tex. 2005); *see also* West Orange-Cove I.S.D. v. Alanis, 107 S.W.3d 558 (Tex. 2003).

[179] Caroline M. Hoxby and Ilyana Kuziemko, "Robin Hood and His Not-So-Merry Plan: Capitalization and the Self-Destruction of Texas' School Finance Equalization Plan", http://www.nber.org/papers/w10722.pdf

[180] *See* Neeley v. W. Orange-Cove Consol. Indep. Sch. Dist., *supra* n.178.

According to the Comptroller's estimate, additional deposits of $5.5 billion are expected to be made to this fund during the 2010-2011 period.[181] In 2008, $4,231,466,000 were spent on public school education from this fund.[182] State law currently permits certain cities, counties and hospital districts also to grant additional property tax relief by enacting their own additional sales tax beyond the levels for which they would otherwise have authority, but still subject to the overall limitation that combined local taxes may not exceed 2% anywhere within the taxing jurisdiction, and subject to certain limitations on use of the revenues raised.[183]

One way to characterize the Texas Supreme Court's jurisprudence on school finance is to describe state-established educational standards as a "mandate" that may or may not be "unfunded", depending upon the extent to which the state arranges funding adequate to meet them. Regardless of the other constitutional considerations, from the point of view of local school districts, this represents a meaningful justification for their insistence on a predominantly state-funded system. The state-funded relief implemented so far has come without discernible loss of control at the local level over school district policies and practices, and the districts may be expected to remain vigilant on this point as such funding continues its projected growth. At the same time, local communities enjoy the both the fundamental right and duty to direct and provide for the education of their children, including the provision of enrichment opportunities to the extent that local resources permit.[184] The current system as summarized in the paragraph above represents one frame in the evolving storyboard of the effort to strike this balance, but in the present context, it seems clear that this evolution points inexorably to a solution that more

---

[181] Texas Comptroller of Public Accounts, *Biennial Revenue Estimate 2010-2011*, January 12, 2010, http://www.window.state.tx.us/taxbud/bre2010/letter.html.

[182] *CAFR 2008*, p. 158.

[183] Texas Tax Code, Sections 321.101 and 323.101; Texas Health and Safety Code, Section 285.061.

[184] The Neeley court rejected arguments that the differences in funding available for education among the state's school districts constituted a failure to meet the Constitution's requirements for "efficiency," or "suitability", whether in terms of the provision of school facilities or in terms of funding for ongoing maintenance and operations. Quoting from its earlier opinion in Edgewood Indep. Sch. Dist. v. Kirby, 777 S.W.2d 391 (Tex. 1989), the court reminded us that

> "the constitutional standard of efficiency requires substantially equivalent access to revenue only up to a point, after which a local community can elect higher taxes to "supplement" and "enrich" its own schools."

Id. at 791. However, the court held out the possibility that evolving curriculum standards might in effect transform today's "supplemental" enrichment into tomorrow's minimally adequate standards, for the funding of which the state would be constitutionally required to make provision one way or another:

> "The danger is that what the Legislature today considers to be "supplementation" may tomorrow become necessary to satisfy the constitutional mandate for a general diffusion of knowledge."

Id. at 792, quoting from its earlier opinion in West Orange-Cove ISD, *supra* n.178, at 571-572.

optimally serves all the goals of adequacy, fairness, constitutionality, liberty and economic and tax efficiency.

B.   Elimination of the School District Property Tax

There is no reason in theory why the measures recently adopted to provide local school district property tax relief could not be extended to fund the entirety of school district expenditures, at least up to the level at which a constitutionally adequate standard of support for all Texas schoolchildren is being met. The two-tier sales tax system described in this report has been designed so as to generate revenues sufficient in the aggregate to fully replace the local *ad valorem* property tax on a pro-forma, statewide basis during fiscal 2008. After allowing for local tax allocations in accordance with the principles described in Section V, this means that the state's general revenues would be able to accommodate appropriations to fund a greatly expanded Foundation School Program, whether to cover the school districts' maintenance and operation (M&O) costs alone, or both M&O as well as interest and sinking fund (I&S) costs. **Table 34** describes in full the extent to which this final step completes the abolition of property taxes in Texas. Such a solution raises concerns among those who seek to ensure that some jurisdictions are not being subsidized by others, the very issue that has roiled Texas school finance reform for years. Yet the state's constitutional mandate to "make suitable provision for" free public education to Texas children should serve as the determining consideration.[185] After all, if the state were to be limited to spending in local jurisdictions the revenues generated in those jurisdictions, we would have no need of state government in the first place.

At the same time, allocation formulas would require careful maintenance and review to prevent the state's "basic" education funding from being used for or diverted to local "enrichment" facilities, programs and activities, whether directly or indirectly. For this reason the enabling legislation might identify current or potential interest and sinking (I&S) obligations or projections, either by category or by jurisdiction, that would be ineligible for substitution with state funding. It is important to ensure, for example, that some districts are not funded or subsidized for mega-stadia while others struggle to keep the roof patched. In turn, local jurisdictions might be

---

[185] TEX. CONST. art. 7, section 1:

> "A general diffusion of knowledge being essential to the preservation of the liberties and rights of the people, it shall be the duty of the Legislature of the State to establish and make suitable provision for the support and maintenance of an efficient system of public free schools."

See also Neeley, *supra*, n. 184.

Table 34

Summary of Property Taxes Abolished (Pro Forma 2008)

Tax Jurisdictions	Property Taxes Abolished	%	Property Taxes Retained	%	Total	% of Aggregate
Top 39 Counties	$4,784,390,135.00	100%	$0.00	0%	$4,784,390,135.00	12.27%
Remaining Counties	$1,558,314,768.00	100%	$0.00	0%	$1,558,314,768.00	4%
Municipalities in Top 39 Counties	$4,378,086,064.89	73.32%	$1,592,877,943.11	26.68%	$5,970,964,008.00	15.32%
Remaining Municipalities	$351,985,605.41	73.32%	$128,062,833.59	26.68%	$480,048,439.00	1.23%
SPD's in Top 39 Counties	$4,569,780,623.00	100%	$0.00	0%	$4,569,780,623.00	11.72%
Remaining SPD's	$382,954,346.00	100%	$0.00	0%	$382,954,346.00	0.98%
Subtotal:	$16,025,511,542.30	90.30%	$1,720,940,776.70	9.70%	$17,746,452,319.00	45.53%
School Districts	$21,233,517,226.00	100%	$0.00	0%	$21,233,517,226.00	54.47%
Aggregate Property Taxes Statewide	$37,259,028,768.30	95.59%	$1,720,940,776.70	4.41%	$38,979,969,545.00	100%

permitted, within limits, to impose additional sales taxes approved by voters to fund such programs. But, although we do not have data sufficient to determine with confidence the taxable sales base within many if not most individual school districts, our findings in those dual-tax jurisdictions we did examine suggest that we should expect to find among them widely divergent balances -- or imbalances -- between their taxable sales bases and their taxable property bases. Such imbalances may render it difficult if not impossible for some jurisdictions to fund even minimal enrichment programs exclusively through reliance exclusively on locally generated sales tax revenues. For this reason, local school districts might also be permitted the right to maintain some portion of their local property tax system, but subject to strict legislative and constitutional constraints.

At the risk of pushing our proposed reforms even further beyond the collective comfort zone, policymakers might also treat this as an opportunity to revisit the current structure of Texas school districts. Like special purpose districts, school districts in many cases are conceived, expanded and gerrymandered – often across city or even county lines – for reasons that have far more to do with the ongoing quest to command a sufficient taxable property base than with effective teaching, responsive relationships with the local community, or personal accountability for teachers and faculty. How much more responsive to the needs of students and parents might school districts be if, rather than being organized into bureaucracy-laden leviathans encompassing populations in the millions, they were instead organized at the truly local, community level, with direct political accountability to the voters being served, and freed from the feudal imperative of having to capture their own sources of financing? The harm in persisting to try to finance public schools through the local property tax extends beyond the evils inherent in the tax itself, and beyond the system's constitutional infirmities. Texans are ready for a fresh start in their relationships with state and local government. Perhaps our public school districts offer a fruitful place to begin.

APPENDIX A

Table A1

Dual-Tax Jurisdictions' Replacement Factors
(Current All-Industry Taxable Sales Base ($US))

Rank	County	Tax Jurisdiction	Property Tax Levy (2008)	Sales Tax Allocation (2008)	Local Tax Replacement Factor
1	Harris	City of Baytown	$22,755,668.00	$11,796,333.75	1.929046
1	Harris	City of Bellaire	$11,645,491.00	$2,261,630.19	5.149158
1	Harris	City of Bunker Hill Village	$3,456,771.00	$71,217.80	48.538020
1	Harris	City of Deer Park	$11,836,630.00	$4,171,743.09	2.837334
1	Harris	City of El Lago	$812,337.00	$128,046.84	6.344061
1	Harris	City of Galena Park	$3,811,099.00	$1,213,637.60	3.140228
1	Harris	City of Hedwig Village	$1,373,398.00	$1,396,175.34	0.983686
1	Harris	City of Hilshire Village	$1,240,299.00	$40,100.29	30.929926
1	Harris, Fort Bend, Montgomery	City of Houston	$963,104,951.00	$504,416,609.93	1.909344
1	Harris	City of Humble	$2,291,689.00	$11,713,515.02	0.195645
1	Harris	City of Hunters Creek Village	$3,127,457.00	$302,501.18	10.338660
1	Harris	City of Jacinto City	$2,691,813.00	$602,504.96	4.467703
1	Harris	City of Jersey Village	$5,543,419.00	$2,466,914.59	2.247106
1	Harris, Fort Bend	City of Katy	$6,071,412.00	$7,967,102.76	0.762060
1	Harris	City of La Porte	$15,971,521.00	$5,422,539.37	2.945395
1	Harris	City of Morgans Point	$1,122,152.00	$270,907.59	4.142195
1	Harris	City of Nassau Bay	$2,464,418.00	$710,315.24	3.469471
1	Harris	City of Pasadena	$29,798,137.00	$23,980,086.96	1.242620
1	Harris	City of Piney Point Village	$3,386,735.00	$92,715.70	36.528172
1	Harris	City of Seabrook	$4,341,373.00	$2,394,265.37	1.813238
1	Harris	City of Shoreacres	$607,925.00	$67,861.49	8.958321
1	Harris	City of South Houston	$2,745,841.00	$2,520,041.01	1.089602
1	Harris	City of Southside Place	$1,674,590.00	$290,800.75	5.758548
1	Harris	City of Spring Valley	$3,307,145.00	$1,195,773.11	2.765696
1	Harris	City of Taylor Lake Village	$1,012,845.00	$43,927.64	23.057123
1	Harris	City of Tomball	$2,652,830.00	$9,443,513.51	0.280916
1	Harris	City of Waller	$214,392.00	$1,041,915.86	0.205767
1	Harris	City of Webster	$2,436,714.00	$14,739,256.38	0.165321
1	Harris	City of West University Place	$13,715,506.00	$1,062,798.59	12.905085
1	Harris	Harris County Emergency Services District #21	$481,876.00	$475,330.66	1.013770
1	Harris	Harris County Emergency Services District #5	$335,335.00	$1,221,983.15	0.274419
1	Harris	Harris County Emergency Services District #80	$550,358.00	$1,212,642.64	0.453850
2	Dallas	City of Addison	$16,748,125.00	$10,654,091.08	1.571990
2	Dallas	City of Balch Springs	$4,552,022.00	$5,049,420.74	0.901494
2	Dallas, Collin, Denton	City of Carrollton	$58,429,252.00	$21,836,423.02	2.675770
2	Dallas, Ellis	City of Cedar Hill	$20,138,143.00	$12,285,802.93	1.639139
2	Dallas	City of Cockrell Hill	$654,545.00	$179,656.38	3.643316
2	Dallas, Denton	City of Coppell	$31,330,600.00	$20,551,374.85	1.524501
2	Dallas, Collin, Denton	City of Dallas	$670,443,483.00	$227,067,964.29	2.952612
2	Dallas	City of De Soto	$21,567,876.00	$6,944,720.86	3.105651
2	Dallas	City of Duncanville	$13,309,800.00	$7,205,081.71	1.847280
2	Dallas	City of Farmers Branch	$20,447,707.00	$13,167,777.63	1.552859
2	Dallas, Collin	City of Garland	$78,693,954.00	$22,059,916.21	3.567283
2	Dallas, Ellis	City of Glenn Heights	$2,965,146.00	$235,384.84	12.597013

2	Dallas, Tarrant, Ellis	City of Grand Prairie	$66,292,699.00	$38,295,770.52	1.731071
2	Dallas	City of Highland Park	$9,609,331.00	$2,392,831.70	4.015883
2	Dallas	City of Hutchins	$1,391,954.00	$1,288,575.84	1.080227
2	Dallas	City of Irving	$100,335,203.00	$51,022,274.29	1.966498
2	Dallas	City of Lancaster	$13,493,595.00	$5,559,770.27	2.427006
2	Dallas, Kaufman	City of Mesquite	$42,376,457.00	$33,888,471.88	1.250468
2	Dallas, Collin	City of Richardson	$56,008,881.00	$23,041,843.35	2.430747
2	Dallas	City of Rowlett	$21,546,428.00	$5,920,354.90	3.639381
2	Dallas, Collin	City of Sachse	$7,366,665.00	$15,663,220.81	0.470316
2	Dallas, Kaufman	City of Seagoville	$3,160,386.00	$2,774,134.67	1.139233
2	Dallas	City of Sunnyvale	$2,495,140.00	$2,089,751.68	1.193989
2	Dallas	City of University Park	$15,490,904.00	$3,090,482.04	5.012456
2	Dallas	City of Wilmer	$674,445.00	$170,935.33	3.945615
3	Tarrant	City of Arlington	$119,903,861.00	$81,851,456.56	1.464896
3	Tarrant, Parker	City of Azle	$4,183,151.00	$2,150,973.27	1.944771
3	Tarrant	City of Bedford	$13,740,400.00	$9,585,193.58	1.433503
3	Tarrant	City of Benbrook	$9,769,989.00	$2,622,176.53	3.725908
3	Tarrant	City of Blue Mound	$483,059.00	$104,637.36	4.616506
3	Tarrant, Johnson	City of Burleson	$13,937,164.00	$11,385,608.92	1.224104
3	Tarrant	City of Colleyville	$13,066,166.00	$3,754,327.21	3.480295
3	Tarrant, Johnson	City of Crowley	$4,040,146.00	$1,321,141.61	3.058072
3	Tarrant	City of Dalworthington Gardens	$808,539.00	$320,292.17	2.524380
3	Tarrant	City of Edgecliff Village	$562,946.00	$71,611.48	7.861114
3	Tarrant	City of Euless	$12,975,885.00	$12,620,520.17	1.028158
3	Tarrant	City of Everman	$1,220,887.00	$471,143.69	2.591326
3	Tarrant	City of Forest Hill	$3,980,780.00	$2,075,965.44	1.917556
3	Tarrant, Denton	City of Fort Worth	$356,015,812.00	$106,259,647.55	3.350433
3	Tarrant, Dallas, Denton	City of Grapevine	$22,461,118.00	$34,379,187.56	0.653335
3	Tarrant	City of Haltom City	$10,182,944.00	$8,819,932.85	1.154538
3	Tarrant, Denton	City of Haslet	$1,449,917.00	$866,698.29	1.672920
3	Tarrant	City of Hurst	$12,789,781.00	$15,105,065.79	0.846721
3	Tarrant	City of Keller	$16,807,193.00	$7,422,637.10	2.264316
3	Tarrant	City of Kennedale	$3,563,291.00	$1,332,866.65	2.673404
3	Tarrant	City of Lake Worth	$1,344,833.00	$5,727,421.46	0.234806
3	Tarrant	City of Lakeside	$111,658,241.00	$81,989.10	1361.866895
3	Tarrant, Johnson, Ellis	City of Mansfield	$29,304,002.00	$14,498,323.45	2.021199
3	Tarrant	City of North Richland Hills	$21,767,577.00	$13,220,143.78	1.646546
3	Tarrant	City of Pantego	$965,011.00	$2,334,132.75	0.413434
3	Tarrant	City of Pelican Bay	$222,336.00	$4,174.49	53.260638
3	Tarrant	City of Richland Hills	$2,120,553.00	$1,809,894.92	1.171644
3	Tarrant	City of River Oaks	$1,865,998.00	$469,960.47	3.970542
3	Tarrant	City of Saginaw	$5,281,554.00	$4,608,783.15	1.145976
3	Tarrant	City of Sansom Park	$612,987.00	$257,409.02	2.381373
3	Tarrant, Denton	City of Southlake	$10,518,520.00	$14,519,650.90	0.724433
3	Tarrant	City of Watauga	$6,090,935.00	$3,900,317.64	1.561651
3	Tarrant	City of Westworth Village	$722,525.00	$1,374,539.45	0.525649
3	Tarrant	City of White Settlement	$3,858,108.00	$2,803,179.54	1.376333
4	Bexar	Cibolo Canyon Special Improvement District	$983,622.00	$34,164.49	28.790771
4	Bexar	City of Alamo Heights	$4,835,020.00	$791,758.82	6.106683
4	Bexar	City of Balcones Heights	$1,110,115.00	$1,288,256.57	0.861719
4	Bexar	City of Castle Hills	$2,066,647.00	$1,005,693.32	2.054948
4	Bexar	City of China Grove	$68,154.00	$96,624.85	0.705347
4	Bexar	City of Converse	$3,890,498.00	$2,233,986.00	1.741505
4	Bexar	City of Elmendorf	$93,397.00	$53,198.26	1.755640
4	Bexar	City of Grey Forest	$32,828.00	$22,519.00	1.457791
4	Bexar	City of Helotes	$2,575,260.00	$730,148.36	3.527037
4	Bexar	City of Hill Country Village	$264,347.00	$1,217,290.04	0.217160
4	Bexar	City of Hollywood Park	$1,524,245.00	$860,605.63	1.771131

4	Bexar	City of Kirby	$1,352,227.00	$215,296.37	6.280770
4	Bexar	City of Leon Valley	$3,670,396.00	$1,840,217.29	1.994545
4	Bexar	City of Live Oak	$3,240,789.00	$5,482,594.69	0.591105
4	Bexar	City of Lytle	$2,247.00	$483,539.08	0.004647
4	Bexar	City of Olmos Park	$2,401,309.00	$495,261.87	4.848564
4	Bexar	City of San Antonio	$414,315,114.00	$215,808,945.20	1.919824
4	Bexar, Guadalupe, Comal	City of Selma	$1,466,842.00	$3,921,111.80	0.374088
4	Bexar	City of Shavano Park	$2,346,924.00	$157,890.74	14.864228
4	Bexar	City of Somerset	$235,718.00	$209,297.04	1.126237
4	Bexar	City of Terrell Hills	$4,406,026.00	$161,844.90	27.223756
4	Bexar	City of Universal City	$4,857,584.00	$2,646,476.27	1.835491
4	Bexar	City of Windcrest	$2,051,283.00	$2,170,380.08	0.945126
5	Travis, Hays, Williamson	City of Austin	$309,093,265.00	$147,051,782.33	2.101935
5	Travis	City of Bee Cave	$163,658.00	$5,647,110.75	0.028981
5	Travis	City of Briarcliff	$194,851.00	$30,003.30	6.494319
5	Travis, Williamson	City of Cedar Park	$19,699,598.00	$13,660,223.14	1.442114
5	Travis	City of Creedmoor	$78,750.00	$111,431.64	0.706711
5	Travis	City of Elgin	$312,835.00	$1,202,575.49	0.260138
5	Travis	City of Jonestown	$2,037,212.00	$106,800.57	19.074917
5	Travis	City of Lago Vista	$3,870,154.00	$296,443.60	13.055279
5	Travis	City of Lakeway	$4,246,346.00	$1,727,348.72	2.458303
5	Travis	City of Manor	$1,466,735.00	$387,028.97	3.789729
5	Travis	City of Mustang Ridge	$130,603.00	$32,067.86	4.072707
5	Travis	City of Point Venture	$90,790.00	$31,924.11	2.843932
5	Travis	City of Rollingwood	$502,032.00	$565,984.69	0.887006
5	Travis	City of Volente	$186,845.00	$39,719.06	4.704165
5	Travis	City of Webberville	$46,113.00	$16,761.55	2.751118
5	Travis	Travis County Emergency Services District #11	$667,063.00	$1,137,695.72	0.586328
5	Travis	Travis County Emergency Services District #2	$5,765,793.00	$2,710,081.17	2.127535
5	Travis	Travis County Emergency Services District #3	$2,011,926.00	$1,531,484.49	1.313710
5	Travis	Travis County Emergency Services District #4	$1,618,619.00	$1,199,774.95	1.349102
5	Travis	Travis County Emergency Services District #8	$1,352,059.00	$80,445.87	16.807065
6	Collin	City of Allen	$39,057,659.00	$20,156,179.50	1.937751
6	Collin	City of Anna	$2,207,496.00	$707,742.97	3.119065
6	Collin	City of Blue Ridge	$152,129.00	$71,871.03	2.116694
6	Collin, Denton	City of Celina	$2,980,969.00	$572,896.74	5.203327
6	Collin	City of Fairview	$35,179,810.00	$586,462.49	59.986462
6	Collin	City of Farmersville	$879,294.00	$503,966.14	1.744748
6	Collin, Denton	City of Frisco	$61,152,866.00	$39,809,254.00	1.536147
6	Collin	City of Josephine	$133,559.00	$16,003.76	8.345476
6	Collin	City of Lavon	$597,523.00	$111,280.93	5.369500
6	Collin	City of Lowry Crossing	$217,104.00	$35,264.93	6.156371
6	Collin	City of Lucas	$1,901,585.00	$163,132.62	11.656682
6	Collin	City of McKinney	$61,834,900.00	$33,592,023.47	1.840761
6	Collin	City of Melissa	$2,074,957.00	$1,393,022.69	1.489536
6	Collin	City of Murphy	$7,321,275.00	$1,249,623.63	5.858784
6	Collin	City of Nevada	$61,568.00	$46,904.13	1.312635
6	Collin	City of New Hope	$75,197.00	$17,810.54	4.222051
6	Collin	City of Parker	$1,849,422.00	$133,145.56	13.890227
6	Collin, Denton	City of Plano	$122,477,976.00	$64,180,104.26	1.908348
6	Collin	City of Princeton	$2,006,014.00	$738,341.67	2.716918
6	Collin, Denton	City of Prosper	$5,177,422.00	$1,742,461.62	2.971326
6	Collin	City of Royse City	$495,906.00	$1,089,458.04	0.455186
6	Collin	City of Saint Paul	$314,556.00	$30,054.52	10.466179
6	Collin	City of Weston	$79,346.00	$3,101.48	25.583270
6	Collin, Dallas	City of Wylie	$19,908,149.00	$5,207,168.92	3.823219
7	El Paso	City of Anthony	$521,365.00	$402,443.63	1.295498
7	El Paso	City of Clint	$159,080.00	$53,305.06	2.984332

TEXAS CENTER FOR ECONOMICS, LAW & POLICY

7	El Paso	City of El Paso	$182,526,356.00	$67,821,673.07	2.691269
7	El Paso	City of Horizon City	$1,773,283.00	$493,534.89	3.593025
7	El Paso	City of Socorro	$3,550,210.00	$932,713.65	3.806324
7	El Paso	City of Vinton	$223,685.00	$228,405.05	0.979335
7	El Paso	El Paso County	$111,493,605.00	$35,509,011.57	3.139868
7	El Paso	El Paso Emergency Medical Services District #2	$2,457,901.00	$1,760,007.59	1.396529
8	Hidalgo	City of Alamo	$2,756,681.00	$2,864,070.74	0.962505
8	Hidalgo	City of Alton	$971,438.00	$462,817.42	2.098966
8	Hidalgo	City of Donna	$3,329,430.00	$1,574,754.37	2.114254
8	Hidalgo	City of Edcouch	$376,824.00	$185,488.50	2.031522
8	Hidalgo	City of Edinburg	$19,025,142.00	$14,215,364.48	1.338351
8	Hidalgo	City of Elsa	$904,137.00	$612,594.63	1.475914
8	Hidalgo	City of Granjeno	$13,847.00	$4,485.69	3.086928
8	Hidalgo	City of Hidalgo	$1,546,389.00	$1,790,169.00	0.863823
8	Hidalgo	City of La Joya	$598,454.00	$387,729.77	1.543482
8	Hidalgo	City of La Villa	$279,149.00	$38,785.63	7.197227
8	Hidalgo	City of McAllen	$31,890,678.00	$58,864,799.64	0.541761
8	Hidalgo	City of Mercedes	$3,445,145.00	$5,730,074.64	0.601239
8	Hidalgo	City of Mission	$17,124,534.00	$13,062,252.74	1.310994
8	Hidalgo	City of Palmview	$770,930.00	$726,969.04	1.060472
8	Hidalgo	City of Penitas	$356,490.00	$214,044.30	1.665496
8	Hidalgo	City of Pharr	$14,584,419.00	$11,418,295.63	1.277285
8	Hidalgo	City of Progreso	$261,969.00	$209,388.10	1.251117
8	Hidalgo	City of San Juan	$5,047,450.00	$2,552,800.70	1.977221
8	Hidalgo	City of Weslaco	$9,281,021.00	$8,981,280.93	1.033374
9	Denton	City of Argyle	$1,504,706.00	$469,965.91	3.201734
9	Denton	City of Aubrey	$677,835.00	$600,522.91	1.128741
9	Denton	City of Bartonville	$431,162.00	$167,711.70	2.570852
9	Denton	City of Copper Canyon	$305,838.00	$174,167.80	1.755996
9	Denton	City of Corinth	$8,175,924.00	$1,792,584.89	4.560969
9	Denton	City of Corral City	$12,221.00	$115,751.51	0.105580
9	Denton	City of Denton	$41,856,644.00	$20,546,337.83	2.037183
9	Denton	City of Double Oak	$742,335.00	$95,036.70	7.811035
9	Denton, Tarrant	City of Flower Mound	$30,813,577.00	$8,735,126.09	3.527548
9	Denton	City of Hackberry	$94,442.00	$24,521.10	3.851459
9	Denton	City of Hickory Creek	$1,439,118.00	$1,367,389.03	1.052457
9	Denton	City of Highland Village	$9,210,527.00	$2,719,056.44	3.387398
9	Denton	City of Justin	$1,144,732.00	$1,203,466.26	0.951196
9	Denton	City of Krugerville	$264,605.00	$67,899.70	3.896998
9	Denton	City of Krum	$1,138,481.00	$252,327.26	4.511922
9	Denton	City of Lake Dallas	$2,315,475.00	$1,082,829.13	2.138357
9	Denton, Dallas	City of Lewisville	$29,908,774.00	$23,516,031.66	1.271846
9	Denton	City of Little Elm	$8,702,529.00	$2,757,031.70	3.156485
9	Denton	City of Northlake	$634,970.00	$404,696.46	1.569003
9	Denton	City of Oak Point	$1,417,196.00	$126,146.51	11.234524
9	Denton	City of Pilot Point	$1,294,144.00	$780,045.42	1.659062
9	Denton	City of Ponder	$404,029.00	$198,903.92	2.031277
9	Denton, Tarrant	City of Roanoke	$4,665,433.00	$8,472,289.64	0.550670
9	Denton	City of Sanger	$2,112,387.00	$872,370.72	2.421433
9	Denton	City of Shady Shores	$619,366.00	$62,643.10	9.887218
9	Denton	City of The Colony	$14,705,317.00	$5,916,751.00	2.485370
9	Denton, Tarrant	City of Trophy Club	$3,594,948.00	$958,166.01	3.751905
10	Fort Bend	City of Arcola	$634,075.00	$527,964.62	1.200980
10	Fort Bend	City of Beasley	$84,152.00	$81,055.53	1.038202
10	Fort Bend	City of Fulshear	$190,201.00	$356,009.22	0.534259
10	Fort Bend	City of Kendleton	$84,740.00	$19,045.23	4.449408
10	Fort Bend	City of Meadows Place	$2,265,713.00	$1,055,797.78	2.145972
10	Fort Bend, Harris	City of Missouri City	$22,915,240.00	$5,751,816.15	3.984001

10	Fort Bend	City of Needville	$512,550.00	$409,680.68	1.251096
10	Fort Bend	City of Orchard	$49,129.00	$45,742.85	1.074026
10	Fort Bend	City of Richmond	$3,109,598.00	$3,690,657.68	0.842559
10	Fort Bend	City of Rosenberg	$7,603,807.00	$10,707,648.18	0.710129
10	Fort Bend	City of Simonton	$129,238.00	$53,063.68	2.435527
10	Fort Bend	City of Sugar Land	$26,245,626.00	$39,539,273.71	0.663786
11	Montgomery	City of Conroe	$13,527,579.00	$30,795,283.92	0.439274
11	Montgomery	City of Magnolia	$385,477.00	$1,945,730.95	0.198114
11	Montgomery	City of Montgomery	$246,274.00	$1,289,610.69	0.190968
11	Montgomery	City of Oak Ridge North	$1,440,187.00	$1,679,175.84	0.857675
11	Montgomery	City of Patton Village	$59,777.00	$17,780.98	3.361851
11	Montgomery	City of Shenandoah	$1,577,421.00	$5,618,880.36	0.280736
11	Montgomery	City of Splendora	$109,089.00	$192,131.70	0.567782
11	Montgomery	City of Stagecoach	$133,574.00	$11,052.72	12.085170
11	Montgomery	City of Willis	$673,192.00	$1,556,118.13	0.432610
11	Montgomery	Montgomery County Emergency Services District #12	$256,344.00	$169,560.29	1.511816
11	Montgomery	Montgomery County Emergency Services District #3	$1,304,804.00	$967,838.91	1.348162
11	Montgomery	Montgomery County Emergency Services District #6	$1,393,324.00	$1,130,064.28	1.232960
11	Montgomery	Montgomery County Emergency Services District #7	$655,565.00	$291,336.09	2.250202
11	Montgomery	Montgomery County Emergency Services District #9	$374,525.00	$618,030.08	0.605998
12	Williamson	City of Florence	$184,778.00	$124,713.22	1.481623
12	Williamson	City of Georgetown	$15,231,755.00	$13,862,929.09	1.098740
12	Williamson	City of Granger	$357,780.00	$46,734.21	7.655634
12	Williamson	City of Hutto	$3,812,970.00	$1,980,551.43	1.925206
12	Williamson	City of Jarrell	$208,178.00	$439,174.18	0.474021
12	Williamson, Travis	City of Leander	$9,761,592.00	$1,656,760.01	5.891977
12	Williamson	City of Liberty Hill	$326,803.00	$472,161.32	0.692143
12	Williamson, Travis	City of Pflugerville	$30,413,144.00	$4,171,220.94	7.291185
12	Williamson, Travis	City of Round Rock	$2,172,946.00	$67,029,667.41	0.032418
12	Williamson	City of Taylor	$6,013,107.00	$3,896,109.83	1.543362
12	Williamson	City of Thrall	$124,401.00	$26,139.28	4.759159
12	Williamson	City of Weir	$53,882.00	$12,164.38	4.429490
13	Cameron	City of Brownsville	$34,817,465.00	$33,686,132.61	1.033585
13	Cameron	City of Combes	$308,908.00	$53,144.78	5.812575
13	Cameron	City of Harlingen	$15,144,399.00	$19,677,365.84	0.769635
13	Cameron	City of La Feria	$1,245,607.00	$986,151.66	1.263099
13	Cameron	City of Laguna Vista	$905,657.00	$123,327.93	7.343487
13	Cameron	City of Los Fresnos	$1,044,184.00	$514,111.41	2.031046
13	Cameron	City of Palm Valley	$473,594.00	$43,770.61	10.819909
13	Cameron	City of Port Isabel	$1,849,141.00	$1,966,045.18	0.940538
13	Cameron	City of Primera	$558,884.00	$132,348.64	4.222816
13	Cameron	City of Rancho Viejo	$745,346.00	$60,067.32	12.408511
13	Cameron	City of Rio Hondo	$417,652.00	$149,013.29	2.802784
13	Cameron	City of San Benito	$3,791,385.00	$3,992,420.84	0.949646
13	Cameron	City of Santa Rosa	$172,920.00	$59,139.95	2.923912
13	Cameron	City of South Padre Island	$6,140,687.00	$2,403,511.62	2.554881
14	Nueces	City of Agua Dulce	$55,179.00	$28,936.86	1.906876
14	Nueces	City of Bishop	$668,206.00	$191,643.83	3.486708
14	Nueces	City of Corpus Christi	$78,473,461.00	$62,076,565.58	1.264140
14	Nueces	City of Driscoll	$118,531.00	$45,503.34	2.604886
14	Nueces	City of Port Aransas	$3,864,853.00	$1,335,480.81	2.893979
14	Nueces	City of Robstown	$2,291,628.00	$3,420,150.91	0.670037
15	Brazoria	Brazoria County	$81,314,274.00	$15,399,459.88	5.280333
15	Brazoria	City of Alvin	$7,312,087.00	$5,550,980.16	1.317261
15	Brazoria	City of Angleton	$4,887,109.00	$3,068,687.55	1.592573
15	Brazoria	City of Brazoria	$705,671.00	$754,055.44	0.935834
15	Brazoria	City of Brookside Village	$372,660.00	$33,484.78	11.129235
15	Brazoria	City of Clute	$2,006,931.00	$1,812,280.66	1.107406

TEXAS CENTER FOR ECONOMICS, LAW & POLICY

15	Brazoria	City of Danbury	$437,241.00	$51,084.87	8.559110
15	Brazoria	City of Freeport	$2,399,625.00	$1,903,555.61	1.260601
15	Brazoria	City of Holiday Lakes	$86,011.00	$8,319.97	10.337898
15	Brazoria	City of Jones Creek	$154,927.00	$52,828.60	2.932635
15	Brazoria	City of Lake Jackson	$5,666,890.00	$7,019,720.95	0.807281
15	Brazoria	City of Liverpool	$26,660.00	$21,259.10	1.254051
15	Brazoria	City of Manvel	$1,984,528.00	$1,008,161.99	1.968461
15	Brazoria	City of Oyster Creek	$239,861.00	$315,399.43	0.760499
15	Brazoria, Harris, Fort Bend	City of Pearland	$38,253,989.00	$18,717,188.67	2.043789
15	Brazoria	City of Quintana	$1,485.00	$6,017.28	0.246789
15	Brazoria	City of Richwood	$908,057.00	$286,713.95	3.167118
15	Brazoria	City of Surfside Beach	$560,122.00	$46,201.18	12.123543
15	Brazoria	City of Sweeny	$867,861.00	$347,081.54	2.500453
15	Brazoria	City of West Columbia	$991,168.00	$720,368.42	1.375918
16	Galveston	City of Bayou Vista	$514,525.00	$65,614.89	7.841589
16	Galveston	City of Dickinson	$3,136,368.00	$4,790,211.83	0.654745
16	Galveston, Harris	City of Friendswood	$13,197,006.00	$3,792,017.05	3.480207
16	Galveston	City of Galveston	$21,345,999.00	$16,965,085.13	1.258231
16	Galveston	City of Hitchcock	$1,544,467.00	$641,181.23	2.408784
16	Galveston	City of Jamaica Beach	$606,076.00	$80,954.34	7.486640
16	Galveston	City of Kemah	$628,255.00	$3,006,157.28	0.208989
16	Galveston	City of La Marque	$3,272,748.00	$3,219,583.97	1.016513
16	Galveston, Harris	City of League City	$30,993,445.00	$10,358,170.04	2.992174
16	Galveston	City of Santa Fe	$1,380,170.00	$1,783,971.90	0.773650
16	Galveston	City of Texas City	$26,098,116.00	$20,526,175.44	1.271455
17	Bell	Bell County	$52,341,759.00	$13,581,106.98	3.854013
17	Bell	City of Bartlett	$95,644.00	$61,310.31	1.559999
17	Bell	City of Belton	$4,548,867.00	$3,295,233.73	1.380438
17	Bell	City of Harker Heights	$8,553,869.00	$3,604,473.66	2.373126
17	Bell	City of Holland	$117,102.00	$57,782.54	2.026598
17	Bell	City of Killeen	$30,570,785.00	$19,233,876.81	1.589424
17	Bell	City of Nolanville	$669,515.00	$145,497.76	4.601549
17	Bell	City of Rogers	$217,059.00	$30,093.14	7.212906
17	Bell	City of Salado	$97,625.00	$357,682.26	0.272938
17	Bell	City of Temple	$18,063,763.00	$15,588,430.70	1.158793
17	Bell	City of Troy	$312,188.00	$173,233.26	1.802125
18	Lubbock	City of Idalou	$384,318.00	$97,031.89	3.960739
18	Lubbock	City of Lubbock	$52,247,474.00	$49,341,426.47	1.058897
18	Lubbock	City of New Deal	$140,622.00	$25,603.60	5.492275
18	Lubbock	City of Ransom Canyon	$665,963.00	$4,947.59	-34.603514
18	Lubbock	City of Shallowater	$506,779.00	$71,802.68	7.057940
18	Lubbock	City of Slaton	$1,067,434.00	$486,889.13	2.192355
18	Lubbock	City of Wolfforth	$1,125,910.00	$441,685.38	2.549122
18	Lubbock	Lubbock County	$45,864,361.00	$16,702,888.42	2.745894
19	Jefferson	City of Beaumont	$40,526,079.00	$38,636,269.00	1.048913
19	Jefferson	City of Bevil Oaks	$104,374.00	$15,324.04	6.811128
19	Jefferson	City of Groves	$4,217,195.00	$1,912,984.23	2.204511
19	Jefferson	City of Nederland	$4,955,410.00	$3,877,394.53	1.278026
19	Jefferson	City of Port Arthur	$13,919,608.00	$13,199,004.05	1.054595
19	Jefferson	City of Port Neches	$5,444,181.00	$1,138,892.45	4.780242
19	Jefferson	Jefferson County	$75,745,190.00	$24,131,865.51	3.138804
20	Webb	City of El Cenizo	$157,672.00	$12,361.96	12.754612
20	Webb	City of Laredo	$66,158,661.00	$32,762,178.36	2.019361
20	Webb	City of Rio Bravo	$333,983.00	$36,795.55	9.076723
20	Webb	Webb County	$57,241,570.00	$12,840,163.17	4.458010
21	McLennan	City of Bellmead	$783,990.00	$3,010,178.54	0.260446
21	McLennan	City of Beverly Hills	$229,673.00	$609,814.03	0.376628
21	McLennan	City of Crawford	$128,018.00	$47,319.15	2.705416

21	McLennan	City of Gholson	$57,764.00	$23,308.59	2.478228
21	McLennan	City of Hewitt	$2,831,415.00	$1,401,983.75	2.019578
21	McLennan	City of Lorena	$416,461.00	$245,135.27	1.698903
21	McLennan	City of Mart	$370,607.00	$107,672.86	3.441972
21	McLennan	City of Moody	$194,209.00	$32,753.96	5.929329
21	McLennan	City of Riesel	$78,204.00	$244,680.13	0.319617
21	McLennan	City of Robinson	$2,089,897.00	$906,182.57	2.306265
21	McLennan	City of Waco	$46,571,291.00	$28,081,494.18	1.658434
21	McLennan	City of West	$499,074.00	$372,770.29	1.338825
21	McLennan	City of Woodway	$3,545,206.00	$1,841,969.39	1.924682
21	McLennan	McLennan County	$46,790,326.00	$12,329,961.09	3.794848
22	Smith	City of Arp	$162,243.00	$85,539.51	1.896702
22	Smith	City of Bullard	$620,738.00	$226,427.67	2.741441
22	Smith	City of Lindale	$1,774,131.00	$1,978,838.38	0.896552
22	Smith	City of Overton	$29,808.00	$332,467.93	0.089657
22	Smith	City of Troup	$443,444.00	$260,853.54	1.699973
22	Smith	City of Tyler	$13,417,800.00	$37,534,024.42	0.357484
22	Smith	City of Whitehouse	$2,095,089.00	$577,157.50	3.630013
22	Smith	City of Winona	$52,856.00	$33,698.75	1.568485
22	Smith	Smith County	$38,802,286.00	$16,337,162.53	2.375093
23	Brazos	Brazos County	$48,827,914.00	$11,555,847.68	4.225386
23	Brazos	City of Bryan	$21,921,973.00	$13,801,372.06	1.588391
23	Brazos	City of College Station	$22,076,134.00	$18,837,146.62	1.171947
24	Johnson	City of Alvarado	$1,316,824.00	$1,181,659.37	1.114385
24	Johnson	City of Cleburne	$12,633,280.00	$10,646,871.54	1.186572
24	Johnson	City of Godley	$354,523.00	$638,840.77	0.554947
24	Johnson	City of Grandview	$466,186.00	$405,583.17	1.149421
24	Johnson	City of Joshua	$1,751,256.00	$1,067,020.68	1.641258
24	Johnson	City of Keene	$1,478,305.00	$414,692.34	3.564824
24	Johnson	City of Rio Vista	$169,209.00	$163,901.39	1.032383
24	Johnson, Ellis	City of Venus	$763,182.00	$251,644.41	3.032779
25	Hays	City of Buda	$1,118,547.00	$3,250,526.51	0.344113
25	Hays	City of Dripping Springs	$191,829.00	$722,197.41	0.265619
25	Hays	City of Hays	$12,396.00	$17,794.61	0.696615
25	Hays	City of Kyle	$4,716,232.00	$2,295,398.68	2.054646
25	Hays	City of Mountain City	$52,323.00	$4,115.76	12.712840
25	Hays	City of Niederwald	$34,581.00	$22,204.51	1.557386
25	Hays	City of San Marcos	$12,217,863.00	$18,382,874.13	0.664633
25	Hays	City of Uhland	$19,252.00	$32,317.42	0.595716
25	Hays	City of Woodcreek	$140,821.00	$42,628.55	3.303443
25	Hays	Hays County	$46,467,079.00	$9,758,657.29	4.761626
26	Ellis	City of Bardwell	$18,228.00	$11,178.07	1.630693
26	Ellis	City of Ennis	$8,694,524.00	$4,356,259.20	1.995869
26	Ellis	City of Ferris	$628,038.00	$271,882.04	2.309965
26	Ellis	City of Garrett	$38,665.00	$26,335.56	1.468167
26	Ellis	City of Italy	$565,906.00	$260,572.52	2.171779
26	Ellis	City of Maypearl	$205,146.00	$86,283.80	2.377573
26	Ellis	City of Midlothian	$13,436,453.00	$3,698,659.39	3.632790
26	Ellis	City of Milford	$84,840.00	$10,517.80	8.066326
26	Ellis	City of Oak Leaf	$338,373.00	$29,511.24	11.465902
26	Ellis, Dallas	City of Ovilla	$1,807,620.00	$162,134.07	11.148921
26	Ellis	City of Palmer	$389,048.00	$169,803.57	2.291165
26	Ellis	City of Pecan Hill	$94,673.00	$5,364.66	17.647530
26	Ellis	City of Red Oak	$3,594,001.00	$1,712,016.97	2.099279
26	Ellis	City of Waxahachie	$13,034,289.00	$10,934,925.72	1.191987
27	Ector	City of Goldsmith	$11,560.00	$209,406.49	0.055204
27	Ector	City of Odessa	$19,142,850.00	$24,951,525.76	0.767202
27	Ector	Ector County Hospital District	$5,528,695.00	$23,300,723.42	0.237276

28	Midland	City of Midland	$29,214,680.00	$39,487,873.86	0.739839
28	Midland	Midland County	$23,489,746.00	$20,851,281.82	1.126537
29	Wichita	City of Burkburnett	$2,360,948.00	$1,171,803.81	2.014798
29	Wichita	City of Electra	$527,193.00	$498,771.91	1.056982
29	Wichita	City of Iowa Park	$1,483,933.00	$667,265.30	2.223903
29	Wichita	City of Wichita Falls	$26,375,510.00	$28,408,793.50	0.928428
30	Taylor	City of Buffalo Gap	$40,707.00	$75,444.05	0.539565
30	Taylor	City of Lawn	$26,363.00	$6,586.28	4.002715
30	Taylor	City of Merkel	$431,830.00	$274,821.76	1.571309
30	Taylor	City of Trent	$10,026.00	$8,482.66	1.181941
30	Taylor	City of Tuscola	$53,414.00	$46,898.26	1.138934
30	Taylor	City of Tye	$177,868.00	$538,054.56	0.330576
31	Potter	City of Amarillo	$30,124,234.00	$59,442,045.37	0.506783
31	Potter	City of Canyon	$1,793,891.00	$2,108,469.41	0.850802
31	Potter	City of Happy	$4,250.00	$19,367.48	0.219440
32	Grayson	City of Bells	$227,144.00	$191,126.98	1.188446
32	Grayson	City of Collinsville	$130,871.00	$95,038.65	1.377029
32	Grayson	City of Denison	$5,645,727.00	$5,042,175.79	1.119701
32	Grayson	City of Gunter	$409,849.00	$112,202.87	3.652750
32	Grayson	City of Howe	$400,267.00	$187,330.78	2.136686
32	Grayson	City of Knollwood	$5,253.00	$22,486.05	0.233612
32	Grayson	City of Pottsboro	$503,317.00	$418,344.78	1.203115
32	Grayson	City of Sherman	$6,690,569.00	$14,175,283.86	0.471988
32	Grayson	City of Southmayd	$162,876.00	$494,121.88	0.329627
32	Grayson	City of Tioga	$186,741.00	$90,859.55	2.055271
32	Grayson	City of Tom Bean	$150,620.00	$38,457.75	3.916506
32	Grayson	City of Van Alstyne	$1,024,923.00	$595,868.39	1.720049
32	Grayson	City of Whitesboro	$598,895.00	$731,334.35	0.818907
32	Grayson	City of Whitewright	$326,055.00	$416,706.35	0.782457
33	Gregg	City of Clarksville	$302,578.00	$342,227.54	0.884143
33	Gregg	City of Easton	$12,712.00	$8,078.83	1.573495
33	Gregg	City of Gladewater	$1,218,416.00	$1,001,251.82	1.216893
33	Gregg	City of Kilgore	$3,954,912.00	$11,710,910.83	0.337712
33	Gregg	City of Lakeport	$184,318.00	$108,580.13	1.697530
33	Gregg	City of Longview	$23,722,647.00	$28,656,883.47	0.827817
33	Gregg	City of White Oak	$1,637,002.00	$985,610.18	1.660902
33	Gregg	Gregg County	$21,466,344.00	$14,857,802.83	1.444786
34	Guadalupe	City of Cibolo	$3,224,519.00	$710,382.17	4.539133
34	Guadalupe	City of Luling	$9,596.00	$1,035,423.27	0.009268
34	Guadalupe	City of Marion	$140,778.00	$115,516.47	1.218683
34	Guadalupe, Comal, Bexar	City of Schertz	$8,860,134.00	$6,264,333.20	1.414378
34	Guadalupe	City of Seguin	$5,890,658.00	$5,055,804.88	1.165128
34	Guadalupe	Guadalupe County	$29,936,492.00	$4,736,481.95	6.320407
36	Parker	City of Aledo	$629,692.00	$351,937.50	1.789215
36	Parker	City of Millsap	$42,494.00	$24,659.83	1.723207
36	Parker	City of Mineral Wells	$551,808.00	$4,767,055.17	0.115754
36	Parker	City of Reno (Parker Co.)	$417,338.00	$56,870.52	7.338389
36	Parker	City of Springtown	$875,585.00	$898,168.65	0.974856
36	Parker	City of Weatherford	$7,626,780.00	$8,899,445.09	0.856995
36	Parker	City of Willow Park	$1,452,792.00	$666,850.81	2.178586
36	Parker	Parker County	$31,172,032.00	$6,566,470.80	4.747152
37	Comal	City of Bulverde	$758,087.00	$854,963.19	0.886690
37	Comal	City of Fair Oaks Ranch	$130,712.00	$10,892.62	12.000051
37	Comal	City of Garden Ridge	$1,140,246.00	$172,341.28	6.616209
37	Comal, Guadalupe	City of New Braunfels	$15,520,969.00	$17,893,985.55	0.867385
37	Comal	Comal County	$31,557,508.00	$7,727,470.63	4.083808
37	Comal	Comal County Emergency Services District #3	$2,035,148.00	$905,273.78	2.248102
37	Comal	Comal County Emergency Services District #6	$319,450.00	$307,459.40	1.038999

38	Tom Green	City of San Angelo	$27,603,106.00	$19,784,960.18	1.395156
38	Tom Green	Tom Green County	$20,719,737.00	$6,578,545.20	3.149593
39	Kaufman, Dallas	City of Combine	$192,820.00	$23,486.86	8.209697
39	Kaufman	City of Crandall	$1,209,382.00	$356,161.64	3.395599
39	Kaufman	City of Forney	$6,308,290.00	$3,300,618.11	1.911245
39	Kaufman	City of Heath	$7,004.00	$724,776.77	0.009664
39	Kaufman	City of Kaufman	$1,743,006.00	$1,523,685.46	1.143941
39	Kaufman	City of Kemp	$275,637.00	$175,041.15	1.574698
39	Kaufman	City of Mabank	$674,019.00	$1,131,795.63	0.595531
39	Kaufman	City of Oak Ridge	$12,865.00	$80,768.04	0.159283
39	Kaufman	City of Terrell	$6,824,283.00	$7,200,897.16	0.947699
				Average:	6.687148
			Totals: $6,832,566,185.00	$3,742,032,505.94	

TABLE A2

Expanded Jurisdictions' Normalized Replacement Factors
(Current All-Industry Taxable Sales Base ($US))

Cnty Rank	County	Tax Jurisdiction	Property Tax Levy (2008)	Normalized Sales Tax Allocation (2008)	Adjusted RF
1	Harris	City of Baytown	22,755,668.00	9,437,067.00	2.411307242
1	Harris	City of Bellaire	11,645,491.00	2,261,630.19	5.149157918
1	Harris	City of Bunker Hill Village	3,456,771.00	71,217.80	48.538019989
1	Harris	City of Deer Park	11,836,630.00	4,171,743.09	2.837334358
1	Harris	City of El Lago	812,337.00	128,046.84	6.344061283
1	Harris	City of Galena Park	3,811,099.00	1,213,637.60	3.140228187
1	Harris	City of Hedwig Village	1,373,398.00	1,396,175.34	0.983685903
1	Harris	City of Hilshire Village	1,240,299.00	40,100.29	30.929925943
1	Harris	City of Humble	2,291,689.00	11,713,515.02	0.195644859
1	Harris	City of Hunters Creek Village	3,127,457.00	302,501.18	10.338660497
1	Harris	City of Jacinto City	2,691,813.00	602,504.96	4.467702639
1	Harris	City of Jersey Village	5,543,419.00	1,644,609.73	3.370659257
1	Harris	City of La Porte	15,971,521.00	3,098,593.93	5.154441461
1	Harris	City of Morgans Point	1,122,152.00	180,605.06	6.213292141
1	Harris	City of Nassau Bay	2,464,418.00	405,894.42	6.071573939
1	Harris	City of Pasadena	29,798,137.00	15,986,724.64	1.863930084
1	Harris	City of Piney Point Village	3,386,735.00	92,715.70	36.528171604
1	Harris	City of Seabrook	4,341,373.00	1,596,176.91	2.719857031
1	Harris	City of Shoreacres	607,925.00	67,861.49	8.958320839
1	Harris	City of South Houston	2,745,841.00	1,440,023.43	1.906802997
1	Harris	City of Southside Place	1,674,590.00	290,800.75	5.758547734
1	Harris	City of Spring Valley	3,307,145.00	1,195,773.11	2.765696078
1	Harris	City of Taylor Lake Village	1,012,845.00	43,927.64	23.057123032
1	Harris	City of Tomball	2,652,830.00	4,721,756.76	0.561831144
1	Harris	City of Waller	214,392.00	520,957.93	0.411534190
1	Harris	City of Webster	2,436,714.00	7,369,628.19	0.330642732
1	Harris	City of West University Place	13,715,506.00	1,062,798.59	12.905084867
1	Harris	Harris County	1,095,133,426.00	662,280,674.06	1.653579017
1	Harris	Harris County Emergency Services District #21	481,876.00	475,330.66	1.013770077
1	Harris	Harris County Emergency Services District #5	335,335.00	1,221,983.15	0.274418678
1	Harris	Harris County Emergency Services District #80	550,358.00	1,212,642.64	0.453850114
1	Harris, Fort Bend	City of Katy	6,071,412.00	7,967,102.76	0.762060210
1	Harris, Fort Bend, Montgomery	City of Houston	963,104,951.00	504,416,609.93	1.909344244
2	Dallas	City of Addison	16,748,125.00	10,654,091.08	1.571990034
2	Dallas	City of Balch Springs	4,552,022.00	2,524,710.37	1.802987802
2	Dallas	City of Cockrell Hill	654,545.00	179,656.38	3.643316202
2	Dallas	City of De Soto	21,567,876.00	3,472,360.43	6.211301054
2	Dallas	City of Duncanville	13,309,800.00	3,602,540.86	3.694559073
2	Dallas	City of Farmers Branch	20,447,707.00	13,167,777.63	1.552859380
2	Dallas	City of Highland Park	9,609,331.00	2,392,831.70	4.015882521
2	Dallas	City of Hutchins	1,391,954.00	644,287.92	2.160453358
2	Dallas	City of Irving	100,335,203.00	51,022,274.29	1.966498052
2	Dallas	City of Lancaster	13,493,595.00	2,779,885.14	4.854011711
2	Dallas	City of Rowlett	21,546,428.00	5,920,354.90	3.639381146
2	Dallas	City of Sunnyvale	2,495,140.00	1,044,875.84	2.387977504
2	Dallas	City of University Park	15,490,904.00	3,090,482.04	5.012455597

2	Dallas	City of Wilmer	674,445.00	170,935.33	3.945614988
2	Dallas	Dallas County	388,038,362.00	451,039,181.33	0.860320739
2	Dallas, Collin	City of Garland	78,693,954.00	22,059,916.21	3.567282543
2	Dallas, Collin	City of Richardson	56,008,881.00	23,041,843.35	2.430746540
2	Dallas, Collin	City of Sachse	7,366,665.00	10,442,147.21	0.705474157
2	Dallas, Collin, Denton	City of Dallas	670,443,483.00	227,067,964.29	2.952611502
2	Dallas, Denton	City of Coppell	31,330,600.00	10,275,687.43	3.049002826
2	Dallas, Denton Collin	City of Carrollton	58,429,252.00	21,836,423.02	2.675770292
2	Dallas, Ellis	City of Cedar Hill	20,138,143.00	6,142,901.47	3.278278695
2	Dallas, Ellis	City of Glenn Heights	2,965,146.00	235,384.84	12.597013470
2	Dallas, Kaufman	City of Mesquite	42,376,457.00	16,944,235.94	2.500936433
2	Dallas, Kaufman	City of Seagoville	3,160,386.00	1,387,067.34	2.278466171
2	Dallas, Tarrant, Ellis	City of Grand Prairie	66,292,699.00	21,883,297.44	3.029374306
3	Tarrant	City of Arlington	119,903,861.00	46,772,260.89	2.563567780
3	Tarrant	City of Bedford	13,740,400.00	4,792,596.79	2.867005217
3	Tarrant	City of Benbrook	9,769,989.00	1,748,117.69	5.588862280
3	Tarrant	City of Blue Mound	483,059.00	104,637.36	4.616505997
3	Tarrant	City of Colleyville	13,066,166.00	2,502,884.81	5.220442413
3	Tarrant	City of Dalworthington Gardens	808,539.00	213,528.11	3.786569306
3	Tarrant	City of Edgecliff Village	562,946.00	71,611.48	7.861113888
3	Tarrant	City of Euless	12,975,885.00	7,211,725.81	1.799275976
3	Tarrant	City of Everman	1,220,887.00	269,224.97	4.534820895
3	Tarrant	City of Forest Hill	3,980,780.00	1,186,265.97	3.355723012
3	Tarrant	City of Haltom City	10,182,944.00	5,039,961.63	2.020440779
3	Tarrant	City of Hurst	12,789,781.00	10,070,043.86	1.270081956
3	Tarrant	City of Keller	16,807,193.00	4,567,776.68	3.679512855
3	Tarrant	City of Kennedale	3,563,291.00	666,433.33	5.346807950
3	Tarrant	City of Lake Worth	1,344,833.00	3,272,812.26	0.410910523
3	Tarrant	City of Lakeside	111,658,241.00	81,989.10	1361.866894502
3	Tarrant	City of North Richland Hills	21,767,577.00	8,813,429.19	2.469819243
3	Tarrant	City of Pantego	965,011.00	1,167,066.38	0.826868994
3	Tarrant	City of Pelican Bay	222,336.00	4,174.49	53.260637826
3	Tarrant	City of Richland Hills	2,120,553.00	1,608,795.48	1.318099796
3	Tarrant	City of River Oaks	1,865,998.00	313,306.98	5.955813688
3	Tarrant	City of Saginaw	5,281,554.00	3,072,522.10	1.718963714
3	Tarrant	City of Sansom Park	612,987.00	171,606.01	3.572060140
3	Tarrant	City of Watauga	6,090,935.00	2,600,211.76	2.342476522
3	Tarrant	City of Westworth Village	722,525.00	916,359.63	0.788473186
3	Tarrant	City of White Settlement	3,858,108.00	1,868,786.36	2.064499229
3	Tarrant	Tarrant County	329,368,255.00	225,361,849.22	1.461508486
3	Tarrant, Dallas, Denton	City of Grapevine	22,461,118.00	22,919,458.37	0.980002129
3	Tarrant, Denton	City of Fort Worth	356,015,812.00	106,259,647.55	3.350432833
3	Tarrant, Denton	City of Haslet	1,449,917.00	433,349.15	3.345840223
3	Tarrant, Denton	City of Southlake	10,518,520.00	9,679,767.27	1.086650093
3	Tarrant, Johnson	City of Crowley	4,040,146.00	880,761.07	4.587107812
3	Tarrant, Johnson, Ellis	City of Mansfield	29,304,002.00	7,249,161.73	4.042398709
3	Tarrant, Parker	City of Azle	4,183,151.00	1,720,778.62	2.430964077
4	Bexar	Bexar County	319,364,761.00	205,385,342.14	1.554954008
4	Bexar	Cibolo Canyon Special Improvement District	983,622.00	22,776.33	43.186156152
4	Bexar	City of Alamo Heights	4,835,020.00	791,758.82	6.106682841
4	Bexar	City of Balcones Heights	1,110,115.00	1,288,256.57	0.861718873
4	Bexar	City of Castle Hills	2,066,647.00	804,554.66	2.568684408
4	Bexar	City of China Grove	68,154.00	96,624.85	0.705346502
4	Bexar	City of Converse	3,890,498.00	1,489,324.00	2.612257642
4	Bexar	City of Elmendorf	93,397.00	53,198.26	1.755640128
4	Bexar	City of Grey Forest	32,828.00	18,015.20	1.822238998

4	Bexar	City of Helotes	2,575,260.00	486,765.57	5.290554922
4	Bexar	City of Hill Country Village	264,347.00	608,645.02	0.434320485
4	Bexar	City of Hollywood Park	1,524,245.00	430,302.82	3.542261279
4	Bexar	City of Kirby	1,352,227.00	172,237.10	7.850962606
4	Bexar	City of Leon Valley	3,670,396.00	1,840,217.29	1.994544894
4	Bexar	City of Live Oak	3,240,789.00	2,741,297.35	1.182209951
4	Bexar	City of Lytle	2,247.00	322,359.39	0.006970481
4	Bexar	City of Olmos Park	2,401,309.00	396,209.50	6.060705319
4	Bexar	City of San Antonio	414,315,114.00	191,830,173.51	2.159801591
4	Bexar	City of Shavano Park	2,346,924.00	157,890.74	14.864228263
4	Bexar	City of Somerset	235,718.00	104,648.52	2.252473327
4	Bexar	City of Terrell Hills	4,406,026.00	161,844.90	27.223755583
4	Bexar	City of Universal City	4,857,584.00	1,323,238.14	3.670982472
4	Bexar	City of Windcrest	2,051,283.00	1,240,217.19	1.653970787
4	Bexar, Guadalupe, Comal	City of Selma	1,466,842.00	2,614,074.53	0.561132432
5	Travis	City of Bee Cave	163,658.00	2,823,555.38	0.057961675
5	Travis	City of Briarcliff	194,851.00	30,003.30	6.494318958
5	Travis	City of Creedmoor	78,750.00	111,431.64	0.706711307
5	Travis	City of Elgin	312,835.00	801,716.99	0.390206273
5	Travis	City of Jonestown	2,037,212.00	106,800.57	19.074916922
5	Travis	City of Lago Vista	3,870,154.00	296,443.60	13.055279318
5	Travis	City of Lakeway	4,246,346.00	1,381,878.98	3.072878359
5	Travis	City of Manor	1,466,735.00	387,028.97	3.789729229
5	Travis	City of Mustang Ridge	130,603.00	32,067.86	4.072707066
5	Travis	City of Point Venture	90,790.00	31,924.11	2.843932063
5	Travis	City of Rollingwood	502,032.00	377,323.13	1.330509488
5	Travis	City of Volente	186,845.00	39,719.06	4.704164701
5	Travis	City of Webberville	46,113.00	9,578.03	4.814456300
5	Travis	Travis County	394,444,444.00	149,153,992.13	2.644544999
5	Travis	Travis County Emergency Services District #11	667,063.00	1,137,695.72	0.586328126
5	Travis	Travis County Emergency Services District #2	5,765,793.00	5,420,162.34	1.063767584
5	Travis	Travis County Emergency Services District #3	2,011,926.00	765,742.25	2.627419361
5	Travis	Travis County Emergency Services District #4	1,618,619.00	1,199,774.95	1.349102180
5	Travis	Travis County Emergency Services District #8	1,352,059.00	107,261.16	12.605299066
5	Travis, Williamson, Hays	City of Austin	309,093,265.00	147,051,782.33	2.101934843
6	Collin	City of Allen	39,057,659.00	10,078,089.75	3.875502200
6	Collin	City of Anna	2,207,496.00	353,871.49	6.238129077
6	Collin	City of Blue Ridge	152,129.00	35,935.52	4.233388613
6	Collin	City of Fairview	35,179,810.00	293,231.25	119.972924441
6	Collin	City of Farmersville	879,294.00	251,983.07	3.489496338
6	Collin	City of Josephine	133,559.00	16,003.76	8.345476313
6	Collin	City of Lavon	597,523.00	74,187.29	8.054250625
6	Collin	City of Lowry Crossing	217,104.00	35,264.93	6.156371216
6	Collin	City of Lucas	1,901,585.00	163,132.62	11.656681539
6	Collin	City of McKinney	61,834,900.00	16,796,011.74	3.681522791
6	Collin	City of Melissa	2,074,957.00	696,511.35	2.979071360
6	Collin	City of Murphy	7,321,275.00	624,811.82	11.717568113
6	Collin	City of Nevada	61,568.00	26,802.36	2.297111150
6	Collin	City of New Hope	75,197.00	17,810.54	4.222050539
6	Collin	City of Parker	1,849,422.00	133,145.56	13.890226606
6	Collin	City of Princeton	2,006,014.00	369,170.84	5.433836614
6	Collin	City of Royse City	495,906.00	544,729.02	0.910371913
6	Collin	City of Saint Paul	314,556.00	30,054.52	10.466179463
6	Collin	City of Weston	79,346.00	3,101.48	25.583269923
6	Collin	Collin County	173,926,405.00	95,202,832.83	1.826903673
6	Collin, Dallas	City of Wylie	19,908,149.00	2,603,584.46	7.646438710

6	Collin, Denton	City of Celina	2,980,969.00	286,448.37	10.406653737
6	Collin, Denton	City of Frisco	61,152,866.00	19,904,627.00	3.072293995
6	Collin, Denton	City of Plano	122,477,976.00	64,180,104.26	1.908348037
6	Collin, Denton	City of Prosper	5,177,422.00	871,230.81	5.942652556
7	Hidalgo	City of Alamo	2,756,681.00	1,432,035.37	1.925009017
7	Hidalgo	City of Alton	971,438.00	231,408.71	4.197931876
7	Hidalgo	City of Donna	3,329,430.00	787,377.19	4.228507078
7	Hidalgo	City of Edcouch	376,824.00	92,744.25	4.063044340
7	Hidalgo	City of Edinburg	19,025,142.00	7,107,682.24	2.676701259
7	Hidalgo	City of Elsa	904,137.00	306,297.32	2.951828030
7	Hidalgo	City of Granjeno	13,847.00	4,485.69	3.086927541
7	Hidalgo	City of Hidalgo	1,546,389.00	895,084.50	1.727645826
7	Hidalgo	City of La Joya	598,454.00	193,864.89	3.086964408
7	Hidalgo	City of La Villa	279,149.00	38,785.63	7.197227427
7	Hidalgo	City of McAllen	31,890,678.00	29,432,399.82	1.083522859
7	Hidalgo	City of Mercedes	3,445,145.00	2,865,037.32	1.202478228
7	Hidalgo	City of Mission	17,124,534.00	6,531,126.37	2.621987852
7	Hidalgo	City of Palmview	770,930.00	484,646.03	1.590707357
7	Hidalgo	City of Penitas	356,490.00	142,696.20	2.498244522
7	Hidalgo	City of Pharr	14,584,419.00	5,709,147.82	2.554570222
7	Hidalgo	City of Progreso	261,969.00	104,694.05	2.502233890
7	Hidalgo	City of San Juan	5,047,450.00	1,276,400.35	3.954441097
7	Hidalgo	City of Weslaco	9,281,021.00	4,490,640.47	2.066747733
7	Hidalgo	Hidalgo County	159,961,800.00	54,249,623.56	2.948625069
8	El Paso	City of Anthony	521,365.00	402,443.63	1.295498204
8	El Paso	City of Clint	159,080.00	53,305.06	2.984332069
8	El Paso	City of El Paso	182,526,356.00	67,821,673.07	2.691268849
8	El Paso	City of Horizon City	1,773,283.00	329,023.26	5.389536898
8	El Paso	City of Socorro	3,550,210.00	932,713.65	3.806323624
8	El Paso	City of Vinton	223,685.00	228,405.05	0.979334739
8	El Paso	El Paso County	111,493,605.00	71,018,023.14	1.569933942
8	El Paso	El Paso Emergency Medical Services District #2	2,457,901.00	3,520,015.18	0.698264318
9	Denton	City of Argyle	1,504,706.00	268,551.95	5.603035122
9	Denton	City of Aubrey	677,835.00	300,261.46	2.257482566
9	Denton	City of Bartonville	431,162.00	95,835.26	4.498991424
9	Denton	City of Copper Canyon	305,838.00	174,167.80	1.755996229
9	Denton	City of Corinth	8,175,924.00	1,024,334.22	7.981695640
9	Denton	City of Corral City	12,221.00	66,143.72	0.184764328
9	Denton	City of Denton	41,856,644.00	13,697,558.55	3.055774052
9	Denton	City of Double Oak	742,335.00	95,036.70	7.811035105
9	Denton	City of Hackberry	94,442.00	24,521.10	3.851458540
9	Denton	City of Hickory Creek	1,439,118.00	781,365.16	1.841799550
9	Denton	City of Highland Village	9,210,527.00	1,812,704.29	5.081097360
9	Denton	City of Justin	1,144,732.00	601,733.13	1.902391514
9	Denton	City of Krugerville	264,605.00	33,949.85	7.793996144
9	Denton	City of Krum	1,138,481.00	144,187.01	7.895864085
9	Denton	City of Lake Dallas	2,315,475.00	541,414.57	4.276713538
9	Denton	City of Little Elm	8,702,529.00	1,378,515.85	6.312969851
9	Denton	City of Northlake	634,970.00	202,348.23	3.138006199
9	Denton	City of Oak Point	1,417,196.00	72,083.72	19.660417082
9	Denton	City of Pilot Point	1,294,144.00	390,022.71	3.318124732
9	Denton	City of Ponder	404,029.00	113,659.38	3.554735120
9	Denton	City of Sanger	2,112,387.00	436,185.36	4.842865428
9	Denton	City of Shady Shores	619,366.00	62,643.10	9.887218225
9	Denton	City of The Colony	14,705,317.00	2,958,375.50	4.970740530
9	Denton	Denton County	123,891,269.00	51,262,463.72	2.416802861

9	Denton, Dallas	City of Lewisville	29,908,774.00	18,812,825.33	1.589807670
9	Denton, Tarrant	City of Flower Mound	30,813,577.00	8,735,126.09	3.527548049
9	Denton, Tarrant	City of Roanoke	4,665,433.00	4,236,144.82	1.101339354
9	Denton, Tarrant	City of Trophy Club	3,594,948.00	479,083.01	7.503810326
10	Fort Bend	City of Arcola	634,075.00	263,982.31	2.401960192
10	Fort Bend	City of Beasley	84,152.00	40,527.77	2.076403670
10	Fort Bend	City of Fulshear	190,201.00	178,004.61	1.068517270
10	Fort Bend	City of Kendleton	84,740.00	19,045.23	4.449408067
10	Fort Bend	City of Meadows Place	2,265,713.00	527,898.89	4.291944997
10	Fort Bend	City of Needville	512,550.00	204,840.34	2.502192683
10	Fort Bend	City of Orchard	49,129.00	22,871.43	2.148051553
10	Fort Bend	City of Richmond	3,109,598.00	1,845,328.84	1.685118626
10	Fort Bend	City of Rosenberg	7,603,807.00	5,353,824.09	1.420257161
10	Fort Bend	City of Simonton	129,238.00	42,450.94	3.044408153
10	Fort Bend	City of Sugar Land	26,245,626.00	19,769,636.86	1.327572489
10	Fort Bend	Fort Bend County	190,736,711.00	47,382,746.59	4.025446491
10	Fort Bend, Harris	City of Missouri City	22,915,240.00	5,751,816.15	3.984000775
11	Montgomery	City of Conroe	13,527,579.00	15,397,641.96	0.878548744
11	Montgomery	City of Magnolia	385,477.00	972,865.48	0.396228471
11	Montgomery	City of Montgomery	246,274.00	644,805.35	0.381935420
11	Montgomery	City of Oak Ridge North	1,440,187.00	839,587.92	1.715349835
11	Montgomery	City of Patton Village	59,777.00	17,780.98	3.361850697
11	Montgomery	City of Shenandoah	1,577,421.00	2,809,440.18	0.561471645
11	Montgomery	City of Splendora	109,089.00	192,131.70	0.567782412
11	Montgomery	City of Stagecoach	133,574.00	11,052.72	12.085169985
11	Montgomery	City of Willis	673,192.00	778,059.07	0.865219660
11	Montgomery	Montgomery County	146,759,893.00	51,269,348.83	2.862526955
11	Montgomery	Montgomery County Emergency Services District #12	256,344.00	339,120.58	0.755908120
11	Montgomery	Montgomery County Emergency Services District #3	1,304,804.00	483,919.46	2.696324743
11	Montgomery	Montgomery County Emergency Services District #6	1,393,324.00	2,260,128.56	0.616479976
11	Montgomery	Montgomery County Emergency Services District #7	655,565.00	582,672.18	1.125100910
11	Montgomery	Montgomery County Emergency Services District #9	374,525.00	309,015.04	1.211996025
12	Williamson	City of Florence	184,778.00	71,264.70	2.592840599
12	Williamson	City of Georgetown	15,231,755.00	6,931,464.55	2.197480042
12	Williamson	City of Granger	357,780.00	46,734.21	7.655633849
12	Williamson	City of Hutto	3,812,970.00	990,275.72	3.850412509
12	Williamson	City of Jarrell	208,178.00	219,587.09	0.948042984
12	Williamson	City of Liberty Hill	326,803.00	269,806.47	1.211249685
12	Williamson	City of Taylor	6,013,107.00	1,948,054.92	3.086723559
12	Williamson	City of Thrall	124,401.00	26,139.28	4.759159395
12	Williamson	City of Weir	53,882.00	12,164.38	4.429490036
12	Williamson	Williamson County	156,664,266.00	51,172,626.15	3.061485755
12	Williamson, Travis	City of Cedar Park	19,699,598.00	6,830,111.57	2.884227849
12	Williamson, Travis	City of Leander	9,761,592.00	1,656,760.01	5.891977076
12	Williamson, Travis	City of Pflugerville	30,413,144.00	2,780,813.96	10.936777662
12	Williamson, Travis	City of Round Rock	2,172,946.00	33,514,833.71	0.064835351
13	Cameron	Cameron County	54,590,290.00	27,320,374.66	1.998153052
13	Cameron	City of Brownsville	34,817,465.00	16,843,066.31	2.067169028
13	Cameron	City of Combes	308,908.00	53,144.78	5.812574631
13	Cameron	City of Harlingen	15,144,399.00	9,838,682.92	1.539270970
13	Cameron	City of La Feria	1,245,607.00	493,075.83	2.526197644
13	Cameron	City of Laguna Vista	905,657.00	82,218.62	11.015229883
13	Cameron	City of Los Fresnos	1,044,184.00	257,055.71	4.062092300
13	Cameron	City of Palm Valley	473,594.00	43,770.61	10.819908610
13	Cameron	City of Port Isabel	1,849,141.00	983,022.59	1.881076812
13	Cameron	City of Primera	558,884.00	66,174.32	8.445632687

13	Cameron	City of Rancho Viejo	745,346.00	60,067.32	12.408510984
13	Cameron	City of Rio Hondo	417,652.00	74,506.65	5.605567128
13	Cameron	City of San Benito	3,791,385.00	1,996,210.42	1.899291258
13	Cameron	City of Santa Rosa	172,920.00	59,139.95	2.923911840
13	Cameron	City of South Padre Island	6,140,687.00	1,201,755.81	5.109762690
14	Nueces	City of Agua Dulce	55,179.00	28,936.86	1.906875867
14	Nueces	City of Bishop	668,206.00	127,762.55	5.230061411
14	Nueces	City of Corpus Christi	78,473,461.00	45,146,593.15	1.738192309
14	Nueces	City of Driscoll	118,531.00	30,335.56	3.907328561
14	Nueces	City of Port Aransas	3,864,853.00	890,320.54	4.340968029
14	Nueces	City of Robstown	2,291,628.00	2,280,100.61	1.005055651
14	Nueces	Nueces County	67,677,701.00	41,751,782.15	1.620953586
15	Brazoria	Brazoria County	81,314,274.00	30,798,919.76	2.640166429
15	Brazoria	City of Alvin	7,312,087.00	3,700,653.44	1.975890777
15	Brazoria	City of Angleton	4,887,109.00	2,045,791.70	2.388859531
15	Brazoria	City of Brazoria	705,671.00	502,703.63	1.403751560
15	Brazoria	City of Brookside Village	372,660.00	33,484.78	11.129235432
15	Brazoria	City of Clute	2,006,931.00	1,208,187.11	1.661109433
15	Brazoria	City of Danbury	437,241.00	51,084.87	8.559109576
15	Brazoria	City of Freeport	2,399,625.00	1,269,037.07	1.890902205
15	Brazoria	City of Holiday Lakes	86,011.00	8,319.97	10.337897853
15	Brazoria	City of Jones Creek	154,927.00	52,828.60	2.932634974
15	Brazoria	City of Lake Jackson	5,666,890.00	4,679,813.97	1.210922067
15	Brazoria	City of Liverpool	26,660.00	21,259.10	1.254051206
15	Brazoria	City of Manvel	1,984,528.00	672,107.99	2.952692156
15	Brazoria	City of Oyster Creek	239,861.00	210,266.29	1.140748732
15	Brazoria	City of Quintana	1,485.00	6,017.28	0.246789247
15	Brazoria	City of Richwood	908,057.00	229,371.16	3.958897884
15	Brazoria	City of Surfside Beach	560,122.00	46,201.18	12.123543165
15	Brazoria	City of Sweeny	867,861.00	231,387.69	3.750679163
15	Brazoria	City of West Columbia	991,168.00	480,245.61	2.063877259
15	Brazoria, Harris, Fort Bend	City of Pearland	38,253,989.00	12,478,125.78	3.065683875
16	Galveston	City of Bayou Vista	514,525.00	37,494.22	13.722780759
16	Galveston	City of Dickinson	3,136,368.00	3,193,474.55	0.982117737
16	Galveston	City of Galveston	21,345,999.00	8,482,542.57	2.516462350
16	Galveston	City of Hitchcock	1,544,467.00	320,590.62	4.817567726
16	Galveston	City of Jamaica Beach	606,076.00	80,954.34	7.486640000
16	Galveston	City of Kemah	628,255.00	1,503,078.64	0.417978796
16	Galveston	City of La Marque	3,272,748.00	1,609,791.99	2.033025404
16	Galveston	City of Santa Fe	1,380,170.00	891,985.95	1.547300156
16	Galveston	City of Texas City	26,098,116.00	10,263,087.72	2.542910741
16	Galveston	City of Tiki Island	549,284.00	6,672.44	82.321309746
16	Galveston	Galveston County	122,071,933.00	25,522,493.04	4.782915713
16	Galveston, Harris	City of Friendswood	13,197,006.00	2,528,011.37	5.220311180
16	Galveston, Harris	City of League City	30,993,445.00	5,918,954.31	5.236304148
17	Bell	Bell County	52,341,759.00	27,162,213.96	1.927006358
17	Bell	City of Bartlett	95,644.00	61,310.31	1.559998636
17	Bell	City of Belton	4,548,867.00	2,196,822.49	2.070657519
17	Bell	City of Harker Heights	8,553,869.00	2,402,982.44	3.559688518
17	Bell	City of Holland	117,102.00	46,226.03	2.533247933
17	Bell	City of Killeen	30,570,785.00	12,822,584.54	2.384135968
17	Bell	City of Nolanville	669,515.00	116,398.21	5.751935631
17	Bell	City of Rogers	217,059.00	30,093.14	7.212906330
17	Bell	City of Salado	97,625.00	357,682.26	0.272937774
17	Bell	City of Temple	18,063,763.00	10,392,287.13	1.738189368

17	Bell	City of Troy	312,188.00	115,488.84	2.703187598
18	Lubbock	City of Abernathy	79,052.00	45,924.14	1.721360487
18	Lubbock	City of Idalou	384,318.00	97,031.89	3.960739093
18	Lubbock	City of Lubbock	52,247,474.00	32,894,284.31	1.588345060
18	Lubbock	City of New Deal	140,622.00	17,069.07	8.238411786
18	Lubbock	City of Ransom Canyon	665,963.00	9,895.18	67.301757017
18	Lubbock	City of Shallowater	506,779.00	71,802.68	7.057939899
18	Lubbock	City of Slaton	1,067,434.00	324,592.75	3.288533059
18	Lubbock	City of Wolfforth	1,125,910.00	294,456.92	3.823683274
18	Lubbock	Lubbock County	45,864,361.00	33,405,776.84	1.372946997
19	Jefferson	City of Beaumont	40,526,079.00	25,757,512.67	1.573369274
19	Jefferson	City of Bevil Oaks	104,374.00	15,324.04	6.811128136
19	Jefferson	City of Groves	4,217,195.00	1,275,322.82	3.306766674
19	Jefferson	City of Nederland	4,955,410.00	2,584,929.69	1.917038605
19	Jefferson	City of Port Arthur	13,919,608.00	8,799,336.03	1.581892991
19	Jefferson	City of Port Neches	5,444,181.00	759,261.63	7.170362311
19	Jefferson	Jefferson County	75,745,190.00	48,263,731.02	1.569401876
20	Webb	City of El Cenizo	157,672.00	12,361.96	12.754611728
20	Webb	City of Laredo	66,158,661.00	26,209,742.69	2.524201088
20	Webb	City of Rio Bravo	333,983.00	36,795.55	9.076722593
20	Webb	Webb County	57,241,570.00	25,680,326.34	2.229004774
21	McLennan	City of Bellmead	783,990.00	2,006,785.69	0.390669518
21	McLennan	City of Beverly Hills	229,673.00	406,542.69	0.564941905
21	McLennan	City of Crawford	128,018.00	31,546.10	4.058124459
21	McLennan	City of Gholson	57,764.00	15,539.06	3.717341976
21	McLennan	City of Hewitt	2,831,415.00	934,655.83	3.029366425
21	McLennan	City of Lorena	416,461.00	163,423.51	2.548354221
21	McLennan	City of Mart	370,607.00	86,138.29	4.302465357
21	McLennan	City of Moody	194,209.00	32,753.96	5.929328851
21	McLennan	City of Riesel	78,204.00	195,744.10	0.399521612
21	McLennan	City of Robinson	2,089,897.00	604,121.71	3.459397260
21	McLennan	City of Waco	46,571,291.00	18,720,996.12	2.487650267
21	McLennan	City of West	499,074.00	248,513.53	2.008236762
21	McLennan	City of Woodway	3,545,206.00	1,227,979.59	2.887023546
21	McLennan	McLennan County	46,790,326.00	24,659,922.18	1.897423911
22	Smith	City of Arp	162,243.00	85,539.51	1.896702471
22	Smith	City of Bullard	620,738.00	150,951.78	4.112160850
22	Smith	City of Lindale	1,774,131.00	1,319,225.59	1.344827615
22	Smith	City of Overton	29,808.00	221,645.29	0.134485152
22	Smith	City of Troup	443,444.00	173,902.36	2.549959644
22	Smith	City of Tyler	13,417,800.00	25,022,682.95	0.536225473
22	Smith	City of Whitehouse	2,095,089.00	384,771.67	5.445018907
22	Smith	City of Winona	52,856.00	22,465.83	2.352728217
22	Smith	Smith County	38,802,286.00	32,674,325.06	1.187546672
23	Brazos	Brazos County	48,827,914.00	23,111,695.36	2.112692870
23	Brazos	City of Bryan	21,921,973.00	9,200,914.71	2.382586264
23	Brazos	City of College Station	22,076,134.00	12,558,097.75	1.757920224
24	Johnson	City of Alvarado	1,316,824.00	590,829.69	2.228770885
24	Johnson	City of Cleburne	12,633,280.00	7,097,914.36	1.779858048
24	Johnson	City of Godley	354,523.00	319,420.39	1.109894724
24	Johnson	City of Grandview	466,186.00	202,791.59	2.298842923
24	Johnson	City of Joshua	1,751,256.00	533,510.34	3.282515574
24	Johnson	City of Keene	1,478,305.00	207,346.17	7.129647005
24	Johnson	City of Rio Vista	169,209.00	109,267.59	1.548574420
24	Johnson	Johnson County	42,393,245.00	12,964,331.17	3.269990904
24	Johnson, Ellis	City of Venus	763,182.00	143,796.81	5.307364070

24	Johnson, Tarrant	City of Burleson	13,937,164.00	5,692,804.46	2.448207048
25	Hays	City of Buda	1,118,547.00	2,167,017.67	0.516168841
25	Hays	City of Dripping Springs	191,829.00	577,757.93	0.332023138
25	Hays	City of Hays	12,396.00	17,794.61	0.696615436
25	Hays	City of Kyle	4,716,232.00	1,530,265.79	3.081969185
25	Hays	City of Mountain City	52,323.00	4,115.76	12.712840399
25	Hays	City of Niederwald	34,581.00	22,204.51	1.557386315
25	Hays	City of San Marcos	12,217,863.00	12,255,249.42	0.996949355
25	Hays	City of Uhland	19,252.00	32,317.42	0.595715871
25	Hays	City of Woodcreek	140,821.00	42,628.55	3.303443350
25	Hays	Hays County	46,467,079.00	19,517,314.58	2.380813140
26	Ellis	City of Bardwell	18,228.00	11,178.07	1.630692955
26	Ellis	City of Ennis	8,694,524.00	2,904,172.80	2.993803950
26	Ellis	City of Garrett	38,665.00	26,335.56	1.468166995
26	Ellis	City of Italy	565,906.00	130,286.26	4.343558561
26	Ellis	City of Maypearl	205,146.00	57,522.53	3.566358923
26	Ellis	City of Midlothian	13,436,453.00	1,849,329.70	7.265580084
26	Ellis	City of Milford	84,840.00	10,517.80	8.066325657
26	Ellis	City of Oak Leaf	338,373.00	16,863.57	20.065329346
26	Ellis	City of Palmer	389,048.00	84,901.79	4.582330042
26	Ellis	City of Pecan Hill	94,673.00	5,364.66	17.647530319
26	Ellis	City of Red Oak	3,594,001.00	856,008.49	4.198557681
26	Ellis	City of Waxahachie	13,034,289.00	5,467,462.86	2.383973944
26	Ellis	Ellis County	40,457,240.00	9,602,906.40	4.213020341
26	Ellis, Dallas	City of Ferris	628,038.00	135,941.02	4.619930026
26	Ellis, Dallas	City of Ovilla	1,807,620.00	162,134.07	11.148921383
27	Ector	City of Goldsmith	11,560.00	209,406.49	0.055203638
27	Ector	City of Odessa	19,142,850.00	19,961,220.61	0.959001976
27	Ector	Ector County	34,267,631.00	27,204,729.22	1.259620367
27	Ector	Ector County Hospital District	5,528,695.00	31,067,631.23	0.177956760
28	Midland	City of Midland	29,214,680.00	26,325,249.24	1.109758914
28	Midland	Midland County	23,489,746.00	41,702,563.64	0.563268633
29	Wichita	City of Burkburnett	2,360,948.00	585,901.91	4.029596046
29	Wichita	City of Electra	527,193.00	249,385.96	2.113964277
29	Wichita	City of Iowa Park	1,483,933.00	333,632.65	4.447805093
29	Wichita	City of Wichita Falls	26,375,510.00	14,204,396.75	1.856855343
29	Wichita	Wichita County	26,852,904.00	13,042,896.01	2.058814544
30	Taylor	City of Abilene	32,557,861.00	14,652,360.48	2.222021567
30	Taylor	City of Buffalo Gap	40,707.00	37,722.03	1.079130826
30	Taylor	City of Lawn	26,363.00	6,586.28	4.002714734
30	Taylor	City of Merkel	431,830.00	137,410.88	3.142618692
30	Taylor	City of Trent	10,026.00	8,482.66	1.181940571
30	Taylor	City of Tuscola	53,414.00	37,518.61	1.423666891
30	Taylor	City of Tye	177,868.00	269,027.28	0.661152282
30	Taylor	Taylor County	29,273,799.00	15,666,780.78	1.868526752
31	Potter	City of Amarillo	30,124,234.00	29,721,022.69	1.013566536
31	Potter	City of Canyon	1,793,891.00	1,054,234.71	1.701604957
31	Potter	City of Happy	4,250.00	19,367.48	0.219440010
31	Potter	Potter County	36,552,270.00	21,256,277.74	1.719598814
32	Grayson	City of Bells	227,144.00	95,563.49	2.376891007
32	Grayson	City of Collinsville	130,871.00	47,519.33	2.754058480
32	Grayson	City of Denison	5,645,727.00	2,521,087.90	2.239401098
32	Grayson	City of Gunter	409,849.00	56,101.44	7.305499405
32	Grayson	City of Howe	400,267.00	93,665.39	4.273371413
32	Grayson	City of Knollwood	5,253.00	22,486.05	0.233611506
32	Grayson	City of Pottsboro	503,317.00	209,172.39	2.406230574

32	Grayson	City of Sherman	6,690,569.00	8,100,162.21	0.825979632
32	Grayson	City of Southmayd	162,876.00	395,297.50	0.412033970
32	Grayson	City of Tioga	186,741.00	45,429.78	4.110542040
32	Grayson	City of Tom Bean	150,620.00	38,457.75	3.916505776
32	Grayson	City of Van Alstyne	1,024,923.00	297,934.20	3.440098576
32	Grayson	City of Whitesboro	598,895.00	365,667.18	1.637814496
32	Grayson	City of Whitewright	326,055.00	208,353.18	1.564914957
32	Grayson	Grayson County	29,524,189.00	10,581,520.90	2.790164975
33	Gregg	City of Clarksville	302,578.00	228,151.69	1.326214132
33	Gregg	City of Easton	12,712.00	8,078.83	1.573495172
33	Gregg	City of Gladewater	1,218,416.00	667,501.21	1.825339004
33	Gregg	City of Kilgore	3,954,912.00	7,807,273.89	0.506567601
33	Gregg	City of Lakeport	184,318.00	108,580.13	1.697529741
33	Gregg	City of Longview	23,722,647.00	19,104,588.98	1.241725065
33	Gregg	City of White Oak	1,637,002.00	657,073.45	2.491353123
33	Gregg	Gregg County	21,466,344.00	29,715,605.66	0.722392949
34	Guadalupe	City of Cibolo	3,224,519.00	473,588.11	6.808699182
34	Guadalupe	City of Luling	9,596.00	690,282.18	0.013901561
34	Guadalupe	City of Marion	140,778.00	77,010.98	1.828025043
34	Guadalupe	City of Seguin	5,890,658.00	3,370,536.59	1.747691458
34	Guadalupe	Guadalupe County	29,936,492.00	9,472,963.90	3.160203323
34	Guadalupe, Comal, Bexar	City of Schertz	8,860,134.00	4,176,222.13	2.121566746
35	Randall	Randall County	25,265,410.00	7,363,231.39	3.431293771
36	Parker	City of Aledo	629,692.00	351,937.50	1.789215415
36	Parker	City of Millsap	42,494.00	24,659.83	1.723207338
36	Parker	City of Mineral Wells	551,808.00	3,178,036.78	0.173631722
36	Parker	City of Reno (Parker Co.)	417,338.00	56,870.52	7.338389028
36	Parker	City of Springtown	875,585.00	598,779.10	1.462283837
36	Parker	City of Weatherford	7,626,780.00	5,932,963.39	1.285492509
36	Parker	City of Willow Park	1,452,792.00	444,567.21	3.267879363
36	Parker	Parker County	31,172,032.00	13,132,941.60	2.373575772
37	Comal	City of Bulverde	758,087.00	854,963.19	0.886689636
37	Comal	City of Fair Oaks Ranch	130,712.00	21,785.24	6.000025705
37	Comal	City of Garden Ridge	1,140,246.00	172,341.28	6.616209419
37	Comal	Comal County	31,557,508.00	15,454,941.26	2.041904105
37	Comal	Comal County Emergency Services District #3	2,035,148.00	905,273.78	2.248102226
37	Comal	Comal County Emergency Services District #6	319,450.00	614,918.80	0.519499485
37	Comal, Guadalupe	City of New Braunfels	15,520,969.00	11,929,323.70	1.301077026
38	Tom Green	City of San Angelo	27,603,106.00	13,189,973.45	2.092734007
38	Tom Green	Tom Green County	20,719,737.00	13,157,090.40	1.574796279
39	Kaufman	City of Crandall	1,209,382.00	178,080.82	6.791197390
39	Kaufman	City of Forney	6,308,290.00	1,650,309.06	3.822490085
39	Kaufman	City of Heath	7,004.00	362,388.39	0.019327330
39	Kaufman	City of Kaufman	1,743,006.00	761,842.73	2.287881647
39	Kaufman	City of Kemp	275,637.00	100,023.51	2.755722012
39	Kaufman	City of Mabank	674,019.00	565,897.82	1.191061323
39	Kaufman	City of Oak Ridge	12,865.00	53,845.36	0.238924951
39	Kaufman	City of Terrell	6,824,283.00	3,600,448.58	1.895397990
39	Kaufman	Kaufman County	33,943,708.00	6,380,979.23	5.319513946
39	Kaufman, Dallas	City of Combine	192,820.00	15,657.91	12.314545239
		Totals:	10,886,912,294.00	5,447,796,922.45	

Table A3

Estimated 2008 Tax Pyramiding Factors for NAICS Industry Sub-classifications in Texas

Description	Pyramid Factor
Chocolate and confectionery manufacturing from cacao beans	9.64
Wet corn milling	7.65
Soybean and other oilseed processing	7.61
Secondary smelting and alloying of aluminum	7.11
Cheese manufacturing	7.07
Funds, trusts, and other financial vehicles	6.62
Animal (except poultry) slaughtering, rendering, and processing	6.61
Petroleum refineries	5.98
Flour milling and malt manufacturing	5.85
Military armored vehicle, tank, and tank component manufacturing	5.77
Dry, condensed, and evaporated dairy product manufacturing	5.52
Fluid milk and butter manufacturing	5.38
Other animal food manufacturing	5.16
Other basic organic chemical manufacturing	5.01
Fertilizer manufacturing	4.78
All other transportation equipment manufacturing	4.61
Copper rolling, drawing, extruding and alloying	4.54
Artificial and synthetic fibers and filaments manufacturing	4.49
Womens and girls cut and sew apparel manufacturing	4.33
Soft drink and ice manufacturing	4.31
Wineries	4.30
Motorcycle, bicycle, and parts manufacturing	4.08
Cattle ranching and farming	4.02
Leather and hide tanning and finishing	3.98
Primary smelting and refining of copper	3.93
Iron and steel mills and ferroalloy manufacturing	3.92
Dog and cat food manufacturing	3.91
Ice cream and frozen dessert manufacturing	3.88
Frozen food manufacturing	3.83
Petrochemical manufacturing	3.81
Cable and other subscription programming	3.66
Sugar cane mills and refining	3.63
Steel product manufacturing from purchased steel	3.60
Poultry and egg production	3.55
Seafood product preparation and packaging	3.53
Heavy duty truck manufacturing	3.50
Audio and video equipment manufacturing	3.49
Light truck and utility vehicle manufacturing	3.46
Fruit and vegetable canning, pickling, and drying	3.33
Carbon black manufacturing	3.31

Fats and oils refining and blending	3.25
Aluminum product manufacturing from purchased aluminum	3.24
Seasoning and dressing manufacturing	3.23
Synthetic rubber manufacturing	3.23
All other food manufacturing	3.22
Irradiation apparatus manufacturing	3.21
Railroad rolling stock manufacturing	3.19
Sound recording industries	3.17
Coffee and tea manufacturing	3.17
Adhesive manufacturing	3.16
Printing ink manufacturing	3.16
Sawmills and wood preservation	3.16
Commercial Fishing	3.15
Nonferrous metal (except copper and aluminum) rolling, drawing, extruding and alloying	3.13
Automobile manufacturing	3.13
Tortilla manufacturing	3.12
Construction machinery manufacturing	3.12
Poultry processing	3.11
Alumina refining and primary aluminum production	3.08
Computer storage device manufacturing	3.07
Computer terminals and other computer peripheral equipment manufacturing	3.07
Telephone apparatus manufacturing	3.05
Totalizing fluid meters and counting devices manufacturing	3.05
Nonchocolate confectionery manufacturing	3.01
Other engine equipment manufacturing	2.99
Magnetic and optical recording media manufacturing	2.99
Semiconductor and related device manufacturing	2.96
Farm machinery and equipment manufacturing	2.95
Cookie, cracker, and pasta manufacturing	2.95
Electromedical and electrotherapeutic apparatus manufacturing	2.95
Electronic computer manufacturing	2.94
Alkalies and chlorine manufacturing	2.93
Fabric coating mills	2.93
Electronic connector manufacturing	2.92
Internet publishing and broadcasting	2.90
Broadcast and wireless communications equipment manufacturing	2.89
Travel trailer and camper manufacturing	2.86
Paint and coating manufacturing	2.83
Primary smelting and refining of nonferrous metal (except copper and aluminum)	2.83
Household refrigerator and home freezer manufacturing	2.82
Aircraft engine and engine parts manufacturing	2.79
Plastics packaging materials and unlaminated film and sheet manufacturing	2.78
Watch, clock, and other measuring and controlling device manufacturing	2.74
Analytical laboratory instrument manufacturing	2.69
Other communications equipment manufacturing	2.68
All other crop farming	2.67
Custom roll forming	2.67
Plastics material and resin manufacturing	2.66
Paperboard Mills	2.65
Grantmaking, giving, and social advocacy organizations	2.65

Nonwoven fabric mills	2.65
Plastics bottle manufacturing	2.60
Metal can, box, and other metal container (light gauge) manufacturing	2.60
Plastics pipe and pipe fitting manufacturing	2.58
Unlaminated plastics profile shape manufacturing	2.57
Electron tube manufacturing	2.57
Boat building	2.57
All other paper bag and coated and treated paper manufacturing	2.56
Electronic capacitor, resistor, coil, transformer, and other inductor manufacturing	2.56
Semiconductor machinery manufacturing	2.55
Commercial logging	2.54
Motor vehicle parts manufacturing	2.54
Air and gas compressor manufacturing	2.51
Synthetic dye and pigment manufacturing	2.51
Other major household appliance manufacturing	2.50
Automatic environmental control manufacturing	2.50
Apparel knitting mills	2.50
Construction of other new residential structures	2.48
Pulp mills	2.46
Apparel accessories and other apparel manufacturing	2.45
Motor home manufacturing	2.45
Civic social, professional, and similar organizations	2.45
Textile and fabric finishing mills	2.45
Wood kitchen cabinet and countertop manufacturing	2.42
All other basic inorganic chemical manufacturing	2.42
Household cooking appliance manufacturing	2.42
In-vitro diagnostic substance manufacturing	2.41
Electricity and signal testing instruments manufacturing	2.41
Confectionery manufacturing from purchased chocolate	2.41
Lawn and garden equipment manufacturing	2.41
Pump and pumping equipment manufacturing	2.40
Other information services	2.39
Blind and shade manufacturing	2.39
Optical instrument and lens manufacturing	2.37
All other chemical product and preparation manufacturing	2.37
Paperboard container manufacturing	2.36
Other plastics product manufacturing	2.36
Fruit farming	2.34
Transport by water	2.32
Motion picture and video industries	2.31
Other amusement and recreation industries	2.30
Industrial gas manufacturing	2.30
Amusement parks, arcades, and gambling industries	2.30
Periodical publishers	2.29
All other forging, stamping, and sintering	2.29
Search, detection, and navigation instruments manufacturing	2.28
Biological product (except diagnostic) manufacturing	2.28
Manufactured home (mobile home) manufacturing	2.28
Miscellaneous nonmetallic mineral product manufacturing	2.28
Truck trailer manufacturing	2.28

Mining and oil and gas field machinery manufacturing	2.27
Metal and other household furniture manufacturing	2.27
Other commercial and service industry machinery manufacturing	2.27
Industrial process variable instruments manufacturing	2.26
Material handling equipment manufacturing	2.26
Urethane and other foam product (except polystyrene) manufacturing	2.25
Nonferrous metal foundries	2.25
Stationery product manufacturing	2.24
Securities, commodity contracts, investments, and related activities	2.24
Polystyrene foam product manufacturing	2.23
Motor vehicle body manufacturing	2.22
Aircraft manufacturing	2.22
Religious organizations	2.22
Ready-mix concrete manufacturing	2.22
Breweries	2.22
Coated and laminated paper, packaging paper and plastics film manufacturing	2.21
Forestry, forest products, and timber tract production	2.20
Printed circuit assembly (electronic assembly) manufacturing	2.20
Other aircraft parts and auxiliary equipment manufacturing	2.18
Software, audio, and video media for reproduction	2.18
Wood windows and doors and millwork manufacturing	2.18
Fluid power process machinery manufacturing	2.16
Mattress manufacturing	2.15
Packaging machinery manufacturing	2.15
Bread and bakery product manufacturing	2.15
Asphalt paving mixture and block manufacturing	2.15
Vending, commercial, industrial, and office machinery manufacturing	2.14
Other general purpose machinery manufacturing	2.13
Laminated plastics plate, sheet (except packaging), and shape manufacturing	2.13
Flavoring syrup and concentrate manufacturing	2.13
Air purification and ventilation equipment manufacturing	2.12
Petroleum lubricating oil and grease manufacturing	2.12
Air conditioning, refrigeration, and warm air heating equipment manufacturing	2.12
Ferrous metal foundries	2.12
Snack food manufacturing	2.11
Ornamental and architectural metal products manufacturing	2.10
Construction of new residential permanent site single- and multi-family structures	2.10
Other leather and allied product manufacturing	2.10
Metal tank (heavy gauge) manufacturing	2.09
Mechanical power transmission equipment manufacturing	2.09
Metal cutting and forming machine tool manufacturing	2.09
Plumbing fixture fitting and trim manufacturing	2.08
All other converted paper product manufacturing	2.07
Power-driven handtool manufacturing	2.07
Broadwoven fabric mills	2.06
Dairy cattle and milk production	2.06
Guided missile and space vehicle manufacturing	2.06
Book publishers	2.05
Ship building and repairing	2.05
Footwear manufacturing	2.04

Construction of other new nonresidential structures	2.04
Heating equipment (except warm air furnaces) manufacturing	2.03
Breakfast cereal manufacturing	2.03
Clay and nonclay refractory manufacturing	2.03
Plate work and fabricated structural product manufacturing	2.03
Telecommunications	2.03
Communication and energy wire and cable manufacturing	2.02
Doll, toy and game manufacturing	2.02
Turbine and turbine generator set units manufacturing	2.02
Pesticide and other agricultural chemical manufacturing	2.02
Engineered wood member and truss manufacturing	2.01
Lime and gypsum product manufacturing	2.00
Crown and closure manufacturing and metal stamping	2.00
Other rubber product manufacturing	2.00
Other industrial machinery manufacturing	1.99
Construction of new nonresidential commercial and health care structures	1.99
Power, distribution, and specialty transformer manufacturing	1.99
All other miscellaneous wood product manufacturing	1.98
Vegetable and melon farming	1.98
Showcase, partition, shelving, and locker manufacturing	1.98
Insurance carriers	1.98
Soap and cleaning compound manufacturing	1.98
Tire manufacturing	1.97
Other cut and sew apparel manufacturing	1.97
Transport by air	1.97
Textile bag and canvas mills	1.97
Fiber, yarn, and thread mills	1.97
Industrial process furnace and oven manufacturing	1.96
Storage battery manufacturing	1.95
Flat glass manufacturing	1.95
Commercial and industrial machinery and equipment rental and leasing	1.95
Mens and boys cut and sew apparel manufacturing	1.94
Veneer and plywood manufacturing	1.94
Bare printed circuit board manufacturing	1.92
Reconstituted wood product manufacturing	1.92
Rubber and plastics hoses and belting manufacturing	1.92
Paper mills	1.92
Rolling mill and other metalworking machinery manufacturing	1.92
Cement manufacturing	1.91
Fabricated pipe and pipe fitting manufacturing	1.91
Speed changer, industrial high-speed drive, and gear manufacturing	1.91
Bowling centers	1.91
Other electronic component manufacturing	1.91
Sugarcane and sugar beet farming	1.91
Oilseed farming	1.90
Small electrical appliance manufacturing	1.89
Hardware manufacturing	1.87
Toilet preparation manufacturing	1.87
Glass product manufacturing made of purchased glass	1.85
Carbon and graphite product manufacturing	1.85

Wood container and pallet manufacturing	1.85
Commercial hunting and trapping	1.85
Promoters of performing arts and sports and agents for public figures	1.85
All other petroleum and coal products manufacturing	1.84
Broom, brush, and mop manufacturing	1.84
Data processing, hosting, ISP, web search portals and related services	1.84
Power boiler and heat exchanger manufacturing	1.84
Institutional furniture manufacturing	1.83
Medicinal and botanical manufacturing	1.83
Sporting and athletic goods manufacturing	1.83
Prefabricated wood building manufacturing	1.82
Mining iron ore	1.82
Photographic services	1.82
Curtain and linen mills	1.82
Mineral wool manufacturing	1.82
Lighting fixture manufacturing	1.81
All other textile product mills	1.81
Cutlery, utensil, pot, and pan manufacturing	1.81
Handtool manufacturing	1.80
Spring and wire product manufacturing	1.80
Coating, engraving, heat treating and allied activities	1.79
Support activities for other mining	1.79
Transport by truck	1.78
Surgical and medical instrument, laboratory and medical instrument manufacturing	1.78
Construction of new nonresidential manufacturing structures	1.78
All other miscellaneous electrical equipment and component manufacturing	1.78
Waste management and remediation services	1.78
Other fabricated metal manufacturing	1.78
Relay and industrial control manufacturing	1.78
Sanitary paper product manufacturing	1.77
All other miscellaneous professional, scientific, and technical services	1.77
Automotive equipment rental and leasing	1.76
Industrial mold manufacturing	1.76
Other concrete product manufacturing	1.76
Photographic and photocopying equipment manufacturing	1.75
Fitness and recreational sports centers	1.75
Cotton farming	1.74
Glass container manufacturing	1.74
Wiring device manufacturing	1.74
All other miscellaneous manufacturing	1.74
Custom architectural woodwork and millwork manufacturing	1.74
Insurance agencies, brokerages, and related activities	1.74
Pottery, ceramics, and plumbing fixture manufacturing	1.73
Software publishers	1.73
Greenhouse, nursery, and floriculture production	1.72
Concrete pipe, brick, and block manufacturing	1.72
Other private educational services	1.72
Abrasive product manufacturing	1.71
Switchgear and switchboard apparatus manufacturing	1.71
Other personal services	1.69

Support activities for oil and gas operations	1.69
Grain farming	1.68
Turned product and screw, nut, and bolt manufacturing	1.68
Valve and fittings other than plumbing manufacturing	1.67
Pharmaceutical preparation manufacturing	1.67
Video tape and disc rental	1.67
Death care services	1.66
Other accommodations	1.66
Performing arts companies	1.66
Nonupholstered wood household furniture manufacturing	1.65
Food services and drinking places	1.65
Special tool, die, jig, and fixture manufacturing	1.65
Motor and generator manufacturing	1.65
Gasket, packing, and sealing device manufacturing	1.65
Scientific research and development services	1.65
Dental equipment and supplies manufacturing	1.64
Upholstered household furniture manufacturing	1.64
Transport by pipeline	1.63
Machine shops	1.63
Advertising and related services	1.63
Total	1.63
Directory, mailing list, and other publishers	1.63
Radio and television broadcasting	1.62
Veterinary services	1.62
Plastics and rubber industry machinery manufacturing	1.62
Office supplies (except paper) manufacturing	1.62
Ground or treated mineral and earth manufacturing	1.62
Services to buildings and dwellings	1.62
Cut stone and stone product manufacturing	1.61
Cutting tool and machine tool accessory manufacturing	1.60
Jewelry and silverware manufacturing	1.60
Propulsion units and parts for space vehicles and guided missiles manufacturing	1.60
Community food, housing, and other relief services, including rehabilitation services	1.59
Facilities support services	1.59
Asphalt shingle and coating materials manufacturing	1.59
Private junior colleges, colleges, universities, and professional schools	1.59
Animal production, except cattle and poultry and eggs	1.59
Specialized design services	1.58
Cut and sew apparel contractors	1.57
Ophthalmic goods manufacturing	1.56
Printing	1.55
Management of companies and enterprises	1.55
Surgical appliance and supplies manufacturing	1.54
Other pressed and blown glass and glassware manufacturing	1.54
Private hospitals	1.54
Natural gas distribution	1.53
Newspaper publishers	1.53
Management, scientific, and technical consulting services	1.53
Architectural, engineering, and related services	1.52
Narrow fabric mills and schiffli machine embroidery	1.52

Lessors of nonfinancial intangible assets	1.52
Electric lamp bulb and part manufacturing	1.51
Ball and roller bearing manufacturing	1.51
Car washes	1.51
Office Furniture	1.51
Maintenance and repair construction of nonresidential structures	1.51
Individual and family services	1.50
Sign manufacturing	1.50
Environmental and other technical consulting services	1.50
Travel arrangement and reservation services	1.49
Primary battery manufacturing	1.49
Arms, ordnance, and accessories manufacturing	1.49
Transport by rail	1.47
Brick, tile, and other structural clay product manufacturing	1.47
Custom computer programming services	1.47
Nondepository credit intermediation and related activities	1.46
Child day care services	1.46
Tobacco product manufacturing	1.46
Retail Stores - Furniture and home furnishings	1.46
Museums, historical sites, zoos, and parks	1.45
Personal care services	1.45
Hotels and motels, including casino hotels	1.45
Retail Stores - Sporting goods, hobby, book and music	1.44
Automotive repair and maintenance, except car washes	1.44
Accounting, tax preparation, bookkeeping, and payroll services	1.44
Tree nut farming	1.43
Carpet and rug mills	1.43
Retail Stores - Food and beverage	1.43
Drilling oil and gas wells	1.43
Medical and diagnostic labs and outpatient and other ambulatory care services	1.42
Mining and quarrying sand, gravel, clay, and ceramic and refractory minerals	1.42
Retail Stores - Clothing and clothing accessories	1.42
Spectator sports companies	1.41
Retail Stores - Building material and garden supply	1.41
Retail Stores - General merchandise	1.41
Personal and household goods repair and maintenance	1.41
Business support services	1.41
Legal services	1.40
Distilleries	1.40
Extraction of oil and natural gas	1.40
Wholesale trade businesses	1.39
Imputed rental activity for owner-occupied dwellings	1.39
Other support services	1.39
Support activities for printing	1.38
Mining and quarrying other nonmetallic minerals	1.38
Mining and quarrying stone	1.38
Mining coal	1.37
General and consumer goods rental except video tapes and discs	1.37
Transit and ground passenger transportation	1.36
Retail Stores - Gasoline stations	1.36

Ammunition manufacturing	1.35
Maintenance and repair construction of residential structures	1.34
Musical instrument manufacturing	1.33
Retail Nonstores - Direct and electronic sales	1.32
Retail Stores - Electronics and appliances	1.32
Electronic and precision equipment repair and maintenance	1.31
Office administrative services	1.31
Monetary authorities and depository credit intermediation activities	1.31
Commercial and industrial machinery and equipment repair and maintenance	1.30
Retail Stores - Health and personal care	1.30
Private elementary and secondary schools	1.29
Offices of physicians, dentists, and other health practitioners	1.29
Independent artists, writers, and performers	1.29
Investigation and security services	1.28
Mining gold, silver, and other metal ore	1.28
Retail Stores - Motor vehicle and parts	1.27
Retail Stores - Miscellaneous	1.27
Couriers and messengers	1.27
Water, sewage and other treatment and delivery systems	1.26
Nursing and residential care facilities	1.25
Employment services	1.24
Home health care services	1.24
Dental laboratories manufacturing	1.23
Real estate establishments	1.23
Other computer related services, including facilities management	1.22
Dry-cleaning and laundry services	1.22
Computer systems design services	1.20
Warehousing and storage	1.19
Support activities for agriculture and forestry	1.17
Electric power generation, transmission, and distribution	1.17
Scenic and sightseeing transportation and support activities for transportation	1.09

Table A4 (part 1 of 3)

Texas Sales and Use Tax Base by Industry Classification/ by County (2008)
(in $US millions)

County	Accommodation and Food Services		Administrative and Support and Waste Management and Remediation Services		Agriculture, Forestry, Fishing and Hunting		Arts, Entertainment, and Recreation		Construction		Educational Services		Finance and Insurance		Health Care and Social Assistance	
	Taxable Sales	Gross Sales	Taxable Sales	Gross Sales	Taxable Sales	Gross Sales	Taxable Sales	Gross Sales	Taxable Sales	Gross Sales	Taxable Sales	Gross Sales	Taxable Sales	Gross Sales	Taxable Sales	Gross Sales
Harris	6311.7	7293.1	2389.0	8677.1	16.2	88.5	582.5	751.9	3547.1	23604.8	51.2	172.1	278.7	4737.6	115.4	2251.9
Dallas	4038.0	4697.4	1693.7	3758.7	10.9	41.1	610.6	868.0	2502.1	12618.8	45.6	252.5	351.8	1983.8	88.6	1410.2
Tarrant	2896.5	3749.8	699.2	1663.4	9.7	48.8	425.2	525.0	824.8	6294.9	10.7	78.2	94.3	202.9	34.7	1109.8
Bexar	2822.2	3243.0	616.5	1353.9	7.9	29.6	504.3	607.4	825.9	5674.6	15.3	67.7	137.5	505.1	170.2	2559.8
Travis	2033.1	2376.0	674.5	1719.1	6.2	14.2	162.8	260.4	616.3	5846.1	16.0	73.0	52.7	285.4	17.5	1075.8
Collin	1124.9	1224.8	308.4	537.4	7.1	90.8	147.0	179.6	245.2	2028.5	4.7	30.6	33.1	83.8	24.6	68.8
El Paso	875.2	981.3	172.3	438.7	0.2	3.5	51.7	61.5	157.0	1547.2	4.9	26.8	23.2	77.1	24.9	86.4
Hidalgo	719.1	793.1	114.8	232.6	1.9	41.4	35.8	43.4	99.6	1100.0	1.2	18.7	28.5	65.0	8.6	36.1
Denton	700.1	775.6	203.4	2215.8	3.8	15.6	115.3	187.2	185.4	1539.0	3.2	35.7	13.3	22.3	10.2	65.8
Fort Bend	517.1	570.5	167.7	354.3	0.7	40.6	93.4	108.8	154.3	1562.5	6.5	18.2	9.8	108.9	2.1	78.4
Montgomery	616.1	679.4	110.3	246.6	1.6	22.2	79.2	86.8	171.0	777.5	2.0	11.5	20.8	27.6	12.5	151.8
Williamson	485.8	530.3	124.8	274.5	5.8	22.5	41.6	52.6	171.0	1646.0	2.0	20.1	10.9	19.4	7.8	22.5
Cameron	407.9	431.7	60.6	94.4	1.7	25.5	31.9	45.8	47.5	352.9	3.2	12.6	14.9	16.9	5.0	59.2
Nueces	550.1	668.0	123.1	345.0	0.7	2.4	31.6	39.7	193.9	1795.3	1.8	6.6	12.7	18.1	9.4	138.1
Brazoria	307.5	337.1	47.1	166.0	2.1	20.4	15.9	27.8	100.7	1250.9	2.7	8.5	6.2	10.9	1.0	15.4
Galveston	433.4	515.7	51.1	251.1	0.4	3.3	44.9	74.2	85.3	472.3	4.1	6.1	34.3	13.4	2.5	16.5
Bell	357.7	393.6	43.4	100.4	0.3	11.6	25.2	28.9	41.3	534.9	8.9	12.7	9.5	15.4	9.2	119.4
Lubbock	423.8	510.8	68.1	118.4	1.3	15.5	22.2	40.5	88.7	884.6	2.3	6.5	12.6	16.4	7.4	42.6
Jefferson	348.7	392.0	93.5	246.6	2.8	6.5	16.4	18.6	199.0	1844.3	0.2	1.0	11.2	15.4	5.4	26.2
Webb	288.3	316.7	42.5	59.9	0.1	10.4	11.6	13.2	21.1	205.3	0.2	7.4	20.5	15.2	8.0	3.6
McLennan	312.7	358.3	48.5	123.2	0.7	31.8	18.5	22.8	95.8	994.8	17.9	21.5	32.9	29.4	6.3	25.7
Smith	292.0	314.8	62.5	115.6	2.8	26.7	24.5	31.1	80.8	636.3	0.3	1.7	7.1	52.4	10.3	107.1
Brazos	292.9	349.2	43.3	94.1	0.7	4.3	18.1	26.1	64.7	444.5	28.2	30.4	2.0	2.9	5.0	130.0
Johnson	135.2	142.6	29.4	68.9	0.7	20.6	6.9	10.3	47.8	605.1	0.1	0.8	2.7	4.7	0.4	10.2
Hays	208.3	222.0	31.5	95.0	0.2	5.3	6.3	9.3	58.5	590.2	1.1	2.6	1.6	2.9	1.3	28.5
Ellis	128.7	139.4	30.9	72.6	0.1	0.3	10.3	11.5	109.4	437.2	2.3	2.6	5.3	9.1	0.9	7.3
Ector	224.5	256.6	16.0	40.3	0.7	3.2	6.8	8.1	162.6	923.5	0.7	2.0	4.1	6.8	3.6	17.9
Midland	226.3	253.4	57.3	98.9	0.5	4.5	26.2	30.3	144.8	537.5	0.6	6.6	5.4	10.9	2.0	17.3
Wichita	177.4	196.6	21.4	53.1	2.1	3.4	11.6	22.9	27.8	266.9	0.2	0.6	6.8	11.5	1.0	66.3
Taylor	199.6	229.2	26.5	74.4	0.0	0.2	11.6	14.4	49.9	461.5	4.8	6.6	6.8	9.8	4.5	772.6
Potter	244.5	291.1	47.5	77.9	0.8	77.7	19.7	22.7	65.8	602.3	4.3	7.7	8.5	129.6	4.5	17.4
Grayson	137.9	149.5	18.9	-167.1	2.1	7.2	11.0	25.1	30.7	291.3	5.7	6.6	5.3	4.5	5.5	21.1
Gregg	231.8	262.6	60.8	128.6	0.3	1.1	10.8	14.6	95.8	543.9	5.2	6.3	6.0	36.0	4.1	742.3
Guadalupe	107.2	116.4	21.4	39.1	1.4	11.3	6.6	13.2	41.7	505.4	3.3	5.1	3.3	5.9	1.1	14.2
Randall	109.6	122.4	19.6	38.8	0.4	4.6	7.1	7.8	20.0	286.5	0.1	0.3	4.1	2.8	0.1	6.7
Parker	107.8	111.6	24.1	73.0	0.8	5.8	6.3	8.4	57.9	329.7	2.9	4.9	4.3	4.3	0.0	8.4
Comal	147.1	292.2	26.4	57.6	1.5	7.4	42.5	65.4	54.2	618.7	1.5	11.6	3.2	6.7	1.6	3.4
Tom Green	149.9	163.1	29.5	48.7	0.9	8.2	10.0	13.1	44.8	247.6	0.4	1.7	2.1	3.0	4.3	911.8
Kaufman	85.6	96.8	17.2	30.7	0.3	3.3	5.6	7.0	41.7	191.4	0.6	1.2	1.4	1.0	0.1	0.3

Table A4 (part 2 of 3)
Texas Sales and Use Tax Base by Industry Classification/ by County (2008)
(in $US millions)

County	Information		Management of Companies and Enterprises		Manufacturing		Mining		Other Services (except Public Administration)		Professional, Scientific, and Technical Services		Public Administration		Real Estate and Rental and Leasing		Retail Trade	
	Taxable Sales	Gross Sales	Taxable Sales	Gross Sales	Taxable Sales	Gross Sales	Taxable Sales	Gross Sales	Taxable Sales	Gross Sales	Taxable Sales	Gross Sales	Taxable Sales	Gross Sales	Taxable Sales	Gross Sales	Taxable Sales	Gross Sales
Harris	1116.2	3294.6	225.0	449.0	6562.1	92002.8	5580.3	13113.7	1668.7	5274.0	1779.6	20460.0	136.7	1045.7	1562.5	4092.7	24086.9	58096.0
Dallas	7534.5	9859.7	33.0	128.9	3441.9	32020.3	709.9	484.1	970.9	3803.6	1345.9	13670.5	177.8	420.7	870.0	5597.4	13835.7	39190.9
Tarrant	381.1	971.3	47.0	216.3	1717.4	14139.4	1104.4	630.7	526.8	1512.8	416.1	1513.2	86.2	99.6	466.4	1014.6	10640.7	25031.6
Bexar	1132.8	2174.3	22.4	60.3	1118.5	5720.3	80.8	228.2	523.2	1275.5	340.9	1727.6	123.6	136.7	415.8	822.0	9197.0	22065.1
Travis	210.8	1099.7	19.8	42.9	1108.0	8617.8	12.3	53.6	411.8	1331.2	429.2	3672.4	444.3	484.7	292.2	443.8	6739.3	14590.2
Collin	537.6	1381.5	18.2	27.1	298.5	5062.0	53.4	242.8	183.9	477.1	736.6	1350.1	26.6	34.8	138.2	234.6	5221.8	11620.6
El Paso	62.4	245.2	6.8	257.1	217.7	5759.0	0.1	2.5	137.4	311.1	36.6	383.5	4.5	9.5	92.8	153.6	3554.7	8373.6
Hidalgo	60.6	79.8	11.4	16.3	121.7	1535.1	60.3	202.2	79.5	438.7	29.6	103.4	8.7	13.2	94.8	171.3	3651.1	8046.3
Denton	75.9	124.7	13.5	34.5	221.6	2450.2	94.6	214.2	159.1	368.9	94.9	568.0	60.9	231.0	68.2	110.1	2693.8	10265.6
Fort Bend	131.6	291.5	17.7	18.1	164.7	2619.4	511.1	80.1	96.7	342.9	92.7	402.9	10.1	11.3	99.3	179.0	2320.1	6411.4
Montgomery	93.4	149.0	6.8	8.1	537.2	7973.8	102.2	316.0	126.3	430.7	81.5	493.1	6.6	33.6	130.9	190.8	2727.4	7506.4
Williamson	63.9	111.3	1.2	12.4	1165.2	3795.8	40.8	116.2	118.8	369.8	103.9	439.8	4.1	4.2	176.9	209.5	2316.8	5731.3
Cameron	39.8	69.1	2.6	32.8	94.8	734.7	0.9	9.7	46.3	136.9	15.6	77.6	11.3	12.6	44.6	73.3	1735.7	3549.3
Nueces	47.8	138.3	6.3	11.8	226.5	21397.1	84.5	296.0	125.0	357.8	24.9	217.0	2.3	2.7	201.9	373.3	1958.3	3967.3
Brazoria	24.7	41.3	4.0	5.9	88.2	1503.8	21.9	235.3	62.7	241.4	33.8	131.1	16.5	18.8	121.0	212.7	1483.4	3140.7
Galveston	37.2	58.6	0.8	10.6	114.6	35438.0	4.7	205.7	60.7	233.8	36.4	143.8	13.9	14.4	55.1	144.6	1478.2	2973.3
Bell	104.0	191.3	0.1	6.4	71.4	1190.2	2.9	29.0	59.0	138.4	21.4	335.6	11.2	11.3	39.9	56.5	1491.6	5060.3
Lubbock	150.1	253.3	6.7	10.4	86.9	1438.1	7.2	40.3	88.9	266.1	37.4	266.9	3.6	6.7	49.9	110.9	1770.4	4314.3
Jefferson	32.1	101.5	357.9	1510.7	157.4	25230.0	17.5	81.0	137.1	496.2	19.3	323.0	13.1	13.8	156.2	393.5	1702.9	3636.5
Webb	20.5	107.1	0.0	0.1	47.1	528.8	35.2	125.3	36.5	90.0	14.0	58.1	0.0	0.0	42.3	59.6	1347.9	3263.3
McLennan	20.9	70.6	3.4	3.6	84.9	1938.9	0.4	18.0	70.1	180.3	21.0	121.0	3.8	11.2	99.6	184.1	1182.4	3132.7
Smith	81.0	118.9	5.4	12.3	137.3	1151.7	159.0	215.8	69.2	246.6	46.0	213.8	1.6	4.0	89.8	139.9	1394.5	3213.1
Brazos	64.2	80.3	0.0	0.0	79.2	437.6	13.0	71.0	52.2	127.2	32.4	186.4	0.2	2.3	67.6	105.2	1116.4	2357.5
Johnson	23.2	177.0	1.9	1.9	160.7	1691.0	99.3	513.2	34.0	97.0	12.7	44.9	5.6	6.9	37.9	66.6	574.7	3003.0
Hays	155.2	162.2	0.9	1.0	81.2	523.0	4.5	50.8	28.9	68.3	12.4	45.3	16.8	34.9	25.1	46.4	1087.6	1980.9
Ellis	3.6	10.0	0.0	0.6	80.4	1753.4	0.0	0.0	27.1	81.5	8.1	31.5	2.5	2.5	15.8	35.0	477.5	1291.9
Ector	34.5	60.0	0.0	0.0	214.8	946.6	279.7	1013.8	137.8	342.5	23.1	81.0	2.3	6.6	190.6	346.7	1029.0	2565.3
Midland	47.5	73.1	0.0	0.0	275.0	760.4	454.1	1012.0	104.8	207.5	71.7	491.9	1.5	1.7	134.4	232.9	1166.3	2354.9
Wichita	32.2	52.5	2.2	2.5	61.9	783.1	11.5	41.5	41.5	90.1	11.4	59.8	0.3	0.4	32.6	43.9	760.6	1685.9
Taylor	37.3	63.0	0.0	0.0	37.0	258.6	54.6	76.6	40.3	98.7	17.9	177.4	10.7	12.1	27.8	49.5	907.5	2052.8
Potter	56.2	99.5	2.9	8.3	88.4	602.3	0.7	17.0	64.0	149.0	17.2	97.3	0.0	0.0	16.0	39.6	1123.9	2568.9
Grayson	27.6	49.6	0.7	1.5	57.6	584.0	3.7	8.9	29.4	63.9	5.3	59.8	6.7	10.8	23.3	30.9	628.5	1429.2
Gregg	53.0	280.0	0.2	0.2	212.0	2263.9	126.1	481.0	97.4	257.6	30.8	176.1	6.9	7.2	189.9	350.6	1154.7	2653.4
Guadalupe	3.6	9.9	0.4	0.0	61.2	1081.3	0.8	1.3	19.6	62.2	3.4	161.8	9.6	40.7	12.3	25.8	430.3	998.2
Randall	12.3	17.1	0.0	0.0	7.4	68.3	0.3	0.3	32.4	116.5	19.4	34.4	0.0	0.0	17.3	31.7	416.8	1300.6
Parker	3.4	12.0	0.0	0.0	37.8	428.6	64.5	289.1	33.2	74.5	8.7	30.1	18.5	63.8	52.5	63.4	530.2	1671.5
Comal	40.5	50.2	0.0	0.0	87.2	467.4	6.0	58.3	31.2	83.8	12.3	58.4	27.8	129.6	18.9	31.6	598.8	1401.9
Tom Green	54.1	127.9	0.0	0.0	50.2	302.6	26.9	64.0	38.7	91.4	13.2	61.2	0.0	0.0	15.0	24.3	671.5	1504.3
Kaufman	11.0	21.7	0.0	0.0	59.2	748.2	7.2	17.3	16.1	51.8	3.6	19.9	1.4	2.1	8.4	15.1	352.8	1584.9

Table A4 (part 3 of 3)
Texas Sales and Use Tax Base by Industry Classification/ by County (2008)
(in $US millions)

County	Transportation and Warehousing		Unclassified Establishments		Utilities		Wholesale Trade		Aggregates	
	Taxable Sales	Gross Sales	Taxable Sales	Gross Sales	Taxable Sales	Gross Sales	Taxable Sales	Gross Sales	Taxable Sales	Gross Sales
Harris	854.0	9381.5	1.0	20.7	3278.7	31299.6	6084.5	103968.6	66228.1	390075.9
Dallas	233.0	1143.4	0.3	9.9	2721.0	28663.3	3888.5	69861.4	45103.9	230484.5
Tarrant	240.9	1037.5	0.0	0.0	195.2	763.6	1718.8	20337.4	22536.2	80940.5
Bexar	674.5	543.5	0.0	0.0	495.8	2913.8	1313.3	65089.9	20538.5	116798.1
Travis	54.2	230.6	0.0	0.0	535.9	1876.5	1078.7	7225.7	14915.4	51319.2
Collin	9.3	28.3	0.0	0.0	7.1	443.4	393.9	5199.2	9520.3	30345.7
El Paso	18.5	155.8	0.0	0.0	227.4	737.6	301.2	3825.2	5969.5	23436.2
Hidalgo	9.3	72.9	0.0	0.0	36.1	287.2	252.3	1928.6	5425.0	15225.1
Denton	42.0	725.8	0.0	0.0	102.8	533.7	264.1	5766.6	5126.2	26250.2
Fort Bend	2.0	49.6	0.0	0.0	15.6	79.4	325.0	4065.2	4738.3	17393.1
Montgomery	4.3	25.1	0.0	0.0	48.0	262.4	248.9	4580.0	5126.9	23972.4
Williamson	3.3	48.5	0.0	0.0	24.1	65.5	248.6	1232.1	5117.3	14724.5
Cameron	4.4	31.2	0.0	0.0	47.2	137.6	116.1	817.7	2732.0	6721.5
Nueces	31.1	132.3	0.0	0.0	26.0	162.1	517.1	1620.8	4175.2	31689.7
Brazoria	21.3	216.7	0.0	0.0	58.3	168.1	85.8	1120.1	2504.7	8873.0
Galveston	11.3	61.1	0.0	0.0	5.9	75.8	77.7	680.5	2552.2	41393.0
Bell	0.9	34.6	0.0	0.0	0.6	0.8	96.0	3572.1	2394.6	11843.6
Lubbock	5.5	15.0	0.0	0.0	55.1	388.6	266.6	2517.3	3154.8	11263.2
Jefferson	9.1	80.5	0.0	0.0	3.6	3.6	244.1	6172.6	3527.8	40593.7
Webb	4.4	24.9	0.0	0.0	0.3	55.1	90.1	1374.9	2030.8	6318.8
McLennan	3.5	48.6	0.0	0.0	5.5	1137.0	119.2	1250.3	2148.1	9703.7
Smith	1.8	12.5	0.0	0.0	3.6	18.1	129.2	619.9	2598.8	7252.2
Brazos	3.9	23.7	0.0	0.0	55.9	204.7	101.7	553.3	2041.6	5230.8
Johnson	2.7	192.6	0.0	0.0	0.0	0.0	120.5	420.3	1296.4	7077.6
Hays	1.1	27.2	0.0	0.0	1.2	422.1	68.6	256.0	1792.3	4573.9
Ellis	1.0	96.0	0.0	0.0	0.2	697.0	56.3	291.0	960.3	4970.2
Ector	10.7	25.6	0.0	0.0	2.1	49.4	377.0	1727.1	2720.5	8422.9
Midland	5.8	140.4	0.0	0.0	4.1	709.0	850.7	2091.0	3579.1	9034.5
Wichita	0.8	124.5	0.0	0.0	15.8	42.4	85.0	426.5	1304.3	3974.3
Taylor	1.4	10.8	0.0	0.0	5.7	105.7	122.9	508.9	1566.7	4982.8
Potter	4.0	30.6	0.0	0.0	199.9	1467.6	156.8	1610.0	2125.6	7916.5
Grayson	4.3	28.0	0.0	0.0	6.4	91.6	47.4	335.2	1058.2	3031.3
Gregg	10.5	1855.8	0.0	0.0	0.2	62.1	280.0	2004.3	2576.4	12127.6
Guadalupe	1.2	33.8	0.0	0.0	5.3	30.4	26.6	278.2	760.6	3434.0
Randall	0.9	14.5	0.0	0.0	0.3	0.5	68.3	703.6	736.3	2757.5
Parker	1.4	969.9	0.0	0.0	0.1	0.4	77.8	416.8	1032.2	4566.2
Comal	1.3	12.7	0.0	0.0	0.4	19.5	255.6	3059.2	1358.1	6435.8
Tom Green	1.0	47.5	0.0	0.0	1.8	28.0	61.1	352.8	1175.6	4001.2
Kaufman	0.9	10.1	0.0	0.0	5.9	84.2	19.1	345.2	638.1	3232.2
								Totals:	264,886.89	1,292,387.38

Table A5 (part 1 of 3)
Relative Concentrations of Taxable Sales Base by Industry Classification & County (2008)

		Harris	Dallas	Tarrant	Bexar	Travis	Collin	El Paso	Hidalgo	Denton	Fort Bend	Montgomery	Williamson	Cameron
Accommodation & Food Svcs.	% of Cnty's Txbl Sales	9.53	8.95	12.85	13.74	13.63	11.82	14.66	13.25	13.66	10.91	12.02	9.49	14.93
	Average %	12.33	12.33	12.33	12.33	12.33	12.33	12.33	12.33	12.33	12.33	12.33	12.33	12.33
	Ratio	0.77	0.73	1.04	1.11	1.11	0.96	1.19	1.08	1.11	0.89	0.97	0.77	1.21
Admin. & Supp. & Waste Mgmt. & Remed. Svcs.	% of Cnty's Txbl Sales	3.61	3.76	3.10	3.00	4.52	3.24	2.89	2.12	3.97	3.54	2.15	2.44	2.22
	Average %	2.49	2.49	2.49	2.49	2.49	2.49	2.49	2.49	2.49	2.49	2.49	2.49	2.49
	Ratio	1.45	1.51	1.25	1.21	1.82	1.30	1.16	0.85	1.60	1.42	0.87	0.98	0.89
Agric., Forestry, Fishing & Hunting	% of Cnty's Txbl Sales	0.02	0.02	0.04	0.04	0.04	0.07	0.00	0.04	0.07	0.01	0.03	0.11	0.06
	Average %	0.05	0.05	0.05	0.05	0.05	0.05	0.05	0.05	0.05	0.05	0.05	0.05	0.05
	Ratio	0.46	0.45	0.80	0.72	0.77	1.39	0.05	0.66	1.39	0.26	0.59	2.09	1.17
Arts, Entertainment & Recreation	% of Cnty's Txbl Sales	0.88	1.35	1.89	2.46	1.09	1.54	0.87	0.66	2.25	1.97	1.54	0.81	1.17
	Average %	1.06	1.06	1.06	1.06	1.06	1.06	1.06	1.06	1.06	1.06	1.06	1.06	1.06
	Ratio	0.83	1.28	1.78	2.31	1.03	1.46	0.82	0.62	2.12	1.86	1.46	0.77	1.10
Construction	% of Cnty's Txbl Sales	5.36	5.55	3.66	4.02	4.13	2.58	2.63	1.84	3.62	3.26	3.34	3.34	1.74
	Average %	3.86	3.86	3.86	3.86	3.86	3.86	3.86	3.86	3.86	3.86	3.86	3.86	3.86
	Ratio	1.39	1.44	0.95	1.04	1.07	0.67	0.68	0.48	0.94	0.84	0.86	0.87	0.45
Educational Svcs.	% of Cnty's Txbl Sales	0.08	0.10	0.05	0.07	0.11	0.05	0.08	0.02	0.06	0.14	0.04	0.04	0.12
	Average %	0.17	0.17	0.17	0.17	0.17	0.17	0.17	0.17	0.17	0.17	0.17	0.17	0.17
	Ratio	0.46	0.61	0.28	0.45	0.64	0.29	0.50	0.13	0.38	0.83	0.23	0.23	0.70
Finance & Insurance	% of Cnty's Txbl Sales	0.42	0.78	0.42	0.67	0.35	0.35	0.39	0.53	0.26	0.21	0.41	0.21	0.55
	Average %	0.43	0.43	0.43	0.43	0.43	0.43	0.43	0.43	0.43	0.43	0.43	0.43	0.43
	Ratio	0.98	1.82	0.98	1.56	0.82	0.81	0.90	1.22	0.60	0.48	0.94	0.49	1.27
Health Care & Social Assistance	% of Cnty's Txbl Sales	0.17	0.20	0.15	0.83	0.12	0.26	0.42	0.16	0.20	0.04	0.24	0.15	0.18
	Average %	0.20	0.20	0.20	0.20	0.20	0.20	0.20	0.20	0.20	0.20	0.20	0.20	0.20
	Ratio	0.86	0.97	0.76	4.10	0.58	1.28	2.06	0.78	0.99	0.22	1.21	0.75	0.90
Information	% of Cnty's Txbl Sales	1.69	16.70	1.69	5.52	1.41	5.65	1.05	1.12	1.48	2.78	1.82	1.25	1.46
	Average %	2.64	2.64	2.64	2.64	2.64	2.64	2.64	2.64	2.64	2.64	2.64	2.64	2.64
	Ratio	0.64	6.34	0.64	2.09	0.54	2.14	0.40	0.42	0.56	1.05	0.69	0.47	0.55
Mgmt. Companies & Enterprises	% of Cnty's Txbl Sales	0.34	0.07	0.21	0.11	0.13	0.19	0.11	0.21	0.26	0.37	0.13	0.02	0.09
	Average %	0.36	0.36	0.36	0.36	0.36	0.36	0.36	0.36	0.36	0.36	0.36	0.36	0.36
	Ratio	0.95	0.20	0.58	0.30	0.37	0.53	0.32	0.59	0.73	1.05	0.37	0.06	0.26
Manufacturing	% of Cnty's Txbl Sales	9.91	7.63	7.62	5.45	7.43	3.14	3.65	2.24	4.32	3.48	10.48	22.77	3.47
	Average %	5.88	5.88	5.88	5.88	5.88	5.88	5.88	5.88	5.88	5.88	5.88	5.88	5.88
	Ratio	1.69	1.30	1.30	0.93	1.26	0.53	0.62	0.38	0.74	0.59	1.78	3.88	0.59
Mining	% of Cnty's Txbl Sales	8.43	1.57	4.90	0.39	0.08	0.56	0.00	1.11	1.84	10.79	1.99	0.80	0.03
	Average %	2.45	2.45	2.45	2.45	2.45	2.45	2.45	2.45	2.45	2.45	2.45	2.45	2.45
	Ratio	3.43	0.64	2.00	0.16	0.03	0.23	0.00	0.45	0.75	4.39	0.81	0.33	0.01
Other Svcs. (except Pub. Admin.)	% of Cnty's Txbl Sales	2.52	2.15	2.34	2.55	2.76	1.93	2.30	1.47	3.10	2.04	2.46	2.32	1.69
	Average %	2.71	2.71	2.71	2.71	2.71	2.71	2.71	2.71	2.71	2.71	2.71	2.71	2.71
	Ratio	0.93	0.79	0.86	0.94	1.02	0.71	0.85	0.54	1.15	0.75	0.91	0.86	0.63
Prof., Sci. & Tech. Services	% of Cnty's Txbl Sales	2.69	2.98	1.85	1.66	2.88	7.74	0.61	0.55	1.85	1.96	1.59	2.03	0.57
	Average %	1.45	1.45	1.45	1.45	1.45	1.45	1.45	1.45	1.45	1.45	1.45	1.45	1.45
	Ratio	1.86	2.06	1.28	1.15	1.99	5.35	0.42	0.38	1.28	1.35	1.10	1.41	0.40
Public Admin.	% of Cnty's Txbl Sales	0.21	0.39	0.38	0.60	2.98	0.28	0.08	0.16	1.19	0.21	0.13	0.08	0.41
	Average %	0.47	0.47	0.47	0.47	0.47	0.47	0.47	0.47	0.47	0.47	0.47	0.47	0.47
	Ratio	0.44	0.84	0.82	1.29	6.37	0.60	0.16	0.34	2.54	0.46	0.27	0.17	0.89
Real Estate & Rental & Leasing	% of Cnty's Txbl Sales	2.36	1.93	2.07	2.02	1.96	1.45	1.55	1.75	1.33	2.10	2.55	3.46	1.63
	Average %	2.65	2.65	2.65	2.65	2.65	2.65	2.65	2.65	2.65	2.65	2.65	2.65	2.65
	Ratio	0.89	0.73	0.78	0.76	0.74	0.55	0.59	0.66	0.50	0.79	0.96	1.30	0.61
Retail Trade	% of Cnty's Txbl Sales	36.37	30.68	47.22	44.78	45.18	54.85	59.55	67.30	52.55	48.96	53.20	45.27	63.53
	Average %	52.04	52.04	52.04	52.04	52.04	52.04	52.04	52.04	52.04	52.04	52.04	52.04	52.04
	Ratio	0.70	0.59	0.91	0.86	0.87	1.05	1.14	1.29	1.01	0.94	1.02	0.87	1.22
Transportation & Warehousing	% of Cnty's Txbl Sales	1.29	0.52	1.07	3.28	0.36	0.10	0.31	0.17	0.82	0.04	0.08	0.06	0.16
	Average %	0.37	0.37	0.37	0.37	0.37	0.37	0.37	0.37	0.37	0.37	0.37	0.37	0.37
	Ratio	3.53	1.41	2.92	8.98	0.99	0.27	0.85	0.47	2.24	0.12	0.23	0.18	0.44
Unclassified Establishments	% of Cnty's Txbl Sales	0.00	0.00	0.00	0.00	0.00	0.00	0.00	0.00	0.00	0.00	0.00	0.00	0.00
	Average %	0.00	0.00	0.00	0.00	0.00	0.00	0.00	0.00	0.00	0.00	0.00	0.00	0.00
	Ratio	28.02	10.98	0.00	0.00	0.00	0.00	0.00	0.00	0.00	0.00	0.00	0.00	0.00
Utilities	% of Cnty's Txbl Sales	4.95	6.03	0.87	2.41	3.59	0.07	3.81	0.67	2.00	0.33	0.94	0.47	1.73
	Average %	1.28	1.28	1.28	1.28	1.28	1.28	1.28	1.28	1.28	1.28	1.28	1.28	1.28
	Ratio	3.88	4.72	0.68	1.89	2.81	0.06	2.98	0.52	1.57	0.26	0.73	0.37	1.35
Wholesale Trade	% of Cnty's Txbl Sales	9.19	8.62	7.63	6.39	7.23	4.14	5.05	4.65	5.15	6.86	4.86	4.86	4.25
	Average %	7.13	7.13	7.13	7.13	7.13	7.13	7.13	7.13	7.13	7.13	7.13	7.13	7.13
	Ratio	1.29	1.21	1.07	0.90	1.01	0.58	0.71	0.65	0.72	0.96	0.68	0.68	0.60

Table A5 (part 2 of 3)
Relative Concentrations of Taxable Sales Base by Industry Classification & County (2008)

		Nueces	Brazoria	Galveston	Bell	Lubbock	Jefferson	Webb	McLennan	Smith	Brazos	Johnson	Hays	Ellis
Accommodation & Food Svcs.	% of Cnty's Txbl Sales	13.18	12.28	16.98	14.94	13.43	9.89	14.20	14.56	11.24	14.35	10.43	11.62	13.40
	Average %	12.33	12.33	12.33	12.33	12.33	12.33	12.33	12.33	12.33	12.33	12.33	12.33	12.33
	Ratio	1.07	1.00	1.38	1.21	1.09	0.80	1.15	1.18	0.91	1.16	0.85	0.94	1.09
Admin. & Supp. & Waste Mgmt. & Remed. Svcs.	% of Cnty's Txbl Sales	2.95	1.88	2.00	1.81	2.16	2.65	2.09	2.26	2.40	2.12	2.27	1.76	3.21
	Average %	2.49	2.49	2.49	2.49	2.49	2.49	2.49	2.49	2.49	2.49	2.49	2.49	2.49
	Ratio	1.19	0.76	0.80	0.73	0.87	1.07	0.84	0.91	0.97	0.85	0.91	0.71	1.29
Agric., Forestry, Fishing & Hunting	% of Cnty's Txbl Sales	0.02	0.08	0.02	0.01	0.04	0.08	0.01	0.03	0.11	0.03	0.06	0.01	0.01
	Average %	0.05	0.05	0.05	0.05	0.05	0.05	0.05	0.05	0.05	0.05	0.05	0.05	0.05
	Ratio	0.31	1.54	0.32	0.27	0.75	1.46	0.11	0.58	2.03	0.64	1.04	0.16	0.23
Arts, Entertainment & Recreation	% of Cnty's Txbl Sales	0.76	0.64	1.76	1.05	0.70	0.47	0.57	0.86	0.94	0.89	0.54	0.35	1.07
	Average %	1.06	1.06	1.06	1.06	1.06	1.06	1.06	1.06	1.06	1.06	1.06	1.06	1.06
	Ratio	0.71	0.60	1.66	0.99	0.66	0.44	0.54	0.81	0.89	0.84	0.51	0.33	1.01
Construction	% of Cnty's Txbl Sales	4.64	4.02	3.34	1.73	2.81	5.64	1.04	4.46	3.11	3.17	3.63	3.26	11.40
	Average %	3.86	3.86	3.86	3.86	3.86	3.86	3.86	3.86	3.86	3.86	3.86	3.86	3.86
	Ratio	1.20	1.04	0.87	0.45	0.73	1.46	0.27	1.16	0.81	0.82	0.93	0.85	2.95
Educational Svcs.	% of Cnty's Txbl Sales	0.04	0.11	0.16	0.37	0.07	0.01	0.01	0.83	0.01	1.38	0.01	0.06	0.24
	Average %	0.17	0.17	0.17	0.17	0.17	0.17	0.17	0.17	0.17	0.17	0.17	0.17	0.17
	Ratio	0.26	0.64	0.95	2.22	0.44	0.03	0.06	4.98	0.08	8.26	0.05	0.37	1.43
Finance & Insurance	% of Cnty's Txbl Sales	0.30	0.25	1.34	0.40	0.40	0.32	1.01	1.53	0.27	0.10	0.21	0.09	0.55
	Average %	0.43	0.43	0.43	0.43	0.43	0.43	0.43	0.43	0.43	0.43	0.43	0.43	0.43
	Ratio	0.71	0.58	3.13	0.92	0.93	0.74	2.35	3.57	0.64	0.23	0.49	0.21	1.27
Health Care & Social Assistance	% of Cnty's Txbl Sales	0.22	0.04	0.10	0.39	0.23	0.15	0.39	0.29	0.39	0.24	0.03	0.07	0.09
	Average %	0.20	0.20	0.20	0.20	0.20	0.20	0.20	0.20	0.20	0.20	0.20	0.20	0.20
	Ratio	1.11	0.20	0.48	1.91	1.16	0.76	1.95	1.46	1.95	1.20	0.14	0.36	0.46
Information	% of Cnty's Txbl Sales	1.15	0.99	1.46	4.34	4.76	0.91	1.01	0.97	3.12	3.15	1.73	8.66	0.38
	Average %	2.64	2.64	2.64	2.64	2.64	2.64	2.64	2.64	2.64	2.64	2.64	2.64	2.64
	Ratio	0.43	0.37	0.55	1.65	1.80	0.34	0.38	0.37	1.18	1.19	0.63	3.28	0.14
Mgmt. Companies & Enterprises	% of Cnty's Txbl Sales	0.15	0.16	0.03	0.00	0.21	10.15	0.00	0.16	0.21	0.00	0.15	0.05	0.00
	Average %	0.36	0.36	0.36	0.36	0.36	0.36	0.36	0.36	0.36	0.36	0.36	0.36	0.36
	Ratio	0.42	0.45	0.09	0.01	0.59	28.33	0.00	0.44	0.58	0.00	0.41	0.14	0.00
Manufacturing	% of Cnty's Txbl Sales	5.42	3.52	4.49	2.98	2.76	4.46	2.32	3.95	5.28	3.88	12.39	4.53	8.37
	Average %	5.88	5.88	5.88	5.88	5.88	5.88	5.88	5.88	5.88	5.88	5.88	5.88	5.88
	Ratio	0.92	0.60	0.76	0.51	0.47	0.76	0.40	0.67	0.90	0.66	2.11	0.77	1.42
Mining	% of Cnty's Txbl Sales	2.02	0.87	0.18	0.12	0.23	0.50	1.73	0.02	6.12	0.64	7.66	0.25	0.00
	Average %	2.45	2.45	2.45	2.45	2.45	2.45	2.45	2.45	2.45	2.45	2.45	2.45	2.45
	Ratio	0.82	0.36	0.07	0.05	0.09	0.20	0.71	0.01	2.49	0.26	3.12	0.10	0.00
Other Svcs. (except Pub. Admin.)	% of Cnty's Txbl Sales	2.99	2.50	2.38	2.46	2.82	3.89	1.80	3.26	2.66	2.56	2.62	1.61	2.82
	Average %	2.71	2.71	2.71	2.71	2.71	2.71	2.71	2.71	2.71	2.71	2.71	2.71	2.71
	Ratio	1.11	0.92	0.88	0.91	1.04	1.44	0.66	1.20	0.98	0.94	0.97	0.59	1.04
Prof., Sci. & Tech. Services	% of Cnty's Txbl Sales	0.60	1.35	1.42	0.89	1.19	0.55	0.69	0.98	1.77	1.58	0.98	0.69	0.84
	Average %	1.45	1.45	1.45	1.45	1.45	1.45	1.45	1.45	1.45	1.45	1.45	1.45	1.45
	Ratio	0.41	0.93	0.99	0.62	0.82	0.38	0.48	0.68	1.23	1.10	0.68	0.48	0.58
Public Admin.	% of Cnty's Txbl Sales	0.06	0.66	0.54	0.47	0.11	0.37	0.00	0.18	0.06	0.01	0.43	0.94	0.26
	Average %	0.47	0.47	0.47	0.47	0.47	0.47	0.47	0.47	0.47	0.47	0.47	0.47	0.47
	Ratio	0.12	1.41	1.16	1.00	0.24	0.79	0.00	0.38	0.13	0.02	0.92	2.00	0.55
Real Estate & Rental & Leasing	% of Cnty's Txbl Sales	4.84	4.83	2.16	1.66	1.58	4.43	2.08	4.64	3.45	3.31	2.93	1.40	1.65
	Average %	2.65	2.65	2.65	2.65	2.65	2.65	2.65	2.65	2.65	2.65	2.65	2.65	2.65
	Ratio	1.82	1.82	0.81	0.63	0.60	1.67	0.78	1.75	1.30	1.25	1.10	0.53	0.62
Retail Trade	% of Cnty's Txbl Sales	46.90	59.22	57.92	62.29	56.12	48.27	66.38	55.05	53.66	54.68	44.33	60.68	49.72
	Average %	52.04	52.04	52.04	52.04	52.04	52.04	52.04	52.04	52.04	52.04	52.04	52.04	52.04
	Ratio	0.90	1.14	1.11	1.20	1.08	0.93	1.28	1.06	1.03	1.05	0.85	1.17	0.96
Transportation & Warehousing	% of Cnty's Txbl Sales	0.75	0.85	0.44	0.04	0.17	0.26	0.22	0.16	0.07	0.19	0.21	0.06	0.11
	Average %	0.37	0.37	0.37	0.37	0.37	0.37	0.37	0.37	0.37	0.37	0.37	0.37	0.37
	Ratio	2.04	2.33	1.22	0.10	0.48	0.71	0.59	0.45	0.19	0.52	0.57	0.16	0.30
Unclassified Establishments	% of Cnty's Txbl Sales	0.00	0.00	0.00	0.00	0.00	0.00	0.00	0.00	0.00	0.00	0.00	0.00	0.00
	Average %	0.00	0.00	0.00	0.00	0.00	0.00	0.00	0.00	0.00	0.00	0.00	0.00	0.00
	Ratio	0.00	0.00	0.00	0.00	0.00	0.00	0.00	0.00	0.00	0.00	0.00	0.00	0.00
Utilities	% of Cnty's Txbl Sales	0.62	2.33	0.23	0.03	1.75	0.10	0.02	0.26	0.14	2.74	0.00	0.07	0.02
	Average %	1.28	1.28	1.28	1.28	1.28	1.28	1.28	1.28	1.28	1.28	1.28	1.28	1.28
	Ratio	0.49	1.82	0.18	0.02	1.37	0.08	0.01	0.20	0.11	2.14	0.00	0.05	0.02
Wholesale Trade	% of Cnty's Txbl Sales	12.38	3.42	3.04	4.01	8.45	6.92	4.44	5.55	4.97	4.98	9.30	3.83	5.86
	Average %	7.13	7.13	7.13	7.13	7.13	7.13	7.13	7.13	7.13	7.13	7.13	7.13	7.13
	Ratio	1.74	0.48	0.43	0.56	1.19	0.97	0.62	0.78	0.70	0.70	1.30	0.54	0.82

Table A5 (part 3 of 3)
Relative Concentrations of Taxable Sales Base by Industry Classification & County (2008)

		Midland	Wichita	Taylor	Potter	Grayson	Gregg	Guadalupe	Randall	Parker	Comal	Tom Green	Kaufman
Accommodation & Food Svcs.	% of Cnty's Txbl Sales	6.32	13.60	12.74	11.50	13.03	9.00	14.10	14.89	10.44	10.83	12.75	13.42
	Average %	12.33	12.33	12.33	12.33	12.33	12.33	12.33	12.33	12.33	12.33	12.33	12.33
	Ratio	0.51	1.10	1.03	0.93	1.06	0.73	1.14	1.21	0.85	0.88	1.03	1.09
Admin. & Supp. & Waste Mgmt. & Remed. Svcs.	% of Cnty's Txbl Sales	1.60	1.64	1.69	2.23	1.79	2.36	2.81	2.66	2.34	1.95	2.51	2.69
	Average %	2.49	2.49	2.49	2.49	2.49	2.49	2.49	2.49	2.49	2.49	2.49	2.49
	Ratio	0.64	0.66	0.68	0.90	0.72	0.95	1.13	1.07	0.94	0.78	1.01	1.08
Agric., Forestry, Fishing & Hunting	% of Cnty's Txbl Sales	0.01	0.16	0.00	0.04	0.20	0.01	0.19	0.06	0.08	0.11	0.08	0.04
	Average %	0.05	0.05	0.05	0.05	0.05	0.05	0.05	0.05	0.05	0.05	0.05	0.05
	Ratio	0.23	3.03	0.03	0.70	3.73	0.24	3.49	1.03	1.47	2.07	1.48	0.79
Arts, Entertainment & Recreation	% of Cnty's Txbl Sales	0.73	0.89	0.74	0.93	1.04	0.42	0.87	0.96	0.61	3.13	0.85	0.87
	Average %	1.06	1.06	1.06	1.06	1.06	1.06	1.06	1.06	1.06	1.06	1.06	1.06
	Ratio	0.69	0.84	0.70	0.88	0.98	0.40	0.82	0.91	0.57	2.95	0.80	0.82
Construction	% of Cnty's Txbl Sales	4.05	2.13	3.18	3.10	2.90	3.72	5.48	2.71	5.61	3.99	3.81	6.54
	Average %	3.86	3.86	3.86	3.86	3.86	3.86	3.86	3.86	3.86	3.86	3.86	3.86
	Ratio	1.05	0.55	0.82	0.80	0.75	0.96	1.42	0.70	1.45	1.03	0.99	1.69
Educational Svcs.	% of Cnty's Txbl Sales	0.02	0.01	0.31	0.20	0.54	0.20	0.43	0.01	0.28	0.11	0.04	0.09
	Average %	0.17	0.17	0.17	0.17	0.17	0.17	0.17	0.17	0.17	0.17	0.17	0.17
	Ratio	0.10	0.07	1.84	1.22	3.21	1.20	2.56	0.05	1.68	0.67	0.21	0.54
Finance & Insurance	% of Cnty's Txbl Sales	0.15	0.52	0.43	0.40	0.50	0.23	0.44	0.56	0.41	0.23	0.18	0.22
	Average %	0.43	0.43	0.43	0.43	0.43	0.43	0.43	0.43	0.43	0.43	0.43	0.43
	Ratio	0.35	1.22	1.01	0.93	1.17	0.54	1.02	1.29	0.96	0.55	0.43	0.52
Health Care & Social Assistance	% of Cnty's Txbl Sales	0.06	0.07	0.28	0.21	0.52	0.16	0.14	0.01	0.00	0.12	0.37	0.02
	Average %	0.20	0.20	0.20	0.20	0.20	0.20	0.20	0.20	0.20	0.20	0.20	0.20
	Ratio	0.28	0.36	1.41	1.06	2.57	0.78	0.71	0.04	0.02	0.59	1.82	0.11
Information	% of Cnty's Txbl Sales	1.33	2.47	2.38	2.64	2.60	2.06	0.47	1.67	0.33	2.99	4.61	1.73
	Average %	2.64	2.64	2.64	2.64	2.64	2.64	2.64	2.64	2.64	2.64	2.64	2.64
	Ratio	0.50	0.94	0.90	1.00	0.99	0.78	0.18	0.63	0.12	1.13	1.75	0.66
Mgmt. Companies & Enterprises	% of Cnty's Txbl Sales	0.00	0.17	0.00	0.14	0.07	0.01	0.05	0.00	0.00	0.00	0.00	0.00
	Average %	0.36	0.36	0.36	0.36	0.36	0.36	0.36	0.36	0.36	0.36	0.36	0.36
	Ratio	0.00	0.48	0.00	0.38	0.19	0.02	0.14	0.00	0.00	0.00	0.00	0.00
Manufacturing	% of Cnty's Txbl Sales	7.68	4.75	2.36	4.16	5.45	8.23	8.05	1.00	3.66	6.42	4.27	9.28
	Average %	5.88	5.88	5.88	5.88	5.88	5.88	5.88	5.88	5.88	5.88	5.88	5.88
	Ratio	1.31	0.81	0.40	0.71	0.93	1.40	1.37	0.17	0.62	1.09	0.73	1.58
Mining	% of Cnty's Txbl Sales	12.69	0.88	3.49	0.03	0.35	4.89	0.11	0.04	6.25	0.44	2.29	1.13
	Average %	2.45	2.45	2.45	2.45	2.45	2.45	2.45	2.45	2.45	2.45	2.45	2.45
	Ratio	5.17	0.36	1.42	0.01	0.14	1.99	0.04	0.01	2.55	0.18	0.93	0.46
Other Svcs. (except Pub. Admin.)	% of Cnty's Txbl Sales	2.93	3.18	2.57	3.01	2.78	3.78	2.58	4.40	3.22	2.30	3.29	2.52
	Average %	2.71	2.71	2.71	2.71	2.71	2.71	2.71	2.71	2.71	2.71	2.71	2.71
	Ratio	1.08	1.17	0.95	1.11	1.03	1.40	0.95	1.62	1.19	0.85	1.22	0.93
Prof., Sci. & Tech. Services	% of Cnty's Txbl Sales	2.00	0.87	1.14	0.81	0.50	1.19	0.45	2.64	0.84	0.91	1.12	0.56
	Average %	1.45	1.45	1.45	1.45	1.45	1.45	1.45	1.45	1.45	1.45	1.45	1.45
	Ratio	1.39	0.60	0.79	0.56	0.34	0.83	0.31	1.83	0.58	0.63	0.77	0.39
Public Admin.	% of Cnty's Txbl Sales	0.04	0.03	0.68	0.00	0.63	0.27	1.27	0.00	1.79	2.05	0.00	0.21
	Average %	0.47	0.47	0.47	0.47	0.47	0.47	0.47	0.47	0.47	0.47	0.47	0.47
	Ratio	0.09	0.06	1.46	0.00	1.36	0.57	2.71	0.00	3.83	4.38	0.00	0.46
Real Estate & Rental & Leasing	% of Cnty's Txbl Sales	3.76	2.50	1.77	0.75	2.21	7.37	1.62	2.35	5.08	1.39	1.28	1.32
	Average %	2.65	2.65	2.65	2.65	2.65	2.65	2.65	2.65	2.65	2.65	2.65	2.65
	Ratio	1.41	0.94	0.67	0.28	0.83	2.78	0.61	0.89	1.92	0.52	0.48	0.50
Retail Trade	% of Cnty's Txbl Sales	32.59	58.32	57.92	52.87	59.40	44.82	56.58	56.61	51.36	44.09	57.12	55.30
	Average %	52.04	52.04	52.04	52.04	52.04	52.04	52.04	52.04	52.04	52.04	52.04	52.04
	Ratio	0.63	1.12	1.11	1.02	1.14	0.86	1.09	1.09	0.99	0.85	1.10	1.06
Transportation & Warehousing	% of Cnty's Txbl Sales	0.16	0.06	0.09	0.19	0.41	0.41	0.16	0.12	0.14	0.09	0.09	0.14
	Average %	0.37	0.37	0.37	0.37	0.37	0.37	0.37	0.37	0.37	0.37	0.37	0.37
	Ratio	0.45	0.17	0.24	0.51	1.11	1.12	0.43	0.34	0.37	0.26	0.24	0.40
Unclassified Establishments	% of Cnty's Txbl Sales	0.00	0.00	0.00	0.00	0.00	0.00	0.00	0.00	0.00	0.00	0.00	0.00
	Average %	0.00	0.00	0.00	0.00	0.00	0.00	0.00	0.00	0.00	0.00	0.00	0.00
	Ratio	0.00	0.00	0.00	0.00	0.00	0.00	0.00	0.00	0.00	0.00	0.00	0.00
Utilities	% of Cnty's Txbl Sales	0.12	1.21	0.37	9.41	0.61	0.01	0.70	0.03	0.01	0.03	0.16	0.92
	Average %	1.28	1.28	1.28	1.28	1.28	1.28	1.28	1.28	1.28	1.28	1.28	1.28
	Ratio	0.09	0.95	0.29	7.37	0.48	0.01	0.55	0.03	0.01	0.03	0.12	0.72
Wholesale Trade	% of Cnty's Txbl Sales	23.77	6.51	7.85	7.38	4.48	10.87	3.50	9.28	7.54	18.82	5.20	2.99
	Average %	7.13	7.13	7.13	7.13	7.13	7.13	7.13	7.13	7.13	7.13	7.13	7.13
	Ratio	3.33	0.91	1.10	1.03	0.63	1.52	0.49	1.30	1.06	2.64	0.73	0.42

Table A6

Relative Concentrations of Taxable Sales Base by Industry Classification & Municipality (2008)
(as a percentage of taxable sales in all classifications)

Rank	County	City	Accommodation & Food Svcs.	Admin. & Supp. & Waste Mgmt. & Remed. Svcs.	Agric., Forestry, Fish'g & Hunt'g	Arts, Entertainment & Rec.	Construction	Educational Svcs.	Finance & Insurance	Health Care & Social Assist.	Information	Mgmt. Companies & Enterprises	Manufacturing	Mining	Other Svcs. (ex. Pub. Admin.)	Prof., Sci. & Tech. Services	Public Admin.	Real Estate & Rental & Leasing	Retail Trade	Transportation & Warehousing	Unclassified Establishments	Utilities	Wholesale Trade	Aggregates
1	Harris	Baytown	15.4	1.5	0	1.1	1.6	0.4	0.3	0.2	1.3	0	1.2	0	2.6	0.5	0.4	2.6	68.7	0.1	0	0	2.4	100
1	Harris	Bellaire	9.9	6.1	0	0.1	3.5	0	5.5	0.2	1.4	0	1.8	3.1	3.5	8.3	0	0.8	41.8	0	0	0	14	100
1	Harris	Bunker Hill Village	0	4.8	0	0	0	0	0	0	0	0	0	0	6.7	48.4	0	0	40.1	0	0	0	0	100
1	Harris	Deer Park	9.3	2.3	0	0.4	9	0	0	0	0.2	0	12.3	0	2.1	0.5	0	8.1	38	0.3	0	0	17.4	100
1	Harris	El Lago	41	10.4	0	0	0	0	0	0	0	0	0.4	0	25.7	1.6	0	0	20.8	0	0	0	0.1	100
1	Harris	Galena Park	4.4	0.3	0	0	1.4	0.1	0	0	0	0	0.4	0	7.1	0.1	0	0	6.4	5.5	0	0	74.4	100
1	Harris	Hedwig Village	15.3	2	0	0	5.6	0.2	0	0	2.7	0	0.3	0	7.2	4.5	0	0.4	59	0	0	0	2.8	100
1	Harris	Hilshire Village	0	0	0	0	0	0	0	0	0	0	0	0	0	87.4	0	0	12.6	0	0	0	0	100
1	Harris	Humble	12.4	0.8	0	0.5	1.7	0	0.1	0.4	2.6	0	1	0.7	4	0.6	0	1.6	70.9	0	0	0	2.6	100
1	Harris	Hunters Creek Village	0	13.2	0	36.1	0	0	0	0	0	0	0	0	0	35.5	0	0	15.3	0	0	0	0	100
1	Harris	Jacinto City	23.5	0.1	0	0	0.4	0	0.8	0	0	0	6.9	0	3.5	0.1	0	0	52	0	0	0	12.7	100
1	Harris	Jersey Village	12.7	3.1	0	0	4.7	0	0	0	0	0	0.7	0	1.9	0.4	0	10.4	63.4	0	0	0	2.8	100
1	Harris	La Porte	15.3	10.2	0	0.1	7.1	0	0.1	0	0.1	0	12.8	0	5.2	1.6	0	6.7	25.8	0.1	0	0	14.8	100
1	Harris	Morgans Point	-	-	-	-	-	-	-	-	-	-	-	-	-	-	-	-	-	-	-	-	-	-
1	Harris	Nassau Bay	29.6	3.8	0	0	1.8	0	0	1.5	0	0	0.7	0	1	10.5	0	0	16.7	0	0	0	34.4	100
1	Harris	Pasadena	12.1	2.9	0.1	1	3.1	0	0.6	0.2	1.4	0	13.4	0.1	3	0.7	0	3.7	54.1	0.2	0	0.1	3.4	100
1	Harris	Piney Point Village	0	12.1	0	0	0	0	0	0	0	0	0	0	2.1	11.8	0	0	73.6	0	0	0	0.4	100
1	Harris	Seabrook	29.4	1.8	0	2.7	0.7	0	0	0	0.1	0	1.9	0	7.2	0.4	0	1.6	49.4	0	0	0	4.7	100
1	Harris	Shoreacres	0	0	0	0	0	0	0	0	0	0	0	0	0	0	0	0	100	0	0	0	0	100
1	Harris	South Houston	13	2.5	0	1.4	11.2	0	0.4	0	0.3	0	3.4	0	4.8	0.7	0	4.5	44.4	0.8	0	0	12.6	100
1	Harris	Southside Place	31.2	0	0	0	0	0	0	0	0	0	0	0	0	4.9	1	0	62.3	0	0	0	0.7	100
1	Harris	Spring Valley	0.7	33	0	0	15.6	0	0	0	1.2	0	0.8	0	0.1	17.1	0	0	28.9	0	0	0	2.6	100
1	Harris	Taylor Lake Village	0	0	0	0	1.1	0	0	0	0	0	0	0	8.7	18.7	0	0	71.5	0	0	0	0	100
1	Harris	Tomball	13.2	1.1	0	0.2	1.2	0.2	1.4	0.1	0.9	0	10.6	0	1.3	0.9	0	2.2	62.6	0.8	0	0	3.5	100
1	Harris	Waller	17.7	2.6	0	0	12.4	0	0	0	0	0	6.4	0	5.5	0.4	0	0.5	52.5	0	0	0	2	100
1	Harris	Webster	16.6	3.1	0	1.5	0.3	0.1	0.1	1.1	2.2	0	0.9	0	1.8	0.4	0	1.3	69.1	0	0	0	1.5	100
1	Harris	West University Place	14.5	3.3	0	0.1	1.5	0.1	0	0	0	0	0.2	0	2.5	10	0	0	64.3	0	0	0	3.3	100
2	Dallas	Addison	22.8	2.9	0	1	8.5	0.5	1.7	0.3	3.6	0.2	5.7	1.9	1.5	9.6	0	2.7	29.9	0.6	0	0	6.6	100
2	Dallas	Balch Springs	9.2	7.6	0	0	5.5	0	0	0	0	0	3.7	0	2	0.5	0	0.4	63.9	0.3	0	0	6.8	100
2	Dallas	Cedar Hill	13.8	0.6	0	0.6	2.2	0.1	0	0	2.1	0	2.8	0	2.6	0.4	0	1.2	69.9	0.1	0	0	3.5	100
2	Dallas	Cockrell Hill	1.4	0	0	0	0	0	0	0	0	0	14.6	0	2.2	0	0	0	81.8	0	0	0	0.1	100
2	Dallas	Combine	0	24	0	0	4.6	0	0	0	0	0	0.5	0	4.4	0	0	0	66.5	0	0	0	0	100

Rank	County	City	Accommodation & Food Svcs.	Admin. & Supp. & Waste Mgmt. & Remed. Svcs.	Agric., Forestry, Fish'g & Hunt'g	Arts, Entertainment & Rec.	Construction	Educational Svcs.	Finance & Insurance	Health Care & Social Assist.	Information	Mgmt Companies & Enterprises	Manufacturing	Mining	Other Svcs. (ex. Pub. Admin.)	Prof., Sci. & Tech. Services	Public Admin.	Real Estate & Rental & Leasing	Retail Trade	Transportation & Warehousing	Unclassified Establishments	Utilities	Wholesale Trade	Aggregates
2	Dallas	Coppell	6.1	5.1	0	0.8	2.4	0	0.5	0	3.8	0	4.2	0	5.3	2	0	3.7	42.2	0.2	0	0	23.7	100
2	Dallas	De Soto	21.6	3.8	0	1.9	7.8	0	0.4	0.1	1.3	0	5.9	0	2.5	0.7	0	1.2	48.7	0.1	0	0	4	100
2	Dallas	Duncanville	19.2	2.4	0	1.6	2.2	0.1	0.5	0.1	1.2	0	9.4	0	5.6	0.7	0	1.3	52.1	0.2	0	0	3.5	100
2	Dallas	Farmers Branch	5	10.6	0	1.3	10.6	0.1	2.2	0.4	1.3	0	7.3	0	3.1	5	0	1.8	35.4	0	0	0.1	16	100
2	Dallas	Ferris	13.5	31.5	0	0	1.6	0	0	0	0	0	1.2	0	0.5	1	0	0	50.6	0	0	0	0	100
2	Dallas	Glenn Heights	37.2	5.7	0	0	6.6	0	0	0	0	0	7.5	0	4.1	3.5	0	0	35.3	0	0	0	0.1	100
2	Dallas	Grand Prairie	10.8	3	0	2.2	8	0.1	0.2	0	0.8	0	8.3	0.1	2.2	0.7	0	4.4	44.4	0.2	0	0	14.8	100
2	Dallas	Grapevine	22.1	1.8	0	1.5	1.8	0	0.2	0.2	1.2	0.1	17.2	0	1.1	1.5	0	1.8	45.9	0.5	0	0	3.1	100
2	Dallas	Highland Park	10	1.9	0	14.4	0	0	0	0	0.2	0	4.6	0	2.6	4.2	0	1	61.1	0	0	0	0	100
2	Dallas	Hutchins	5.6	40.4	0	0	0	0	0	0	0	0	10.3	0	1.3	0	0	12.5	6.6	0	0	0	23.2	100
2	Dallas	Irving	7.9	2.8	0	1.5	6.6	0.1	0.5	0.1	18.6	0.2	5.3	8	1.6	7.1	0.1	4.3	25.2	2	0	2.3	5.8	100
2	Dallas	Lancaster	13.4	1	0	0	3.1	0	0.4	0.2	0.3	0	6.5	0	3.8	0.8	0	3.3	62.7	0.2	0	0	4.4	100
2	Dallas	Lewisville	12.2	5.4	0	1	2.6	0	1	0.2	1.5	0.4	5.6	0	2.9	1.9	0	2	55.7	2.2	0	0	5.3	100
2	Dallas	Mesquite	15.4	1.4	0	0.8	3.1	0.2	0.1	0.1	2	0.2	2.7	0	2.7	0.8	0	1.4	64.7	0.1	0	0	4.2	100
2	Dallas	Ovilla	0	7.6	0	0.9	29	0	0	0	0	0	0.3	0	12.4	7.4	0	0	42	0	0	0	0.2	100
2	Dallas	Rowlett	9.9	3.2	0	1	4.8	0	0	0.4	0.3	0	3.3	0	4	0.9	0	0.4	69.8	0.1	0	0	1.9	100
2	Dallas	Seagoville	12.6	3.1	0	0	20.8	0	0	0	0.1	0	1.9	0	2.4	0.1	0	2.3	54.9	0	0	0	1.7	100
2	Dallas	Sunnyvale	2	6.8	0	0	14.3	0	0	0	0	0	43.9	0	0.9	1	0	0	15.9	0	0	0	15.2	100
2	Dallas	University Park	18.4	2.7	0	0.1	1.9	3.2	0	0	0.3	0	1.1	0	4.7	4.4	0	0.6	61.9	0	0	0	0.6	100
2	Dallas	Wilmer	24.6	13.3	0	0	0	0	0	0	0	0	0	0	1.1	0	0	0	61	0	0	0	0	100
3	Tarrant	Arlington	14.6	3.1	0	5	2	0.1	0.8	0.2	3.4	0.1	2.9	0	2.2	1.8	0.4	1.4	55.9	0.1	0	0	6.1	100
3	Tarrant	Bedford	26.2	2.6	0	1.3	1.2	0.1	0.5	0.4	1.6	0	1.9	0	2.8	3.8	1.2	1.9	52.9	0	0	0	1.6	100
3	Tarrant	Benbrook	19.4	7.7	0.6	0.3	5	0	0.4	0	0.4	0	9	2.9	5.5	2.6	0	0.6	41.8	0	0	0	3.7	100
3	Tarrant	Blue Mound	0	0	0	0	0	0	0	0	0	0	0	0	23.8	0	0	0	62.5	0	0	0	13.7	100
3	Tarrant	Colleyville	17.1	4.4	0	8.3	3	0.1	2.8	0.1	0.3	0	2.8	0	7.1	4.7	0	1.3	40.4	0	0	0	7.6	100
3	Tarrant	Dalworthington Gardens	3.3	18.5	0	0	22.9	0.1	0	0	0.2	0	8.1	0	16.9	4.3	0	0	21.1	0	0	0	4.7	100
3	Tarrant	Edgecliff Village	0	11.5	0	0	0	0	0	0	0	0	0	0	26.6	0	0	0	61.9	0	0	0	0	100
3	Tarrant	Euless	11.8	5.8	0	2.2	1.8	0	0.2	0	0.2	0	21	0	3	0.7	0	0.5	43.9	0.1	0	0	8.7	100
3	Tarrant	Everman	7.7	6.3	0	0.1	13.7	0	0	0	0	0	39.5	0	2.3	0	0	0	30.3	0	0	0	0.2	100
3	Tarrant	Forest Hill	28.5	2.1	0	0	5.6	0	0	0	0	0	2.5	0	3.5	0	0	0	49.8	0	0	0	7.9	100
3	Tarrant	Haltom City	7.1	9.4	0	0.9	6.5	0	0.2	0	0.2	0	5.7	0	6.9	0.3	0	8.8	30.9	0.1	0	0	23.1	100
3	Tarrant	Hurst	9.3	1	0	0.6	1.7	0	0	0	2.3	0	0.8	0	1.4	0.9	0	0.4	80.4	0	0	0	1.1	100
3	Tarrant	Keller	17.4	2.4	0	3.2	3.6	0	0.4	0.1	0.6	0.8	1.1	0	2.9	1.6	0.5	3	60.5	0	0	0	1.9	100
3	Tarrant	Kennedale	5	2.4	0	1.5	8.7	0	0	0	0	0	22.2	2.4	6.5	4.1	0	6.8	34.7	0	0	0	5.6	100
3	Tarrant	Lake Worth	14.3	11.2	0	0.1	0.8	0	0.2	0	1.1	0	0.2	0	0.5	0.1	0	0.3	70.5	0	0	0	0.7	100
3	Tarrant	Lakeside	0	17.3	0	0	4.3	0	0	0	0	0	0	0	2.7	0.1	0	0	75.6	0	0	0	0	100
3	Tarrant	North Richland Hills	13.4	4.7	0	0.9	1.6	0	0.3	0.5	1.3	0	2	0	2.8	0.8	0.5	1.4	67.1	0	0	0	2.6	100
3	Tarrant	Pantego	14	6.4	0	0	7.8	0	0	0	0.4	0	1.9	0	9.6	3.7	0	1.5	50.3	0	0	0	4.4	100

Rank	County	City	Accommodation & Food Svcs.	Admin. & Supp. & Waste Mgmt. & Remed. Svcs.	Agric., Forestry, Fish'g & Hunt'g	Arts, Entertainment & Rec.	Construction	Educational Svcs.	Finance & Insurance	Health Care & Social Assist.	Information	Mgmt. Companies & Enterprises	Manufacturing	Mining	Other Svcs. (ex. Pub. Admin.)	Prof., Sci. & Tech. Services	Public Admin.	Real Estate & Rental & Leasing	Retail Trade	Transportation & Warehousing	Unclassified Establishments	Utilities	Wholesale Trade	Aggregates
3	Tarrant	Pelican Bay	-	-	-	-	-	-	-	-	-	-	-	-	-	-	-	-	-	-	-	-	-	-
3	Tarrant	Richland Hills	4	28.1	0	0	16.4	0	0	0.1	0.7	0	4.3	0	3.9	2.2	0	0	6	0	0	0	34.2	100
3	Tarrant	River Oaks	27.1	2.6	0	0	2.2	0	0	0	0	0	1.1	0	15.1	0.1	0	0.8	51	0	0	0	0	100
3	Tarrant	Saginaw	15.3	1	0	0.3	2.2	0	0.2	0	1.4	0	10.9	0	1.8	0.3	0	2.7	51.3	0	0	0	12.6	100
3	Tarrant	Sansom Park	16.2	20.1	0	0	5.7	0	0	0	0	0	1.6	0	8.9	0	0	0	47.1	0	0	0	0.3	100
3	Tarrant	Watauga	22.4	0.4	0	1.8	0.8	0.1	0.5	0	2	0	1	0	2.6	0.4	0	0.4	64.9	0	0	0	2.6	100
3	Tarrant	Westworth Village	0	0	0	11.2	0.1	0	0	0	0	0	0	0	0	0	0	0	88.7	0	0	0	0	100
3	Tarrant	White Settlement	9.1	1.1	0	0	2.2	0	1.5	0	0.4	0	8.5	0	2.5	2.4	0	1.2	56	0	0	0	15	100
4	Bexar	Alamo Heights	22.5	3	0	3.3	0.8	0	0	0	0.1	0	0.2	0	6.5	7.7	0	0	54.2	0	0	0	1.6	100
4	Bexar	Balcones Heights	21.7	0	0	0	0	0	0	0	2.2	0	0.1	0	1.5	0	0	1.1	73.4	0	0	0	0	100
4	Bexar	Castle Hills	20.4	3.1	0	0.4	1.6	0	2.3	0	0	0	3.1	0	4.4	2.4	0	0.5	54.2	0	0	0	7.7	100
4	Bexar	China Grove	11	1.4	0	0	38.1	0	0	0	0	0	0	0	2.5	0	0	0	42.1	0	0	0	4.8	100
4	Bexar	Converse	18.3	0.7	0	0	1.4	0.1	0	0	0.1	0	9.9	0	3.7	0.3	0	0.2	63.4	0	0	0	1.9	100
4	Bexar	Elmendorf	0	38.7	0	0	33.4	0	0	0	0	0	0	0	0	0	0	0	27.9	0	0	0	0	100
4	Bexar	Grey Forest	0	0	0	0	0	0	0	0	0	0	0	0	0	0	0	0	100	0	0	0	0	100
4	Bexar	Helotes	51.3	6.6	0	0.7	1.5	0	0	0	0.8	0	1.8	0	11.7	0.5	0	0.7	18.3	0	0	0	6.1	100
4	Bexar	Hill Country Village	10.4	0	0	0	0	0	0	0	0	0	0	0	5.2	4.1	0	1.7	78.6	0	0	0	0.1	100
4	Bexar	Hollywood Park	23.7	5.5	0	0.1	0.2	0	0	0	0.2	0	0	0	3.1	6.6	0	0.5	57.2	0	0	0	2.8	100
4	Bexar	Kirby	31.9	3.3	0	0	15.6	0	0	0	0	0	2.4	0	9.3	0.4	0	0	37	0	0	0	0	100
4	Bexar	Leon Valley	17.2	2.9	0	2.7	2.1	0	0.4	0	0.7	0	1.4	0	4.3	0.4	0	1.7	51.2	0	0	0	15.2	100
4	Bexar	Live Oak	14.1	2.3	0	1	0.2	0	0	0.1	5.4	0	0	0	2.1	0.2	0	0.5	73.1	0	0	0	0.9	100
4	Bexar	Lytle	25.7	0.7	0	0	0	0	0	0	0	0	3.5	0	2.7	0	0	0	66.8	0	0	0	0.6	100
4	Bexar	Olmos Park	22.3	4.3	0	0	0.2	0	0	0	0	0	0	0	3	4.5	0	0	65.7	0	0	0	0.1	100
4	Bexar	San Antonio	13.4	3	0	2.5	4	0.1	0.7	0.9	5.9	0.1	5.6	0.3	2.4	1.7	0.6	2.1	43.9	3.6	0	2.7	6.5	100
4	Bexar	Schertz	13.7	3.8	0	0.4	2.5	0	0.5	0	0.2	0	13.2	0	2.9	0.2	0	2	52.1	0.2	0	0	8.2	100
4	Bexar	Selma	12.5	1.3	0	0.1	3.5	0	0	0	0	0	2.6	0	0.1	0.5	0	3.3	75.7	0	0	0	0.5	100
4	Bexar	Shavano Park	0	0.2	0	0	3.9	0	0	0	0	0	0.3	0	0.8	63	0	0	24.5	0	0	0	7.3	100
4	Bexar	Somerset	14.9	0.6	0	0	0.3	0	0	0	0	0	0	0	3.7	0	0	0	80.5	0	0	0	0	100
4	Bexar	Terrell Hills	17.6	15.9	0	0.1	1.4	0	0	0	0	0	0.3	0	3.2	11.8	0	0	47.7	0	0	0	2.1	100
4	Bexar	Universal City	24.9	2.3	0	3.1	2.9	0.1	0.6	0	0.8	0	1.8	0	7.5	0.5	0	2.9	50.9	0	0	0	1.8	100
4	Bexar	Windcrest	28.1	0.8	0	0.6	0.5	0.3	0	0	1.1	0	0.4	0	0.4	0.2	0	0.5	67.1	0	0	0	0	100
5	Travis	Bee Cave	6.6	0.8	0	1.8	0.8	0	0	0	2.4	0	1.2	0	2.1	0.1	0	0.3	82	0	0	0	1.9	100
5	Travis	Briarcliff	0	56.4	0	12.4	0	0	0	0	0	0	0	0	0	23.3	0	0	8	0	0	0	0	100
5	Travis	Cedar Park	14.4	5.4	0.2	0.4	6.4	0	0.2	1.4	1.8	0	2.3	0	4.3	2.1	0.1	2.2	55.6	0	0	0	3.3	100
5	Travis	Creedmoor	0	95.5	0	0	0	0	0	0	0	0	0	0	0	0	0	0	4.5	0	0	0	0	100
5	Travis	Elgin	31.3	0.2	0	0.3	1.7	0	0.1	0	0	0	1.2	0	2.3	0.6	0	4.1	58.2	0	0	0	0.1	100
5	Travis	Jonestown	10.2	0.9	0	0	5.2	0	0	0	0	0	0	0	22.2	3.2	0	0	57.7	0	0	0	0.6	100

Rank	County	City	Accommodation & Food Svcs.	Admin. & Supp. & Waste Mgmt. & Remed. Svcs.	Agric., Forestry, Fish'g & Hunt'a	Arts, Entertainment & Rec.	Construction	Educational Svcs.	Finance & Insurance	Health Care & Social Assist.	Information	Mgmt. Companies & Enterprises	Manufacturing	Mining	Other Svcs. (ex. Pub. Admin.)	Prof., Sci. & Tech. Services	Public Admin.	Real Estate & Rental & Leasing	Retail Trade	Transportation & Warehousing	Unclassified Establishments	Utilities	Wholesale Trade	Aggregates
5	Travis	Lago Vista	14	2.5	0	3.4	0.3	0	0	0	0	0	8.9	0	1.3	2	0	2	64.2	0	0	0	1.2	100
5	Travis	Leander	6.5	7.9	0.2	0.6	17.2	0.3	0	0	0.4	0	6.1	0.5	2	0.7	0	1.9	55.3	0	0	0	0.3	100
5	Travis	Manor	27.2	0.9	0	6.6	1.5	0	0	0	0	0	0	0	0.5	0	0	0	29.4	0	0	0	33.8	100
5	Travis	Mustang Ridge	0	0	0	0	0	0	0	0	0	0	0	0	1.2	0	0	0	98.8	0	0	0	0	100
5	Travis	Pflugerville	16.1	3.5	0	0.9	1.8	0.1	1.6	0	0.4	0	1.9	0	6.8	0.8	0	2.5	57.8	0	0	0	5.6	100
5	Travis	Point Venture	0	0	0	17.5	0	0	0	0	0	0	0	0	0	0	0	0	82.5	0	0	0	0	100
5	Travis	Rollingwood	21.5	0.7	0	0	0	0	0	0.8	6.2	0	0.6	0	7.4	11.9	0	0	50.9	0	0	0	0	100
5	Travis	Round Rock	7.6	1.4	0	0.3	1.6	0.1	0.1	0	0.6	0	38.2	0	1.7	0.9	0	4.8	36.4	0	0	0	6.4	100
5	Travis	Volente	89.4	3	0	7.3	0	0	0	0	0	0	0	0	0	0	0	0	0.3	0	0	0	0	100
5	Travis	Webberville	0	0	0	0	0	0	0	0	0	0	0	0	0	0	0	0	100	0	0	0	0	100
6	Collin	Allen	14.1	2.5	0	2.7	2.3	0	0.1	0.1	7.5	0	1.8	0	1.4	2.5	0	0.6	61.9	0	0	0	2.5	100
6	Collin	Anna	14.9	2.4	0	0.2	0.6	0	0	0	0	0	4.4	0	2.1	0.4	0	0	74.9	0	0	0	0	100
6	Collin	Blue Ridge	2.2	0	0	0	0	0	0	0	0	0	0	0	0	0	0	0	97.8	0	0	0	0	100
6	Collin	Carrollton	7	6.1	0	1.1	7.8	0.3	1.1	0.2	3.7	0.1	10.5	0	3.4	3.1	0	3.2	34.4	0.5	0	0	17.4	100
6	Collin	Celina	12	12.2	0	0.3	4.8	0	0	0	0	0	19	0	2.9	0.6	0	0	46.2	0	0	0	2.1	100
6	Collin	Dallas	8.6	3.8	0	1.4	5.3	0.1	0.7	0.3	21.3	0.1	8.8	1	1.8	2.5	0.3	1.3	26.4	0.4	0	9.6	6.4	100
6	Collin	Fairview	27.7	26.7	0	0.5	4.4	0	0	0	0	0	0.6	0	7.5	5.9	0	0	24.5	0	0	0	2.2	100
6	Collin	Farmersville	12.9	4	0	0.1	0.8	0	0	0	0	0	43.4	0	3.4	1.6	0	0	33.1	0	0	0	0.6	100
6	Collin	Frisco	13.7	1.8	0.3	2.3	0.6	0	0.6	0.3	1.4	0.1	2.6	0	2.3	2	0	0.8	68	0.1	0	0	3.1	100
6	Collin	Garland	12.6	3.5	0	1.3	5	0.1	0.7	0.1	1.2	0	2.8	0	2.9	0.8	2.7	1.6	54.1	0	0	0	10.5	100
6	Collin	Josephine	0	0	0	0	0	0	0	0	0	0	0	0	0	0	0	0	100	0	0	0	0	100
6	Collin	Lavon	51.8	0.8	0	0	0	0	0	0	0.3	0	0	0	7.6	10.5	0	0	29	0	0	0	0	100
6	Collin	Lowry Crossing	0	95	0	0	0	0	0	0	0	0	0	0	1.9	0	0	0	3.1	0	0	0	0	100
6	Collin	Lucas	2.7	23.7	0.2	0	39.6	0	0	0	0	0	0.1	0	10.5	7	0	0	10.8	0	0	0	5.3	100
6	Collin	McKinney	14.6	5.5	0	2.1	1.9	0.1	0.2	0.2	1	0.4	1.7	0.1	2.4	0.8	0	4.7	58.6	0.2	0	0.1	5.5	100
6	Collin	Melissa	3	2.1	0	0	16.6	0	0	0	0	0	10.5	0	0	0.1	0	0	37.3	0	0	0	30.5	100
6	Collin	Murphy	19.5	5.6	0	1.9	5	0	0	0	0.1	0	1.2	0	4.2	2.1	0	1.7	57.3	0	0	0	1.4	100
6	Collin	Nevada	0	34.6	0	0	0.1	0	0	0	0	0	0	0	0	12.1	0	0	53.2	0	0	0	0	100
6	Collin	New Hope	0	15.3	0	0	0	0	0	0	0	0	0	0	0	0	0	0	84.7	0	0	0	0	100
6	Collin	Parker	0	59.4	0	0	0	0	0	0	0	0	4.4	0	0.5	14.1	0	0	21.6	0	0	0	0	100
6	Collin	Plano	9.9	2.7	0	1.2	2.2	0.1	0.4	0.3	8.2	0.1	2.6	0.6	1.6	12.3	0.3	1.1	52.5	0.1	0	0	3.9	100
6	Collin	Princeton	32.8	1.6	0	0.1	2.9	0	0	0	0	0	6.2	0	2.1	0.5	0	0	36.8	0	0	0	17.1	100
6	Collin	Prosper	5.9	9.7	0	0	3.3	0	0	0	0	0	14.6	0	0.8	0.3	0	2	60.2	0	0	0	3.1	100
6	Collin	Richardson	8	4.2	0	0.7	4.6	0	1.7	0	29.1	0	6.3	0	1.9	3.2	0	0.4	24.2	0	0	6.1	9.5	100
6	Collin	Royse City	27.4	2.5	0	2.3	6.7	0	0	0	0	0	11.2	0	1.8	1.4	0	0	37.1	0	0	0	9.6	100
6	Collin	Sachse	1.2	0.4	0	0.1	8.7	0	0	0	10.5	0	0	0	0.3	0	0	0	19.7	0	0	0	59.1	100
6	Collin	Saint Paul	55.9	12.4	0	0	0	0	0	0	0	0	0	0	8.7	0	0	0	23	0	0	0	0	100
6	Collin	Weston	0	0	0	0	0	0	0	0	0	0	0	0	93.9	0	0	0	6.1	0	0	0	0	100

Rank	County	City	Accommodation & Food Svcs.	Admin. & Supp. & Waste Mgmt. & Remed. Svcs.	Agric., Forestry, Fish'g & Hunt'g	Arts, Entertainment & Rec.	Construction	Educational Svcs.	Finance & Insurance	Health Care & Social Assist.	Information	Mgmt. Companies & Enterprises	Manufacturing	Mining	Other Svcs. (ex. Pub. Admin.)	Prof., Sci. & Tech. Services	Public Admin.	Real Estate & Rental & Leasing	Retail Trade	Transportation & Warehousing	Unclassified Establishments	Utilities	Wholesale Trade	Aggregates
6	Collin	Wylie	14	6	0	1	11.3	0	0.2	0	0.5	0	4.2	0	3.3	2	0	0.4	54.9	0	0	0	2.2	100
7	El Paso	Anthony	19.7	0	0	0	0	0	0	0	0	0	2.5	0	1.3	0	0	0	76.5	0	0	0	0	100
7	El Paso	Clint	2.8	0.1	0	0	0	0	0	0	0	0	0	0	0.4	0	0	0	92.3	0	0	0	4.4	100
7	El Paso	El Paso	14.6	3	0	0.9	2.6	0.1	0.4	0.4	1.1	0.1	3.2	0	2.2	0.6	0.1	1.4	60	0.3	0	4	5.1	100
7	El Paso	Horizon City	22.3	0.2	0	0	1.1	0	0	0	0	0	4.1	0	1.5	0	0	0	69.6	0	0	0	1.1	100
7	El Paso	Socorro	25.7	1.6	0	0.3	0.9	0	1	0	0	0	4.4	0	3.7	3.8	0	4.5	50.3	0.3	0	0	3.5	100
7	El Paso	Vinton	5.9	0.4	0	0	13.8	0	0	0	0	0	21.2	0	0.4	0	0	0	51.1	0	0	0	7.2	100
8	Hidalgo	Alamo	17.2	0.2	0	0	1.2	0	0.1	0	0.6	0	0.2	0	0.7	0.1	0	3.1	73.4	0	0	0	3.1	100
8	Hidalgo	Alton	4.5	2.4	0	0	5.1	0	0	0	0	0	0.4	0	0.7	0	0	0.5	86.4	0	0	0	0	100
8	Hidalgo	Donna	21.5	2.7	0	0	0.4	0	0.4	0	0	0	5.8	0	1.2	0.4	0	10.6	48.7	0	0	0	8.1	100
8	Hidalgo	Edcouch	17.3	7.9	0	0	0	0	0	0	0	0	0	0	3.3	0	0	0	71.5	0	0	0	0	100
8	Hidalgo	Edinburg	16	3.5	0	0.7	2.1	0	0.6	0.3	2.1	0	0.9	5.4	1.2	0.9	0	3.4	57.7	0.5	0	0	4.6	100
8	Hidalgo	Elsa	39.2	1.5	0	0	0	0	0.5	0	0	0	0	0	1.4	0	0	0	57.3	0	0	0	0	100
8	Hidalgo	Granjeno	-	-	-	-	-	-	-	-	-	-	-	-	-	-	-	-	-	-	-	-	-	-
8	Hidalgo	Hidalgo	17.7	0.1	0	0	0	0	1.8	0	0	0	0.1	0	1.6	1.1	0	0	73.4	0.1	0	0	4.2	100
8	Hidalgo	La Joya	54.7	0	0	0	0	0	0	0	0	0	0	0	0.2	0	0	0	45.1	0	0	0	0	100
8	Hidalgo	La Villa	0	0	0	0	0	0	0	0	0	0	0	0	0	0	0	0	100	0	0	0	0	100
8	Hidalgo	McAllen	12.3	2.2	0	0.6	1.7	0	0.5	0.2	1.1	0	1.6	0.1	1.2	0.7	0	0.9	73.6	0.1	0	0	3	100
8	Hidalgo	Mercedes	5.4	0	0	0	0.2	0	0.1	0	0.2	0	1.5	0	3.1	0	0	0.3	85	0	0	0	4.3	100
8	Hidalgo	Mission	17.2	0.5	0	1.6	1.1	0	0.4	0.1	2.3	0	3.7	0.2	1.3	0.4	0	0.9	66.9	0.1	0	0	3.3	100
8	Hidalgo	Palmview	20.5	1.8	0	0	0	0	0	0	0.1	0	0.5	0	1.7	0.5	0	0.7	61.5	0	0	0	12.7	100
8	Hidalgo	Penitas	1.3	2.1	0	0	2.9	0	0	0	0	0	0.1	0	2	0	0	0	79.8	0	0	0	11.9	100
8	Hidalgo	Pharr	12.7	3.7	0	0.7	3.2	0	0.7	0	0.4	0	2.6	0.2	2	0.4	0	1.3	57.7	0.1	0	0	14.4	100
8	Hidalgo	Progreso	8.9	0	0	0	0	0	0	0	0	0	0	0	0	0	0	0	91	0	0	0	0.1	100
8	Hidalgo	San Juan	15.9	2.6	0	0	1.4	0	0	0	0.5	0	10.6	0	1.3	0.1	0	2.5	61.2	0	0	0	3.9	100
8	Hidalgo	Weslaco	17.5	1.6	0	0.2	0.3	0	0.5	0.1	1.7	0	1.2	0	1.8	0.3	0	7	62.9	0.4	0	0	4.3	100
9	Denton	Argyle	20.5	29.2	0	0	2.2	2.9	0	0	0	0	0.6	0	12.5	5.4	0	0	24.5	0	0	0	2.2	100
9	Denton	Aubrey	34.1	0.2	0	0	0.4	0	0	0	0	0	0	0	3.6	0.1	0	0	61.4	0	0	0	0.2	100
9	Denton	Bartonville	29.8	5.4	0	0	0.2	0	0	0	0	0	0.4	0	3.8	0.5	0	0	59.5	0	0	0	0.4	100
9	Denton	Copper Canyon	0	6.3	0	0.1	90.2	0	0	0	0	0	0.2	0	0	0	0	0	3.3	0	0	0	0	100
9	Denton	Corinth	6.5	1.2	0	2	2.1	0.1	0	0	1.1	0	1.9	0	3	1	0	0.4	14.5	0	0	64.6	1.6	100
9	Denton	Corral City	0	0	0	0	0	0	0	0	0	0	0	0	0	0	0	0	100	0	0	0	0	100
9	Denton	Denton	15.9	1.2	0	0.4	2.5	0	0.2	0.3	1.4	0	4	6.1	3.1	0.9	0	1.7	58.7	0.4	0	0	3.3	100
9	Denton	Double Oak	0	29.4	0	0.1	1.2	0	0	0	0	0	2.9	0	1.4	6.9	0	0	56.8	0	0	0	1.2	100
9	Denton	Flower Mound	16.2	2.1	0	3.7	3.8	0.1	0.3	0.1	1	0	0.6	0	3.2	3.4	0	0.6	58.6	0	0	0	6.3	100
9	Denton	Fort Worth	10.7	2.5	0	1.3	3.6	0.1	0.4	0.2	1.4	0.1	9	11.6	2.3	2.6	0.5	2.6	38.2	2.5	0	1.5	9	100
9	Denton	Hackberry	0	0	0	0	0	0	0	0	0	0	0	0	0	0	0	0	100	0	0	0	0	100
9	Denton	Haslet	39.5	2.1	0	0	8.4	0	0	0	0	0	2.6	0	2	2.4	0	0	41.8	0	0	0	1.3	100

Rank	County	City	Accommodation & Food Svcs.	Admin. & Supp. & Waste Mgmt. & Remed. Svcs.	Agric., Forestry, Fish'g & Hunt'g	Arts, Entertainment & Rec.	Construction	Educational Svcs.	Finance & Insurance	Health Care & Social Assist.	Information	Mgmt. Companies & Enterprises	Manufacturing	Mining	Other Svcs. (ex. Pub. Admin.)	Prof., Sci. & Tech. Services	Public Admin.	Real Estate & Rental & Leasing	Retail Trade	Transportation & Warehousing	Unclassified Establishments	Utilities	Wholesale Trade	Aggregates
9	Denton	Hickory Creek	20	0	0	0	0.3	0	0.1	0	0	0	0	0	1.7	0.3	0	1.2	76.3	0	0	0	0	100
9	Denton	Highland Village	15.1	1	0	2.5	0.8	0.1	0	0	3.2	0	0.3	0	1.3	1.4	0	0.3	73	0	0	0	0.9	100
9	Denton	Justin	17.6	2.8	0	0	2.2	0	0	0	0	0	0.4		1.6	0.3	0	0	36.4	0	0	0	38.7	100
9	Denton	Krugerville	0	0	0	0	70.8	0	0	0	0	0	0	0	0.4	0	0	0	28.7	0	0	0	0	100
9	Denton	Krum	30.4	0.2	0	0	7.2	0	0	0	0	0	0.4	0	4.4	2.7	0	0	45	9.4	0	0	0.3	100
9	Denton	Lake Dallas	5.1	3.5	0	0	38.1	0	0	0	3.8	0	1.8	0	1.1	2	0	0	44.4	0	0	0	0.2	100
9	Denton	Little Elm	25.6	3.5	0	1.8	1.7	0	0	0	1.2	0	0.3	0	2.9	0.4	0	1.3	60	0.1	0	0	1.1	100
9	Denton	Northlake	0	0	0	0	0	0	0	0	0	0	78.9	0	0	0	0	0	21.1	0	0	0	0	100
9	Denton	Oak Point	0	19.4	0	2.5	55.5	0	0	0	0	0	0	0	0.1	11.1	0	0	2	0	0	0	9.2	100
9	Denton	Pilot Point	17.1	0.3	0	0.2	5.7	0	0	0	0	0	8.1	0	10.1	0.4	0	0	55.9	0	0	0	2.2	100
9	Denton	Ponder	28.3	0	0	0	0	0	0	0	0	0	0.1	0	5.7	0	0	0	63.1	0	0	0	2.8	100
9	Denton	Roanoke	18.3	0.4	0	0.4	4.1	0	0	0	0.2	0	2.3	0	1.7	0.3	0	0.1	64.9	0	0	0	7.3	100
9	Denton	Sanger	30.3	1.9	0	0	7	0	0	0	0.8	0	0.3	0	14.4	0.8	0	5.9	36.9	0.5	0	0	1.2	100
9	Denton	Shady Shores	0	17.3	0	0	42.3	0	0	0	0	0	0.1	0	1.3	1	0	0	12.5	0	0	0	25.5	100
9	Denton	Southlake	14.3	1.8	0.3	1.7	3	0	0	0.1	3.2	0	6.5	0	1.2	1.9	0	1.7	58.2	0.1	0	0	6	100
9	Denton	The Colony	13.6	1.9	0	3.2	2.3	0	0.2	0	0.2	0.2	0.5	0	1.9	0.3	0	1.4	53.3	0	0	0	21.1	100
9	Denton	Trophy Club	16.1	6.6	0	9.3	2.8	0	0	0	0.1	0	0.1	0	4.9	5.2	0	1.3	50.2	0	0	0	3.3	100
10	Fort Bend	Arcola	4.8	0	0	0	0	0	0	0	0	0	28.8	0	6	0	0	33.3	27.1	0	0	0	0	100
10	Fort Bend	Beasley	0	0	0	0	0	0	0	0	0	0	0	0	0	0	0	0	100	0	0	0	0	100
10	Fort Bend	Fulshear	23.6	4.3	0	0	8.5	0	0	0	0	0	0	0	3.9	0.5	0	0	37.1	0	0	0	22.1	100
10	Fort Bend	Houston	9.5	3.5	0	0.8	4.6	0.1	0.4	0.2	1.5	0.4	10.1	10.2	2.3	2.9	0.2	1.9	34.8	1.5	0	6.1	8.9	100
10	Fort Bend	Katy	9.4	3.4	0	0.2	1.5	0.1	0.1	0	5.6	0	3.3	0.2	1.1	0.5	0	0.1	73.4	0	0	0	1	100
10	Fort Bend	Kendleton	-	-	-	-	-	-	-	-	-	-	-	-	-	-	-	-	-	-	-	-	-	-
10	Fort Bend	Meadows Place	23.6	0.1	0	0	0	0	0	0	0	0	0	0	0.9	1	0	0	74.5	0	0	0	0	100
10	Fort Bend	Missouri City	12.9	4.3	0	1.3	9.3	0.1	0	0	2.4	0	0.8	0	2.5	1.4	0.1	1.7	57.2	0	0	0	6.1	100
10	Fort Bend	Needville	13.6	0.2	0	0	3.6	0	0	0	0	0	7.4	0	3.3	0	0	2.1	69.7	0	0	0	0	100
10	Fort Bend	Orchard	0	0	0	0	59.5	0	0	0	0	0	0	0	0	0	0	0	40.5	0	0	0	0	100
10	Fort Bend	Richmond	14.2	2.9	0	3.1	0.5	0	0.1	0.2	0.3	0	1.7	0	3.5	2.6	0	0	70.7	0	0	0	0.1	100
10	Fort Bend	Rosenberg	13.6	1.1	0	0.1	1.6	0	0.4	0	1.4	0	2	0	1.4	0.4	0	2.8	63.6	0	0	0	11.5	100
10	Fort Bend	Simonton	0	0	0	0	0	0	0	0	0	0	2	0	0	4.4	0	0	93.7	0	0	0	0	100
10	Fort Bend	Sugar Land	9.5	0.9	0	2	3.8	0	0.1	0.1	2.8	0.3	1.7	24.7	1.2	2.2	0	0.9	41.8	0.1	0	0.7	7.2	100
11	Montgomery	Conroe	9.9	0.9	0	0.4	3.4	0	0.3	0.4	4.1	0	6.1	0.9	1.9	1.1	0.1	2.7	60.7	0.2	0	0.3	6.7	100
11	Montgomery	Magnolia	37.5	0.2	0	0.6	0.3	0	0	0	0	0	3	0	2.9	0.1	0	5	49.3	0	0	0	1.1	100
11	Montgomery	Montgomery	35.2	0	0	1.2	0.3	0	0	0	0	0	1.5	0	4.8	0	0	0	55.2	0	0	0	1.7	100
11	Montgomery	Oak Ridge North	12.3	3.4	0	0.5	4.4	0	0	0	0.3	0	3.3	0	2.5	1.5	0	0	70.1	0	0	0	1.7	100
11	Montgomery	Panorama Village	0	18.6	0	0	0	0	0	0	0	0	12.8	0	0	7.4	0	0	61.1	0	0	0	0	100
11	Montgomery	Patton Village	-	-	-	-	-	-	-	-	-	-	-	-	-	-	-	-	-	-	-	-	-	-
11	Montgomery	Shenandoah	21.7	0	0	0	0.2	0	0.1	0.7	0	0	0.2	0	0.2	0.2	0	0	75.7	0	0	0	1	100

Rank	County	City	Accommodation & Food Svcs.	Admin. & Supp. & Waste Mgmt. & Remed. Svcs.	Agric., Forestry, Fish'g & Hunt'g	Arts, Entertainment & Rec.	Construction	Educational Svcs.	Finance & Insurance	Health Care & Social Assist.	Information	Mgmt. Companies & Enterprises	Manufacturing	Mining	Other Svcs. (ex. Pub. Admin.)	Prof., Sci. & Tech. Services	Public Admin.	Real Estate & Rental & Leasing	Retail Trade	Transportation & Warehousing	Unclassified Establishments	Utilities	Wholesale Trade	Aggregates
11	Montgomery	Splendora	29.4	9.9	0	0	0.1	0	0	0	0	0	10	0	3.5	0	0	1.8	45.2	0	0	0	0.1	100
11	Montgomery	Stagecoach	0	0	0	0	0	0	0	0	0	0	0	0	0	0	0	0	100	0	0	0	0	100
11	Montgomery	Willis	26.9	0.1	0	0	0.4	0	0.4	0	0.3	0	10.8	0	2.5	0.2	0	0.2	52.4	0	0	0	5.7	100
12	Williamson	Florence	0	0	0	0	6	0	0	0	0	0	0.3	0	2	0	0	0	91.7	0	0	0	0	100
12	Williamson	Georgetown	13.4	0.6	0	1.8	0.7	0	0.1	0	4.8	0	1.4	0.1	2.5	1.1	0	0.7	66.7	0.3	0	3.1	2.7	100
12	Williamson	Granger	33	0	0	0	0	0	0	0	0	0	0	0	8	0	0	0	59	0	0	0	0	100
12	Williamson	Hutto	21.2	0.5	0	0.1	1.3	0	0	0	0.3	0	0.7	0	3	0.3	0	0.4	72.1	0	0	0	0.1	100
12	Williamson	Jarrell	8.9	21.9	0	0	0.6	0	0	0	0	0	0.5	8.2	4.5	0	0	0	44.6	0	0	0	10.8	100
12	Williamson	Liberty Hill	19.2	0.9	0	0	7.3	0	0	0	0	0	5.1	0	4.2	1.1	0	3.3	53.4	0	0	0	5.5	100
12	Williamson	Taylor	15.5	1.4	0	0.3	12.6	0	0.2	0	0.4	0	8.1	0	2.8	1	0	1.8	54.8	0	0	0	1	100
12	Williamson	Thorndale	13.6	0	0	0	0.6	0	0	0	0	0	0	0	0.2	0.1	0	0	85.6	0	0	0	0	100
12	Williamson	Thrall	0	0	0	0	0	0	0	0	0	0	0	0	0	0	0	0	100	0	0	0	0	100
12	Williamson	Weir	0	0	0	0	0	0	0	0	0	0	0	0	0	0	0	0	100	0	0	0	0	100
13	Cameron	Brownsville	13.6	1.5	0	0.8	0.7	0.1	0.4	0.2	1.4	0	3.2	0	0.9	0.4	0	1.1	69.4	0.1	0	3	3.4	100
13	Cameron	Combes	3.1	17.5	0	0	0.4	0	0	0	0	0	0	0	0.3	0	0	0	78.8	0	0	0	0	100
13	Cameron	Harlingen	14.9	3.9	0	0.4	2.3	0.3	0.8	0.3	2.4	0	1.7	0	2.7	0.7	0	1.1	61	0.1	0	0.6	6.9	100
13	Cameron	La Feria	26.4	0	0	0	4.8	0	1.1	0	0.4	0	16.1	0	10.4	0	0	6	32.9	0	0	0	1.8	100
13	Cameron	Laguna Vista	25.9	27.3	0	15.3	0.4	0	0	0	0	0	0	0	11.2	0	0	0	20	0	0	0	0	100
13	Cameron	Los Fresnos	27.4	0.7	0	1.8	9.9	0	0	0	0.1	0	0	0	1.1	0.7	0	0	58.3	0	0	0	0	100
13	Cameron	Palm Valley	-	-	-	-	-	-	-	-	-	-	-	-	-	-	-	-	-	-	-	-	-	-
13	Cameron	Port Isabel	18.9	0.4	0	0.8	2	0	0	0	0	0	0.3	0	1.3	0.1	0	0.2	76	0	0	0	0	100
13	Cameron	Primera	0	5.7	0	0	43.8	0	0	0	0	0	0	0	0	0	0	0	50.5	0	0	0	0	100
13	Cameron	Rancho Viejo	87.8	2.1	0	0	0	0	0	0	0	0	0	0	0	0	0	0	9.3	0	0	0	0.7	100
13	Cameron	Rio Hondo	5.6	0.2	0	0	0	0	0	0	0	0	0	0	1.3	0	0	0	92.9	0	0	0	0	100
13	Cameron	San Benito	13.9	0.9	0	2.5	1.6	0	0.9	0	0.1	0	8.5	0	0.5	1.7	0	3.8	60.7	0	0	0	4.9	100
13	Cameron	Santa Rosa	2.4	0	0	0	9.1	0	0	0	0	0	0	0	0.7	0	0	0	87.8	0	0	0	0	100
13	Cameron	South Padre Island	43.9	0.9	0	9.4	1.3	0	0	0	0	0	0	0	1.4	0.4	0	1.4	39.8	1.5	0	0	0.1	100
14	Nueces	Agua Dulce	0	9.9	0	0	0	0	0	0	0	0	0	0	32.6	0	0	0	43.8	0	0	0	13.7	100
14	Nueces	Aransas Pass	8.6	0.1	0	0.5	20.2	0	0.7	0	0.9	0	0.4	0	1.2	0.8	0	2.1	63.6	0.2	0	0	0.6	100
14	Nueces	Bishop	31.4	0	0	0	0	0	0	0	0	0	0	0	2.9	0	0	0	65.6	0	0	0	0	100
14	Nueces	Corpus Christi	13.8	3.1	0	0.8	4.8	0	0.3	0.3	1.3	0.2	4.1	2	3.3	0.6	0	4.5	51.2	0.8	0	0.3	8.6	100
14	Nueces	Driscoll	0	0	0	0	0	0	0	0	0	0	0	0	0	0	0	0	100	0	0	0	0	100
14	Nueces	Port Aransas	36.7	2.1	0	2	5	0	0	0	0	0	0.7	0	1.1	1.2	0	1.3	49.2	0.6	0	0	0.1	100
14	Nueces	Robstown	5.5	1.7	0	0	0.1	0	0	0	0	0	1.7	2.6	0.5	0	0	3.3	6.7	0	0	5.7	72.2	100
15	Brazoria	Alvin	13.2	5.4	0	0.1	2.4	0.7	0.3	0	0.5	0	2.5	0.5	2.2	3.7	0	5.9	58.2	0	0	0	4.4	100
15	Brazoria	Angleton	17.3	3.5	0	0.2	3.1	0	0.5	0.1	0.3	0	1.1	0	2.3	0.8	0	2.8	66.4	0	0	0	1.6	100
15	Brazoria	Brazoria	10.2	0.4	0	0	13.2	0	0	0	7.6	0	0.8	0	3.5	0.3	0	0.1	62	0	0	0	2	100
15	Brazoria	Brookside Village	0	19.9	0	0	38.2	0	0	0	0	0	7	0	3.1	0	0	0	31.7	0	0	0	0	100

Rank	County	City	Accommodation & Food Svcs.	Admin. & Supp. & Waste Mgmt. & Remed. Svcs.	Agric., Forestry, Fish'g & Hunt'g	Arts, Entertainment & Rec.	Construction	Educational Svcs.	Finance & Insurance	Health Care & Social Assist.	Information	Mgmt. Companies & Enterprises	Manufacturing	Mining	Other Svcs. (ex. Pub. Admin.)	Prof., Sci. & Tech. Services	Public Admin.	Real Estate & Rental & Leasing	Retail Trade	Transportation & Warehousing	Unclassified Establishments	Utilities	Wholesale Trade	Aggregates
15	Brazoria	Clute	19	0.8	0	0.5	10.4	0.1	1	0	0	0	4.3	0	3.4	1.3	0	3.8	46.9	0	0	0	8.4	100
15	Brazoria	Danbury	8.7	0	0	0	0.2	0	0	0	0	0	0	0	0.6	0	0	0	90.4	0	0	0	0	100
15	Brazoria	Freeport	12.1	0.9	0	0	16.9	0	0.5	0	0	0	13.2	0.1	2.2	1.2	0	9.6	36.2	0.9	0	0	6.1	100
15	Brazoria	Holiday Lakes	-	-	-	-	-	-	-	-	-	-	-	-	-	-	-	-	-	-	-	-	-	-
15	Brazoria	Jones Creek	0	0	0	0	0	0	0	0	0	0	0	0	0	0	0	0	100	0	0	0	0	100
15	Brazoria	Lake Jackson	12.8	0.8	0	0.5	0.5	0	0.1	0.1	1.6	0	0.1	0	1.3	0.3	0	0.9	80.6	0	0	0	0.3	100
15	Brazoria	Liverpool	0	0	0	0	0	0	0	0	0	0	0.4	0	0	0	0	0	99.6	0	0	0	0	100
15	Brazoria	Manvel	12.8	0.7	0	0.1	4	0	0	0	0	0	12.1	0	1.7	0.6	0	0.5	66.2	0	0	0	1.2	100
15	Brazoria	Oyster Creek	26.1	0	0	0	0	0	0	0	0	0	0	0	2	0	0	0	13.8	0	0	0	58	100
15	Brazoria	Pearland	12.5	1.3	0.1	1	1.6	0	0.1	0	1.2	0.3	4.6	1	2.3	0.5	0	5.2	65.1	0	0	0	3.2	100
15	Brazoria	Quintana	-	-	-	-	-	-	-	-	-	-	-	-	-	-	-	-	-	-	-	-	-	-
15	Brazoria	Richwood	0	0.1	0	0	1.3	0	0	0	0	0	0	0	11.4	0	0	0	83	0	0	0	4.1	100
15	Brazoria	Surfside Beach	38.7	0	0	0	0	0	0	0	0	0	0	0	0	0	0	0	61.3	0	0	0	0	100
15	Brazoria	Sweeny	33.7	0	0	0	0.1	0	0	0	0	0	2.2	0	1.7	0	0	0	62.4	0	0	0	0	100
15	Brazoria	West Columbia	25.2	0.4	0	0	0.8	0	0	0	0	0	0.3	0	1.3	0.3	0	0	71.5	0	0	0	0	100
16	Galveston	Bayou Vista	0	4.8	0	0	0	0	0	0	0	0	6.8	0	0	0	0	0	76.7	0	0	0	11.7	100
16	Galveston	Clear Lake Shores	7.5	0	0	0.1	0	0	0	0	0	0	0	0	4.1	0.3	0	0	84.6	2.3	0	0	1.3	100
16	Galveston	Dickinson	7.2	0.5	0	0.2	1.2	0	0	0	0.1	0	0.3	0	1.1	0.2	0	0.9	87.7	0.1	0	0	0.6	100
16	Galveston	Friendswood	23.4	4.2	0	4.1	4.7	0	0.3	0	1.2	0	1.3	0	3.6	5.9	0.3	1	46.9	0	0	0	3.3	100
16	Galveston	Galveston	23.2	1.2	0	3.2	2.1	0.5	4.8	0.1	3.6	0	3.5	0.6	1.7	0.7	0.8	2	46.5	1	0	0	4.4	100
16	Galveston	Hitchcock	17.2	1.6	0	0	9	0	0	0	0	0	6	0	12.1	0.5	0	0.3	51.7	0	0	0	1.5	100
16	Galveston	Jamaica Beach	17.2	0	0	0	2.1	0	0	0	0	0	0	0	0	0	0	0	80.7	0	0	0	0	100
16	Galveston	Kemah	36.1	0.4	0	2.3	1	0	0	0	0.1	0	0.5	0	1.3	0.2	0	0.1	54.9	0	0	0	3.2	100
16	Galveston	La Marque	13.9	1	0	0.9	3.1	0	0	0	1.6	0	1.6	0	1.5	0.1	0	1.8	68.5	0	0	0	6	100
16	Galveston	League City	12.4	3.9	0	2.4	3.6	0.1	0.2	0	0.9	0	9.7	0	3.3	2.7	0	1.6	57.2	0.4	0	0.1	1.7	100
16	Galveston	Santa Fe	20.3	1	0	0.1	4.2	0	0	0	0	0	1.8	0	4.3	3.1	0	2.2	61	0	0	0	2.1	100
16	Galveston	Texas City	14.2	0.6	0	0.1	6.1	0	0.2	0.5	1.2	0	6.4	0	1.8	0.6	0	6.5	57.9	0.3	0	0	3.5	100
16	Galveston	Tiki Island	0	0	0	0	0	0	0	0	0	0	0	0	0	0	0	0	100	0	0	0	0	100
17	Bell	Bartlett	12.7	0.6	0	0	0	0	0	0	0	0	0	0	0.8	0	0	0	85.7	0	0	0	0.3	100
17	Bell	Belton	15.5	1.8	0	0.8	4.7	0.7	0.2	0.3	0.1	0	7	0	2.6	0.7	0	0.6	60.1	0	0	0	4.8	100
17	Bell	Harker Heights	13.4	1.3	0	0.4	1.4	0.2	0	0	2.5	0	0.5	0	0.9	0.3	0	0.9	77.4	0	0	0	0.8	100
17	Bell	Holland	4.3	0	0	0	0	0	0	0	0	0	0	0	5.6	0	0	0	90.1	0	0	0	0	100
17	Bell	Killeen	16.5	0.8	0	1.9	0.8	0.4	0.5	0.2	8.1	0	1.5	0	2.7	0.6	0	1.8	62.3	0	0	0	1.8	100
17	Bell	Nolanville	6.5	0.5	0	0	0	0	0	0	0	0	0	0	14.7	0	0	0	78.3	0	0	0	0	100
17	Bell	Rogers	10.9	0	0	0	1.3	0	0	0	0	0	0	0	0.2	0	0	0	87.6	0	0	0	0	100
17	Bell	Salado	27.1	1.7	0	0.1	0.2	0	0	0	0.2	0	5.3	0	0.9	2.2	0	0	62.4	0	0	0	0	100
17	Bell	Temple	14	2.1	0	0.3	2	0.1	0.4	0.7	1.5	0	4.8	0	2.4	1.3	0.2	2.1	62.2	0	0	0	5.9	100
17	Bell	Troy	3.3	0.7	0	0	0.3	0	0	0	0	0	4.8	0	0.8	0	0	0	79.3	0	0	0	10.7	100

Rank	County	City	Accommodation & Food Svcs.	Admin. & Supp. & Waste Mgmt. & Remed. Svcs.	Agric., Forestry, Fish'g & Hunt'g	Arts, Entertainment & Rec.	Construction	Educational Svcs.	Finance & Insurance	Health Care & Social Assist.	Information	Mgmt. Companies & Enterprises	Manufacturing	Mining	Other Svcs. (ex. Pub. Admin.)	Prof., Sci. & Tech. Services	Public Admin.	Real Estate & Rental & Leasing	Retail Trade	Transportation & Warehousing	Unclassified Establishments	Utilities	Wholesale Trade	Aggregates
18	Lubbock	Abernathy	24.3	0.2	0	0	8.5	0	0	0	0	0	0	0	6.2	0	0	0	58.8	0	0	0	2.1	100
18	Lubbock	Idalou	4.2	2.4	0	0	0.2	0	0	0	0	0	0.4	0	5.2	0.2	0	0	86	0	0	0	1.4	100
18	Lubbock	Lubbock	13.9	2	0	0.7	2.3	0.1	0.4	0.2	5	0.2	2.3	0.2	2.8	1.2	0.1	1.5	56.4	0.2	0	1.8	8.7	100
18	Lubbock	New Deal	13	0	0	0	0	0	0	0	0	0	0	0	0	0	0	0	87	0	0	0	0	100
18	Lubbock	Ransom Canyon	0	0	0	0	0	0	0	0	0	0	0	0	0	66	0	0	34	0	0	0	0	100
18	Lubbock	Shallowater	9.8	1.7	0	0	7.6	0	0	0	0	0	0	0	1.7	0	1.3	0	56.7	0	0	0	21.3	100
18	Lubbock	Slaton	14.7	0.8	0	0.7	3.4	0	0	0	0.2	0	3.6	0	2.4	0	0	0	73.1	0	0	0	1.1	100
18	Lubbock	Wolfforth	8.3	1.4	0	0	2.2	0.6	0	0	0	0	0	0	0	0.9	0	0	84.2	0	0	0	2.5	100
19	Jefferson	Beaumont	9.8	2.3	0.1	0.5	4.9	0	0.4	0.2	1.1	12	5	0.3	4.8	0.5	0	3.2	47.2	0.3	0	0	7.3	100
19	Jefferson	Bevil Oaks	0	10.8	0	0	0	0	0	0	0	0	0	0	0	24.6	0	0	64.5	0	0	0	0	100
19	Jefferson	Groves	16.8	1.9	0	0	23.3	0	0	0	0	0	1.3	0	2.4	0.2	0	7.3	35.5	0	0	0	11.3	100
19	Jefferson	Nederland	16.7	8.9	0	0.8	4.5	0	0.2	0	0	0	1.5	0	3.9	0.6	0	8.9	45.8	0	0	0	8.1	100
19	Jefferson	Port Arthur	10	2.7	0	0.4	3	0	0.1	0.2	1	0	3.6	0	1.2	0.4	0	2.9	69.7	0.2	0	0	4.6	100
19	Jefferson	Port Neches	20.4	4.1	0	0.2	12.2	0	0	0	0	0	1.6	0	7.5	2.9	0	0.9	47.3	0	0	0	2.9	100
20	Webb	El Cenizo	2.2	0	0	0	0	0	0	0	0	0	0	0	0	0	0	0	97.8	0	0	0	0	100
20	Webb	Laredo	14.3	2.1	0	0.6	0.9	0	1	0.4	1	0	2.3	1.7	1.8	0.7	0	2	66.6	0.2	0	0	4.4	100
20	Webb	Rio Bravo	1.1	0	0	0	0	0	0	0	0	0	0	0	0.5	0	0	0	97	0	0	0	1.3	100
21	McLennan	Bellmead	11.7	0.1	0	0	0.7	0	0	0	0	0	1.3	0	1.2	0.1	0	2.1	82.6	0	0	0	0.3	100
21	McLennan	Beverly Hills	20.6	0.1	0	0	0	0	0	0	0	0	2.1	0	4.6	0	0	3.1	67.4	0	0	0	2.1	100
21	McLennan	Crawford	0	0	0	0	0	0	0	0	0	0	0	0	0	0	0	0	100	0	0	0	0	100
21	McLennan	Gholson	0	0	0	0	0	0	0	0	0	0	0	0	0	0	0	0	100	0	0	0	0	100
21	McLennan	Hewitt	12.4	4.9	0	0	16.7	0	0	0	0	0	6.2	0	8.1	0.9	0.4	0.8	34	0	0	0	15.6	100
21	McLennan	Lorena	34.1	15.7	0	0	4.7	0	0	0	0	0	0.2	0	2.2	0	0	0	42.1	0	0	0	1	100
21	McLennan	Mart	15.9	0	0	0	0	0	0	0	0	0	0	0	0.8	0	0	0	83.3	0	0	0	0	100
21	McLennan	Moody	10.3	8.1	0	0	0	0	0	0	0	0	0.5	0	0.1	0.3	0	0	79.9	0	0	0	0.9	100
21	McLennan	Riesel	0	0	0	0	79.5	0	0	0	0	0	0	0	2	0	0	0	18.5	0	0	0	0	100
21	McLennan	Robinson	18.4	2.4	0	0.3	18.2	0	0	0	0	0	3.1	0	10.9	1.7	0	0	42.2	0	0	0	2.7	100
21	McLennan	Valley Mills	15.8	2.2	0	0	2	0	0	0	0	0	0.3	0	1.3	0	0	0	78.4	0	0	0	0	100
21	McLennan	Waco	15.4	1.9	0	1.1	1.4	1.2	1.8	0.4	1.1	0.2	3.5	0	2.9	1.1	0	5.1	56.7	0.2	0	0.2	5.9	100
21	McLennan	West	25.1	0.6	0	0.2	1.1	0	0	0	0	0	0.7	0	8.6	0	0	0	63.3	0	0	0	0.4	100
21	McLennan	Woodway	2.3	5.3	0	0.2	15	0	0	0	0.7	0	8.9	0	2.1	1	0	9.8	44	0	0	0	10.6	100
22	Smith	Arp	4.1	0	0	0	80.9	0	0	0	0	0	0	0	0.3	0	0	0	14.7	0	0	0	0	100
22	Smith	Bullard	21.5	8.8	0	0.6	0	0	0	0	0.1	0	0.2	0	3.8	1.6	0	0	62.9	0	0	0	0.4	100
22	Smith	Lindale	22.4	0.5	0	0.3	1.4	0	0	0.1	0.1	0	0.2	0	1.9	0.3	0	0.1	72.1	0.1	0	0	0.6	100
22	Smith	Overton	18.3	1	0	0	8.9	0	0	0	0	0	1.8	0	0.9	0	0	0	69	0	0	0	0	100
22	Smith	Troup	21.2	0	0	0	0	0	0	0	0	0	3	0	0.4	0	0	0	73.9	0	0	0	1.5	100
22	Smith	Tyler	12	1.4	0	0.9	1.6	0	0.3	0.4	3.5	0.2	3	6.4	2.2	2	0	1.5	59.5	0	0	0	4.9	100
22	Smith	Whitehouse	24.5	3.3	0	0	4.5	0	0	0	0	0	2.7	0	4	2.8	0	0	58	0	0	0	0.1	100
22	Smith	Winona	34.9	0.3	0	0	0	0	0	0	0	0	0	0	0	0	0	0	64.7	0	0	0	0	100

Rank	County	City	Accommodation & Food Svcs.	Admin. & Supp. & Waste Mgmt. & Remed. Svcs.	Agric., Forestry, Fish'g & Hunt'g	Arts, Entertainment & Rec.	Construction	Educational Svcs.	Finance & Insurance	Health Care & Social Assist.	Information	Mgmt. Companies & Enterprises	Manufacturing	Mining	Other Svcs. (ex. Pub. Admin.)	Prof., Sci. & Tech. Services	Public Admin.	Real Estate & Rental & Leasing	Retail Trade	Transportation & Warehousing	Unclassified Establishments	Utilities	Wholesale Trade	Aggregates
23	Brazos	Bryan	11.1	2.4	0	1.1	2.5	0.1	0.2	0.3	6.3	0	5.7	0.4	3.7	0.7	0	3.2	51.6	0.5	0	0	10.3	100
23	Brazos	College Station	19.1	1.7	0	0.8	1.5	2.6	0.1	0.3	1.4	0	1.5	0	1.3	2.4	0	1.7	64.3	0	0	0	1.3	100
24	Johnson	Alvarado	42.7	0.4	0	0	2.4	0	0	0	0	0	6.6	0	2	0.1	0	1.6	43.7	0	0	0	0.6	100
24	Johnson	Burleson	16.1	1.3	0.1	0.7	1.6	0	0.1	0	1	0.4	4.6	0.1	1.9	1	0	4.3	64.4	0	0	0	2.5	100
24	Johnson	Cleburne	10.9	1.2	0	0.4	4.2	0	0.3	0.1	1.3	0	5.1	2.1	2.9	0.3	0	1.4	53.5	0.1	0	0	16.1	100
24	Johnson	Crowley	27.7	2	0	0.5	0.3	0	0	0	0.2	0	4.8	0	3.4	0.3	0	0.5	59.2	0	0	0	0.9	100
24	Johnson	Godley	13.3	0	0	0	21.6	0	0	0	0	0	50.6	0	0.5	0	0	0	14	0	0	0	0	100
24	Johnson	Grandview	9.9	0.1	0	0	0.4	0	0	0	0	0	0.6	0	0.2	0.7	0	0	32.3	0	0	0	55.8	100
24	Johnson	Joshua	24.5	0.9	0	1.2	4.1	0	0	0	4.9	0	7.7	0	7.3	1.5	0	1.8	33	0	0	0	13.1	100
24	Johnson	Keene	18.9	6.1	0	0	17.6	0	0	0	0	0	5.5	0	9.4	1.5	0	0	40.9	0	0	0	0	100
24	Johnson	Rio Vista	1.9	0	0	0	0	0	0	0	0	0	0	0	0.5	0	0	0	97.6	0	0	0	0	100
25	Hays	Austin	13.9	3.9	0.1	0.9	3.3	0.1	0.4	0.1	1.5	0.1	7.4	0.1	2.6	3.2	3.3	1.5	46.1	0.4	0	4.1	7.1	100
25	Hays	Buda	15.4	1	0	0	1.4	0	0	0	0.5	0	6.8	0	0.5	0.4	0	0	71.4	0	0	0	2.5	100
25	Hays	Dripping Springs	12.4	0.9	0	0.1	3.3	0.3	0	0	0.1	0	2.3	0	2.5	2	0	1.1	71.9	0	0	0	3.1	100
25	Hays	Hays	0	0	0	0	0	0	0	0	0	0	0	0	0	0	0	0	100	0	0	0	0	100
25	Hays	Kyle	11.9	0.8	0	0.9	1.6	0.2	0	0	0.1	0	9.3	0	2.5	0.3	0	0.7	70.2	0	0	0	1.4	100
25	Hays	Mountain City	0	0	0	0	0	0	0	0	0	0	0	0	94.4	0	0	0	5.6	0	0	0	0	100
25	Hays	Niederwald	0	0	0	0	0	0	0	0	0	0	0	0	0	0	0	0	100	0	0	0	0	100
25	Hays	San Marcos	11.9	0.4	0	0.3	0.5	0	0.1	0.1	12.5	0	3	0	0.9	0.3	1.2	1	64.9	0	0	0	2.9	100
25	Hays	Uhland	0	0	0	0	0	0	0	0	0	0	0	0	###	0	0	0	0	0	0	0	0	100
25	Hays	Woodcreek	0	0	0	13.7	0	0	0	0	0	0	0.6	0	0	5.3	0	0	80.4	0	0	0	0	100
26	Ellis	Bardwell	-	-	-	-	-	-	-	-	-	-	-	-	-	-	-	-	-	-	-	-	-	-
26	Ellis	Ennis	12.3	1.4	0	0.7	26	0	0.1	0.3	0.1	0	4.2	0	2.5	0.3	0	1.5	43.7	0	0	0	7	100
26	Ellis	Garrett	-	-	-	-	-	-	-	-	-	-	-	-	-	-	-	-	-	-	-	-	-	-
26	Ellis	Italy	26.5	0	0	0	0	0	0	0	0	0	0	0	0.1	0	0	0	73.4	0	0	0	0	100
26	Ellis	Mansfield	15.3	2.4	0	3.1	2.4	0	0.5	0.1	1.8	0	4.2	0	1.8	0.7	0	1.5	61	0.1	0	0	5	100
26	Ellis	Maypearl	28.2	0	0	0	0	0	0	0	0	0	0	0	5.2	0	0	0	66.6	0	0	0	0	100
26	Ellis	Midlothian	15.5	3.6	0	1.1	1.6	0	0.1	0	0	0	5.4	0	2.1	2.5	0	5.2	59.3	0.6	0	0	2.9	100
26	Ellis	Milford	0	0	0	0	16.7	0	0	0	0	0	0	0	0	0	0	0	83.3	0	0	0	0	100
26	Ellis	Oak Leaf	0	0	0	0	0	0	0	0	0.7	0	0	0	90.6	8.1	0	0	0.6	0	0	0	0	100
26	Ellis	Palmer	6	6.5	0	0	4.8	0	0	0	0	0	0.1	0	22	0.3	0	0	60.4	0	0	0	0	100
26	Ellis	Pecan Hill	0	0	0	0	0	0	0	0	0	0	0	0	0	0	0	0	100	0	0	0	0	100
26	Ellis	Red Oak	23.4	8.1	0	0.6	6.5	0.1	0	0	0.2	0	3.1	0	5.5	0.9	0.3	0.9	47.9	0	0	0	2.4	100
26	Ellis	Venus	48.2	3.7	0	0	0	0	0	0	0	0	0	0	1.8	0	0	0	46.3	0	0	0	0	100
26	Ellis	Waxahachie	14.4	1.5	0	0.4	8.2	0.1	0	0.1	0.4	0	8	0	2	0.4	0	1.2	57.4	0	0	0	6	100
27	Ector	Goldsmith	6.9	0	0	0	0	0	0	0	0	0	0	93.1	0	0	0	0	0	0	0	0	0	100
27	Ector	Odessa	13.1	0.9	0	0.4	2.4	0	0.2	0.2	2.1	0	4.4	2.7	4.3	1.1	0.1	3	52	0.5	0	0	12.5	100
28	Midland	Midland	9.5	1.7	0	1.1	2.9	0	0.2	0.1	1.9	0	2.4	8.2	2.2	3.1	0.1	2	46.3	0.2	0	0.2	17.9	100

Rank	County	City	Accommodation & Food Svcs.	Admin. & Supp. & Waste Mgmt. & Remed. Svcs.	Agric., Forestry, Fish'g & Hunt'a	Arts, Entertainment & Rec.	Construction	Educational Svcs.	Finance & Insurance	Health Care & Social Assist.	Information	Mgmt. Companies & Enterprises	Manufacturing	Mining	Other Svcs. (ex. Pub. Admin.)	Prof., Sci. & Tech. Services	Public Admin.	Real Estate & Rental & Leasing	Retail Trade	Transportation & Warehousing	Unclassified Establishments	Utilities	Wholesale Trade	Aggregates
29	Wichita	Burkburnett	26.4	0.5	0	0.2	3.8	0	0	0	0	0	9.2	0	3.2	0.5	0	0	54.4	0	0	0	1.8	100
29	Wichita	Electra	3.3	1.8	0	0	4.6	0	0	0	0	0	20.1	4.9	4.1	0	0	0	50.1	0	0	0	11.1	100
29	Wichita	Iowa Park	26.1	1.4	0	0	4	0	0	0	0	0	3.1	11.9	11.6	0.1	0	0.6	36.9	0	0	0	4.2	100
29	Wichita	Wichita Falls	14.1	1.6	0.2	0.9	1.8	0	0.6	0.1	2.7	0	3	0.3	2.8	0.8	0	2.7	61.6	0	0	0	6.8	100
30	Taylor	Abilene	13.4	1.5	0	0.7	3	0.3	0.5	0.4	2.3	0	2.3	1.7	2.5	1.1	0.2	1.9	60.6	0.1	0	0	7.6	100
30	Taylor	Buffalo Gap	74.1	0	0	0	5.4	0	0	0	0	0	0	0	0	0	0	0	20.5	0	0	0	0	100
30	Taylor	Lawn	-	-	-	-	-	-	-	-	-	-	-	-	-	-	-	-	-	-	-	-	-	-
30	Taylor	Merkel	14.8	0.9	0	0	0.2	0	0	0	0	0	31	0	0.1	0	0.7	0	52.3	0	0	0	0	100
30	Taylor	Trent	-	-	-	-	-	-	-	-	-	-	-	-	-	-	-	-	-	-	-	-	-	-
30	Taylor	Tuscola	24.7	5.4	0	0	1.1	0	0	0	0	0	0	0	1.6	0	0	0	67.2	0	0	0	0	100
30	Taylor	Tye	0	0	0	0	3.8	0	0	0	0	0	0	0	4.9	0	0	0	62	0	0	0	29.3	100
31	Potter	Amarillo	12.7	1.7	0	0.9	2.8	0.2	0.4	0.2	2.6	0.1	3	0	3.1	1.3	0	1.1	55.7	0.1	0	7.6	6.3	100
31	Potter	Canyon	23.6	1.6	0	0.2	0.8	0	0.1	0	0.1	0	0.3	0	4	1.3	0	0.1	67.4	0	0	0	0.3	100
31	Potter	Happy	0	0	0	0	0	0	0	0	0	0	0	0	0	0	0	0	100	0	0	0	0	100
32	Grayson	Bells	3.7	0	0	0	0	0	0	0	0	0	0	0	0	0	0	0	96.3	0	0	0	0	100
32	Grayson	Collinsville	6.6	0	0	0	0	0	0	0	0	0	0	0	2.6	0	0	0	90.9	0	0	0	0	100
32	Grayson	Denison	17.8	1.7	0	0.3	5	0	0.1	2.6	0.3	0	5.1	0	2	0.7	0	2.7	59.7	0	0	0	1.9	100
32	Grayson	Gunter	20.6	3.5	0	0	9.6	0	0	0	0	0	0	0	1.1	1.5	0	0	63.7	0	0	0	0	100
32	Grayson	Howe	10.6	2	0	0	1	0	0	0	0	0	5	0	25.9	0	0	0	55	0	0	0	0.5	100
32	Grayson	Knollwood	-	-	-	-	-	-	-	-	-	-	-	-	-	-	-	-	-	-	-	-	-	-
32	Grayson	Pottsboro	16.3	5.7	0	0	16.8	0	0	0	0	0	0.3	0	8.8	0.4	0	0	40.5	0	0	0	11.2	100
32	Grayson	Sherman	12.8	1.5	0	0.3	1.4	0.5	0.2	0.1	3.9	0	1.7	0	2.2	0.4	0	2.5	68.1	0	0	0	4.3	100
32	Grayson	Southmayd	0	0.5	0	0	1.6	0	0	0	0	0	97.8	0	0	0	0	0	0	0	0	0	0	100
32	Grayson	Tioga	0	8.1	0	0	0	0	0	0	0	0	0	0	5.3	0	0	0	86.6	0	0	0	0	100
32	Grayson	Tom Bean	0	0	0	0	0	0	0	0	0	0	0	0	1.5	0	0	0	98.5	0	0	0	0	100
32	Grayson	Van Alstyne	17.7	1.7	0	0.2	1.4	0	0	0	0.2	0	2.7	0	2.6	0.1	0	0	66.8	0	0	0	6.6	100
32	Grayson	Whitesboro	22.3	0.9	0	0.2	4.2	0	0	0	0	0	1.7	0	7.5	0.4	0	0	62.7	0	0	0	0.1	100
32	Grayson	Whitewright	18.1	1.7	0	0	0	0	0	0	0	0	0.3	0	0.5	0	0	0	79.3	0	0	0	0	100
33	Gregg	Clarksville	29	0.4	0	0	4.8	0	0.3	0	0	0	1.5	0	2.5	0.1	0	0	59.9	0	0	0	1.4	100
33	Gregg	Easton	-	-	-	-	-	-	-	-	-	-	-	-	-	-	-	-	-	-	-	-	-	-
33	Gregg	Gladewater	11.4	1.3	0	0.2	11.7	0	0	0	6.1	0	16.5	0	4.1	1.7	0	5.2	40.6	0.8	0	0	0.3	100
33	Gregg	Kilgore	4.5	1.8	0	0.2	2.5	0	0.1	0	0.9	0	10.3	11.8	1.8	2	0	12.2	24.5	0	0	0	27.3	100
33	Gregg	Lakeport	0	0	0	0	0	0	0	0	0	0	0	0	0	0	0	0	100	0	0	0	0	100
33	Gregg	Longview	11	2	0	0.4	2.7	0.1	0.3	0.2	2.7	0	5.6	0.6	5.2	0.7	0.3	4.8	56.2	0.2	0	0	7	100
33	Gregg	White Oak	8.2	2	0	0	9.1	0.3	0	0	0	0	10.3	19.7	11.3	0.3	0	14.3	18.3	0	0	0	6.1	100
34	Guadalupe	Cibolo	9.6	13.2	0	0.1	5.8	0	0	0	0.1	0	19.2	0	0.8	2.2	0	1.9	42.5	0	0	0	4.6	100
34	Guadalupe	Luling	14.2	3.2	0	0.1	5	0	0	0	0	0	3.2	5.2	3	0.1	3.5	0	61	0	0	0	1.6	100
34	Guadalupe	Marion	10.7	1.2	0	0	0.6	0	0	0	0	0	0	0	1.9	0	0	0	85.5	0	0	0	0.1	100
34	Guadalupe	Seguin	15.7	0.7	0	1	2.4	1.1	0.5	0.4	1	0	6.4	0	3.2	0.4	0.6	1.3	63.6	0	0	0	1.6	100

Rank	County	City	Accommodation & Food Svcs.	Admin. & Supp. & Waste Mgmt. & Remed. Svcs.	Agric., Forestry, Fish'g & Hunt'g	Arts, Entertainment & Rec.	Construction	Educational Svcs.	Finance & Insurance	Health Care & Social Assist.	Information	Mgmt. Companies & Enterprises	Manufacturing	Mining	Other Svcs. (ex. Pub. Admin.)	Prof., Sci. & Tech. Services	Public Admin.	Real Estate & Rental & Leasing	Retail Trade	Transportation & Warehousing	Unclassified Establishments	Utilities	Wholesale Trade	Aggregates
36	Parker	Aledo	20.2	5.8	0	0	2.9	0	0	0	1.3	0	1.7	0	14.4	11.3	0	0	30.1	0	0	0	12.1	100
36	Parker	Azle	16	1.9	0	0.7	7.6	0.1	0	0	0	0	0.6	0	1.8	0.7	0	2.8	65.5	0	0	0	2.3	100
36	Parker	Millsap	0	3	0	0	3.5	0	0	0	0	0	0	0	2.7	0	0	0	90.7	0	0	0	0	100
36	Parker	Mineral Wells	13.3	0.4	0	0.9	1	0	0	0.1	2.9	0	3.7	2.5	3.9	1.2	0.4	0.6	58.9	0	0	0	10.2	100
36	Parker	Springtown	26	6	0	0.1	0.1	0	0	0	0.3	0	0.2	0	3.1	0.3	0	0	58.9	0	0	0	5.1	100
36	Parker	Weatherford	14.6	0.8	0	0.2	1.4	0.1	0.4	0	0.4	0	2.1	0.3	4.1	0.7	0.8	2.6	66	0	0	0	5.2	100
36	Parker	Willow Park	40.1	2.6	0	0.4	2.6	0	0	0	0	0	0.1	0	5.8	3	0	4.7	35.7	0	0	0	5	100
37	Comal	Bulverde	11.5	0.8	0	0.4	4.1	0	0	0	0	0	12.5	0	1.6	0.6	0	0.5	68	0.1	0	0	0	100
37	Comal	Fair Oaks Ranch	23.5	2.3	0	45.2	5.1	0	0	0	0.4	0	1	0	1.8	0.8	0	0	19.8	0	0	0	0.1	100
37	Comal	Garden Ridge	16.7	0	0	0	19.9	0	0	0	0	0	1.2	0	10.5	3.2	0	0	48.2	0	0	0	0.3	100
37	Comal	New Braunfels	12.1	1.2	0	3.2	2.5	0.1	0.2	0.1	0.6	0	4.4	0	1.9	0.6	2.6	1	47.9	0.1	0	0	21.5	100
38	Tom Green	San Angelo	13.2	2.5	0.1	0.8	3.7	0	0.2	0.4	4.8	0	2.5	2	3.3	1.2	0	1.2	59	0.1	0	0	5	100
39	Kaufman	Crandall	32.7	4.7	0	0	9	0	0	0	0	0	1	0	8	0.1	0	0	44.5	0	0	0	0	100
39	Kaufman	Forney	16.9	1	0	0.3	5.2	0	0	0	2.1	0	3.1	0	1.8	0.5	0	0.3	65.1	0.4	0	0	3.2	100
39	Kaufman	Heath	3.3	9.3	0	15.9	12	0	0	0	8.7	0	0.1	0	6.1	25.3	0	0	16.5	0	0	0	2.7	100
39	Kaufman	Kaufman	22	0.5	0	0.2	0.4	0	0	0	13.3	0	1.7	0	3.4	0.8	0	2.5	51.9	0	0	0	3.3	100
39	Kaufman	Kemp	32	0.5	0	0	0	0	0	0	0	0	0.4	0	2.6	0	0	0	64.5	0	0	0	0	100
39	Kaufman	Mabank	3.8	1.9	0.1	0	0.6	0	0	0	0	0	6.6	0	5.2	1	0	0	80.7	0	0	0	0	100
39	Kaufman	Oak Ridge	0	0	0	0	0	0	0	0	0	0	0	0	0	0	0	0	100	0	0	0	0	100
39	Kaufman	Terrell	13.8	1.6	0	0.2	1.1	0.1	0.4	0	0.2	0	15.6	0	1.3	0.3	0	1.9	61.3	0	0	0	2.3	100

Table A7

Relative Concentrations of Taxable Sales Base by Industry Classification & Municipality (2008)
(as a percentage of gross sales in same classification)

Rank	County	City	Accommodation & Food Svcs.	Admin. & Supp. & Waste Mgmt. & Remed. Svcs.	Agric., Forestry, Fish'g & Hunt'g	Arts, Entertainment & Rec.	Construction	Educational Svcs.	Finance & Insurance	Health Care & Social Assist.	Information	Mgmt. Companies & Enterprises	Manufacturing	Mining	Other Svcs. (ex. Pub. Admin.)	Prof., Sci. & Tech. Services	Public Admin.	Real Estate & Rental & Leasing	Retail Trade	Transportation & Warehousing	Unclassified Establishments	Utilities	Wholesale Trade	Aggregates
1	Harris	Baytown	90.8	107.2	-	92.3	17.0	38.3	68.3	24.8	67.5	-	5.1	-	33.5	10.9	100.0	53.6	45.6	6.1	-	-	12.1	40.6
1	Harris	Bellaire	80.4	54.5	-	26.4	5.6	100.0	87.2	13.8	14.8	-	47.1	8.9	44.2	33.7	-	9.9	27.2	-	-	-	17.7	24.0
1	Harris	Bunker Hill Village	-	100.2	-	-	-	-	-	-	-	-	-	-	16.3	30.9	-	-	90.0	-	-	-	-	40.5
1	Harris	Deer Park	80.6	9.2	-	86.9	3.6	100.0	NM	0.9	25.4	-	1.1	-	7.5	3.9	100.0	38.0	44.4	77.5	-	-	18.9	6.1
1	Harris	El Lago	65.5	62.6	-	-	-	-	-	-	-	-	45.1	-	72.1	10.0	-	-	80.1	-	-	-	1.1	59.1
1	Harris	Galena Park	80.3	77.3	-	-	22.5	103.9	-	-	-	-	0.1	-	40.7	8.4	-	-	49.4	89.1	-	-	27.9	16.9
1	Harris	Hedwig Village	94.1	65.8	-	-	9.7	50.3	0.0	2.4	70.6	-	6.0	-	92.7	24.4	-	26.9	66.3	-	-	-	5.2	38.6
1	Harris	Hilshire Village	-	-	-	-	-	-	-	-	-	-	-	-	-	50.8	-	-	58.1	-	-	-	-	51.6
1	Harris	Humble	92.2	57.2	-	89.9	6.2	67.8	57.8	33.5	96.9	-	3.2	85.8	32.4	42.3	-	99.7	68.7	42.4	-	-	11.0	45.1
1	Harris	Hunters Creek Village	-	102.0	-	97.5	-	-	-	-	-	-	-	-	-	74.1	-	-	39.3	-	-	-	-	73.1
1	Harris	Jacinto City	75.9	93.0	-	-	4.3	-	106.9	-	-	-	15.3	-	46.1	79.9	-	-	29.8	-	-	-	1.5	9.1
1	Harris	Jersey Village	87.7	72.6	-	-	2.4	-	1.4	-	-	-	1.0	-	42.7	16.9	-	71.0	25.1	-	-	-	12.5	17.5
1	Harris	La Porte	92.3	25.3	-	94.1	2.8	39.2	77.6	-	26.9	-	9.9	0.0	10.9	26.3	-	79.1	36.7	2.2	-	-	25.4	15.3
1	Harris	Morgans Point	-	-	-	-	-	-	-	-	-	-	-	-	-	-	-	-	-	-	-	-	-	-
1	Harris	Nassau Bay	89.0	50.2	-	-	17.8	-	-	99.8	30.2	-	13.8	-	23.2	9.1	-	-	18.1	-	-	-	34.1	27.0
1	Harris	Pasadena	95.0	36.2	32.6	89.0	12.4	39.2	67.2	5.4	71.7	1.5	18.2	4.2	20.9	6.1	-	65.1	52.9	21.4	-	2.4	8.1	32.2
1	Harris	Piney Point Village	-	92.1	-	-	-	-	-	-	-	-	-	-	2.8	88.8	-	-	47.1	-	-	-	0.0	7.2
1	Harris	Seabrook	78.3	71.2	-	-	9.6	19.5	82.5	-	15.4	-	12.9	-	42.7	1.7	-	24.4	43.4	-	-	-	16.7	35.9
1	Harris	Shoreacres	-	-	-	-	-	-	-	-	-	-	-	-	-	-	-	-	9.6	-	-	-	-	9.6
1	Harris	South Houston	100.8	81.8	-	88.3	32.2	100.0	70.0	-	99.8	-	4.0	-	17.9	24.1	-	99.9	26.5	38.7	-	-	10.0	21.3
1	Harris	Southside Place	89.7	-	-	-	-	-	-	-	-	-	-	-	71.6	30.7	-	-	45.1	-	-	-	33.5	54.1
1	Harris	Spring Valley	95.9	77.4	-	-	13.2	-	-	-	84.0	-	11.5	-	39.7	28.2	-	-	88.8	-	-	-	9.1	34.3
1	Harris	Taylor Lake Village	-	-	-	-	0.2	-	-	-	-	-	-	-	4.1	96.8	-	-	31.0	-	-	-	-	9.3
1	Harris	Tomball	94.3	33.5	100.0	98.7	10.2	24.7	73.3	24.9	67.0	-	21.9	-	45.2	26.6	-	64.1	52.7	36.7	-	-	22.2	43.9
1	Harris	Waller	96.6	91.2	-	-	43.7	-	-	-	-	-	31.3	-	34.2	5.6	-	31.3	21.1	-	-	-	25.2	28.4
1	Harris	Webster	90.8	53.0	-	70.2	0.7	181.4	62.0	0.5	98.3	-	9.1	-	28.9	7.0	-	42.3	69.4	13.8	-	-	9.5	23.4
1	Harris	West University Place	91.1	86.0	-	10.8	6.4	58.6	-	-	1.6	-	9.4	-	61.5	51.8	-	29.0	52.6	-	-	-	9.3	43.5
2	Dallas	Addison	84.9	37.3	-	57.0	12.1	17.9	47.0	91.7	29.4	NM	6.5	6.6	23.5	24.4	-	34.1	16.3	9.4	-	-	3.3	14.5
2	Dallas	Balch Springs	99.0	36.3	-	-	7.6	-	-	-	-	-	13.6	-	23.8	3.2	-	36.2	52.8	18.2	-	-	40.7	34.1
2	Dallas	Cedar Hill	96.3	32.9	-	75.0	9.6	52.6	36.6	0.9	87.6	-	14.6	-	34.3	36.9	-	34.4	66.7	5.0	-	-	18.8	50.0
2	Dallas	Cockrell Hill	96.9	-	-	-	-	-	-	-	-	-	31.8	-	81.1	-	-	-	49.0	-	-	-	6.3	45.8
2	Dallas	Combine	-	99.2	-	-	21.1	-	-	-	-	-	5.2	-	41.0	-	-	-	47.3	-	-	-	-	48.4

Rank	County	City	Accommodation & Food Svcs.	Admin. & Supp. & Waste Mgmt. & Remed. Svcs.	Agric., Forestry, Fish'g & Hunt'g	Arts, Entertainment & Rec.	Construction	Educational Svcs.	Finance & Insurance	Health Care & Social Assist.	Information	Mgmt. Companies & Enterprises	Manufacturing	Mining	Other Svcs. (ex. Pub. Admin.)	Prof., Sci. & Tech. Services	Public Admin.	Real Estate & Rental & Leasing	Retail Trade	Transportation & Warehousing	Unclassified Establishments	Utilities	Wholesale Trade	Aggregates
2	Dallas	Coppell	95.5	81.4	-	36.0	21.4	5.5	34.5	2.9	78.3	-	10.3	-	57.6	34.7	-	29.0	44.1	1.7	-	-	16.2	28.1
2	Dallas	De Soto	97.3	65.6	-	77.7	9.6	37.9	83.9	NM	96.5	-	12.5	-	35.3	2.7	-	99.3	29.8	171.4	-	-	5.0	22.8
2	Dallas	Duncanville	96.3	74.3	-	91.4	10.3	19.4	85.4	10.3	69.8	-	21.5	-	43.0	17.9	-	73.1	29.4	14.7	-	-	9.1	30.5
2	Dallas	Farmers Branch	84.5	31.8	-	93.0	24.4	28.0	48.6	41.2	10.0	100.0	4.5	-	23.2	14.3	-	26.0	44.1	0.9	-	59.2	8.1	16.7
2	Dallas	Ferris	92.3	32.1	-	-	39.4	-	-	-	-	-	1.0	-	43.0	16.4	-	-	38.2	-	-	-	-	26.0
2	Dallas	Glenn Heights	97.2	66.6	-	-	15.2	-	-	-	-	-	50.9	-	48.7	87.0	-	-	65.6	-	-	-	1.1	56.0
2	Dallas	Grand Prairie	26.8	37.4	0.1	44.3	21.8	8.1	19.6	0.6	31.1	-	4.8	14.9	22.0	10.2	-	22.0	34.9	4.4	-	-	5.7	14.3
2	Dallas	Grapevine	84.8	60.6	-	84.6	13.3	3.2	49.5	30.8	86.5	15.4	49.5	-	44.6	29.5	-	91.9	46.0	61.0	-	-	7.0	42.1
2	Dallas	Highland Park	83.2	83.6	-	90.6	0.1	-	-	-	64.1	-	19.1	-	84.5	55.6	-	94.3	59.4	-	-	-	0.2	54.9
2	Dallas	Hutchins	100.1	134.2	-	-	0.0	-	-	-	-	-	9.6	-	11.3	-	-	16.2	5.3	-	-	-	24.5	22.0
2	Dallas	Irving	92.3	53.7	37.5	50.9	27.2	21.1	49.5	10.9	70.7	19.5	6.1	NM	10.3	5.9	91.3	49.1	37.3	62.0	-	68.4	5.8	21.0
2	Dallas	Lancaster	96.1	19.8	-	91.4	3.2	-	34.0	146.0	2.9	-	3.6	-	26.5	80.8	-	84.4	45.4	58.2	-	-	12.4	20.0
2	Dallas	Lewisville	90.5	50.1	0.2	27.8	9.9	8.6	96.3	27.0	64.4	89.0	10.6	27.6	45.6	17.0	-	69.4	43.5	5.0	-	-	11.0	28.3
2	Dallas	Mesquite	97.1	59.5	48.4	83.7	13.0	60.3	43.8	0.3	71.0	97.7	6.6	-	47.2	31.5	-	9.9	52.4	45.1	-	-	8.2	31.1
2	Dallas	Ovilla	-	38.2	-	85.6	24.2	-	-	-	-	-	12.9	-	54.2	19.3	-	-	54.1	-	-	-	1.5	33.4
2	Dallas	Rowlett	94.3	57.8	0.0	96.1	15.6	1.8	-	214.7	34.1	-	15.4	-	51.4	26.0	-	96.4	55.6	14.2	-	-	13.6	44.9
2	Dallas	Seagoville	96.1	59.6	-	-	28.5	-	-	-	65.3	-	3.7	-	42.2	99.1	-	98.8	39.9	-	-	-	22.0	33.7
2	Dallas	Sunnyvale	84.2	90.5	-	91.9	13.0	-	-	-	-	-	39.3	-	30.5	15.7	-	0.5	22.0	-	-	-	13.3	23.4
2	Dallas	University Park	65.7	45.6	-	67.7	19.5	98.6	24.3	-	33.1	-	68.3	-	49.0	42.0	-	75.3	58.0	-	-	-	4.3	52.0
2	Dallas	Wilmer	84.3	12.3	-	-	-	-	-	-	-	-	-	-	36.6	-	-	-	36.4	-	-	-	-	32.5
3	Tarrant	Arlington	91.4	48.5	27.6	89.0	9.9	22.6	81.9	0.9	54.6	102.9	5.9	-	33.3	19.2	99.8	86.3	40.9	4.2	-	3.8	7.9	27.7
3	Tarrant	Bedford	93.4	55.1	-	76.5	14.3	6.1	44.7	16.5	38.2	4.9	35.9	-	28.2	32.5	76.0	65.1	30.5	19.8	-	-	9.7	36.5
3	Tarrant	Benbrook	96.5	66.6	40.3	82.1	11.8	82.3	59.3	-	60.4	-	21.2	NM	42.2	25.5	-	91.1	33.2	-	-	-	17.8	34.3
3	Tarrant	Blue Mound	-	-	-	-	-	-	-	-	-	-	-	-	20.9	-	-	-	22.4	-	-	-	6.1	16.1
3	Tarrant	Colleyville	71.1	27.8	-	60.3	49.5	5.9	81.8	2.7	72.0	-	38.7	-	39.8	20.0	-	44.0	42.0	-	-	-	48.2	43.2
3	Tarrant	Dalworthington Gardens	89.0	32.8	-	-	38.0	16.2	-	-	1.2	-	12.1	-	28.0	24.4	-	-	7.5	-	-	-	6.4	15.7
3	Tarrant	Edgecliff Village	-	97.1	-	-	0.0	-	-	-	-	-	-	-	47.1	-	-	-	65.8	-	-	-	-	45.1
3	Tarrant	Euless	58.8	55.6	-	87.4	8.0	58.6	27.8	0.0	4.9	-	43.8	-	45.6	16.0	-	114.5	41.3	2.0	-	-	22.1	36.6
3	Tarrant	Everman	96.5	70.1	-	54.0	2.7	-	-	-	-	-	13.6	-	37.6	-	-	-	49.6	-	-	-	6.0	11.3
3	Tarrant	Forest Hill	98.6	11.1	-	77.7	14.6	-	-	-	-	-	12.7	-	53.5	7.8	-	-	39.4	-	-	-	18.6	35.5
3	Tarrant	Haltom City	95.9	56.3	-	65.3	19.9	42.7	65.4	-	12.9	-	11.3	-	46.0	8.6	-	53.4	30.6	37.8	-	-	20.9	28.1
3	Tarrant	Hurst	90.9	59.0	-	97.9	21.6	23.1	95.0	3.6	95.8	-	3.9	-	43.7	35.0	-	86.8	64.6	104.1	-	-	29.2	56.4
3	Tarrant	Keller	97.4	60.2	30.8	57.9	21.3	28.8	162.4	3.9	17.6	99.0	17.0	-	38.9	21.7	93.8	75.4	46.5	-	-	-	11.0	44.4
3	Tarrant	Kennedale	65.4	17.3	-	59.8	5.2	-	-	-	-	-	5.9	18.8	15.6	25.8	-	59.6	20.6	-	-	-	3.4	10.1
3	Tarrant	Lake Worth	98.4	16.8	-	90.4	32.1	-	67.2	2.5	99.7	-	20.9	-	31.1	27.4	-	68.3	59.6	-	-	-	82.5	48.2
3	Tarrant	Lakeside	-	89.9	-	-	2.2	-	-	-	-	-	-	-	92.6	78.9	-	-	93.3	-	-	-	-	33.9
3	Tarrant	North Richland Hills	93.4	55.1	-	95.7	11.8	2.5	206.1	4.0	52.4	-	8.5	-	43.3	15.7	94.8	39.2	44.3	0.9	-	-	37.4	39.4
3	Tarrant	Pantego	96.6	74.2	-	-	15.6	-	-	-	108.2	-	9.7	-	37.0	37.8	-	86.0	46.5	0.7	-	-	16.9	37.7

Rank	County	City	Accommodation & Food Svcs.	Admin. & Supp. & Waste Mgmt. & Remed. Svcs.	Agric., Forestry, Fish'g & Hunt'g	Arts, Entertainment & Rec.	Construction	Educational Svcs.	Finance & Insurance	Health Care & Social Assist.	Information	Mgmt. Companies & Enterprises	Manufacturing	Mining	Other Svcs. (ex. Pub. Admin.)	Prof., Sci. & Tech. Services	Public Admin.	Real Estate & Rental & Leasing	Retail Trade	Transportation & Warehousing	Unclassified Establishments	Utilities	Wholesale Trade	Aggregates
3	Tarrant	Pelican Bay	-	-	-	-	-	-	-	-	-	-	-	-	-	-	-	-	-	-	-	-	-	-	-
3	Tarrant	Richland Hills	94.8	69.0	-	36.3	20.6	-	-	2.0	67.2	-	3.0	-	45.4	25.0	-	0.9	19.3	-	-	-	30.7	22.9
3	Tarrant	River Oaks	92.7	63.2	-	-	3.5	-	-	-	-	-	26.0	-	43.3	3.0	-	55.9	41.3	-	-	-	-	38.0
3	Tarrant	Saginaw	97.2	80.3	-	19.4	9.7	99.7	70.9	-	95.3	-	4.3	-	39.9	15.7	-	73.2	40.3	6.5	-	-	16.2	19.6
3	Tarrant	Sansom Park	75.9	73.1	-	-	3.6	-	-	-	-	-	5.6	-	63.7	-	-	-	36.1	-	-	-	43.5	26.3
3	Tarrant	Watauga	90.9	46.3	-	91.6	12.9	59.9	62.3	-	95.8	-	50.9	-	37.7	27.0	-	95.4	61.9	-	-	-	34.8	62.5
3	Tarrant	Westworth Village	-	-	-	82.1	39.5	-	-	-	-	-	0.0	-	-	-	-	-	43.2	-	-	-	-	45.6
3	Tarrant	White Settlement	97.7	66.9	-	96.9	11.2	70.9	128.5	-	83.2	-	7.0	-	29.9	37.0	-	100.4	84.3	-	-	-	28.4	34.6
4	Bexar	Alamo Heights	69.7	53.1	-	29.2	5.4	0.9	-	-	4.3	-	14.1	-	62.9	10.2	-	-	42.7	-	-	-	32.4	34.8
4	Bexar	Balcones Heights	99.3	-	-	-	-	-	-	23.5	98.5	-	16.7	-	74.4	-	-	85.1	49.2	-	-	-	5.0	56.3
4	Bexar	Castle Hills	93.2	33.1	-	50.5	13.5	1.4	91.3	-	-	-	59.9	-	54.5	20.7	-	81.8	37.5	-	-	-	21.0	39.1
4	Bexar	China Grove	103.2	33.0	-	-	17.8	-	-	-	-	-	-	-	44.9	-	-	-	35.8	-	-	-	19.9	26.6
4	Bexar	Converse	98.5	79.0	-	-	5.2	21.2	-	-	59.7	-	30.4	-	47.9	18.5	-	78.6	52.3	4.4	-	-	4.4	39.4
4	Bexar	Elmendorf	-	100.0	-	-	100.0	-	-	-	-	-	-	-	-	-	-	-	30.0	-	-	-	-	60.6
4	Bexar	Grey Forest	-	-	-	-	-	-	-	-	-	-	-	-	-	-	-	-	93.8	-	-	-	-	93.8
4	Bexar	Helotes	94.2	64.4	-	98.6	2.3	-	-	-	33.8	-	11.8	-	39.7	31.5	-	85.4	11.2	-	-	-	27.0	27.4
4	Bexar	Hill Country Village	85.6	-	-	-	-	-	-	-	-	-	-	-	49.5	81.0	-	80.6	85.4	-	-	-	0.7	73.7
4	Bexar	Hollywood Park	89.7	83.6	-	66.6	3.0	-	-	-	2.1	-	4.9	-	51.4	33.4	-	15.4	17.2	-	-	-	11.3	22.9
4	Bexar	Kirby	96.2	69.7	-	-	2.0	-	-	-	-	-	93.6	-	33.9	45.8	-	-	36.3	-	-	-	-	10.3
4	Bexar	Leon Valley	95.1	49.1	-	84.2	9.3	13.4	30.9	-	2.1	-	19.8	-	40.3	2.2	-	46.2	22.2	-	-	-	44.8	25.9
4	Bexar	Live Oak	94.5	63.1	-	74.9	34.5	-	-	0.3	88.1	-	10.7	-	58.3	36.3	-	99.1	46.4	-	-	-	80.8	40.5
4	Bexar	Lytle	96.1	46.9	-	-	-	-	-	-	-	-	71.9	-	47.6	3.2	-	-	24.2	-	-	-	5.7	30.6
4	Bexar	Olmos Park	92.6	54.6	-	-	5.2	-	-	-	-	-	-	-	50.6	52.1	-	-	78.1	-	-	-	67.4	74.8
4	Bexar	San Antonio	86.4	45.4	27.2	83.9	16.3	23.2	26.8	7.0	52.9	30.1	19.3	44.2	41.1	20.0	90.5	52.1	41.8	129.1	-	17.0	1.9	16.8
4	Bexar	Schertz	23.4	74.3	-	58.9	11.9	7.2	64.6	-	63.8	-	18.8	-	35.4	3.4	-	79.1	38.0	4.8	-	-	5.3	21.2
4	Bexar	Selma	96.0	66.5	-	98.3	3.1	-	-	-	-	-	22.7	-	11.8	17.6	-	70.2	61.9	-	-	-	4.4	35.4
4	Bexar	Shavano Park	-	100.0	-	-	12.0	-	-	146.7	-	-	10.1	-	0.2	77.2	-	13.5	-	-	-	-	4.3	11.1
4	Bexar	Somerset	98.9	68.7	-	-	6.6	-	-	-	-	-	-	-	52.1	-	-	-	49.2	-	-	-	-	52.4
4	Bexar	Terrell Hills	86.5	90.2	-	96.2	15.2	-	-	-	-	-	1.1	-	NM	39.4	-	-	33.5	-	-	-	61.3	39.9
4	Bexar	Universal City	94.4	67.0	-	79.5	22.9	36.8	68.8	-	48.7	-	25.0	-	41.2	10.3	-	100.2	36.9	-	-	-	11.1	42.4
4	Bexar	Windcrest	97.9	45.6	-	93.5	38.9	36.0	-	-	73.7	-	20.9	-	46.4	18.6	-	100.0	79.3	-	-	-	21.3	80.9
5	Travis	Bee Cave	97.2	81.1	-	71.3	7.4	-	-	-	115.2	-	68.1	-	46.6	7.3	-	98.6	72.7	-	-	-	49.0	67.9
5	Travis	Briarcliff	-	69.2	-	25.6	-	-	-	-	-	-	-	-	23.2	-	-	-	55.7	-	-	-	-	40.9
5	Travis	Cedar Park	92.7	47.6	45.0	72.3	15.8	10.0	27.0	113.2	28.1	-	16.1	-	38.9	21.2	100.0	66.6	43.9	6.7	-	-	19.3	38.5
5	Travis	Creedmoor	-	44.8	-	-	-	-	-	-	-	-	-	-	-	-	-	-	28.1	-	-	-	-	43.6
5	Travis	Elgin	89.7	10.3	-	66.4	14.9	-	87.5	-	-	-	10.7	-	52.1	3.9	-	100.8	28.3	-	-	-	1.3	33.7
5	Travis	Jonestown	97.0	89.3	-	-	18.1	-	-	-	-	-	0.3	-	72.9	31.9	-	-	41.7	-	-	-	59.6	44.2

TEXAS CENTER FOR ECONOMICS, LAW & POLICY

Rank	County	City	Accommodation & Food Svcs.	Admin. & Supp. & Waste Mgmt. & Remed. Svcs.	Agric., Forestry, Fish'g & Hunt'g	Arts, Entertainment & Rec.	Construction	Educational Svcs.	Finance & Insurance	Health Care & Social Assist.	Information	Mgmt. Companies & Enterprises	Manufacturing	Mining	Other Svcs. (ex. Pub. Admin.)	Prof., Sci. & Tech. Services	Public Admin.	Real Estate & Rental & Leasing	Retail Trade	Transportation & Warehousing	Unclassified Establishments	Utilities	Wholesale Trade	Aggregates
5	Travis	Lago Vista	73.2	44.1	-	76.8	6.3	2.6	-	-	0.8	-	47.8	-	36.0	9.6	-	100.6	37.6	-	-	-	2.0	32.1
5	Travis	Leander	91.0	30.1	11.8	64.6	16.7	17.0	-	0.0	17.9	-	15.3	72.0	51.1	23.7	-	83.3	41.3	-	-	-	1.5	29.1
5	Travis	Manor	81.3	83.3	-	94.7	6.3	-	-	-	69.0	-	10.7	-	100.1	100.0	-	-	22.2	-	-	-	58.1	39.0
5	Travis	Mustang Ridge	-	-	-	-	-	-	-	-	-	-	-	-	44.8	-	-	-	10.4	-	-	-	-	10.5
5	Travis	Pflugerville	72.8	50.5	-	67.6	2.3	91.1	90.9	26.8	3.6	-	3.6	-	45.2	15.6	-	45.4	37.7	3.1	-	-	26.8	26.5
5	Travis	Point Venture	-	-	-	100.5	-	-	-	-	-	-	-	-	-	-	-	-	100.0	-	-	-	-	100.1
5	Travis	Rollingwood	90.2	26.6	-	94.8	-	-	-	20.7	38.8	-	82.7	-	23.7	9.7	-	-	63.2	-	-	-	-	35.5
5	Travis	Round Rock	90.1	55.9	3.9	73.7	9.0	25.8	26.0	9.2	58.4	11.7	30.9	-	41.3	16.7	-	91.5	40.0	10.7	-	-	25.9	35.1
5	Travis	Volente	72.3	75.2	-	47.7	-	-	-	-	-	-	-	-	-	-	-	-	8.4	-	-	-	-	68.4
5	Travis	Webberville	-	-	-	-	-	-	-	-	-	-	-	-	-	-	-	-	8.3	-	-	-	-	8.3
6	Collin	Allen	95.7	46.9	99.4	76.2	19.5	19.3	4.5	17.7	71.4	-	6.2	-	41.5	18.0	-	57.0	59.4	9.2	-	-	10.9	44.6
6	Collin	Anna	85.7	84.3	-	98.4	34.1	-	-	-	59.2	-	5.3	-	57.6	83.4	-	-	22.7	0.3	-	-	3.6	22.8
6	Collin	Blue Ridge	100.0	-	-	-	-	-	-	-	-	-	-	-	-	-	-	-	50.5	-	-	-	-	51.0
6	Collin	Carrollton	85.5	33.1	-	84.0	12.6	24.1	33.3	92.2	33.7	27.3	4.8	-	43.9	18.0	-	51.5	23.8	53.0	-	-	7.1	13.4
6	Collin	Celina	98.2	53.5	-	97.5	13.2	-	-	-	-	-	15.9	-	52.7	3.8	-	-	22.0	-	-	-	42.6	23.5
6	Collin	Dallas	82.4	47.8	32.4	80.5	20.5	14.2	11.0	9.2	79.8	24.0	19.3	120.0	25.6	12.1	49.2	7.7	34.0	13.4	1.9	8.6	3.3	17.8
6	Collin	Fairview	75.2	70.9	-	98.4	25.1	-	-	-	0.1	-	3.1	-	72.3	17.5	-	-	13.8	-	-	-	26.7	26.9
6	Collin	Farmersville	96.0	10.0	-	98.8	39.6	-	-	-	-	-	40.4	-	57.8	43.4	-	-	18.0	-	-	-	1.6	25.5
6	Collin	Frisco	93.4	60.7	46.8	85.4	9.7	18.1	65.5	64.8	87.7	99.0	47.6	3.4	52.3	24.0	-	74.9	58.1	45.0	-	-	3.7	39.8
6	Collin	Garland	93.7	33.3	93.1	65.1	14.1	7.5	59.4	21.9	62.9	5.3	1.3	23.0	35.6	19.2	28.1	62.7	38.2	7.4	-	-	12.2	18.7
6	Collin	Josephine	-	-	-	-	-	-	-	-	-	-	-	-	-	-	-	-	27.1	-	-	-	-	27.1
6	Collin	Lavon	96.5	97.3	-	-	-	-	-	-	46.9	-	-	-	57.1	27.1	-	-	37.3	-	-	-	-	54.0
6	Collin	Lowry Crossing	-	74.4	-	-	-	-	-	-	-	-	0.0	-	74.7	-	-	-	32.6	-	-	-	-	69.1
6	Collin	Lucas	69.6	76.9	12.3	-	58.2	-	-	-	1.9	-	8.7	-	49.8	58.6	-	-	35.1	-	-	-	22.4	51.3
6	Collin	McKinney	92.2	86.9	8.4	82.8	3.6	9.4	37.4	14.7	68.0	60.0	1.4	27.9	47.4	19.1	32.4	86.2	35.9	31.0	-	9.7	16.3	24.1
6	Collin	Melissa	96.4	71.3	-	-	37.7	-	-	-	-	-	39.6	-	1.3	7.8	-	-	82.5	-	-	-	55.3	56.3
6	Collin	Murphy	95.9	69.3	-	94.6	37.3	-	-	-	54.2	-	26.8	-	46.0	56.4	-	84.9	29.1	-	-	-	30.8	37.8
6	Collin	Nevada	-	80.1	-	-	40.8	-	-	-	-	-	-	-	19.0	-	-	-	79.4	-	-	-	-	57.5
6	Collin	New Hope	-	59.0	-	-	-	-	-	-	-	-	-	-	-	-	-	-	10.9	-	-	-	-	12.5
6	Collin	Parker	-	89.2	-	-	-	-	-	-	-	-	31.0	-	82.5	15.0	-	-	47.6	-	-	-	-	45.3
6	Collin	Plano	90.6	55.3	34.7	83.9	15.5	17.2	43.8	45.1	36.4	67.3	5.2	18.0	36.0	70.9	100.0	50.5	43.2	34.7	-	-	9.1	33.6
6	Collin	Princeton	100.5	95.0	-	100.0	25.3	-	-	-	-	-	42.2	-	56.9	23.0	-	-	42.0	-	-	-	48.7	52.9
6	Collin	Prosper	100.3	54.0	0.0	100.0	19.7	-	-	-	-	-	46.0	-	89.3	35.1	-	78.6	56.9	-	-	-	25.9	30.6
6	Collin	Richardson	89.4	42.8	106.2	69.6	23.7	4.4	52.0	2.6	76.3	40.7	10.3	-	29.7	13.6	-	26.8	27.4	5.4	-	47.6	7.8	25.1
6	Collin	Royse City	97.2	96.9	-	96.9	11.5	-	-	-	-	-	6.6	-	64.5	92.7	-	-	29.7	5.4	-	-	32.5	23.8
6	Collin	Sachse	97.9	70.6	-	86.8	80.7	1.6	-	-	99.9	-	8.8	-	45.8	23.1	-	5.2	80.8	-	-	-	79.0	80.7
6	Collin	Saint Paul	100.0	53.8	-	-	-	-	-	-	-	-	-	-	57.8	-	-	-	13.0	-	-	-	-	36.8
6	Collin	Weston	-	-	-	-	-	-	-	-	-	-	-	-	20.7	-	-	-	6.4	-	-	-	-	18.2

Rank	County	City	Accommodation & Food Svcs.	Admin. & Supp. & Waste Mgmt. & Remed. Svcs.	Agric., Forestry, Fish'g & Hunt'g	Arts, Entertainment & Rec.	Construction	Educational Svcs.	Finance & Insurance	Health Care & Social Assist.	Information	Mgmt. Companies & Enterprises	Manufacturing	Mining	Other Svcs. (ex. Pub. Admin.)	Prof., Sci. & Tech. Services	Public Admin.	Real Estate & Rental & Leasing	Retail Trade	Transportation & Warehousing	Unclassified Establishments	Utilities	Wholesale Trade	Aggregates
6	Collin	Wylie	96.8	39.6	-	75.4	22.1	28.6	68.7	-	15.6	-	3.0	-	46.4	40.5	-	10.8	42.9	4.4	-	5.1	21.2	26.4
7	El Paso	Anthony	92.1	-	-	-	-	-	-	-	-	-	64.3	-	44.9	1.5	-	-	10.1	-	-		20.8	12.7
7	El Paso	Clint	80.8	93.8	-	-	-	-	-	-	-	-	-	-	2.2	-	-	-	41.4	-	-		30.5	38.8
7	El Paso	El Paso	89.2	39.1	4.2	84.9	10.5	19.0	29.6	29.0	25.4	2.5	3.4	0.5	45.7	9.7	44.7	59.2	45.4	11.0	-	30.6	8.4	26.5
7	El Paso	Horizon City	96.0	7.1	-	-	1.1	-	-	-	-	-	2.1	-	14.4	-	-	-	35.0	-	-		20.2	18.4
7	El Paso	Socorro	89.5	57.8	-	44.5	1.5	-	82.6	-	-	-	25.8	-	29.9	7.2	-	98.0	20.2	100.0	-		1.2	13.7
7	El Paso	Vinton	98.8	74.4	-	-	16.9	-	-	-	-	-	1.4	-	20.7	-	-	-	12.0	-	-		0.9	3.5
8	Hidalgo	Alamo	98.2	62.1	-	-	19.9	-	102.7	-	76.3	-	0.7	-	47.5	95.5	-	42.0	43.7	43.9	-		24.3	42.1
8	Hidalgo	Alton	90.9	12.0	-	-	28.0	-	-	-	-	-	11.3	-	27.3	72.2	-	94.2	37.0	-	-		0.3	34.0
8	Hidalgo	Donna	91.0	14.1	-	30.0	6.6	-	106.4	-	31.8	-	19.8	-	53.8	61.1	-	57.6	27.6	-	-		20.6	31.7
8	Hidalgo	Edcouch	69.2	150.1	-	-	-	-	-	-	-	-	-	-	45.5	-	-	-	63.9	-	-		-	67.0
8	Hidalgo	Edinburg	89.9	59.3	-	76.9	2.9	-	28.3	71.9	78.3	-	2.8	35.5	29.1	25.5	-	45.4	39.2	27.4	-		17.4	29.3
8	Hidalgo	Elsa	94.6	98.6	-	-	-	-	114.2	-	-	-	-	-	42.2	-	-	-	25.1	-	-		0.2	35.2
8	Hidalgo	Granjeno	-	-	-	-	-	-	-	-	-	-	-	-	-	-	-	-	-	-	-		-	-
8	Hidalgo	Hidalgo	94.9	5.8	-	-	-	-	41.1	-	-	-	1.2	-	20.4	64.1	-	-	19.2	0.4	-		1.5	14.0
8	Hidalgo	La Joya	94.3	-	-	-	0.2	-	-	-	-	-	-	-	40.5	-	-	-	29.3	-	-		100.0	47.0
8	Hidalgo	La Villa	-	-	-	-	-	-	-	-	-	-	-	-	-	-	-	-	78.4	-	-		-	78.4
8	Hidalgo	McAllen	91.5	51.2	28.4	79.2	15.3	5.7	42.3	21.1	79.9	-	5.4	74.9	10.0	30.3	-	55.0	52.6	17.6	-	92.1	7.8	38.5
8	Hidalgo	Mercedes	95.8	100.0	-	-	1.5	-	98.3	-	99.6	-	20.2	-	72.5	100.4	-	68.1	72.1	1.6	-		32.6	61.9
8	Hidalgo	Mission	92.3	61.0	-	88.0	12.7	-	73.7	22.9	103.4	-	12.5	6.8	30.1	14.3	-	69.9	42.7	35.4	-		20.1	40.4
8	Hidalgo	Palmview	99.3	39.8	-	-	1.1	-	-	-	26.1	-	39.5	-	42.3	18.9	-	94.0	30.2	-	-		57.0	38.1
8	Hidalgo	Penitas	68.3	75.5	-	-	24.9	-	-	-	-	-	1.9	-	53.0	-	-	-	56.2	-	-		80.0	55.5
8	Hidalgo	Pharr	79.2	51.7	-	88.7	13.2	-	91.5	5.5	95.3	-	17.2	45.7	33.4	30.8	-	72.3	38.0	6.5	-		33.6	37.1
8	Hidalgo	Progreso	92.0	-	-	-	-	-	-	-	-	-	-	-	-	-	-	-	44.6	-	-		3.8	46.4
8	Hidalgo	San Juan	90.9	27.6	-	100.0	14.8	-	-	-	75.6	-	68.2	-	30.4	24.6	-	86.7	30.7	-	-		7.6	32.2
8	Hidalgo	Weslaco	96.0	53.5	-	88.8	1.1	0.3	78.6	18.6	45.6	-	11.9	-	58.3	19.1	-	58.1	37.0	9.7	-		24.4	36.2
9	Denton	Argyle	99.8	18.6	-	-	7.6	76.2	-	-	0.0	-	9.9	-	59.8	24.7	-	-	9.9	-	-		19.4	19.3
9	Denton	Aubrey	98.2	141.7	-	-	3.1	-	-	-	-	-	1.6	-	63.2	1.2	-	-	43.8	-	-		58.5	49.5
9	Denton	Bartonville	94.9	60.6	-	-	4.0	-	-	-	-	-	1.5	-	70.9	11.4	-	-	50.3	-	-		0.8	39.6
9	Denton	Copper Canyon	-	58.5	-	72.8	26.8	-	-	-	-	-	5.1	-	-	-	-	-	60.8	-	-		1.2	27.8
9	Denton	Corinth	98.0	48.1	-	101.1	24.8	21.5	-	-	68.1	-	110.7	-	44.9	29.1	-	39.3	11.7	-	-	20.9	19.1	21.1
9	Denton	Corral City	-	-	-	-	-	-	-	-	-	-	-	-	-	-	-	-	56.6	-	-		-	56.6
9	Denton	Denton	89.9	46.3	1.2	86.9	14.7	6.2	33.0	15.9	48.3	-	4.7	61.3	41.7	6.4	-	77.1	41.3	16.4	-	0.5	12.9	30.2
9	Denton	Double Oak	-	66.2	-	-	11.4	2.5	-	-	-	-	69.8	-	36.8	50.6	-	-	80.4	-	-		76.5	52.8
9	Denton	Flower Mound	94.3	0.5	46.8	66.6	18.2	4.4	100.0	2.7	63.0	-	4.7	-	38.2	16.4	-	49.4	50.6	-	-	0.0	34.8	16.2
9	Denton	Fort Worth	84.7	40.9	6.3	79.8	12.4	17.5	32.1	15.6	24.6	60.4	12.1	216.0	36.1	38.4	93.1	51.4	37.9	26.8	-	26.8	7.4	25.4
9	Denton	Hackberry	-	-	-	-	-	-	-	-	-	-	-	-	-	-	-	-	20.0	-	-		-	20.0
9	Denton	Haslet	97.0	43.2	-	-	45.6	-	-	-	-	-	76.9	-	79.1	34.4	-	-	69.5	-	-		NM	73.0

Rank	County	City	Accommodation & Food Svcs.	Admin. & Supp. & Waste Mgmt. & Remed. Svcs.	Agric., Forestry, Fish'g & Hunt'g	Arts, Entertainment & Rec.	Construction	Educational Svcs.	Finance & Insurance	Health Care & Social Assist.	Information	Mgmt. Companies & Enterprises	Manufacturing	Mining	Other Svcs. (ex. Pub. Admin.)	Prof., Sci. & Tech. Services	Public Admin.	Real Estate & Rental & Leasing	Retail Trade	Transportation & Warehousing	Unclassified Establishments	Utilities	Wholesale Trade	Aggregates
9	Denton	Hickory Creek	96.4	-	-	-	42.8	-	35.5	-	-	-	100.0	-	33.7	36.6	-	100.1	45.6	-	-	-	-	51.0
9	Denton	Highland Village	84.0	32.7	-	72.7	13.6	29.4	-	-	80.8	-	23.8	-	61.3	18.8	-	25.2	60.1	-	-	-	16.9	57.6
9	Denton	Justin	51.1	5.7	-	26.7	11.8	-	-	-	-	-	19.9	-	43.3	100.0	-	-	35.4	-	-	-	39.3	32.3
9	Denton	Krugerville	-	-	-	-	81.3	-	-	-	-	-	-	-	2.9	6.3	-	-	65.7	-	-	-	-	69.0
9	Denton	Krum	93.8	99.9	-	-	19.9	-	-	-	-	-	5.6	-	59.3	14.9	-	-	42.7	33.6	-	-	6.3	41.8
9	Denton	Lake Dallas	79.3	86.4	-	100.0	36.2	-	-	-	135.6	-	1.9	-	25.0	25.0	-	-	68.5	-	-	-	15.5	34.4
9	Denton	Little Elm	94.0	65.1	-	78.6	20.7	33.1	-	-	67.6	-	20.0	-	57.1	15.0	-	82.7	57.7	17.6	-	-	22.4	60.5
9	Denton	Northlake	-	-	-	-	-	-	-	-	-	-	29.8	-	-	-	-	-	28.9	-	-	-	-	29.6
9	Denton	Oak Point	-	88.9	-	83.3	85.1	-	-	-	-	-	0.7	-	100.0	52.3	-	-	86.9	-	-	-	15.7	56.0
9	Denton	Pilot Point	95.5	21.0	-	90.3	6.9	-	-	-	-	-	14.4	-	38.8	9.3	-	-	37.6	-	-	-	56.7	29.4
9	Denton	Ponder	99.9	103.1	-	-	0.0	-	-	-	-	-	0.0	-	56.0	-	-	-	21.0	-	-	-	44.9	10.9
9	Denton	Roanoke	97.9	38.2	-	96.1	3.6	-	-	-	76.5	-	2.6	-	22.6	16.8	-	21.0	5.5	-	-	-	0.3	2.7
9	Denton	Sanger	85.8	29.3	-	-	22.9	-	100.0	-	16.0	-	1.4	-	76.1	4.4	-	41.1	0.6	33.4	-	-	4.4	1.6
9	Denton	Shady Shores	-	62.1	-	-	61.5	-	-	-	-	-	54.1	-	36.5	9.3	-	-	70.8	-	-	-	95.2	64.4
9	Denton	Southlake	93.4	55.5	53.0	66.6	3.4	6.2	41.8	2.3	58.0	0.2	33.5	-	28.6	21.7	-	48.3	60.9	8.0	-	-	28.7	36.8
9	Denton	The Colony	84.1	32.4	-	82.7	56.9	4.9	92.5	-	49.0	94.0	31.9	-	40.9	13.3	-	76.1	48.6	-	-	-	50.1	51.8
9	Denton	Trophy Club	95.0	46.1	-	96.6	3.4	0.1	-	-	23.0	-	1.2	-	47.9	37.0	-	53.3	26.6	-	-	-	1.2	16.1
10	Fort Bend	Arcola	99.9	-	-	-	-	-	-	-	-	-	39.4	-	20.5	-	-	100.0	14.1	-	-	-	-	30.1
10	Fort Bend	Beasley	-	-	-	-	-	-	-	-	-	-	-	-	-	-	-	-	93.5	-	-	-	-	93.5
10	Fort Bend	Fulshear	73.9	16.4	-	-	15.8	-	-	-	-	-	-	-	23.4	4.3	-	-	36.1	-	-	-	11.4	22.9
10	Fort Bend	Houston	85.9	25.3	12.1	80.4	16.1	28.4	5.1	11.8	28.0	52.4	8.4	46.9	35.7	8.9	79.4	33.3	41.1	8.6	4.8	10.6	5.1	16.9
10	Fort Bend	Katy	91.5	40.2	1.1	99.3	19.4	9.0	34.6	5.3	89.6	0.6	12.1	8.2	45.0	40.3	-	28.1	65.7	34.8	-	-	2.3	44.8
10	Fort Bend	Kendleton	-	-	-	-	-	-	-	-	-	-	-	-	-	-	-	-	-	-	-	-	-	-
10	Fort Bend	Meadows Place	97.4	95.3	-	-	-	-	-	-	-	-	0.2	-	58.1	82.3	-	-	23.0	-	-	-	0.0	26.5
10	Fort Bend	Missouri City	92.7	45.7	-	87.2	48.0	39.5	0.8	2.3	78.4	-	4.5	1.8	45.5	31.8	51.1	60.0	35.8	0.0	-	-	26.4	38.2
10	Fort Bend	Needville	91.8	61.7	-	-	21.9	-	-	-	-	-	48.1	-	51.3	-	-	100.2	37.7	-	-	-	-	41.6
10	Fort Bend	Orchard	-	-	-	-	5.7	-	-	-	-	-	-	-	-	-	-	-	81.4	-	-	-	-	9.1
10	Fort Bend	Richmond	86.5	37.2	-	71.5	7.3	-	17.0	4.0	69.0	-	4.3	-	60.3	44.1	-	100.0	30.7	-	-	-	5.8	30.8
10	Fort Bend	Rosenberg	97.7	54.7	-	100.5	10.0	5.7	36.6	0.3	55.0	-	7.6	-	37.9	18.2	-	91.8	48.5	-	-	-	22.2	39.0
10	Fort Bend	Simonton	-	-	-	-	0.0	-	-	-	-	-	1.4	-	-	46.2	-	-	42.9	-	-	-	-	26.8
10	Fort Bend	Sugar Land	89.7	67.4	-	86.3	11.1	18.5	1.9	2.9	39.1	93.3	3.1	NM	19.9	30.1	-	26.2	60.4	16.6	-	21.1	8.3	34.1
11	Montgomery	Conroe	92.1	46.4	2.1	81.7	22.9	6.3	42.1	4.6	100.7	-	6.5	6.2	43.8	26.2	92.1	59.3	41.3	19.0	-	8.3	3.3	19.4
11	Montgomery	Magnolia	94.5	57.4	-	97.6	9.7	-	-	-	100.0	-	7.6	-	43.0	1.9	-	99.7	35.7	-	-	-	60.0	41.8
11	Montgomery	Montgomery	98.4	-	-	98.8	1.1	-	-	-	-	-	35.9	-	48.4	100.0	-	100.0	31.2	-	-	-	70.2	38.4
11	Montgomery	Oak Ridge North	71.7	92.3	-	46.4	13.5	-	-	-	30.0	-	10.0	-	52.3	20.7	-	68.6	84.4	-	-	-	19.9	51.9
11	Montgomery	Panorama Village	-	69.2	-	-	-	-	-	-	-	-	1.1	-	-	6.1	-	-	43.4	-	-	-	-	6.9
11	Montgomery	Patton Village	-	-	-	-	-	-	-	-	-	-	-	-	-	-	-	-	-	-	-	-	-	-
11	Montgomery	Shenandoah	89.8	32.3	-	-	68.2	-	-	-	13.9	-	1.3	-	27.0	8.1	-	-	78.7	-	-	-	70.6	67.5

Rank	County	City	Accommodation & Food Svcs.	Admin. & Supp. & Waste Mgmt. & Remed. Svcs.	Agric., Forestry, Fish'g & Hunt'g	Arts, Entertainment & Rec.	Construction	Educational Svcs.	Finance & Insurance	Health Care & Social Assist.	Information	Mgmt. Companies & Enterprises	Manufacturing	Mining	Other Svcs. (ex. Pub. Admin.)	Prof., Sci. & Tech. Services	Public Admin.	Real Estate & Rental & Leasing	Retail Trade	Transportation & Warehousing	Unclassified Establishments	Utilities	Wholesale Trade	Aggregates
11	Montgomery	Splendora	96.7	99.8	-	-	1.2	-	-	-	-	-	11.3	-	38.8	-	-	97.6	41.0	-	-	-	5.7	38.7
11	Montgomery	Stagecoach	-	-	-	-	-	-	-	-	-	-	-	-	-	-	-	-	81.0	-	-	-	-	81.0
11	Montgomery	Willis	93.1	99.8	-	-	39.0	-	99.1	-	32.4	-	7.1	-	54.1	8.7	-	102.6	30.5	-	-	-	7.2	22.6
12	Williamson	Florence	-	-	-	-	9.2	-	-	-	-	-	100.0	-	45.2	-	-	-	66.2	-	-	-	-	47.9
12	Williamson	Georgetown	90.7	25.9	-	90.0	3.3	1.7	50.3	12.4	86.2	-	2.4	46.8	32.1	10.1	100.0	74.2	35.2	16.9	-	46.0	12.6	28.9
12	Williamson	Granger	87.9	-	-	-	-	-	-	-	-	-	-	-	24.2	-	-	-	22.6	-	-	-	-	30.2
12	Williamson	Hutto	94.5	12.2	-	100.0	24.2	100.0	-	-	99.8	-	8.4	-	50.7	36.0	-	60.1	79.6	-	-	-	10.0	71.3
12	Williamson	Jarrell	99.8	66.0	-	-	3.0	-	-	-	-	-	17.9	47.3	49.9	-	-	-	44.5	0.3	-	-	48.4	44.8
12	Williamson	Liberty Hill	95.9	15.7	-	87.9	44.5	-	-	-	100.0	-	54.6	-	30.8	29.4	-	66.4	33.0	-	-	-	95.5	41.4
12	Williamson	Taylor	96.5	73.3	-	97.8	28.8	-	130.8	-	13.0	-	9.4	-	42.6	24.4	-	98.7	28.6	-	-	-	2.4	25.2
12	Williamson	Thorndale	70.9	-	-	-	12.2	-	-	-	-	-	-	-	23.0	31.8	-	-	28.9	-	-	-	-	31.1
12	Williamson	Thrall	-	-	-	-	-	-	-	-	-	-	-	-	-	-	-	-	32.3	-	-	-	-	32.3
12	Williamson	Weir	-	-	-	-	-	-	-	-	-	-	-	-	-	-	-	-	50.4	-	-	-	-	50.4
13	Cameron	Brownsville	94.5	55.9	90.3	78.1	9.9	11.6	85.0	5.2	70.8	-	10.9	-	25.7	20.7	-	77.4	50.6	17.6	-	32.5	15.2	42.3
13	Cameron	Combes	91.5	66.0	-	-	0.4	-	-	-	-	-	-	-	9.6	-	-	-	71.9	-	-	-	-	41.1
13	Cameron	Harlingen	96.8	75.8	43.6	66.4	11.8	74.8	90.0	20.5	68.9	-	10.5	-	36.5	35.5	-	31.2	50.4	4.6	-	97.8	18.6	42.3
13	Cameron	La Feria	97.8	2.2	-	-	24.1	-	99.0	-	36.5	-	28.4	-	48.7	100.0	-	62.3	29.1	-	-	-	10.4	37.2
13	Cameron	Laguna Vista	63.1	100.0	-	97.1	5.4	-	-	-	-	-	-	-	59.9	-	-	-	52.0	-	-	-	-	67.6
13	Cameron	Los Fresnos	95.7	99.7	-	12.6	42.9	-	-	-	100.0	-	-	-	36.8	16.9	-	-	38.6	-	-	-	-	44.4
13	Cameron	Palm Valley	-	-	-	-	-	-	-	-	-	-	-	-	-	-	-	-	-	-	-	-	-	-
13	Cameron	Port Isabel	96.6	83.1	-	81.0	44.5	-	-	-	-	-	57.3	-	58.0	17.6	-	36.4	53.6	4.7	-	-	-	58.1
13	Cameron	Primera	-	14.7	-	-	20.7	-	-	-	-	-	-	-	-	-	-	-	58.9	-	-	-	-	29.8
13	Cameron	Rancho Viejo	93.3	52.7	-	-	-	-	-	-	-	-	-	-	-	-	-	-	86.6	-	-	-	1.1	57.1
13	Cameron	Rio Hondo	58.0	34.5	-	-	-	-	-	-	-	-	-	-	63.9	-	-	-	53.8	-	-	-	-	54.1
13	Cameron	San Benito	97.7	81.7	3.0	65.0	26.6	-	91.6	-	11.5	-	28.4	-	23.7	13.3	-	92.8	36.1	5.6	-	-	29.3	38.3
13	Cameron	Santa Rosa	90.3	-	-	-	62.1	-	-	-	-	-	-	-	50.5	-	-	-	76.7	-	-	-	-	75.1
13	Cameron	South Padre Island	91.1	80.2	-	65.4	39.3	-	-	-	-	-	-	-	92.6	25.8	-	69.7	72.9	96.0	-	-	20.8	77.8
14	Nueces	Agua Dulce	-	93.0	-	-	-	-	-	-	-	-	-	-	3.4	-	-	-	93.7	-	-	-	32.6	9.5
14	Nueces	Aransas Pass	90.4	60.3	0.9	81.6	231.3	100.0	84.0	-	70.4	-	25.0	-	22.8	73.1	-	94.2	43.0	12.3	-	-	16.7	52.9
14	Nueces	Bishop	63.1	-	-	-	-	-	-	-	-	-	-	-	55.1	-	-	-	46.6	-	-	-	-	51.0
14	Nueces	Corpus Christi	82.4	38.6	49.0	83.9	20.6	26.6	70.3	6.8	34.5	62.4	1.5	36.0	36.0	11.1	100.3	52.4	50.1	27.4	-	8.4	25.1	19.7
14	Nueces	Driscoll	-	-	-	-	-	-	-	-	-	-	-	-	-	-	-	-	30.8	-	-	-	-	30.8
14	Nueces	Port Aransas	78.1	88.5	-	41.9	22.1	-	-	-	-	-	52.5	-	69.5	54.8	-	66.9	58.9	15.8	-	-	3.2	57.5
14	Nueces	Robstown	93.4	32.2	-	-	1.8	100.0	-	-	-	-	31.2	68.0	33.1	7.3	-	53.8	18.0	0.3	-	50.7	63.5	49.9
15	Brazoria	Alvin	96.6	23.4	6.4	100.0	15.7	89.4	57.8	-	47.9	-	4.6	10.8	46.7	52.5	-	50.0	32.2	12.6	-	-	32.0	30.3
15	Brazoria	Angleton	98.8	62.4	-	100.0	16.8	39.9	39.8	24.7	99.4	-	3.3	-	45.2	12.9	-	55.2	35.0	-	-	-	1.3	24.8
15	Brazoria	Brazoria	96.3	97.9	-	-	17.8	-	-	-	87.5	-	100.0	-	53.3	43.5	-	100.3	42.4	-	-	-	23.8	39.0
15	Brazoria	Brookside Village	-	95.4	-	-	21.4	-	-	-	-	-	21.9	-	53.4	-	-	-	60.1	-	-	-	-	34.5

154

Rank	County	City	Accommodation & Food Svcs.	Admin. & Supp. & Waste Mgmt. & Remed. Svcs.	Agric., Forestry, Fish'g & Hunt'g	Arts, Entertainment & Rec.	Construction	Educational Svcs.	Finance & Insurance	Health Care & Social Assist.	Information	Mgmt. Companies & Enterprises	Manufacturing	Mining	Other Svcs. (ex. Pub. Admin.)	Prof., Sci. & Tech. Services	Public Admin.	Real Estate & Rental & Leasing	Retail Trade	Transportation & Warehousing	Unclassified Establishments	Utilities	Wholesale Trade	Aggregates
15	Brazoria	Clute	80.4	64.3	-	34.5	2.4	11.4	73.9	-	-	-	22.8	-	29.6	19.9	-	42.3	41.3	-	-	-	9.9	14.1
15	Brazoria	Danbury	100.0	-	-	-	25.5	-	-	-	-	-	-	-	41.2	-	-	-	36.7	-	-	-	-	38.8
15	Brazoria	Freeport	46.9	3.9	26.9	1.4	129.4	-	94.2	-	-	-	6.5	0.4	29.9	10.3	-	57.6	38.5	1.7	-	-	10.2	18.8
15	Brazoria	Holiday Lakes	-	-	-	-	-	-	-	-	-	-	-	-	-	-	-	-	-	-	-	-	-	-
15	Brazoria	Jones Creek	-	-	-	-	-	-	-	-	-	-	-	-	-	-	-	-	23.4	-	-	-	-	23.4
15	Brazoria	Lake Jackson	91.2	64.1	-	89.2	11.8	23.5	22.6	14.0	94.0	-	22.9	-	31.0	30.4	-	70.3	59.3	-	-	-	10.4	59.4
15	Brazoria	Liverpool	-	-	-	-	-	-	-	-	-	-	0.1	-	-	-	-	-	80.0	-	-	-	-	19.2
15	Brazoria	Manvel	100.0	79.8	-	100.0	49.2	18.0	-	-	-	-	13.2	-	21.0	28.2	-	100.6	58.8	-	-	-	42.0	41.6
15	Brazoria	Oyster Creek	96.9	-	-	-	-	-	-	-	-	-	-	-	3.2	-	-	-	37.0	-	-	-	13.7	18.1
15	Brazoria	Pearland	96.4	42.3	78.8	78.8	8.9	32.9	49.2	1.1	95.1	98.6	10.6	24.7	38.6	28.8	-	63.5	57.8	13.5	-	2.3	9.5	40.3
15	Brazoria	Quintana	-	-	-	-	-	-	-	-	-	-	-	-	-	-	-	-	-	-	-	-	-	-
15	Brazoria	Richwood	-	98.1	-	-	4.0	-	-	-	-	-	-	-	19.1	-	-	-	32.5	-	-	-	71.4	28.2
15	Brazoria	Surfside Beach	95.5	-	-	-	-	-	-	-	-	-	-	-	-	-	-	-	53.8	-	-	-	-	64.7
15	Brazoria	Sweeny	98.5	-	-	-	10.3	-	-	-	-	-	24.1	-	67.5	-	-	-	29.0	-	-	-	-	38.2
15	Brazoria	West Columbia	96.9	14.9	-	-	39.5	-	-	-	-	-	42.7	-	65.8	39.7	-	-	40.0	-	-	-	10.6	46.8
16	Galveston	Bayou Vista	-	19.7	-	-	-	-	-	-	-	-	92.3	-	-	-	-	-	82.4	-	-	-	27.7	59.8
16	Galveston	Clear Lake Shores	100.0	-	-	8.6	-	-	-	-	-	-	39.3	-	82.5	73.7	-	72.3	88.5	-	-	-	8.2	67.3
16	Galveston	Dickinson	87.5	78.2	-	73.8	43.3	-	80.9	-	78.5	-	2.6	-	36.1	10.0	-	99.7	68.7	9.6	-	-	2.3	53.9
16	Galveston	Friendswood	83.5	8.3	-	83.5	13.3	16.7	72.7	1.2	28.0	-	12.5	0.0	23.9	36.2	100.0	50.6	29.5	23.0	-	-	14.5	28.6
16	Galveston	Galveston	76.1	12.9	100.0	61.5	10.6	100.0	NM	12.2	59.6	-	11.9	1.8	29.0	23.5	90.3	45.5	56.0	30.4	-	-	11.8	36.8
16	Galveston	Hitchcock	90.9	66.5	-	-	27.4	-	-	-	-	-	10.0	-	29.1	0.9	-	7.4	41.3	-	-	-	41.9	29.0
16	Galveston	Jamaica Beach	47.1	-	-	-	5.0	-	-	-	-	-	-	-	-	-	-	-	57.4	-	-	-	-	45.5
16	Galveston	Kemah	95.8	16.0	-	91.3	18.1	-	-	-	90.1	-	4.7	-	31.0	5.2	-	30.4	53.5	-	-	-	18.1	53.3
16	Galveston	La Marque	84.9	14.6	-	73.3	11.4	-	-	-	99.7	-	3.5	-	17.5	77.8	-	49.0	38.4	-	-	-	26.0	31.9
16	Galveston	League City	91.4	58.8	-	55.3	18.0	39.0	65.2	2.5	54.8	-	78.0	-	45.2	26.4	-	59.4	44.5	55.3	-	5.0	13.6	44.8
16	Galveston	Santa Fe	91.3	53.1	-	100.0	31.8	5.7	-	-	10.3	-	15.7	-	36.0	33.3	-	58.2	47.2	-	-	-	15.5	46.1
16	Galveston	Texas City	94.1	16.5	-	56.2	29.2	-	43.8	34.1	97.7	21.4	0.1	-	8.9	36.1	-	27.7	44.9	5.5	-	-	9.7	1.0
16	Galveston	Tiki Island	-	-	-	-	-	-	-	-	-	-	-	-	-	-	-	-	52.3	-	-	-	-	52.3
17	Bell	Bartlett	26.7	91.5	-	-	-	-	-	-	-	-	21.9	-	-	-	-	-	38.0	-	-	-	36.0	36.0
17	Bell	Belton	95.6	49.4	-	83.5	17.6	96.3	91.3	5.5	93.9	-	7.2	-	40.2	13.2	-	72.6	35.0	-	-	-	10.6	26.2
17	Bell	Harker Heights	99.6	60.1	-	63.9	14.9	51.5	-	-	74.5	-	21.9	-	45.5	26.8	-	85.3	49.3	-	-	-	23.4	50.9
17	Bell	Holland	100.0	-	-	-	100.0	-	-	-	-	-	-	-	46.2	-	-	-	33.4	-	-	-	-	35.0
17	Bell	Killeen	92.7	57.6	-	92.2	20.7	77.0	70.7	68.5	54.5	-	47.0	-	44.0	9.6	-	83.0	42.4	7.2	-	-	39.9	47.3
17	Bell	Nolanville	100.0	81.9	-	-	-	-	-	-	-	-	-	-	79.6	-	-	-	23.5	-	-	-	-	27.9
17	Bell	Rogers	100.0	-	-	-	39.9	-	-	-	-	-	-	-	7.9	-	-	-	28.1	-	-	-	-	30.5
17	Bell	Salado	95.4	25.5	-	64.9	1.8	-	-	-	99.4	-	31.7	-	47.0	84.1	-	-	58.4	-	-	-	-	58.1
17	Bell	Temple	86.8	35.4	-	73.5	4.5	22.3	48.7	5.5	53.6	-	4.1	-	42.9	30.3	100.0	61.7	18.7	8.5	-	-	4.9	15.0
17	Bell	Troy	100.0	11.2	-	-	8.7	-	-	-	-	-	1.9	-	24.6	-	-	-	12.5	-	-	-	21.2	10.4

Rank	County	City	Accommodation & Food Svcs.	Admin. & Supp. & Waste Mgmt. & Remed. Svcs.	Agric., Forestry, Fish'g & Hunt'g	Arts, Entertainment & Rec.	Construction	Educational Svcs.	Finance & Insurance	Health Care & Social Assist.	Information	Mgmt. Companies & Enterprises	Manufacturing	Mining	Other Svcs. (ex. Pub. Admin.)	Prof., Sci. & Tech. Services	Public Admin.	Real Estate & Rental & Leasing	Retail Trade	Transportation & Warehousing	Unclassified Establishments	Utilities	Wholesale Trade	Aggregates
18	Lubbock	Abernathy	99.5	100.0	-	-	50.5	-	-	-	-	-	-	-	42.9	-	-	-	16.8	-	-	-	0.8	14.6
18	Lubbock	Idalou	97.9	12.9	-	-	13.0	-	-	-	-	-	1.4	-	88.0	0.4	-	-	30.6	-	-	-	1.9	21.5
18	Lubbock	Lubbock	83.4	61.3	10.9	55.4	9.3	46.4	73.8	17.3	59.1	63.9	5.5	18.7	33.3	14.3	47.7	45.6	41.4	44.4	-	14.4	11.2	28.8
18	Lubbock	New Deal	32.1	-	-	-	-	-	-	-	-	-	-	-	-	-	-	-	11.1	-	-	-	-	12.1
18	Lubbock	Ransom Canyon	-	-	-	-	-	-	-	-	-	-	-	-	-	71.1	-	-	5.9	-	-	-	-	15.0
18	Lubbock	Shallowater	100.0	44.1	-	-	22.5	-	-	-	-	-	-	-	82.1	6.5	51.5	-	16.2	-	-	-	65.9	23.1
18	Lubbock	Slaton	99.3	76.0	-	96.4	30.2	-	-	-	44.5	-	23.5	-	57.5	-	-	-	22.9	-	-	-	0.9	20.4
18	Lubbock	Wolfforth	40.8	42.5	-	-	34.1	13.1	-	-	-	-	0.0	-	8.8	4.8	-	-	62.4	-	-	-	38.8	48.6
19	Jefferson	Beaumont	87.1	41.2	40.7	88.5	14.4	15.4	74.8	27.0	28.8	18.6	5.5	18.0	27.7	4.6	-	35.6	46.5	49.6	-	-	15.1	24.8
19	Jefferson	Bevil Oaks	-	33.1	-	-	-	-	-	-	-	-	-	-	47.0	-	-	-	27.7	-	-	-	-	31.4
19	Jefferson	Groves	93.2	89.7	-	-	18.6	-	-	-	75.4	-	3.1	-	32.6	6.9	-	30.0	39.1	-	-	-	27.8	28.3
19	Jefferson	Nederland	93.9	58.6	-	-	93.3	32.1	35.3	62.2	-	10.3	-	-	13.3	44.8	3.4	26.5	43.2	12.0	-	-	65.2	42.2
19	Jefferson	Port Arthur	92.5	39.2	-	87.0	8.9	-	54.1	13.4	54.9	-	0.1	-	24.2	17.4	-	77.5	53.8	2.0	-	-	23.0	2.6
19	Jefferson	Port Neches	96.3	14.5	-	100.0	12.3	25.7	-	-	-	-	0.2	-	27.8	75.8	-	43.8	33.8	-	-	-	0.2	3.4
20	Webb	El Cenizo	100.0	-	-	-	-	-	-	-	-	-	-	-	-	-	-	-	42.3	-	-	-	-	42.9
20	Webb	Laredo	91.1	70.7	1.2	88.0	9.2	2.8	134.8	NM	19.2	0.6	8.9	30.1	40.4	24.1	-	71.4	41.4	15.6	-	-	6.5	32.4
20	Webb	Rio Bravo	54.4	-	-	-	-	-	-	-	-	-	28.9	-	-	-	-	-	26.1	-	-	-	29.4	26.3
21	McLennan	Bellmead	91.4	55.4	-	-	7.5	68.1	-	-	-	-	8.5	-	52.5	35.6	-	96.1	41.1	-	-	-	8.9	40.6
21	McLennan	Beverly Hills	99.2	12.6	-	-	-	-	-	-	-	-	5.3	-	41.3	-	-	91.9	21.1	-	-	-	32.6	24.8
21	McLennan	Crawford	-	-	-	-	-	-	-	-	-	-	-	-	-	-	-	-	50.9	-	-	-	-	50.9
21	McLennan	Gholson	-	-	-	-	-	-	-	-	-	-	-	-	-	-	-	-	41.0	-	-	-	-	41.0
21	McLennan	Hewitt	90.3	56.6	-	85.7	35.5	-	-	-	-	-	5.8	-	47.9	24.4	21.2	39.0	25.9	-	-	-	25.5	25.5
21	McLennan	Lorena	97.1	42.6	-	-	0.5	-	-	-	-	-	96.4	-	33.6	-	-	-	24.6	-	-	-	17.0	7.8
21	McLennan	Mart	99.6	-	-	-	-	-	-	-	-	-	-	-	16.1	-	-	-	24.3	-	-	-	-	27.5
21	McLennan	Moody	99.8	91.3	-	-	0.0	-	-	-	-	-	0.8	-	6.2	98.4	-	-	17.4	-	-	-	0.2	9.1
21	McLennan	Riesel	-	-	-	-	5.8	-	-	-	-	-	0.0	-	42.1	-	-	-	19.1	-	-	-	-	6.8
21	McLennan	Robinson	91.7	54.3	-	-	49.9	18.4	-	-	-	-	7.6	-	38.2	49.3	-	-	10.8	-	-	-	8.2	16.1
21	McLennan	Valley Mills	98.1	32.8	-	-	40.2	-	-	-	-	-	14.2	-	27.5	0.0	-	-	15.2	-	-	-	-	18.2
21	McLennan	Waco	85.6	34.9	17.8	80.2	9.4	85.6	116.4	24.9	25.4	96.1	3.5	-	41.1	16.2	0.0	51.1	47.6	6.4	-	0.2	9.4	23.2
21	McLennan	West	85.4	100.0	-	-	100.0	29.1	-	-	-	-	0.7	-	39.4	25.3	-	-	10.8	-	-	-	31.3	13.5
21	McLennan	Woodway	59.1	37.1	-	83.6	17.1	100.0	-	-	4.9	55.9	-	-	11.4	56.6	10.0	67.4	29.4	-	-	-	19.1	23.8
22	Smith	Arp	83.3	-	-	-	14.7	-	-	-	-	-	-	-	8.5	-	-	-	22.8	-	-	-	-	16.0
22	Smith	Bullard	95.9	62.0	-	-	99.3	-	-	-	30.1	-	100.0	-	48.3	60.7	-	-	23.2	-	-	-	12.9	31.0
22	Smith	Lindale	96.0	86.0	0.5	-	93.0	41.4	-	-	39.9	64.0	19.4	-	55.8	36.8	-	98.5	40.4	47.3	-	-	32.2	46.3
22	Smith	Overton	99.7	100.8	-	-	22.1	-	-	-	-	-	92.6	-	11.1	-	-	-	37.5	-	-	-	-	39.3
22	Smith	Troup	99.8	-	-	-	-	-	-	-	-	-	4.3	-	26.0	-	-	-	51.3	-	-	-	8.2	39.2
22	Smith	Tyler	92.8	60.2	7.1	76.0	13.9	19.9	12.8	8.1	65.7	51.6	12.3	108.2	48.5	25.9	-	48.5	46.6	34.2	-	0.2	27.1	42.7
22	Smith	Whitehouse	96.9	68.6	-	-	17.1	-	-	-	-	-	58.1	-	38.3	26.2	-	-	32.5	-	-	-	0.6	35.6
22	Smith	Winona	100.0	2.2	-	-	-	-	-	-	-	-	-	-	-	-	-	-	31.5	-	-	-	-	39.0

Rank	County	City	Accommodation & Food Svcs.	Admin. & Supp. & Waste Mgmt. & Remed. Svcs.	Agric., Forestry, Fish'g & Hunt'g	Arts, Entertainment & Rec.	Construction	Educational Svcs.	Finance & Insurance	Health Care & Social Assist.	Information	Mgmt. Companies & Enterprises	Manufacturing	Mining	Other Svcs. (ex. Pub. Admin.)	Prof., Sci. & Tech. Services	Public Admin.	Real Estate & Rental & Leasing	Retail Trade	Transportation & Warehousing	Unclassified Establishments	Utilities	Wholesale Trade	Aggregates
23	Brazos	Bryan	87.8	62.8	15.3	70.9	13.2	18.6	77.0	21.4	83.6	-	13.1	6.8	42.2	20.0	28.8	82.2	35.3	16.8	-	-	18.4	31.6
23	Brazos	College Station	82.3	67.3	8.1	71.7	14.4	98.9	57.7	2.4	73.8	58.8	77.0	14.8	38.3	16.9	0.2	79.8	58.6	10.4	-	-	37.9	53.1
24	Johnson	Alvarado	97.8	100.0	-	57.5	8.0	-	-	-	-	-	6.1	-	25.7	1.1	-	100.0	27.6	-	-	-	86.6	27.8
24	Johnson	Burleson	96.2	45.5	67.8	70.8	7.7	6.8	38.9	0.3	52.0	98.8	9.1	1.1	26.9	30.6	-	64.5	51.8	2.6	-	-	40.0	40.0
24	Johnson	Cleburne	92.6	45.3	-	63.4	4.9	-	53.0	4.6	55.7	-	3.5	8.9	49.9	22.9	-	60.0	10.9	1.5	-	-	33.4	12.0
24	Johnson	Crowley	94.4	89.2	-	100.2	6.9	-	-	0.9	91.9	-	2.9	-	46.5	14.2	-	99.4	26.9	-	-	-	17.1	22.8
24	Johnson	Godley	88.2	-	-	-	81.5	-	-	-	-	-	53.2	-	98.5	-	-	-	23.3	-	-	-	-	50.7
24	Johnson	Grandview	99.9	89.8	-	-	2.2	-	-	-	-	-	44.6	-	38.6	18.5	-	-	32.9	-	-	-	28.7	30.5
24	Johnson	Joshua	92.9	45.8	-	58.6	40.7	-	-	-	80.6	-	18.3	-	22.4	13.1	-	41.5	21.0	-	-	-	55.7	31.5
24	Johnson	Keene	95.7	44.5	-	-	12.4	-	-	-	-	-	6.0	-	24.2	81.5	-	-	29.9	-	-	-	-	22.4
24	Johnson	Rio Vista	84.7	-	-	-	-	-	-	-	-	-	-	-	100.0	-	-	-	75.8	-	-	-	-	76.1
25	Hays	Austin	85.7	37.6	46.2	61.1	10.3	19.9	19.1	1.5	19.3	33.1	13.2	72.6	28.2	12.3	94.9	68.9	47.0	28.3	-	29.0	14.2	29.4
25	Hays	Buda	99.5	63.5	-	-	20.4	-	441.3	-	98.9	-	17.7	-	36.9	12.2	-	95.0	45.7	-	-	-	44.9	43.6
25	Hays	Dripping Springs	100.2	52.9	-	37.3	23.4	78.8	-	-	84.6	-	9.2	-	50.5	65.0	-	45.6	47.7	-	-	-	32.2	44.5
25	Hays	Hays	-	-	-	-	-	-	-	-	-	-	-	-	-	-	-	-	39.4	-	-	-	-	39.4
25	Hays	Kyle	81.9	14.6	-	97.5	12.6	43.3	-	0.3	70.0	-	15.6	-	48.5	16.2	-	96.0	37.1	22.6	-	-	44.7	33.9
25	Hays	Mountain City	-	-	-	-	-	-	-	-	-	-	-	-	94.8	-	-	68.1	-	-	-	-	-	92.8
25	Hays	Niederwald	-	-	-	-	-	-	-	-	-	-	-	-	-	-	-	76.5	-	-	-	-	-	76.5
25	Hays	San Marcos	95.6	17.7	99.2	73.0	4.7	25.6	76.1	4.4	101.9	-	14.1	-	40.1	23.2	45.8	70.6	64.8	2.2	-	-	63.7	56.9
25	Hays	Uhland	-	-	-	-	-	-	-	-	-	-	-	-	57.5	-	-	-	-	-	-	-	-	57.5
25	Hays	Woodcreek	-	-	-	99.0	-	-	-	-	-	-	10.4	-	-	20.9	-	-	45.2	-	-	-	-	44.9
26	Ellis	Bardwell	-	-	-	-	-	-	-	-	-	-	-	-	-	-	-	-	-	-	-	-	-	-
26	Ellis	Ennis	93.3	77.7	-	93.4	37.5	-	5.5	13.9	101.4	-	1.9	-	47.1	48.3	-	67.1	31.8	-	-	-	36.6	21.2
26	Ellis	Garrett	-	-	-	-	-	-	-	-	-	-	-	-	-	-	-	-	-	-	-	-	-	-
26	Ellis	Italy	98.1	-	-	-	-	-	-	-	-	-	-	-	7.3	-	-	-	47.0	-	-	-	-	54.2
26	Ellis	Mansfield	97.4	23.4	0.1	68.0	7.3	6.9	94.3	2.5	62.1	-	3.7	-	29.2	7.5	-	64.9	48.8	3.8	-	-	11.4	26.8
26	Ellis	Maypearl	72.3	-	-	-	-	-	-	-	-	-	-	-	44.3	-	-	-	24.0	-	-	-	-	30.5
26	Ellis	Midlothian	87.2	36.5	-	95.5	9.7	82.5	99.8	-	22.6	-	1.5	-	47.6	38.0	-	37.3	31.6	0.7	-	-	8.1	13.8
26	Ellis	Milford	-	-	-	-	100.0	-	-	-	-	-	-	-	-	-	-	-	72.0	-	-	-	-	75.6
26	Ellis	Oak Leaf	-	-	-	-	-	-	-	100.0	-	-	-	-	61.3	4.9	-	-	0.2	-	-	-	-	14.9
26	Ellis	Palmer	100.0	81.7	-	-	3.5	-	-	-	-	-	7.0	-	55.2	-	-	-	43.1	-	-	-	-	29.9
26	Ellis	Pecan Hill	-	-	-	-	-	-	-	-	-	-	-	-	-	-	-	-	100.0	-	-	-	-	100.0
26	Ellis	Red Oak	95.8	81.3	-	43.3	37.0	59.5	-	-	85.3	-	19.7	-	52.5	27.5	100.0	55.8	31.5	17.7	-	-	13.9	39.2
26	Ellis	Venus	99.5	2.5	-	-	-	-	-	-	-	-	-	-	75.2	-	-	-	46.9	-	-	-	-	33.4
26	Ellis	Waxahachie	93.3	59.3	30.2	84.2	24.1	97.3	45.5	10.1	23.0	-	5.1	-	46.3	13.3	-	56.3	43.9	5.4	-	0.0	25.0	26.7
27	Ector	Goldsmith	99.7	-	-	-	-	-	-	-	-	-	-	35.9	-	-	-	-	-	-	-	-	-	37.5
27	Ector	Odessa	87.9	53.8	77.2	81.8	9.3	36.0	61.7	20.7	62.0	-	19.6	29.2	42.7	26.2	35.7	54.3	41.7	57.2	-	-	23.4	35.9
28	Midland	Midland	95.3	63.2	0.7	88.1	23.7	53.4	49.0	14.1	63.6	-	29.0	103.3	45.2	14.9	84.3	54.7	52.6	13.3	-	0.6	43.1	41.9

Rank	County	City	Accommodation & Food Svcs.	Admin. & Supp. & Waste Mgmt. & Remed. Svcs.	Agric., Forestry, Fish'g & Hunt'g	Arts, Entertainment & Rec.	Construction	Educational Svcs.	Finance & Insurance	Health Care & Social Assist.	Information	Mgmt. Companies & Enterprises	Manufacturing	Mining	Other Svcs. (ex. Pub. Admin.)	Prof., Sci. & Tech. Services	Public Admin.	Real Estate & Rental & Leasing	Retail Trade	Transportation & Warehousing	Unclassified Establishments	Utilities	Wholesale Trade	Aggregates
29	Wichita	Burkburnett	96.7	90.3	-		61.0	30.2	-	112.4	-		30.7	-	46.8	96.8	-		17.1	-		-	4.7	23.0
29	Wichita	Electra	100.2	100.2	-		91.8	-		-	-		38.2	25.1	23.0	-		-	67.5	-		-	83.9	53.3
29	Wichita	Iowa Park	93.7	57.0	-		36.8	-	8.6	-	-		41.7	48.9	37.8	4.8	-	30.4	36.4	-		-	52.6	46.0
29	Wichita	Wichita Falls	89.8	39.9	64.0	48.5	9.9	23.0	59.6	1.4	61.2	-	8.9	19.7	47.8	16.7	-	75.2	47.0	0.5	-	-	20.3	36.4
30	Taylor	Abilene	87.7	33.6	3.4	82.0	11.8	73.3	69.0	0.5	57.1	-	13.2	69.3	40.4	9.3	85.2	64.5	47.3	14.7	-	0.7	25.0	29.8
30	Taylor	Buffalo Gap	61.4	-		-	1.6	-		-	-		-	-	-	-	-	-	61.2	-		-	-	20.1
30	Taylor	Lawn	-																					
30	Taylor	Merkel	98.5	72.5	-		3.6	-		-	100.3	-	85.9	-	14.3	-		-	16.1	-		-	-	26.2
30	Taylor	Trent	-																					
30	Taylor	Tuscola	69.1	38.5	-		44.2	-		-	-		-	-	24.4	-		-	34.8	-		-	0.0	7.2
30	Taylor	Tye	-	-		-	6.1	-		-	-		-	-	35.4	-		-	8.1	-		-	13.3	9.4
31	Potter	Amarillo	85.9	55.4	1.4	87.6	9.4	54.8	8.9	23.4	58.6	34.9	14.0	6.8	36.5	27.4	-	48.9	41.7	19.0	-	13.6	10.5	28.5
31	Potter	Canyon	78.4	59.0	-	89.4	13.9	22.1	NM	-	59.5	-	7.1	-	55.3	38.5	-	93.4	35.9	-		-	2.5	39.1
31	Potter	Happy	-																5.2				-	5.2
32	Grayson	Bells	99.8	-															42.3				-	43.2
32	Grayson	Collinsville	69.9	-											60.9				35.2				-	36.8
32	Grayson	Denison	93.2	59.3	-	64.9	14.3	0.5	294.1	68.5	6.1	-	9.2	-	41.2	4.7	-	85.6	32.2	-		-	14.4	29.1
32	Grayson	Gunter	99.7	51.3	-		8.1	-		-	-		-	-	59.6	27.3	-		58.1				-	38.1
32	Grayson	Howe	91.2	94.0	-		64.7	-		-	-		2.7	-	48.8	-		-	35.4	-		-	0.2	15.6
32	Grayson	Knollwood	-																					
32	Grayson	Pottsboro	87.6	78.8	-		32.6	-		-	-		31.4	-	60.1	61.4	-		43.3	-		-	23.5	42.6
32	Grayson	Sherman	93.0	-5.1	0.0	79.8	5.6	91.4	157.0	7.6	69.5	99.4	3.7	-	52.9	9.6	-	73.5	51.9	1.1	-		17.0	42.3
32	Grayson	Southmayd	-	62.9	-		8.0	-		-	-		63.5	-	-	-								56.9
32	Grayson	Tioga	-	99.3	-								7.0	-	58.5	-			26.1				-	28.6
32	Grayson	Tom Bean	-												33.2				30.6				-	30.7
32	Grayson	Van Alstyne	97.3	80.3	-	49.0	5.2	-		-	15.1	-	1.7	-	21.1	22.3	-		27.8				3.9	15.8
32	Grayson	Whitesboro	99.0	81.7	-	99.9	46.9	-		-	5.2	-	23.4	-	57.4	39.2	-		33.0				32.6	40.9
32	Grayson	Whitewright	76.9	80.5	-		-	-		-	-		9.1	-	42.5	-			29.8				-	33.7
33	Gregg	Clarksville	99.7	95.6	-		52.6	-	138.0	-	-		0.4	-	26.9	95.4	-		28.5	-		-	0.3	9.5
33	Gregg	Easton	-																					
33	Gregg	Gladewater	98.4	76.6	-	47.0	49.3	-		-	100.8	-	21.1	-	25.1	10.5	-	43.4	32.2	26.4	-		19.4	33.6
33	Gregg	Kilgore	94.4	29.9	-	83.9	18.3	38.3	63.7	3.3	60.6	-	19.5	24.1	70.8	29.4	-	76.9	36.4	14.7	-	0.3	14.3	23.7
33	Gregg	Lakeport	-																24.7				-	24.7
33	Gregg	Longview	90.6	37.8	41.2	70.7	13.8	96.7	14.8	0.5	16.4	79.2	3.6	17.3	41.5	12.7	98.6	43.3	48.6	0.3	-		12.2	19.5
33	Gregg	White Oak	85.5	69.5	-		32.7	39.5	-		-	-	6.5	54.2	45.8	45.8	-	99.0	33.4	5.5	-		30.0	28.4
34	Guadalupe	Cibolo	94.8	35.4	-	85.4	6.5	5.4	-		42.0	-	15.4	-	11.9	0.4	-	24.9	56.6	0.2	-		15.4	10.7
34	Guadalupe	Luling	89.8	41.0	-		50.4	81.6	-		-	-	36.0	11.8	52.2	12.9	23.4	-	23.9	-		-	21.3	27.3
34	Guadalupe	Marion	94.0	55.9	-		20.0	-		-	-		100.0	-	59.1	0.5	-		34.9				36.1	37.1
34	Guadalupe	Seguin	93.9	65.5	2.4	35.3	9.5	73.8	53.1	18.0	33.9	-	9.4	5.7	32.1	15.7	9.8	41.6	44.5	0.3	-		4.6	30.6

Rank	County	City	Accommodation & Food Svcs.	Admin. & Supp. & Waste Mgmt. & Remed. Svcs.	Agric., Forestry, Fish'g & Hunt'g	Arts, Entertainment & Rec.	Construction	Educational Svcs.	Finance & Insurance	Health Care & Social Assist.	Information	Mgmt Companies & Enterprises	Manufacturing	Mining	Other Svcs. (ex. Pub. Admin.)	Prof., Sci. & Tech. Services	Public Admin.	Real Estate & Rental & Leasing	Retail Trade	Transportation & Warehousing	Unclassified Establishments	Utilities	Wholesale Trade	Aggregates
36	Parker	Aledo	91.0	15.2	-	-	31.6	-	-	-	6.6	-	0.6	-	61.4	15.9	-	-	21.1	-	-	-	18.9	14.3
36	Parker	Azle	97.4	85.8	-	77.3	33.9	52.5	-	-	-	-	3.0	-	38.5	43.4	-	97.2	40.5	-	-	-	82.4	42.4
36	Parker	Millsap	-	100.0	-	-	1.4	-	-	-	-	-	-	-	18.4	-	-	-	35.8	-	-	-	157.1	19.2
36	Parker	Mineral Wells	90.8	75.9	-	78.7	26.1	-	-	5.3	72.9	-	3.1	14.7	58.9	31.6	100.0	72.5	45.1	15.4	-	-	38.3	30.0
36	Parker	Springtown	99.4	19.1	-	100.0	7.4	-	-	-	14.5	-	3.3	-	41.6	92.1	-	-	38.5	-	-	-	38.5	41.7
36	Parker	Weatherford	98.7	71.4	-	76.0	12.3	20.5	101.9	0.5	32.2	-	6.2	2.1	49.8	31.3	30.2	88.1	40.8	100.1	-	-	50.7	36.9
36	Parker	Willow Park	90.0	39.5	-	100.0	67.2	-	-	-	100.0	-	7.9	-	63.5	90.2	-	85.6	30.8	-	-	-	34.8	48.9
37	Comal	Bulverde	98.5	72.2	-	79.7	18.6	-	-	-	5.3	-	54.3	-	71.6	14.9	-	93.8	47.4	2.1	-	-	3.4	47.1
37	Comal	Fair Oaks Ranch	51.6	72.5	-	98.2	11.0	-	-	-	62.6	-	0.9	-	14.5	5.1	-	-	14.1	-	-	-	0.4	22.0
37	Comal	Garden Ridge	73.8		-	-	2.5	-	-	-	-	-	72.4	-	96.2	31.5	-	-	16.0	-	-	-	7.2	8.6
37	Comal	New Braunfels	92.9	51.9	28.9	64.7	21.9	16.9	65.9	12.7	43.4	-	36.3	100.0	40.4	21.4	21.1	71.3	45.3	10.7	-	-	68.0	48.3
38	Tom Green	San Angelo	92.1	60.9	29.0	78.2	18.1	24.1	71.2	0.5	42.4	-	15.1	51.0	43.4	21.3	-	65.2	46.1	1.3	-	7.9	21.9	30.8
39	Kaufman	Crandall	94.3	25.2	-	-	33.3	-	-	-	-	-	4.7	-	55.8	3.5	-	-	34.5	-	-	-	-	40.3
39	Kaufman	Forney	96.2	35.9	-	65.2	19.5	31.7	-	-	99.5	-	1.4	-	35.1	13.2	-	46.3	39.5	5.9	-	-	3.4	18.1
39	Kaufman	Heath	100.0	78.1	-	97.0	38.8	4.5	-	-	72.7	-	27.9	-	26.6	53.6	-	0.0	66.7	-	-	-	31.6	55.8
39	Kaufman	Kaufman	98.2	49.3	-	99.7	7.3	-	-	-	90.2	-	5.4	-	54.1	29.1	-	98.0	24.1	-	-	-	1.3	18.2
39	Kaufman	Kemp	99.8	7.2	-	-	-	-	-	-	-	-	19.5	-	53.2	-	-	-	32.8	-	-	-	-	41.3
39	Kaufman	Mabank	91.8	50.6	21.5	-	21.6	-	-	-	-	-	16.3	-	13.4	52.5	-	-	49.5	-	-	-	99.4	39.1
39	Kaufman	Oak Ridge	-	-	-	-	-	-	-	-	-	-	-	-	-	-	-	-	51.2	-	-	-	-	51.2
39	Kaufman	Terrell	81.8	65.7	-	64.8	29.6	53.7	197.5	118.2	30.4	-	12.3	-	40.2	14.7	-	97.2	16.3	36.2	-	-	10.7	18.0

www.ingramcontent.com/pod-product-compliance
Lightning Source LLC
Chambersburg PA
CBHW041239020426
42333CB00002B/18